The
RED LAND

The
RED LAND

The Illustrated Archaeology of
Egypt's Eastern Desert

Steven E. Sidebotham
Martin Hense
Hendrikje M. Nouwens

The American University in Cairo Press
Cairo   New York

Dar el Kutub No. 3130/07
ISBN 978 977 416 094 3

Dar el Kutub Cataloging-in-Publication Data

Sidebotham, Steven
        The Red Land: The Illustrated Archaeology of Egypt's Eastern Desert /
    Steven Sidebotham.—Cairo: The American University in Cairo Press, 2007
        p.   cm.
        ISBN 977 416 094 0
        1. Deserts—Egypt 2. Eastern Desert—Egypt   I. Hense, Martin (jt. auth.)
        II. Nouwens, Hendrikje M. (jt. author.)   III. Title
        916.35

1 2 3 4 5 6 7 8   12 11 10 09 08

Designed by Sally Boylan / AUC Press Design Center
Printed in Egypt

Contents

Illustrations

Plates

Preface

W orking in the Eastern Desert of Egypt over the years has had its share of challenges, but its haunting beauty, the incredible state of preservation of many of its ancient archaeological remains, and the friendliness of its Bedouin inhabitants have completely captivated us. This book is a snapshot of our experiences in the Eastern Desert and cannot begin to convey a complete impression of this arid wilderness, nor can it adequately express our dedication to the protection and preservation of its beautiful natural and historical treasures and its rich Bedouin heritage from the ravages of the modern world. We hope this book will inspire in our readers an appreciation for this remote and often overlooked area of the world.

There are numerous individuals and institutions that have helped us in our fieldwork over the decades. They are too many to mention here, but their names can be found listed in our many publications. Of most immediate help were those who actually made this book possible. These include Ms. Mary Caulfield on whose computer much of this text was composed and who spent countless hours scanning hundreds of slides as digital images. Ms. Angie Hoseth, Ms. Tracy Jentzsch of the History Media Center, History Department, University of Delaware, USA, and Ruud Koningen from the Netherlands also cheerfully and tirelessly scanned hundreds of slides as digital images. Prof. William Leadbetter of Edith Cowen University, Perth, Australia generously provided his personal computer on which much of this text was edited while Sidebotham was a visiting scholar there in December 2006. Prof. James A. Harrell of the University of Toledo read and commented on the geology sections of the book.

There is always the vexing question of the transliteration of Arabic words and proper names into the Latin alphabet. We have attempted to use the most commonly accepted and most recognizable spellings. With the *el/al* prefixes, we have opted to use *al.* For many proper Eastern Desert place names we have presented here our transcriptions of Ma'aza and 'Ababda pronunciations, which do not always coincide with spellings that appear on modern maps. All ruling/reigning dates are based on J. Baines and J. Málek, *Cultural Atlas of Ancient Egypt* (New York: Checkmark Books, 2000).

We would like to dedicate this book to all our Ma'aza and 'Ababda Bedouin friends who, over the years, have taught us so much about themselves and their lives in the Eastern Desert.

Historical Overview

Prehistory

The earliest traces of human occupation in the Nile Valley and the surrounding deserts survive along the desert hills and terraces in Upper Egypt
and Nubia. They consist of large, roughly shaped flint tools, such as hand-
axes and scrapers, dated about 250,000 BC. These primitive tools, similar to
those found in Europe in the Lower Paleolithic period, were made by
nomads and hunters ranging over all of North Africa.

Toward Late Paleolithic times, in approximately 25,000 BC, the climate of
the region underwent a drastic change and grass steppes began to turn into
desert. As a result, early man had to withdraw from his old hunting grounds
toward sources of water; in this period traces of more settled occupation
have been found in the Nile Valley.

During the Mesolithic period (about 10,000–5000 BC) the population of
Egypt comprised different groups of semi-nomadic fishermen and hunters living in comparative isolation one from another. The use of flint during this time
was much developed and smaller, finer tools for specialized purposes have
been discovered, including arrowheads, while blade industries became common. It is possible that the last survivors of these fishing and hunting bands
were those who executed the rock-carvings in the cliffs overlooking the Nile
Valley and in the wadis leading to the Red Sea in southern Egypt and Nubia.

The first positive evidence for the domestication of cereal crops in Egypt
comes with the remains of the first settlements in the Neolithic period

(about 5000–4000 BC). The inhabitants of sites on the western edge of the Nile Delta, in the Fayyum region (a large fertile depression in the Libyan Desert southwest of Cairo), and in Middle Egypt clearly lived a settled agricultural life. They cultivated cereals and flax and raised domesticated animals. Climatic conditions improved in the sixth millennium BC and a moist interval probably facilitated agriculture and stock breeding. Furthermore, fishing, weaving, basketry, and pottery-making played an important role in the economy of these early farmers.

The Predynastic Period

The late Neolithic period in Egypt is generally described as 'Predynastic' and began in the fourth millennium BC. This was a time of great innovation and development, which ended with the unification of Egypt at the beginning of the First Dynasty (approximately 3000 BC).

The early Predynastic cultures were not homogenous; rather there were two main regions, Upper and Lower Egypt, and these developed along different lines. Little was known about the earliest inhabitants of Egypt until the end of the nineteenth century when discoveries of Predynastic cemeteries were made in Upper Egypt, and excavations in Lower Egypt led to the recovery of settlement remains.

Most of the Predynastic cultures in Egypt are named after the village place names where the culture was first identified. The earliest known phase of the Upper Egyptian Predynastic period, which was not discovered until the 1920s, is known as the Badarian period (5500–about 4000 BC). The al-Badari region, between Matmar and Qaw, includes several Predynastic cemeteries which yielded numerous finds, including the earliest copper objects found in Egypt, as well as terra-cotta and ivory anthropomorphic figures, palettes of slate for grinding eye-paint, stone vases, and flint tools. The pottery of the Badarian period is particularly fine and was to become very common in later times: the distinctive black-topped red ware, with its carefully polished surface.

The Naqada I period (also described as the Amratian period, 4000–3500 BC), which succeeded the Badarian, is named after the ruins at Naqada, one of the largest Predynastic sites in Egypt. It is located about twenty-six kilometers north of Luxor on the west bank of the Nile and includes thousands of graves and the remains of a Predynastic walled town, founded at least as early as 3600 BC. The historical name for Naqada was Nubt, meaning 'Gold[town],' suggesting that the inhabitants may well have benefited from their location opposite Coptos and Wadi Hammamat, through which they would have been able to exploit the precious minerals of the Eastern Desert. Distinctive styles of pottery, including polished red ware, highly burnished, often with black, carbonized rims, or with white-painted incised decorations characterize the Naqada I period. Furthermore, slate palettes of simple shapes, pressure-flaked flints, disc-shaped mace-heads, and ivory combs are commonly found in the graves of the Naqada I period.

The more advanced Naqada II (or Gerzean) period (3500–3100 BC) forms the turning point in the development of Predynastic Egypt. The remains of this era, which occur at many sites throughout Egypt, show that it was a time of considerable progress. Social stratification appeared and significant population centers developed. Discovered in Gerzean graves were flint tools, copper implements, stone vases, slate palettes in animal form, pear-shaped mace-heads, and buff pottery vessels with reddish decoration. The tombs themselves show improvements in design over the simple pits of earlier times, and have reed matting and wood used to protect the burials. The Naqada II culture gradually spread over the entire Nile Valley and into the Delta.

The Lower Egyptian sequence of Predynastic cultures includes many cultural traditions from different regions. The earliest Lower Egyptian Predynastic remains are the so-called 'Fayyum A' encampments, from the shores of Lake Fayyum, dating back to about 5000 BC. Other important Lower Egyptian sites include Merimda Beni Salama, a Predynastic settlement in the western margin of the Delta, al-Omari, between modern Cairo and Helwan, and the sites of Ma'adi and Tell al-Fara'in (Buto).

Most likely, the inhabitants of Lower Egypt gradually assimilated various aspects of Upper Egyptian material culture in the late fourth millennium BC. Although nothing is certain about the political organization in Upper and Lower Egypt during the early Predynastic era, by the late Predynastic period two clearly defined confederations started to emerge with political heads who can be defined as kings. The political centers seem to have been Hierakonpolis in the south and Buto in the north. The period may have been one of continuous struggle. Finally the Delta was subsumed politically into a unified state dominated by Upper Egypt in about 3000 BC. With the unification of the two kingdoms begins the historic period in Egypt.

The Early Dynastic or the Archaic Period

The Early Dynastic period (2920–2649 BC), often described as the Archaic, comprises the first two dynasties and marks the formative phase of pharaonic civilization. During this time a considerable administrative reorganization was effected and writing, art, and architecture all underwent rapid development.

According to the historian Manetho, an Egyptian priest of the early third century BC, the First Dynasty began with the legendary Menes, considered the founder of the Egyptian state and responsible for the unification of Upper and Lower Egypt. Unfortunately, it is not clear whether Menes should be identified with the historical figure of Narmer, who is primarily known from a stone ceremonial palette which was discovered at Hierakonpolis, or with King Aha, to whose reign dates the earliest tomb at Saqqara.

The increased use of writing, notably for year names which served dating purposes, marks the beginning of the First Dynasty (2920–2770 BC). Also founded at this time was a new political capital at Memphis, located in an area reclaimed from the Nile at the junction of Upper and Lower Egypt. Tradition credits Menes with its foundation. Little is known of the other pharaohs of the First Dynasty except that they were buried in royal tombs at a cemetery in the desert at Abydos, while their high officials had imposing mud-brick tombs at north Saqqara.

The Second Dynasty replaced the First Dynasty in about 2770 BC. The dynasties were probably connected in the matriarchal line. During this period the royal necropolis was relocated to Saqqara, although the last two kings of this dynasty (Peribsen and Khasekhemwy) were both buried at Abydos. A hiatus in the royal succession in the middle of the dynasty may indicate a political upheaval and a struggle for power involving the transfer of religious loyalty of the ruling house from the god Horus to Seth. The change was, however, transitory and order seems to have been restored after a relatively short time.

Unfortunately, preservation of large-scale monuments from the Early Dynastic period is poor as they were made mainly of mud brick. Furthermore, most tombs were thoroughly ransacked in later periods. The royal tombs at Abydos were relatively modest in size. Brick enclosures for the mortuary cult were constructed near the cultivated area. The high officials had larger mud-brick tombs of a different design.

The tombs at Abydos and Saqqara have yielded thousands of small objects that reflect the cultural sophistication of the early royal court and the technical skill and artistic achievement of the Egyptian craftsmen at the beginning of the historic period. The tombs also contained some of the earliest Egyptian textual evidence, primarily in the form of stone steles, wooden and ivory labels, inscribed pottery jars, and clay seal impressions. Some objects, made of materials not native to Egypt, such as lapis lazuli, further testify to the existence of trade connections with Asia and tropical Africa.

The Old Kingdom

The Old Kingdom (2649–2152 BC) corresponds to the Pyramid age, consisting of the Third to Sixth Dynasties. It was a period in Egyptian history of strong central control during which techniques of craft production and industries were highly developed and court culture reached unprecedented heights.

The first significant ruler of the Third Dynasty (2649–2575 BC) was Djoser (2630–2611 BC), best known as builder of the step pyramid at Saqqara. The pyramid, surrounded by a vast funerary complex containing several buildings connected with the king's revitalization for eternity, was Egypt's earliest example of large-scale stone architecture. Previously most buildings had been made of less permanent materials such as mud brick. It was Imhotep, the pharaoh's chief architect, who designed the step pyramid and his importance in later times was so great that he was deified and equated by the Greeks with their god of medicine and healing, Asklepios. Despite the fame of his pyramid, we know very little about Djoser himself or his reign. Records left in Sinai suggest that the king sent an expedition to this area, probably in search of copper and turquoise.

During the Fourth Dynasty (2575–2465 BC) pyramid building in Egypt reached its zenith. These complexes were surrounded by a large number of so-called *mastaba* tombs where the great nobles and priests who served the kings were buried.

The Fourth Dynasty began with the reign of pharaoh Sneferu (2575–2551 BC), who is associated with no fewer than three pyramids: one at Meidum, which he either built or completed, and two at Dahshur, near Saqqara. During his reign there was a major campaign to Nubia, and at Buhen an Egyptian settlement was founded, which lasted for perhaps 250 years. It probably served as a base for mining expeditions and for trade with regions farther south.

Sneferu's son, Khufu (2551–2528 BC), and his grandson, Khafra (2520–2494 BC), were responsible for the construction of two impressive pyramids at Giza, which dominate the desert-plateau. It was likely during the reign of Khafra that the famous Sphinx was carved; it probably portrays Khafra's features and possibly represents the king as the sun-god protecting the royal cemetery. Solar religion was considered very important in the Fourth and Fifth Dynasties (2575–2323 BC). The true pyramid is most probably a solar symbol and the adoption of the royal title 'Son of Re' represented the apogee of the cult of the sun-god. The pyramid of Menkaura (2490–2472 BC) completes the trio of large pyramids at Giza.

With the Fifth Dynasty (2465–2323 BC) the centralized power of the crown declined somewhat and the concept of kingship also underwent modifications, partly because of the increased popularity of the cult of the sun-god Re and the growing influence of the myths of the Osiris legend. The Fifth Dynasty rulers, among whom were Djedkare-Isesi (2388–2356 BC) and Unas (2356–2323 BC), were buried either at Abusir or Saqqara, and several of the earlier successive kings of this period also built sun-temples in honor of Re and in commemoration of the relationship between the king and the sun-god.

Although smaller than those of the preceding dynasty, the pyramids of the Fifth Dynasty were greatly enhanced by fine painted decorations in relief, and by a variety of architectural details. An innovation of great importance in this period was introduced into the pyramid of Unas: its internal walls were inscribed with religious incantations, which are now known as the 'Pyramid Texts.'

During the Fifth Dynasty the pharaohs began to delegate power to various high officials and nobles. The tombs of the nobles during the Fourth Dynasty were of modest size and were grouped around the royal pyramid. As the centuries passed, construction of private tombs grew on a far more ambitious scale and were less closely associated with royal burials. This indicates a further diminution of the dependence of nobles on their monarchs. Some of the great nobles set up virtually independent courts in the various nomes or districts where they lived.

The pyramids and tombs of the Sixth Dynasty rulers (2323–2152 BC) were all constructed at Saqqara. The greater number of surviving texts from this period, especially the inscriptions from the tombs of high officials, indicates that during the reigns of Pepi I (2289–2255 BC), Merenre (2255–2246 BC) and Pepi II (2246–2152 BC), military and trading campaigns were sent to Nubia, western Asia, and Sinai.

It was during the long reign of Pepi II, who is said to have ruled for ninety-four years, that the central administration finally collapsed. A variety of factors precipitated the fall of the Old Kingdom. These included climatic deterioration, consisting of lower Nile inundations causing a series of bad harvests, incursions by foreigners, and an increase in the power of provincial governors.

The First Intermediate Period

A period of relative political instability known as the First Intermediate Period (2150/2134–2040 BC) followed the collapse of the Old Kingdom. It comprised the Seventh to Tenth and the early part of the Eleventh Dynasties (2150–2040 BC). Unfortunately, not much is known about this era.

The rulers of the Seventh and Eighth Dynasties (2150–2134 BC) might still have governed Egypt from the Old Kingdom capital at Memphis. They might even have been accepted throughout the entire land, although central control was only nominal as some provincial nobles had become virtual princes who treated their nomes as their own domains. The nomarchs defended their territories against their neighbors, which often resulted in inter-nome wars.

The kings of the Ninth and Tenth Dynasties (2134–2040 BC), who originated from Heracleopolis, were probably recognized as the sole legitimate authority at the time, although they never succeeded in gaining control of southern Egypt. They undoubtedly established a strong stabilizing regime in Lower Egypt, while in Upper Egypt a struggle for power developed between changing confederacies of nomes.

A clash between the Heracleopolitan rulers and the early Theban Eleventh Dynasty (2134–2040 BC) from the south was inevitable, especially after the position of the Heracleopolitan ruler was challenged by his Theban contemporary who assumed the title "King of Upper and Lower Egypt." The struggle between Heracleopolis and Thebes was finally resolved when the Theban king Mentuhotep II (2061–2010 BC), either by military conquest or by some form of diplomatic arrangement, succeeded in reducing the north. He reunited all of Egypt and made Thebes the capital.

The Middle Kingdom

The Middle Kingdom (2040–1640 BC) began after the reunification of the country under Mentuhotep II in the middle of the Eleventh Dynasty and ended with the political fragmentation of Egypt in the late Thirteenth Dynasty. The Middle Kingdom was a period of strong central government following the First Intermediate Period.

Mentuhotep II is generally regarded as the founder of the Middle Kingdom. After reuniting Egypt under his sole authority, he launched military campaigns in the north against the Libyans and the Bedouin, and in the south against the Nubians. Intensive exploitation of the desert regions involved frequent expeditions, notably to Sinai, Wadi Hammamat, and Wadi al-Hudi where mines and quarries were re-opened. Trade routes were also re-established, such as that to the Red Sea.

Under the kings of the Twelfth Dynasty (1991–1783 BC) there was a considerable development of the Fayyum region. Moreover, the royal residence was moved from Thebes to near Memphis. The new capital was called *Itjtawy* meaning: '[Amenemhat] who takes possession of the two lands.' The site itself, which has not yet been located, is likely to have consisted of an administrative complex and royal residence, and is usually assumed to have been on the west bank of the Nile in the vicinity of the pyramid complexes of Amenemhat I (1991–1962 BC) and his successor Senwosret I (1971–1926 BC) at al-Lisht. Other kings of this period were subsequently buried in pyramid complexes in al-Lahun, Dahshur, and Hawara.

In the Twelfth Dynasty Egypt once more became a highly organized, well-administered state. To ensure continuity of government and to strengthen the royal lines, the practice of co-regency was introduced, probably necessitated by the murder of the first king of this dynasty. To enable a peaceful transfer of power on his death, the reigning king nominated one of his sons to share the throne.

Furthermore, steps were taken to limit the excessive power of the nomarchs that had been attained during the First Intermediate Period. Thus, the re-establishment of nome boundaries characterized the early Twelfth Dynasty. Pharaoh Senwosret III (1878–1841 BC) might even have been responsible for the abolition of the office of nomarch. By the end of the Twelfth Dynasty the independence of the noble princes was completely broken. Their tombs likely reflect the stronger links between the provincial governors and the pharaoh. These were first constructed at elite provincial cemeteries such as Deir al-Bersha and Beni Hasan, but, by the Twelfth Dynasty they surrounded the royal pyramid complexes.

To secure its borders against foreign invaders, the Middle Kingdom rulers built a series of fortifications. To keep infiltrating Asiatics out of the Delta, Amenemhat I (1991–1962 BC) constructed a fort known as 'the Walls of the Prince.' In the south, however, the Nubians also presented a growing threat. Under Amenemhat I Lower Nubia was annexed and later in the dynasty huge mud-brick fortresses, now submerged beneath Lake Nasser, were built not only to secure the southern boundaries of the kingdom, but also to ensure safe access to the mineral-bearing areas in Nubia and to establish the trade routes into the heart of Africa.

In the Thirteenth Dynasty (1783–after 1640 BC) a succession of ephemeral rulers weakened the royal authority and the control of Egypt's borders resulting in increased migrations. Asiatics heavily settled areas of the eastern Delta that had been Egyptian in the Twelfth Dynasty. These apparently peaceful arrivals were absorbed into Egyptian society. The end of the Middle Kingdom was marked by the gradual infiltration of the Egyptian government by these Asiatic immigrants who, as time passed, formed part of its vast bureaucracy. Finally, the Asiatics were able to take advantage of the instability in the country, caused by the many short-lived pharaohs of the Thirteenth Dynasty, and usurped power around 1640 BC.

The Second Intermediate Period

After the decline of the Middle Kingdom, the Second Intermediate Period (1640–1532 BC) began. This existed during the Fifteenth to Seventeenth Dynasties, two of which were assigned to foreign rulers, the so-called Hyksos. These Asiatics, whose name derives from the Egyptian *heka-khasut* (meaning 'rulers of foreign lands'), appear not to have been invaders, but settlers who took advantage of chaotic conditions to seize power in the Delta. Yet, they never conquered the south and the Seventeenth Dynasty, a line of native Egyptians who ruled from Thebes, remained a bastion of resistance throughout the period of Hyksos rule.

Thus, the Second Intermediate Period began with a separate Hyksos kingdom in the north with their capital at Avaris (modern Tell al-Dab'a). Antiquities found on Crete, at Kerma in the Sudan, and in Palestine, as well as the remains of Minoan-style frescoes surviving at Avaris, suggest that the foreign peoples maintained diplomatic or trading relations with the Aegean and the Near East. Contact abroad brought with it a number of technical innovations including bronze working, an improved potter's wheel, the introduction of horse and chariot, composite bows, and new shapes of several weapons.

The Sixteenth Dynasty seems to have ruled concurrently with the Hyksos kings, consisting of minor Hyksos rulers, who proclaimed themselves as kings, wherever they may have resided.

The movement which ended in the liberation of Egypt from the Hyksos' domination began in Thebes. The last two rulers of the Seventeenth Dynasty (1640–1550 BC), Seqenenra Taa II and Kamose (about 1555–1550 BC), campaigned openly against the Hyksos, who at that time were allied with the Nubian kings. By 1550 BC pharaoh Ahmose I (1550–1525 BC), the first ruler of the Eighteenth Dynasty, had expelled the Hyksos and reunited the country.

The New Kingdom

The New Kingdom (1550–1070 BC), comprising the Eighteenth, Nineteenth, and Twentieth Dynasties, spans the period from Ahmose I to Ramesses XI. It was an age that witnessed the creation of a great empire with a strong central government and a strengthened economy. The newly reunified state extended its influence into Syria-Palestine, and annexed and colonized a large part of Nubia, exploiting the area's gold mines.

The New Kingdom is one of the best attested periods of Egyptian history and is often considered the golden age of the pharaohs. Most of the spectacular monuments at Thebes, including the royal mortuary temples and tombs in the Valley of the Kings on the west bank of the Nile, date to this time. Thebes was the religious and political center of the kingdom, while the age-old capital at Memphis remained the principal administrative capital.

During the New Kingdom Amun-Re became Egypt's state god. He was a composite of the Theban god Amun, and the great sun-god Re of Heliopolis. In the New Kingdom great temples were built in his honor particularly at Luxor and Karnak. These grew in size as the empire expanded. Eventually the priests of Amun-Re became an economically and politically powerful force that used the prestige of the cult to legitimize their rivalry with the pharaohs at the end of the New Kingdom.

The Eighteenth Dynasty royal line (1550–1307 BC) comprised a succession of rulers mostly bearing the names Thutmose and Amenhotep. Thutmose I (1504–1492 BC) organized campaigns that extended farther than those of any Egyptian king. He penetrated as far as the Euphrates and continued the work of Ahmose I, who had expelled the Hyksos, rehabilitating the series of fortresses built during the Middle Kingdom at the southern boundaries of Egypt. Similarly, the early Eighteenth Dynasty kings took firm steps to reconstitute the borders of Egypt west of the Delta, campaigning successfully against the Libyans.

Thutmose II (1492–1479 BC), whose reign has left little trace, was succeeded by Thutmose III (1479–1425 BC). Since Thutmose was still young when his father died, Hatshepsut was appointed regent. However, around Thutmose III's seventh year Hatshepsut proclaimed herself 'king,' assumed the full titulary of a pharaoh and ruled in a co-regency with her nephew for about twenty years, until her death. Thutmose III, who finally came to the throne in his own right, was the greatest conqueror that Egypt produced. Following Hatshepsut's death he launched a series of campaigns in the Near East starting with the reconquest of territory in Palestine. He was also active in Syria and in Nubia. A positive and beneficial result of all this activity was a marked increase in Egypt's contacts with distant lands and a consequent development in trade, architecture, and art which profited from the wealth of precious materials now available. The king built at many sites, such as Deir al-Bahari and Medinet Habu as well as numerous locations in Nubia and the Delta.

Amenhotep II (1427–1401 BC) and Thutmose IV (1401–1391 BC) continued the active policies of Thutmose III. Under Amenhotep III (1391–1353 BC) the Egyptian empire reached its zenith. The country was settled and prosperous and the pharaoh devoted himself to extensive building operations; these included the temple of Luxor and a vast mortuary temple at Thebes.

Toward the end of the Eighteenth Dynasty, the son of Amenhotep III took control of the government, first as Amenhotep IV, and then as Akhenaten (1353–1335 BC). The pharaoh set the tone for a new era by a striking departure from the conventions of art and religion. The king abandoned the traditional gods, closed down their temples, and elevated Aten to the position of 'sole' god. Probably as a result of a quarrel with the priesthood of Amun, Akhenaten created a new but short-lived capital city called Akhetaten ('Horizon of the Aten'), which he located on a virgin site at al-Amarna in Middle Egypt. Here two major temples were built, while at the northern and southern ends of the bay of cliffs, to the east of the city, several rock-cut tombs were constructed for the elite. While the pharaoh and his beautiful wife Nefertiti stayed at Akhetaten the empire declined; it has been asserted that Akhenaten neglected foreign affairs and that his position was weakened by opposition movements within Egypt. Akhenaten was succeeded first by an ephemeral figure named Semenkhara (which may even have been a pseudonym for his wife Nefertiti) and soon afterward by Tutankhaten, who changed his name to Tutankhamun (1333–1323 BC). On Akhenaten's death there was a return to the worship of Amun and within a few years the capital at al-Amarna had been abandoned in favor of the traditional administrative center at Memphis. Tutankhamun's tomb preserved an unsurpassed treasure, which was found practically untouched in 1922 by Howard Carter and Lord Carnarvon. The boy-king was succeeded by Ay (1323–1319 BC), an elderly noble, who possibly reinforced his claim to the throne by marrying the widow of Tutankhamun, Ankhesenamun. When Ay died, Horemheb (1319–1307 BC), a former general, became king of Egypt. It was probably during his reign that the demolition of Akhenaten's city at al-Amarna began.

A succession of kings, mostly called Ramesses or Seti, dominated the Nineteenth Dynasty (1307–1196 BC). The reign of Horemheb, who did not belong to the royal family of the Eighteenth Dynasty, served as a transition between both dynasties. Horemheb adopted a fellow army officer as his heir, Ramesses I, who inaugurated the Nineteenth Dynasty and the Ramesside period. Ramesses I, who reigned for a short time only (1307–1306 BC), and his son Seti I (1306–1290 BC) continued the work of Horemheb in restoring monuments, reasserting the authority of Egypt in Nubia and western Asia, where the Hittites had by now become a major threat to the Egyptian empire, and in repulsing the Libyans from the western Delta. In terms of architecture, Seti I constructed a new Osiris temple at Abydos and the reliefs in this temple and the paintings in his tomb in the Valley of the Kings are among the most elegant of the New Kingdom. Ramesses II (1290–1224 BC), who succeeded his father after a period of co-regency, created a vast number of temples, monuments, and statuary during his long reign. These included several Nubian rock-cut temples, the most prominent being that at Abu Simbel. He also founded a new capital city, Pi-Ramesse, in the eastern Delta, near the ancient stronghold of the Hyksos. However, Ramesses II inherited his father's problems in Syria and the major event of his reign was confrontation with the Hittites. Hittite and Egyptian records preserve divergent accounts of the outcome of the Battle of Qadesh, and it is probable that neither side could properly claim a victory. Ultimately, twenty-one years later, Ramesses II concluded a peace treaty with the king of the Hittites.

Merneptah, one of Ramesses' many sons, succeeded him (1224–1214 BC). He faced the threat of invasion from Libya, but won a decisive victory in the western Delta. The later history of the Nineteenth Dynasty is hard to establish as it was a period of confusion that included incursions from Asia and bad harvests.

The most important ruler of the Twentieth Dynasty (1196–1070 BC) was Ramesses III (1194–1163 BC). He successfully defended Egypt against attacks from the Libyans and the 'Sea Peoples.' The glory days, however, were finally over and Egypt's fortunes began to decline. After the reign of Ramesses III the throne became a source of rivalry and in ninety years several kings, all called Ramesses, ruled Egypt. Abroad Egypt lost control of Palestine and Nubia, while toward the end of the Twentieth Dynasty during the last years of Ramesses XI (1100–1070 BC) power in Egypt was virtually divided between the high priest of Amun at Thebes, named Herihor, and Smendes, who governed Lower Egypt from Tanis in the northeastern Delta.

The Late Dynastic Period

After the death of Ramesses XI, Smendes (1070–1044 BC) established the Twenty-first Dynasty (1070–945 BC). He ruled Lower Egypt from Tanis in the northeastern Delta, while the high priests of Amun, under Pinudjem I, controlled the Nile Valley from al-Hiba (south of Fayyum) to Aswan. The regime of the Tanite kings seems to have been without distinction and it was superseded by that of the monarchs of the Twenty-second Dynasty (945–712 BC), with Sheshonq I (945–924 BC) as the first king of the new dynasty. His accession coincided with a decline of the Theban high priests. In an attempt to centralize Egypt he broke the traditional hereditary appointment of the high priests of Amun by placing his son at Thebes in the office.

After nearly a century of internal peace, the Twenty-second Dynasty from the reign of Takelot II (860–835 BC) was a period of conflict and decline. The Thebans apparently objected to the establishment of Osorkon, son of Takelot II, as high priest of Amun, and a long civil war followed with the northern rulers. The result was that several powerful local potentates assumed the title of king. A number of rival dynasties (Twenty-third to Twenty-fifth, about 828–657 BC) were established with all ruling simultaneously in different parts of the country.

While kingship weakened, so did the high priesthood of Amun. Osorkon III (883–855 BC) established his daughter Shepenwepet as 'God's Wife of Amun,' an old Theban office. The god's wife and her adopted successor played an important role in the transference of royal power at this time. It was perhaps by this means that the Nubian king Kashta (770–750 BC), who marked the arrival of the Twenty-fifth Dynasty in Egypt (770–657 BC), demonstrated that he had secured religious as well as political authority in the region.

In the late eighth century the most important factions in Egypt were the descendents of the Twenty-fourth Dynasty (724–712 BC), who were local rulers in Sais in the western Delta, and the Twenty-fifth Dynasty (770–657 BC) of the Kushite kings, whose capital was at Napata in Nubia. Eventually they came into conflict. The Napatan ruler Piye (750–712 BC) campaigned as far as Memphis, but he withdrew to Napata, controlling Egypt from abroad without making himself the sole king.

It was his brother and successor Shabaqa (712–698 BC), the second ruler of the Twenty-fifth Dynasty, who effected the final conquest of the whole land. The Twenty-fourth Dynasty king Bocchoris (717–712 BC) was killed in battle and Shabaqa was finally able to dispose of all other kings in the country as well. He exerted Nubian influence over Egypt, moved the administrative center back from Thebes to Memphis and resided in the country for a while. Local rulers, however, remained largely independent and Egypt does not seem to have been truly unified during this period.

The combined kingdom of Egypt and the Nubian state was a major power, rivaled only by the Assyrian empire, which had been expanding since the ninth century BC. The Egyptian pharaohs attempted to thwart the spread of Assyria into the Levant by joining forces with some of the rulers in Palestine. In 674 BC the Assyrian king Esarhaddon attempted to conquer

Egypt. This attack failed, but his second campaign, in 671 BC, was more successful; Memphis was taken and the country was forced to pay tribute. The Assyrians, however, were not able to suppress all opposition. The Egyptian/Nubian king, Taharqa (690–664 BC), had fled to Nubia and returned within two years to reoccupy Memphis. Esarhaddon died during a counterattack against Egypt, and the next campaign, under his son Assurbanipal—aided by two local rulers from Sais (Necho I, 672–664 BC, and his son Psamtek)—finally established Assyrian rule over Egypt. Necho was left as governor, while his son Psamtek was installed as prince of Athribis. Taharqa had again fled to Nubia, where he died in 664 BC. He was succeeded by his son Tanutamun (664–657 BC), who embarked on a campaign of reconquest and killed Necho of Sais. His success was short-lived as the Assyrians again took over.

Finally, after several campaigns of unification, Necho's son Psamtek (664–610 BC) appointed himself pharaoh of the Twenty-sixth Dynasty (664–525 BC), also called the Saite period. He was the first king to employ foreign mercenaries, notably Greeks and Carians (people who lived in an area of southwestern Asia Minor), who specialized in trade and warfare, to suppress the power of local rulers. Some of them settled in Egypt, building up a nucleus of foreigners in the country. Foreign policy in the Twenty-sixth Dynasty sought to maintain a balance of power, but by the time Psamtek III (526–525 BC) came to the throne, Persia had become the main player in the region.

In 525 BC Cambyses (525–522 BC), king of Achaemenid Persia, defeated Psamtek III at Pelusium. Memphis was besieged and captured, and all of Egypt fell to the Persians who established the Twenty-seventh Dynasty (525–404 BC). Under the Persian kings, Egypt was reorganized as a satrapy of the Persian Empire and new administrative changes seem to have been introduced. Cambyses, the first ruler of the Twenty-seventh Dynasty, appears to have been unpopular, partly because of an attempt to reduce the incomes of the politically influential temples. Darius I (521–486 BC), who succeeded Cambyses, undertook major public works, such as the decoration of the temple of Hibis in al-Kharga oasis and the completion of the canal connecting the Nile with the Red Sea, the construction of which Necho II (610–595 BC) had initiated in the Twenty-sixth Dynasty.

In the years following the defeat of the Persians at the Battle of Marathon in Greece in 490 BC, the Egyptians made several attempts to throw off

Persian rule, supported by military aid from the Athenian-dominated Delian League. The western Delta was the focal point of these revolts, which finally resulted in the expulsion of the Persians. In 404 BC Amyrtaios of Sais gained control of the Delta and within four years the entire country was in his hands. Amyrtaios, like some other anti-Persian rebels, styled himself king, but proved to be the only ruler of the Twenty-eighth Dynasty (404–399 BC). In 399 BC Nepherites I of Mendes (399–393 BC) usurped the throne, founding the Twenty-ninth Dynasty (399–380 BC). The history of this dynasty was a long struggle to maintain the independence of Egypt against repeated attempts by the Persians to re-annex the country. In their struggle the Egyptians relied heavily upon Greek mercenaries.

Finally, the Thirtieth Dynasty began with Nectanebo I (380–362 BC), a general who originated from Sebennytos in the Delta. The dynasty was one of great prosperity, with building activities all over the country and an increased devotion to traditional cults, such as those involving sacred animals. Artistic traditions of the Twenty-sixth Dynasty were resumed and developed. Persian attempts at re-conquest were thwarted until 343 BC when Artaxerxes III Ochus (343-338 BC) launched the final assault, which ended with the flight of Nectanebo II (360–343 BC), the last native pharaoh. Once more Egypt became a satrapy of the Persian Empire; Artaxerxes III established the Thirty-first Dynasty, also known as the Second Persian period (343–332 BC). Finally, in 332 BC Alexander III (the Great) ended Persian rule in Egypt.

The Ptolemaic Period

The Ptolemaic era encompasses almost three centuries, following the death of Alexander the Great to the death of Cleopatra VII (after 304–30 BC). Strictly speaking, the reigns of Alexander the Great (336–323 BC), his half-brother Philip Arrhidaeus (323–316 BC) and his son Alexander IV (316–310 BC) should be classified as the Macedonian period (332–304 BC).

In 332 BC the second Persian occupation of Egypt ended with the arrival of the armies of Alexander the Great. Alexander (born in Macedonia in 356 BC) took possession of Egypt, which became a province of the new Macedonian Empire. Due to the unpopularity of Persian rule, the Egyptians greeted Alexander as a liberator and his arrival in Egypt appears to have been closer to a triumphal procession than an invasion. Alexander was crowned pharaoh by the priests of Memphis and founded a new city, bearing his name, on the shores of the Mediterranean. The foundations of Alexandria were laid in 331 BC on the old site of Rhakotis, and the city became a great Hellenistic center of learning, with a museum and a library, unequalled in the ancient world. However, Alexander never lived to see the city he had founded. He left Egypt to continue his conquest of the Achaemenid Empire and died suddenly in Babylon in 323 BC. His body was eventually buried in Alexandria, the city he had conceived as the cultural and political center of his empire.

Upon Alexander's death, attempts were made on behalf of his half-brother Philip Arrhidaeus and his son Alexander IV to hold the empire together, but finally one of his generals, Ptolemy, took over and founded a successful dynasty that ruled Egypt for approximately the next three centuries. Under the reigns of the first three Ptolemies Egypt flourished and many developments took place. New crops were introduced and by early Roman times the waterwheel (*saqya* in Arabic) had become widespread, increasing the potential of irrigation and the possibility of growing two crops per year. Furthermore, the widespread use of coinage led gradually to a monetized economy, while increased use of the camel opened up new possibilities for long-distance and desert transport. New ports were built as well and contacts with Asia and the classical Mediterranean world were developed. Ptolemaic rule, however, was not popular, and there were native revolts in the Theban area in 208–186 BC and 88–86 BC.

Macedonians and Greeks, as a result of commerce and employment as mercenaries, were familiar to the Egyptians well before the arrival of Alexander the Great. The Ptolemies assimilated much of Egypt's heritage, adopting pharaonic dress and reworking Egyptian gods into a new Greco-Egyptian pantheon, in which the cult of Isis gradually grew and animal worship became very popular. Moreover, throughout the Ptolemaic period traditional Egyptian temples were built, adopting pharaonic building styles; the temples of Dendera, Edfu, Esna, Kom Ombo, and Philae all date from the time of the Ptolemies. The reliefs in these temples regularly depict the Ptolemies as kings in the ancient Egyptian manner. They adopted Egyptian royal titles and their names were written in cartouches.

As Ptolemaic rule weakened and dynastic problems increased the instability of the regime, the Ptolemies relied more heavily on Rome. Under

Ptolemy XII Auletes (80–58/55–51 BC) Roman intervention became a reality, although the last of the Ptolemaic line, Cleopatra VII (51–30 BC), attempted to keep Egypt independent by allying herself with Julius Caesar, to whom she bore a son, Caesarion. In 30 BC the Ptolemaic Dynasty ended with her suicide and Egypt formally became a Roman province.

The Roman Period

The Roman tidal wave that engulfed the Near East during the second and especially the first centuries BC incorporated Egypt into its vast empire in 30 BC. Octavian's (later the emperor Augustus) defeat of Marc Antony and Cleopatra off Actium (west coast of Greece) in 31 BC, and their suicides in the following year, led to the annexation of Egypt as a Roman possession. Alexandria continued to be the capital. One of the four largest cities in the entire Roman Empire, Alexandria had long been a center of economic activity, science, and learning.

The newly acquired province had a special status in supplying Rome with vast amounts of grain each year. Large fleets conveyed this critical commodity to the capital and, when necessary, to other cities of the Mediterranean. Much of the province's governing (keeping irrigation canals operational, requisition of human labor, pack animals, and river transport) revolved around the timely harvest and transport of this staple to Alexandria for onward shipment to Rome.

Due to its important role as a breadbasket, the emperor in power closely supervised access to the province by important Roman officials. He understood that a contender aiming to overthrow him would, if possible, attempt to occupy Egypt to cut off the grain trade from Rome itself, thereby precipitating a crisis in the capital.

Aside from grain, other items of importance produced by Egypt included mineral wealth. Imperial quarries, particularly those at Mons Claudianus, Mons Porphyrites, and a host of smaller operations functioned, especially in the first few centuries of occupation, to provide beautifully colored hard stones for use in massive building projects in Rome and other cities of the empire. Gold, amethyst, and beryl/emerald mines provided other revenue. Egypt also played a pivotal role in the lucrative commerce flowing between the Mediterranean world on the one hand and other areas of the Red Sea and Indian Ocean basins on the other. A lively trade traversed the province via ports including Clysma/Cleopatris (near Suez), Myos Hormos, and Berenike on the Red Sea. That plus merchandise passing along the Nile Valley and in the Western Desert were also important sources of income both to entrepreneurs and to the government in the form of tolls and duties.

In addition to its political insulation, Egypt was also, to some extent, economically distinct among Roman provinces. It produced and was allowed to use only its own unique coinage until the late third century AD when it was finally integrated into the monetary system of the entire empire.

Initially, about twenty thousand troops were stationed in Egypt to insure security. Major bases lay along the Nile Valley with smaller units rotated on temporary duty to outlying desert outposts and along the Red Sea coast. These remote bases monitored activities including banditry as well as commercial endeavors. While there were some initial concerns about external threats (for example from the south), there was little likelihood of invasions from the east (except via Sinai), and less so from the west due to the protective deserts flanking the Nile. The major reason for Roman military presence was for internal security concerns. Roman authorities were well aware of the tumultuous nature of the Egyptian peasantry and of the frequent riots of the unruly urban masses in Alexandria. These had to be kept in check.

Based upon ancient literary and archaeological evidence, peak periods of relative peace and economic growth in Egypt and, more pertinently, in the Eastern Desert during the Roman era took place initially in the first and early second centuries AD. This is especially evident in the reigns of the emperors Augustus (27 BC–AD 14), Tiberius (AD 14–37), the Flavians (Vespasian, Titus, and Domitian, AD 69–96), Trajan (AD 98–117), and Hadrian (AD 117–138). There was also a brief floruit in the late second and early third century AD.

This first era of relative prosperity lasted into the third century, at which time Egypt and much of the rest of the Roman world suffered from political turmoil and economic problems. A renaissance took place beginning in the fourth century AD throughout much of the Roman realm, especially in the eastern part of the empire, including Egypt. This is evident in the Eastern Desert where various gold and emerald mines, and military installations, either continued or began to operate at that time; along the Red Sea coast, Clysma/Cleopatris, Marsa Nakari, and Berenike were especially robust in their activity in this era. This final age of prosperity lasted into the fifth and, to a lesser extent, the sixth centuries, but stagnation and barbarian problems, the latter being a concern for some centuries, became serious. The final blows came in the early seventh century. First was the Sassanian Persian invasion followed soon thereafter by the Muslim Arab occupation beginning in AD 641–642. Prosperity in the Eastern Desert had already declined precipitously in the previous century.

Geography, Climate, and People

Egypt lies in northeastern Africa and, including the Sinai Peninsula, covers an area of approximately 1,002,000 square kilometers (Pl. 2.1). The major geographical feature, which allowed Egypt to prosper for thousands of years, was the Nile (Fig. 2.1), one of the longest rivers in the world. Its sources include Lake Tana in Ethiopia for the Blue Nile, and Lake Victoria, which borders Uganda, Kenya, and Tanzania, for the White Nile. These join at Khartoum. The third branch is the Atbara River, which originates in northern Ethiopia and meets the Nile near a city of the same name. From there all three branches flow northward, as one, into Egypt. In Egypt the river valley itself is divided into Lower Egypt (the Delta region in the north) and Upper Egypt to the south. The Nile flooded every year starting in late summer and early autumn, covering the valley with a layer of fertile silt and clay. When the floods receded, leaving riverine sediments deposited on the floodplain, farmers rejoiced; their fields had been naturally fertilized. The ancient Nile-centric Egyptians called the Nile Valley, where most of them lived, the 'Black Land' *(Kemet)*.

The Nile River divides Egypt into eastern and western portions, both of which are deserts. West of the Nile lies the Western Desert or the Sahara; to its east stretches the Eastern Desert. These deserts, which the valley inhabitants called the 'Red Land' or *Desheret*, cocooned and protected them from numerous invasions. The deserts, however, also initially prevented Egypt from experiencing as much commercial, religious, or

H.M. Nouwens

Fig. 2.1: View of the Nile, one of the longest rivers in the world.

intellectual interaction with her neighbors as the other early Near Eastern river valley civilization in Mesopotamia.

Red Sea

The geography and geology of the Eastern Desert must be seen within the context of the Red Sea (Pl. 2.2) that forms its eastern edge, and the Nile River valley, which acts as its natural western boundary (Pl. 2.3). The Red Sea is a relatively recent creation in geological terms, about twenty-five million years old. It appeared when two of the earth's tectonic plates, which now comprise the African and Arabian landmasses, drew apart, resulting in a long, narrow, and almost totally enclosed salt lake. Today the Red Sea is about 2,250 kilometers long and, at its greatest, about 355 kilometers wide. The maximum depth ever recorded is 2,850 meters. Its only natural outlet is at the Bab al-Mandab (Gate of Tears), an approximately twenty-nine-kilometer-wide strait between Yemen and Djibouti, into the Indian Ocean.

The littorals of the Red Sea are deserts with few good locations for large natural harbors. Those few *marsas* (anchorages) that eventually and temporarily metamorphosed into harbors were formed when seaward ends of valleys were flooded by rising sea levels at the end of the Ice Age (about twelve thousand years ago). The murky marine environments they created precluded the growth of fringing coral reefs or killed off those that had once flourished there. This resulted in natural breaks in the reefs, which were attractive lures for sailors seeking refuge from the strong prevailing northerly winds and dangerous shoals and reefs of the Red Sea. Yet, these *marsas* were themselves doomed. Sediments prevented coral growth, but if unchecked, they also eventually inundated the harbors themselves rendering them so heavily silted and shallow as to become useless as places of refuge except for the smallest boats, such as occurred at Berenike, a Ptolemaic-Roman harbor along the Red Sea coast in southeastern Egypt.

From the floral and faunal points of view, the Red Sea would seem a northern extension of the larger Indian Ocean and, to some extent, it is. Yet there are forms of marine life unique to the Red Sea suggesting an evolutionary trend that sets it somewhat apart from the Indian Ocean. As a result of the creation of the Suez Canal in the nineteenth century, some Red Sea fish species have appeared in the Mediterranean and a lesser number of Mediterranean fauna migrated into the Red Sea. Despite its relatively young geological age—and until recently the dearth of densely inhabited coastal areas—and poor natural harbors, the Red Sea is probably one of the earliest large bodies of water noted in the surviving written records of human history.

Eastern Desert

The Eastern Desert has more in common geologically with the Sinai Peninsula and the Negev than with the Western Desert. Between the Wadi 'Araba and Wadi Sha'ayb in the north, today crossed by the seldom used crumbling paved highway between Za'farana on the coast and the Nile at al-Krymat opposite Beni Suef, and the Sudanese border in the south, the Eastern Desert encompasses an area of about 220,000 square kilometers, which is approximately equivalent to the size of Italy or the American state of Minnesota or Utah. Red Sea coastal plains in the northern and central areas vary dramatically in width from only several hundred meters or less up to fifteen kilometers or more before reaching the multi-hued red and black granite mountains that form the watershed between the Red Sea and the Nile (Pl. 2.4). These, in turn, give way in many, though not all, instances to a riverine plain in the west, or occasionally sandstone or limestone shelves that lead down to the Nile.

Farther south along the Red Sea coast, somewhere between Berenike and Shalateen, about ninety kilometers south of the former, the sharp and craggy mountains of the northern and central parts of the Eastern Desert eventually become large, open plains punctuated by low, flat plateaus and isolated hills and mountains that are scattered some distance apart from one another across a barren, flat landscape.

Climate

Until the beginning of the middle Miocene (about 15 million years ago) the Red Sea hills were stripped of their sedimentary cover. During the early Miocene (beginning about 24 million years ago) these hills must have formed a formidable mountain range. By the middle Miocene the Gulf of Suez area overflowed into the Red Sea. During the late Miocene (about ten million years ago) the lowering of sea level and desiccation of the Mediterranean Sea, with which the Red Sea was connected, severed the Red Sea from the world's oceanic system and converted it into a series of lakes. The Pliocene (5,300,000–1,600,000 years ago) saw a marine transgression from the south, which reached only the southern part of the Gulf of Suez. During the late Pleistocene sea level reached at least three different phases ranging from about one to eleven meters above modern sea level and it was still one meter higher in early recent times (the Holocene Age: about 6500–4500 BC).

By about five thousand years ago the Eastern Desert was in the final stages of becoming the desiccated, hyper-arid region that we know it as today. This was the result of the receding glaciers of the last Ice Age. Thus, the Eastern Desert is a relatively new climatic entity though its sedimentary and volcanic igneous bedrock predates one hundred million years, and its plutonic igneous and metamorphic 'crystalline basement' exceeds 550 million years in age.

As a result of desertification, the savanna fauna of Egypt, including elephant, giraffe, and rhinoceros, disappeared before the Pyramid age beginning in the Third Dynasty (2649–2575 BC). Today, sporadic heavy rains falling in the mountains of the Eastern Desert, and occasionally along the coast, especially in November and December, and the residues of that moisture that either temporarily pool on the surface or percolate down into subterranean strata, are the major sources of water for plants, animals, and humans. Where recorded in the region of Quseir on the Red Sea, average annual precipitation is a paltry four to five millimeters. On those rare occasions when the rains are heavy, huge pools and waterfalls transform this mountain and desert landscape. Floods of great strength, called *seyul,* spew torrents of water down through the wadis (Fig. 2.2) carrying everything in their path. They are death traps for any living thing unfortunate enough to be there. Yet, the immediate after effects are a blossoming of the desert with ephemeral verdant covering, spotted here and there with bright yellows and hues of purple, blue, red, and orange. Sometimes myriads of butterflies briefly appear as miraculous by-products of these torrential downpours and the resultant greening of the desert. Yet the enervating heat and hyper-arid climate soon reclaim the region. Even so, tough and

S.E. Sidebotham

Fig 2.2: Wadi Nugrus in the Eastern Desert.

resilient trees like the acacia, and scrub bushes can be found here and there throughout the desert even during the driest periods; these are mainstays of existence for the nomads who dwell here with their camels, donkeys, and herds of goats and sheep.

With a modern measurable 2,500-millimeter per annum evaporation rate—and it was probably much the same throughout most of the pharaonic period (3000–332 BC) and certainly in Ptolemaic (304–30 BC) and Roman times (30 BC–AD 641/642)—it is no surprise that any humans living in the Eastern Desert had to learn very quickly how to find, protect, store, and distribute water in the most careful and efficient manner possible. It followed that, aside from the indigenous peoples, it would be a highly centralized power that seized control of the principal water sources and the routes emanating to and from them. This tight regulation of the desert by the central government reached its acme during Ptolemaic times and especially during the Roman period.

Historical Background
Prehistory

People long resident in the Eastern Desert from Paleolithic times (about 250,000–10,000 BC) on had discovered the best routes, the most dependable sources of water, the habits and haunts of the animals that they stalked, and the optimal places to live. Later travelers and inhabitants of the area into the Roman period and later made repeated use of the tracks and water supplies exploited by their prehistoric and other more immediate antecedents.

Roads from the pharaonic period followed along paths established and preferred by their Paleolithic, Mesolithic (about 10,000–5000 BC), and Neolithic (about 5000–3400 BC) predecessors; we know this from the survival side-by-side of clearly prehistoric with dynastic graffiti and petroglyphs. Ptolemaic and Roman period roads continued expanding into the region, with soldiers, merchants, quarrymen, miners, and others traveling, exploiting, and living there with increasing regularity and in ever-growing numbers. These terrestrial lines of communication in the northern and central regions of the Eastern Desert crossed in a general east–west pattern, not broad expanses of flat desert plains for the most part, but rather followed wadis, the easiest routes winding through natural passageways amid the peaks of igneous and metamorphic rocks. The mountains in this area range, in general, from about one thousand to 2,200 meters in height, Gebel Shayib al-Banat, southwest of Hurghada, being the tallest (2,187 meters).

It was from the Nile Valley that the earliest recorded explorers entered the Eastern Desert in Paleolithic times. Initially, they sought stones with interesting colors or patterns to make vessels, small figurines, and jewelry. Those peoples, predominantly of the Paleolithic, Mesolithic, and Neolithic periods, and their descendants hunted, made stone tools and weapons, and left crude drawings of animals, mainly gazelle and ibex-like quadrupeds, ostriches and, later, sickle shaped boats, chipped into the rock faces of places they frequented attesting their presence and passing.

Pharaonic Period

At first glance, to those living in the Nile Valley during the pharaonic period, the adjacent deserts were vast, empty, uninviting, and even dangerous. Deserts were places where wrongdoers were sent to perish as exiles or as forced workers in mines or quarries and were also regions of the dead where cemeteries were located. Religion especially linked the Western Desert with the land of the dead; it was regarded as the entrance to the underworld where the sun disappeared each night. The deserts in general were associated with disorder and forces hostile to creation. Seth, the traditional Egyptian god of chaos, received the epithet 'red god,' since he was said to rule over the deserts and the general disorder that they represented, as opposed to the vegetation and fertility of the Nile Valley, which were associated with the god Osiris, Seth's mythical counterpart.

Yet the Eastern Desert formed an unavoidable bridge linking the Nile to the Red Sea whose exploitation followed beginning in the late Predynastic period (before about 3000 BC). Furthermore, the Egyptians knew that the Eastern Desert, a forbidding and otherwise frightening place, was a repository of valuable caches of mineral wealth, which were irresistible draws for them. The god-kings of Egypt understood that the Red Land had varieties of hard stones, mainly volcanic porphyries and other colorful rock types, and gold, copper and iron, and gems, especially amethyst and beryl/emerald, which provided them and their subjects with raw materials they could not live without. Especially favored were metagraywacke and metaconglomerate from Wadi Hammamat (from Early Dynastic to Roman times) and dolerite porphyry from Rod al-Gamra. The latter was quarried, apparently, only in the Thirtieth Dynasty (380–343 BC). These stones were needed to erect both massively impressive and also smaller more or less permanent monuments to the glory of the pharaohs: lithic religious and funerary memorials and their sculptural decoration in and close to the Nile Valley that aggrandized their reigns. Trekking into the desert to acquire these raw materials became, although eventually commonplace, always an ordeal most preferred to forgo.

With the political unification of the Two Lands, Upper and Lower Egypt, beginning in about 3000 BC, and from the Archaic period (Dynasties One–Two, about 2920–2649 BC) and Old Kingdom (Dynasties Three–Six, about 2649–2152 BC) on, incursions into this barren and forbidding 'Red' Land of the Eastern Desert from the comfortable, fertile, and vibrant 'Black' Land of the Nile Valley seem to have been mainly at the urging of the pharaohs. Throughout the Middle (2040–1640 BC) and New (1550–1070 BC) Kingdoms and continuing until Roman times and later, these quarrying expeditions into the Eastern Desert grew in size and number as more sources of ornamental stones, together with gold and other metals, were exploited on a larger scale. These geological riches commemorated the power and prestige of the rulers and the state and supplied the necessary wealth to afford both these expeditions themselves and those of conquest into the more southerly reaches of the Nile and into the eastern Mediterranean.

Ptolemaic Period

The Ptolemies, a foreign dynasty founded by one of Alexander the Great's Macedonian generals, ruled Egypt for about three centuries beginning in the late fourth century BC. During that time the status of the Eastern Desert changed dramatically. Ptolemaic interest in the region was more pervasive and a permanent infrastructure was created to deal with increased and more frequent exploitation of the geological wealth of the area. The trans-Eastern Desert highways also served intrepid entrepreneurs seeking other merchandise in the Red Sea and Indian Ocean, especially at this time aromatics and spices. Diplomatic embassies passed between Ptolemaic Egypt and other Hellenistic states in the Eastern Mediterranean and Aegean on the one hand, and Arabia and India on the other, but we do not know how important such contacts might have been to any of the parties involved.

The Ptolemies, most notably Ptolemy II Philadelphus (285–246 BC), builder of the famous lighthouse at Alexandria, and his immediate successors especially needed the gold of the region to pay for their political and military endeavors within Egypt and particularly throughout the eastern Mediterranean. It was in this latter area that the bulk of their efforts were focused against other former generals of Alexander who had also embarked on their own dynastic state-building aspirations. The major Ptolemaic opponents in the Near East were, initially, the Antigonids, led by Antiginous Monapthalmous (the One-Eyed) and his son Demetrius Poliorcetes (Besieger of Cities) and, after 301 BC, the Seleucids.

In addition to gold, the Ptolemies also believed that their armies required elephants, a species then unavailable in Egypt, but found in relative abundance to the south in areas of what are today Sudan and Eritrea. Soldiers from the Mediterranean discovered in the course of Alexander the Great's conquests in the east during the 330s and 320s BC and his battles with Indian and other forces, that elephants could be effective weapons of war, the armored units of their day. The huge expense and logistical organization required to secure, transport, and train the beasts, and the otherwise increased commercial and naval activities of the Ptolemies in the region, necessitated that various Red Sea ports in Egypt be joined to the Nile with roads and support facilities.

The Ptolemies are reported to have had a massive Mediterranean fleet of several thousand ships with which they retained an empire stretching into the northern Aegean Sea and including parts of mainland Asia Minor and Cyprus. These regions supplied critical timber for shipbuilding, copper (the primary component of bronze) and other important raw materials required by their military. Portions of the Levantine coast of what are today Israel and Lebanon changed hands periodically between the Ptolemies and their most potent and long-term adversaries, the Seleucids. It was in this arena that the mighty Ptolemaic fleet and its elephant phalanxes were dispatched.

A number of ancient authors including Theophrastus from Lesbos, an island in the Aegean, Agatharchides of Cnidus, a city in Asia Minor, and Diodorus Siculus, from Sicily as his name implies, provide details about the Red Sea, and the coastal and inland areas of the Eastern Desert in Ptolemaic times. Their writings, some of which are now lost, and those of other Ptolemaic period authors, are preserved in some instances only in later Roman accounts. Theophrastus, a student of the philosopher Aristotle who lived throughout much of the fourth and into the early third century BC, discussed minerals derived from the Eastern Desert. Agatharchides, although writing in the second century BC, used mainly sources from the previous century when penning his book, *On the Erythraean Sea,* as the Red Sea was then called. He is a font of information and lore about the peoples dwelling along the Red Sea littoral and his stories have an anthropological ring to them. Diodorus visited Egypt in the middle of the first century BC and left some fascinating descriptions of the Eastern Desert in his day in his book *Bibliotheka.* Of special interest to us is Diodorus' detailed account of Ptolemaic period gold mining activities in the Eastern Desert. There are also numerous inscriptions carved on stone, texts on papyri, and records on ostraca (broken pottery shards or flakes of limestone) from the Ptolemaic period that provide copious information on various facets of the Eastern Desert.

Roman Period

In the Roman period, which began after the suicides of Marc Antony and Cleopatra VII in 30 BC and the Roman Emperor Octavian-Augustus' annexation of Egypt, the main interests in the Eastern Desert were mining, quarrying, and international trade. The Romans sought especially gold and hard stones. The latter were hauled with great effort across the desert to the Nile Valley and from there downriver via Alexandria to far-flung corners of the empire to decorate temples and other buildings in Rome, Constantinople, and lesser imperial metropoleis. Extensive archaeological remains and accounts of a number of ancient authors reveal how important mining and quarrying in the Eastern Desert were to the Romans.

The international trade that passed through the Eastern Desert onward to the Nile and Mediterranean from the Indian Ocean via the Red Sea ports especially fascinated some Roman-era authors. They also reported on the names, customs, and physical appearances of peoples living along the coast and in the desert itself. Of particular importance in the history of the Roman occupation of Egypt are several early and late Roman period authors whose 'books' survive. One is Strabo who wrote his lengthy *Geography* in the few decades before and during the Christian Era. The encyclopedist Pliny the Elder composing his *Natural History* in the 50s to 70s AD and dying in the same eruption of Mt. Vesuvius in August AD 79 that buried the Italian cities of Pompeii and Herculaneum, is a great source for anyone interested in the Rome-India trade, and in the Eastern Desert and the mineral wealth of the area.

The anonymously authored *Periplus of the Erythraean Sea* appeared about the middle of the first century AD. It is a handbook written, likely, by a knowledgeable and experienced sea captain or merchant detailing the ports, peoples, and products of many emporia in the Red Sea and Indian Ocean. One later savant, Claudius Ptolemy, who wrote *The Geography* sometime in the middle of the second century AD, provided latitudes and longitudes for the thousands of places he listed from northwest of Britain to Southeast Asia. He is most knowledgeable, of course, about the Roman Empire, but because he underestimated the circumference of the earth by about twenty-five percent, his locations are inaccurate. Yet his was, perhaps, the most detailed account of the location of ancient ports of the Red Sea and he is the only surviving ancient author who reports an emporium called Leukos Limen, somewhere on the Egyptian coast, which has never been conclusively located or identified. Subsequently, maps and itineraries of other authors appeared, the most famous of the latter being the *Antonine Itinerary* and the *Peutinger Table*. The latest 'ancient' itinerary that includes the Eastern Desert is the so-called *Ravenna Cosmography*, the compiler or compilers of which clearly had no firsthand experience with the Red Sea or the Eastern Desert and undoubtedly simply cribbed their data from earlier sources. Other late Roman period authors like the Theban Olympiodorus in the fifth century AD and the court gossip Procopius, writing during the reign of the famous emperor Justinian I (527–565), provide insights into the peoples dwelling in the Eastern Desert in their day and earlier and the relationships these 'Barbarians' had with Roman authorities. Accounts of the mid-sixth- century monk Cosmas Indicopleustes (One who sails to India) in his book *Christian Topography* deal with ports in the Red Sea and Indian Ocean and while his descriptions in some cases are somewhat fanciful, they cannot be totally dismissed.

Controlling the Eastern Desert
Desert Dwellers
From pharaonic times on, the central authorities controlling the Nile Valley always found it difficult to impose their will on the desert regions. Thus, it

was the ideal place for bandits, malcontents, tax evaders, the religiously or politically persecuted, and others to escape the long and often repressive arm of the law. It is fairly clear even in the Ptolemaic and Roman eras that complete domination of the desert was never achieved and, in fact, was deemed impossible by any central power. Placement of the various forts indicates that the Ptolemaic and Roman governments sought only to control the main lines of communications, major sources of water and important nodes of mineral wealth. Monitoring those passing through the region was important, but control of the entirety of this vast area was impractical and unnecessary. This left many of the indigenous peoples relatively free to do as they pleased.

In pharaonic times desert inhabitants such as the Medjay caused problems and later in the Roman period, groups such as the Blemmyes and the Nobadae appear repeatedly in the writings of ancient authors as openly challenging the Nile-based authorities. Occasionally, these seemingly nomadic groups attacked and occupied important cities along the Nile or major mining regions of the desert and possibly one or more of the Red Sea ports, too. The authorities never completely or permanently subdued them. This did not mean that all contacts between the desert dwellers and the 'outsiders' were necessarily confrontational. Occasionally we have evidence that some type of *modus vivendi* existed, which had either been formally ratified by treaty or had been a *de facto* arrangement, which was in all parties' best interests.

Desert Travel

Movement across the Eastern Desert was never easy even at the height of the Roman occupation. Unpaved roads and lack of milestones made travel more risky than in other parts of the Mediterranean world at that time, and modes of transport were limited to human pedestrian traffic, donkeys, and later camels and horses. Although wheeled transport was used in the Roman period, it was mainly, though not exclusively, confined to hauling quarried stone to the Nile especially from the large sites of Mons Porphyrites and Mons Claudianus in the central parts of the desert. Some wagons and chariots carrying water, provisions and passengers are known to have traveled along a road between the Nile at Coptos (modern Quft) and the Red Sea near Quseir. Each type of transport had its advantages. Wagons could carry heavy loads, but required large numbers of draft animals, were very slow, might bog down in sand, and could not negotiate steep terrain; wheels could break leading to long delays or abandonment of heavy cargoes.

Modern Interest in the Eastern Desert

There was some early modern 'western' interest in and exploration of both the Eastern Desert and the Red Sea coast from at least the sixteenth century when the Portuguese naval commander Dom João de Castro (1500–1548) recorded his journeys. Yet, most investigations of the flora, fauna, geology, indigenous human inhabitants, and ancient ruins in the region have taken place during the past two centuries or so. The interest really began after the Napoleonic invasion of Egypt, late in the eighteenth century. Accompanying his army was a separate contingent of scientists and artists who studied and recorded as many of the antiquities as they could. Publication of their research soon thereafter in Europe under the title *Description de l'Égypte* opened the floodgates to other explorers eager to learn more about Egypt. Understandably, most concentrated their efforts on the impressive monuments in the Nile Valley; these were, relatively speaking, easily accessible and offered a wealth of opportunity to study and remove to Europe the more interesting remains. Though some of these men ventured into the deserts, the remote, empty, and inhospitable arid zones were not major attractions. Initially, many European travelers to the Eastern Desert had been commissioned by the Egyptian government to locate sources of gold and precious gemstones, such as emeralds, in order to renew their exploitation for the benefit of the state. This was especially so when Muhammad 'Ali Pasha ruled Egypt in the early part of the nineteenth century. Sometimes, these Europeans explored the region specifically for antiquities and were financed by wealthy patrons or from their own proceeds and were not officially backed by political power brokers in Cairo.

There are a number of travelers whose importance to any discussion of the Eastern Desert cannot be overlooked. These include J. Bruce, F. Cailliaud, G.B. Belzoni, G. Forni, L. de Bellefonds, J.G. Wilkinson, J. Burton, J. Wellstead, G.B. Brocchi, Hekekiyan Bey, K.R. Lepsius, G.A. Schweinfurth, W.S. Golénischeff, A.E.P. Weigall, G.W. Murray, E.A. Floyer, D. Meredith, L.A. Tregenza, and the geologists T. Barron and F.W. Hume. Each of these men made important contributions to our understanding of

JAMES BRUCE

James Bruce was born in Kinnaird, Stirlingshire in 1730. He abandoned the study of law for a life of adventure. He traveled to Spain and Portugal, and married and became a widower within a year. After his wife's death he studied Arabic and the classical languages of Abyssinia, and resolved to travel to the source of the Nile. Bruce arrived in Egypt in 1765 and visited the Valley of the Kings where he partly cleared the tomb of Ramesses III (1194–1163 BC). He also traveled to areas of the Egyptian Red Sea coast and Eastern Desert and published his findings in a book with the lengthy title of *Travels Between the Years 1765 and 1773, Through Part of Africa, Syria, Egypt, and Arabia, into Abyssinia, to Discover the Source of the Nile.* His detailed accounts of Abyssinia reflect firsthand knowledge, but some of his descriptions of regions of Egypt's Eastern Desert, especially those around the beryl/emerald mines of Gebel Sikait are more suspect; they may well be based on second- and third-hand reports. Needless to say, he failed to discover the source of the Nile. James Bruce, who had survived disease, the desert, and the dangerous politics of warring African kingdoms, died in Scotland in 1794, after falling down a flight of stairs.

various aspects of the Eastern Desert providing insightful observations on the flora and fauna, the geology, the indigenous populations, and the ancient archaeological remains. Many of them made etchings, drew plans, and took measurements of ancient remains and, later on, took photographs. While some of these travelers, like James Burton, seldom if ever published their notes and those now linger forgotten in libraries throughout Europe—Burton's are in London—others wrote books and articles on the results of their explorations for scholars and the general public. Their credibility is not uniformly good as some clearly obtained at least some of their information from second or third hand sources (Bruce) or mistakenly located on maps sites they had visited (Bellefonds), or made fanciful rather than accurate drawings of what they had seen (Cailliaud). None of these men really engaged in what we would call scientific archaeology

today for few attempted any actual controlled and fully documented excavations aside from clearing a few grandiose looking structures here and
there. The importance of what they accomplished lies more in their noting
the existence of these places and drawing what they saw or thought they
had seen. Perhaps unconsciously, they left it to scholars of the last half of
the twentieth and early part of the twenty-first centuries to excavate and
provide detailed analyses of the histories of these remote and hauntingly
beautiful desert remains. In a number of cases we have found ancient ruins
that they overlooked.

Archaeological and Anthropological Work in the Eastern Desert

There is a modern popular belief that the Eastern Desert is desolate and
devoid of any significant archaeological remains. Yet this hyper-arid region
is, quite the contrary, the repository of many hundreds of archaeological
sites dating from Paleolithic to Roman times and later. The earliest remains
are burials and caves containing lithic tools. Later there are ancient quarries
and mines. Especially abundant are the myriads of Ptolemaic and especially
Roman remains in the form of roads, thousands of kilometers worth and all
unpaved, mines, quarries, ancient forts (called by the Romans *praesidia*),
many if not most of which protected wells (called *hydreumata* by both Greek
and Latin speakers), and water catchment and storage tanks and cisterns
(called *lakkoi* in Greek and *lacci* in Latin). Additionally, later Christians
escaped to the Eastern Desert to form monasteries and other communities.

Archaeological work in the Eastern desert after 1960 was slow to take off.
Some investigations took place during the decades of the 1960s and 1970s,
but it was really during the course of the 1980s that there was increased
interest in the archaeological remains of the Eastern Desert. This accelerated during the 1990s and continues, albeit on a smaller scale, in this
decade. Unfortunately, work in the area today is greatly hampered by both
logistical and financial considerations and the acquisition, frequently difficult or impossible, of permits from the necessary authorities. More easily
accessible sites along the Red Sea coast or on or near modern major paved
trans-desert highways receive most attention from archaeologists which, of
course, skews any statistical evidence we might have for analysis of ancient
historical trends in the Eastern Desert as a whole. Farther afield in the more
remote regions small mobile teams of scholars engage in surveys. These seek

to locate ancient sites and roads over a broad area and are best described as 'site extensive' surveys. These provide a good general overview of what remains exist, their appearances, locations, and their approximate dates and functions. Those expeditions that concentrate on drawing detailed plans of ancient sites, either because nothing more can be done due to time, money, or the impending destruction of the site as the result of modern mining, quarrying, or other development plans, engage in what we term 'site intensive' surveying. Drawing detailed plans and architectural elevations of ancient remains during a 'site intensive' survey might also be a prelude to future excavations. We have more to say about the different surveying methods and specific examples in Chapter 5.

Some modern anthropological work has attempted to determine the relationship between the ancient inhabitants of the Eastern Desert, like the Medjay, the Blemmyes, and the Nobadae, and those modern Bedouin now residing in the region: the Ma'aza, the 'Ababda, and the Bisharin. We discuss these groups in some detail in Chapter 11.

A Roman Imperial Road and the Northern Part of the Eastern Desert

M any tracks and roads of various sizes and importance criss-crossed the Eastern Desert from prehistoric times onward and these continued in use and were enlarged and extended later, especially in the Ptolemaic and Roman eras. These thoroughfares joined many desert settlements and Red Sea ports to one another and, eventually, to emporia on the Nile. In this chapter we will examine the Via Nova Hadriana, the latest known ancient route built in the Eastern Desert (Fig. 3.1). This highway also reaches farther north and is the longest of any in the region, about eight hundred kilometers. We will also look at some other ancient sites in the northern part of the Eastern Desert.

The Via Nova Hadriana was only one of several major highways that crossed the Eastern Desert in Ptolemaic and Roman times. These thoroughfares all invariably led to western termini on the Nile. The major Nile cities included, from north to south, Sheikh al-'Ibada (ancient Anti-noopolis), Dendera (ancient Tentyris) and nearby Qena (ancient Kainepolis/Maximianopolis), Quft (ancient Coptos), Edfu (ancient Contra Apollonopolis Magna and Apollonopolis Magna), and Aswan (ancient Syene). All these cities, except Kainepolis, had been founded and were active in the pharaonic period. Later in Ptolemaic or Roman times, however, these became more prominent. These Nile entrepôts did not exist solely to serv-ice roads leading into the Eastern Desert; they were self-sustaining without these desert highways. In fact, aside from the recovery of some inscriptions

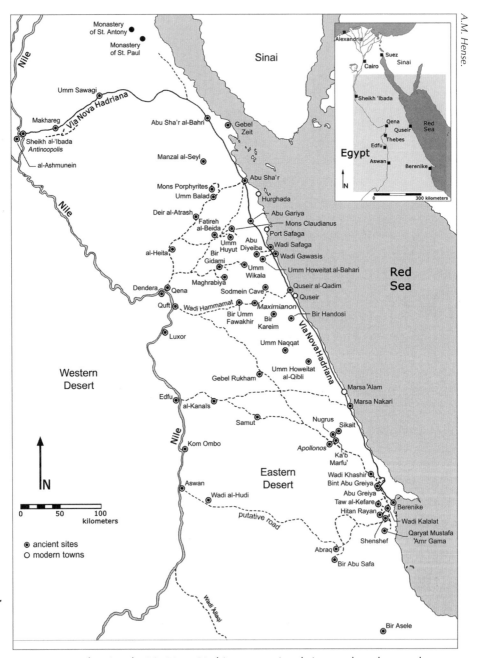

Fig. 3.1: Map showing the Via Nova Hadriana, associated sites, and road networks.

bearing on these Nile ports, little is actually known of the roles they played in Eastern Desert and Red Sea activities.

The one exception is Coptos. This site, about forty kilometers north of Luxor, has been sporadically excavated over the past century or so and has much to tell of its role in Eastern Desert and Red Sea activities. Inscriptions found at Coptos reveal the presence of merchants and troops. Some of the latter hailed from the Syrian Desert caravan city of Palmyra as recorded in one text dated July AD 216. These mounted soldiers patrolled the roads across which caravans bore merchandise from the lucrative Red Sea–Indian Ocean trade. A recent archaeological project conducted at Coptos by Assiut University and the University of Michigan unearthed pottery indicating close connections with many of the forts guarding the roads leading to the Red Sea ports of Myos Hormos and Berenike and with these emporia themselves.

Antinoopolis

Lying on the edge of the Nile, the ruins of the ancient city of Antinoopolis first came to the modern western world's attention as the result of Napoleon's invasion of Egypt in 1798. Accompanying his 25,000-man army was a sizeable and impressive group of 165 scholars, scientists, engineers, and artists who avidly studied, described, and produced measured drawings and sketches of the natural wonders and ancient man-made monuments of Egypt. They were interested in all periods of Egyptian antiquity, including the Roman, and eventually presented their findings to the general public in a monumental publication entitled *Description de l'Égypte*. This *magnum opus*, published between 1809 and 1828, comprised twenty-four tomes including ten folio volumes with over three thousand illustrations, five of which were devoted to antiquities and ancient monuments. In these impressive, often still reproduced and cited publications, the French scholars drew images of the remains of ancient Antinoopolis. Unfortunately, much of what they saw and recorded over two hundred years ago has since disappeared; local villagers have robbed many of the building stones to recycle. However, those Napoleonic-era drawings together with plans sketched by the British savant J.G. Wilkinson (Fig. 3.2), who visited Antinoopolis several decades after Napoleon's scientists, provide us with an idea of what has been lost since the late eighteenth and early nineteenth centuries. Recent

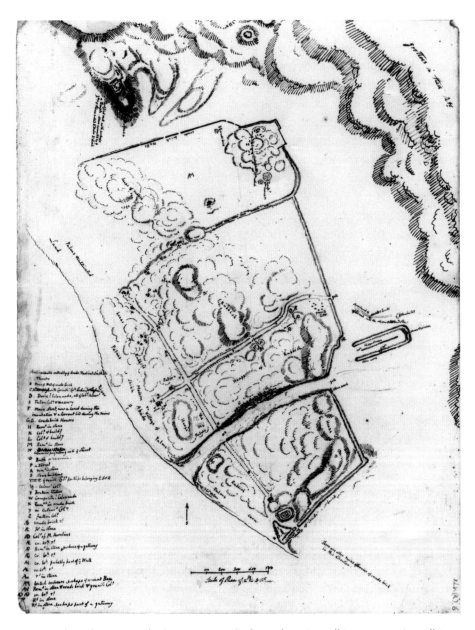

Fig. 3.2: Plan of Antinoopolis (c. 1821–1833), drawn by J.G. Wilkinson. Ms. G. Wilkinson XLV. K.6 dep. a. 15, fol. 158; Gardner Wilkinson papers from Calke Abbey, Bodleian Library, Oxford; courtesy of the National Trust.

excavations at Antinoopolis have added to our knowledge by unearthing ancient texts, a beautiful array of brilliant polychrome textiles and clothing, and other artifacts that bring to light what life was like in this important Middle Egyptian city from the second century AD until late antiquity.

SIR JOHN GARDNER WILKINSON

Sir John Gardner Wilkinson was, from the archaeological point of view, undoubtedly the most important of all the early nineteenth century visitors to the Eastern Desert. He was born in Little Missenden, Buckinghamshire, in 1797. He studied at Exeter College, Oxford, but left in 1818 without taking a degree. In 1820, while visiting Italy, Sir William Gell, an antiquarian, persuaded him to give up his plans for an army career and join, instead, the ranks of archaeologists and Egyptologists.

During his initial visit to Egypt between 1821 and 1833 Wilkinson traveled extensively and took copious but extremely illegible notes, and made many drawings and plans, most of surprising accuracy. Wilkinson was the first to translate correctly many of the ancient Egyptian royal names and he was also the first to make a survey, something he did single-handedly, of all the major sites of Egypt, including the tombs then known in the Valley of the Kings. He assigned numbers to the twenty tombs then identified, establishing the recording system still used today. He published the results of his research in several books and articles. Most important for any study of the Eastern Desert is his volume *Topography of Thebes, and General View of Egypt*, which appeared in 1835. His book, *The Manners and Customs of the Ancient Egyptians*, published in 1837, was the most comprehensive overview of ancient Egypt of its time. In 1839 Wilkinson was dubbed a knight, while in 1852, he was granted a DCL from the Oxford University. His drawings, preserved now in the Bodleian Library in Oxford, and descriptions are important for our understanding of what many of the ancient sites looked like over a century and a half ago. These, in some instances, record features that have since disappeared. Wilkinson died in Llandovery in Wales in 1875.

Hadrian founded Antinoopolis in AD 130 to honor his deceased paramour Antinoos. Originally from Bithynia in Asia Minor, Antinoos had been a favorite of the emperor's for several years. Yet, while on a sightseeing junket and tour of inspection in Egypt with the emperor, Antinoos mysteriously drowned in the Nile. It has never been determined if his death was an accident, suicide, or the result of foul play. In any event, Hadrian was so distraught that he ordered statues carved, coins minted, and a religious cult established in honor of his beloved. He also founded his eponymous city on the east bank of the Nile on the site of an earlier settlement. Hadrian then linked his new metropolis by road to near the Red Sea coast and thence it ran parallel to that littoral terminating at the emporium of Berenike. It was, in fact, the only Roman road in the Eastern Desert to join all the Red Sea ports (except at Suez) to one another by a land route.

The Via Nova Hadriana

According to a famous inscription carved on stone in Greek and dated February 25, AD 137, the Roman Emperor Hadrian (AD 117–138) built the eponymous Via Nova Hadriana as a new road from Antinoopolis to Berenike on the Red Sea. The inscription goes on to record that Hadrian furnished his flat, level highway with wells, stations, and forts. Although similar in appearance to other Roman roads in the Eastern Desert, the function and orientation of the Via Nova Hadriana was, on the whole, different from those older companion routes. While earlier major 'classical' (that is, Ptolemaic and Roman) roads in the Eastern Desert had a generally east–west orientation and connected ports on the Nile with counterparts on the Red Sea coast, or joined mines and quarries in the desert to the Nile, the Via Nova Hadriana seems not to have had these major functions. In other words, while the other highways provided communication networks for commercial and military reasons, as well as for administrative and control purposes, the Via Nova Hadriana primarily seems to have been constructed as an administrative route. In this respect, the Via Nova Hadriana, although unique in the Eastern Desert, was not, however, unusual for the Roman Empire as a whole; other roads in the Roman Near East also seem to have had primarily an administrative function. For example, the famous Via Nova Traiana, built in the neighboring

Roman province of Arabia (basically Jordan and parts of the Negev and southern Syria) during the reign of Hadrian's immediate predecessor, the Emperor Trajan (AD 98–117), seems to have had an analogous function. The Via Nova Traiana linked the southern Syrian city of Bostra to the Red Sea port at Aila/Aelana (modern Aqaba in Jordan). The length and course of the Via Nova Hadriana simply would not have been attractive to merchants shipping goods between the Nile and the Red Sea; the more southerly and older routes in the Eastern Desert were better situated, more direct and shorter for those purposes. As a result, they would have permitted faster and easier travel thereby reducing costs and time on the road, all important considerations to merchants wishing to keep overhead costs down and get products to markets as quickly as possible. Although some small mining and quarrying operations may have benefited from their locations near the Via Nova Hadriana, no major mines or quarries lay close to the road itself. Some gold mines, an amethyst quarry, and some other as yet unidentifiable late Roman settlements located in the desert not far from the Red Sea probably had trunk roads linking them to a coastal road that pre-existed the Via Nova Hadriana. From the time of Hadrian on, the Via Nova Hadriana itself would have replaced this earlier coastal highway. Yet, the need to link desert settlements to a coastal highway probably would not have been a major consideration to those engaged in the initial construction of the Via Nova Hadriana.

The Via Nova Hadriana, like all those ancient roads found thus far in the Eastern Desert, was unpaved. The Romans had similar unmetalled roads elsewhere in the empire; they called these *viae terrenae*. For the vast majority of the Eastern Desert tracks, paving was totally unnecessary. We must assume by their locations in such an arid landscape that any traffic they bore would have been relatively light compared to that carried by their paved counterparts in Europe. Most travel in the desert would also not have been vehicular, but human pedestrian and animal, which would not have required paving, except perhaps in extremely soft sandy areas. Those sandy areas today that preserve paving appear to have been constructed in relatively modern times to assist movement of motor traffic associated with quarrying operations in the earlier part of the twentieth century. In all likelihood, any ancient paving that might have once spanned the sandy zones would probably have been washed away long ago by the *seyul*.

There is an extremely long and impressive paved road section that we stumbled upon in August 1997, but our very sagacious Ma'aza Bedouin guide told us that it had been built by the British about the time of the Second World War to connect Safaga on the Red Sea with Qena on the Nile. For many kilometers this impressive desert highway comprises millions of pieces of cobble-sized stones with the edges bounded by curbing.

Basically, the ancient desert thoroughfares were cleared of major surface debris, mainly cobbles, boulders, and other impediments, and this material was pushed aside forming windrows, which were the roads' boundaries (Fig. 3.3). The resulting smooth surfaces enhanced travel and the windrows also served to mark the course of the road in lieu of paving. The surviving windrows that our surveys have encountered, measured, and photographed are not, on average, wide or tall and seem surprisingly similar in their shape for long stretches. We assume they were created by hand, but there must have been some mechanism for smoothing them to a near uniform appearance; perhaps draft animals pulled timber beams along the route acting as a kind of bulldozer to create this rather even impression.

S.E. Sidebotham

Fig. 3.3: The Via Nova Hadriana: section of the cleared route.

S.E. Sidebotham

Fig. 3.4: Cairns of piled stones flanking the Via Nova Hadriana.

Cairns of piled stones, ranging in diameter from 55 centimeters to 1.5 meters, flanked the Via Nova Hadriana (Fig. 3.4); these could be found just inside the windrows, atop them or some distance outside them. Along some lengths of the Via Nova Hadriana cairns were spaced extremely close together while along other segments they lay farther apart. The placement of those cairns outside the windrows may provide a clue as to the methods employed in the road's construction. If used as route markers, the cairns placed outside the windrows would have been rather superfluous, as the windrows themselves would have served that function well (Pl. 3.1). The cairns that we now see lying outside the windrows may have been markers placed by initial survey crews and intended to signal the actual course that the route would eventually take. They may have been general indicators of where the route should pass leaving it to the judgment of the follow-up crews, who actually cleared the route and created the windrows, where within the lines of cairns they should place the route. There are also sections, and these occur well north of Berenike, but south of Marsa Nakari (perhaps the ancient port of Nechesia), where cairns survive, but there is no evidence that windrows were ever created. This could indicate that these portions of the route were, in fact, never completed. Alternatively, it could suggest that the putative builders following the cairn-laying survey crews determined that the natural surfaces in these areas were sufficiently clear and firm that no windrows were necessary.

As mentioned before the Via Nova Hadriana was only a small part of the massive Roman imperial road network. In the Roman era, the lands surrounding the Mediterranean were crisscrossed by tens of thousands of kilometers of paved and well-maintained roads; one estimate puts these at about eighty thousand kilometers worth, with an additional 320,000 kilometers of secondary routes. These were well marked along their edges by milestones. Generally columnar in shape, made of stone, and standing about two meters high, these Roman milestones provide a great deal of information about the emperors and provincial governors who built and maintained the thoroughfares and the distances in Roman miles (a Roman mile is 1,478.5 meters, less than an English mile) that any particular milestone lay between two important urban centers. Moreover, these ancient highway signs are a bonanza of information on who built the roads and they also inform us when and which urban areas they linked together. Some bore texts in paint, long since worn away by the sun, wind, and rain, while others were carved and the incised letters filled with paint, usually red. Most were written in Latin, but in the eastern portions of the Roman world Greek might also be used and occasionally even more local dialects, such as Palmyrene, are found on some milestones in Syria.

The Via Nova Hadriana, like other Roman-era roads in the Eastern Desert, however, lacked these traditional Roman milestones. It can, for much of its length, as indicated above, be traced by the cleared surfaces and the resulting windrows its builders often provided and by cairns. Unlike other major roads in European portions of the Roman Empire such as the famous Via Appia in Italy or the Via Egnatia—that ran from coastal Albania through northern Greece to Constantinople, and which were elaborately and costly paved engineering marvels marked by milestones—those in many desert regions, including the Eastern Desert, did not require the great expense and high maintenance costs of their European counterparts. We do not understand, however, why those roads in the Eastern Desert also lacked milestones.

Oddly, very few milestones, or possible road markers, have been found anywhere in Egypt. A few, possibly from the Ptolemaic period, but written in hieroglyphs, survived until recently along the banks of the Nile. Some may appear from Roman times marking the route to Saqqara. Other possible mile markers have been found in the Delta areas of Lower Egypt and in the deep south in Nubia, but their absence in the Eastern Desert greatly handicaps those of us looking to reconstruct the history of road building in the area in Roman times. Instead, the relatively good state of preservation of some of the unpaved routes, of the stations and forts along them, and the potshards that we collect from them allow us to date when the roads were used, if not their actual period of construction.

It has been estimated that the durable paved roads of Roman Europe cost about 125,000 denarii (a denarius was a silver coin, about one and a half day's pay for a legionary soldier in the early Roman period) per mile to build. Their sturdy construction meant that repairs, as are also indicated on some of the milestones, were needed only once every twenty years or so. Though undoubtedly laid out by Roman army engineers and created by the military, it was the civilian communities through or near which these highways passed that were usually responsible for their subsequent main-tenance. We have no figures, however, reporting costs for 'building' the cleared thoroughfares of the Eastern Desert. By their very nature, con-struction costs would, indeed, have been relatively cheap compared to the outlays required for their paved counterparts, but who maintained them? Aside from a few scattered desert settlements, mainly mining, quarrying, or military road stations, a few late Roman period communities whose func-tions are still not entirely clear to us but whose locations lay off the main roads, and the Red Sea and Nile ports, there were no civilian settlements along most of the desert roads, so we do not know how the expenses for their maintenance were handled or who actually repaired them when required; we suppose the military dealt with these issues. In any case, repairs would have been relatively simple consisting of filling in areas eroded by *seyul*, and restacking windrows and cairns. Repair of elevated sections would have been the most labor-intensive assignments.

The Via Nova Hadriana, like all of the ancient roads we have investigated in the Eastern Desert, varied dramatically in width. Our survey has taken numerous measurements and we have found that distances separating windrows on the Via Nova Hadriana range from just a few meters to a stag-gering 46.5 meters wide. Unbelievably, our surveys over the years have found Roman road segments that are even broader; one we measured near the quarry at Mons Porphyrites was fifty-three meters wide! These widths are, on average, several times greater than those of paved Roman roads known in Europe and the Near East. Why was there such a great variation in the width of the Via Nova Hadriana, and other desert roads as well? We cannot be certain, but we can speculate. It may be that wider stretches lay nearer the road builders' camps and were attempts to impress their superiors. The broader segments may also reflect operations of larger work crews. Narrower sections, or those that clearly received less attention through lack of windrows or smaller and fewer cairns, may have lain farther from the camps, had fewer laborers engaged in their 'construction,' and attracted less scrutiny by ranking overseers. These, therefore, might have received more desultory attention. We noted where the main road leaves Berenike for the Nile, and is co-terminal with the Via Nova Hadriana, that it is wider closer to the port and becomes narrower farther from it. Yet that 46.5-meter-wide segment of the Via Nova Hadriana noted above lay nowhere near any road station let alone close to any major or even less significant Red Sea port.

But there are other fascinating aspects of the Via Nova Hadriana. For example, in at least two places on the east–west portion of the route artificially elevated sections or ramps were constructed to facilitate movement of traffic from high ground to low. One elevated road segment occurs near Antinoopolis in the Wadi 'Ibada; it measures about eighty-five meters long and directed the highway around the northern edge of a very deep section of the wadi. The other is a ramp about sixty meters long varying from 4.3 to 5.1 meters wide that lay east of the small road station in Tal'at al-Arta and connected high ground on the east down to the wadi floor on the west. In another section of the Via Nova Hadriana, paralleling the coast just north of Wadi Qwei, the road seems to bifurcate as it leaves the wadi floor to the north for higher ground for reasons that remain a mystery. Two kilometers north of Wadi Qwei the two roads join; perhaps each was used at a different period in the long history of this desert highway or they were one-way conduits, one bearing southbound traffic and the other northbound.

The Via Nova Hadriana survives in relatively good condition where it traverses the desert between Antinoopolis and the Red Sea. In some places it is actually overlain by a seldom-used modern paved highway linking Ras Gharib on the Red Sea to Sheikh Fadl on the Nile some 245 kilometers away. Once the Via Nova Hadriana starts its journey parallel to the coast, however, its state of preservation is, in many places, somewhat more deteriorated. The reasons for this are varied. First, the water flowing east from the

Eastern Desert mountain watershed into the Red Sea has washed away large swaths of the road as the *seyul* cut perpendicular to its ancient course. Second, it is along and adjacent to the coast, precisely where the Via Nova Hadriana runs, that much modern building activity has taken place; new roads, pipelines, tourist resorts, scuba diving centers, and the growth of Red Sea towns and cities have all led to the destruction of those lengths of Hadrian's highway that come within a few kilometers of the sea.

At certain points along its course, a number of ancient roads intersected the Via Nova Hadriana running, in general, perpendicular to and west from it. These other highways all seem to predate construction of the Roman period Via Nova Hadriana and were major ones joining the Nile to the Red Sea, such as the ancient Quseir/Quseir al-Qadim (Myos Hormos)–Quft (ancient Coptos) road that linked Marsa Nakari (perhaps the ancient Nechesia) on the coast to Edfu (Apollonopolis Magna) on the Nile, or the two joining Berenike first to Edfu and then later to Coptos on the Nile. We will discuss these other roads in later chapters. In at least one instance a small trunk road linked the Via Nova Hadriana to the major roads connecting Berenike to the Nile.

The Via Nova Hadriana did not, in general, run close to the coast, though in a few places, such as just south of Wadi Safaga and immediately north of Quseir, it came within only a hundred meters or so of the sea. The reasons for this, though nowhere mentioned in any surviving ancient written document, are strikingly obvious. First, if the course of the Via Nova Hadriana had lain very close to or right along the coast it would have had to traverse numerous wadis as they debouch into the Red Sea and this would have resulted in large sections being periodically washed away by the powerful *seyul* flowing into the sea. This would have resulted in the need for frequent repairs. Travel along such a route close to the coast would also have been very troublesome and slow with frequent ups and downs as one ascended and descended the myriads of wadis, which often become more pronounced close to the coast. Fresh water also would not have been found in such close proximity to the Red Sea. Wells dug by a road near the coast would have provided either salty or very brackish water that could not be consumed by humans and, depending upon the extent of its salinity, only with difficulty by donkeys, camels, and horses. Instead, it was the intention of the builders that the road run parallel to the coast, in general, from several kilometers up to fifteen kilometers inland yet, where possible, east of the main chain of the Red Sea Mountains. By opting for this route, the land across which the Via Nova Hadriana ran was, in general, flatter, making road construction, maintenance, and travel along it easier. Any wells dug on or near the road segments this far from the sea would also have provided fresh water. Stations were spaced on average thirty-two kilometers apart with the closest known being about twelve kilometers from one another and the farthest being more or less sixty-five kilometers apart. While our archaeological surveys have traced the Via Nova Hadriana running directly into several Red Sea ports themselves, such as Myos Hormos and Berenike, it bypassed others by four or five kilometers, such as that at Marsa Nakari, or the late Roman fort at Abu Sha'r, which then were joined with it by smaller trunk routes. Clearly some of the larger and more prominent Red Sea entrepôts warranted diversion of the Via Nova Hadriana directly to and through them while smaller coastal towns, like Marsa Nakari, for whatever reason, were not so favored.

Sites along the Via Nova Hadriana

Along the east–west trans-desert portion of the Via Nova Hadriana the Romans apparently built no forts *(praesidia)*, but created, rather, unfortified stations and wells *(hydreumata)*. The lack of fortifications along this stretch of road contrasts sharply with the presence of *praesidia* along the coastal portion of the Via Nova Hadriana. *Praesidia* are also found extensively along other Roman roads in the Eastern Desert. Clearly, Roman officials responsible for construction of the Via Nova Hadriana did not perceive threats to the water supplies or lines of communication along the east–west course of the road to the same extent that they did with the coastal portions of the highway and as they did with other Roman roads in the Eastern Desert. We are not certain why this was the case. Perhaps whatever desert dangers there were, mainly marauding Bedouins or bandits, confined their activities to the roads carrying traffic of a more lucrative nature farther south and found the east–west part of the Via Nova Hadriana not worth their attention.

Along the road across the desert between Antinoopolis and the coast, most stations and the route itself survive in relatively good states of preservation despite the fact that those water stops had little substantial architecture associated with them at any point in their history. The fine

preservation is undoubtedly due to the general remoteness of the road sections, wells, and stations from any modern areas of habitation or
'development' and to the fact that, while subject to some flooding, the road
and stations in this area are not exposed to the same intense waterborne
seyul that occur along the coast.

One excellent example of such an unfortified stop on this east–west part
of the highway is at Makhareg (Pl. 3.2) about forty kilometers east of Antinoopolis. Remains at Makhareg comprise a few buildings and a large well
that were actively used from the second to fifth centuries AD. Our survey also
recovered Pre- or Early Dynastic stone tools suggesting that the station and
route merely exploited earlier ones that passed through the region. Huge
mounds of earth surrounding the well itself indicate its repeated clearing and
excavation over the centuries and its critical importance to people passing
by or dwelling in this part of the Eastern Desert. Nearby is evidence of failed
attempts to irrigate cropland in relatively recent times. While no hydraulic
features except the well survive at Makhareg, other sites along this portion
of the road preserve hydraulic tanks made of kiln-fired bricks and coated
with waterproof plaster, features typically found throughout the Eastern
Desert at Ptolemaic and Roman water stops. The road station at the early
Roman site of Umm Suwagi, about 110 kilometers east–northeast of Antinoopolis and seventy kilometers from Makhareg, is a good example of this.

Once the Via Nova Hadriana arrived close to the coast and began to veer
south–southeast the stations took on a different appearance; we believe that
our survey has not found all of these stops. We also postulate that at least
one trunk road left the east–west component of the Via Nova Hadriana and
veered north toward the Christian monasteries at St. Antony and St. Paul.
Christians from Upper and Middle Egypt making a pilgrimage to either or
both of these two desert monastic centers could best do so by traveling from
the Nile at Antinoopolis along the Via Nova Hadriana. Unfortunately, our
surveys along the Via Nova Hadriana between 1996 and 2000 had insufficient time and resources to investigate the existence of this putative route to
those still functioning monasteries.

All the Roman stops that have survived on the Via Nova Hadriana as it
parallels the Red Sea coast, and that we have examined, take on the appearance of *praesidia* defending intramural *hydreumata* and cisterns
(lakkoi/lacci) or, in some cases, wells located near, but extramural to the

forts. Yet, in some instances these *praesidia* also had other functions as well. For example, the *praesidium* at Abu Sha'r al-Qibli, where we found ostraca indicating use of the fort in the earliest period of the Via Nova Hadriana and immediately preceding its construction, also supported operations at the larger late Roman fort on the coast at Abu Sha'r, about 5.5 kilometers to the east, beginning in the early fourth century AD. Moreover, the *praesidium* at Abu Sha'r al-Qibli supported traffic between the larger fort at Abu Sha'r, during its military phase, and the road that led to the Nile at Qena (Kainepolis/Maximianopolis). Several stations on this latter road operated in late antiquity clearly supporting coastal operations at Abu Sha'r by linking it to Qena. We will discuss this route and some of these stations in a later chapter.

Other especially noteworthy *praesidia* on the Via Nova Hadriana include those at the second and possibly third century AD fort at Abu Gariya, between the modern coastal cities of Hurghada and Safaga, and about sixteen kilometers from the Red Sea, and the early Roman fort in Wadi Safaga (Pl. 3.3), about fifteen kilometers southwest of Safaga. In both these cases, cisterns and rooms inside the ancient fortification walls can still be seen. At Abu Gariya the interior well has been re-excavated in modern times and is still used by the Ma'aza Bedouin; a three chambered cistern also appears that has been refurbished in modern times though it is uncertain who did this. A water trough outside and north of the Abu Gariya installation suggests that pack and transport animals were watered there and not allowed inside the *praesidium* itself. This type of extramural watering facility for animals survives at other forts in the Eastern Desert and, as we will see in Chapter 13, was so placed for very practical reasons. At the Wadi Safaga installation, sections of the perimeter walls at the southern corner have been washed away by powerful *seyul* over the intervening centuries and no indication of an intramural *hydreuma* is now visible, but remains of waterproof plaster coating a kiln-fired brick basin in the interior of the fort do indicate the existence of internal water storage facilities.

Sites in the Northern Eastern Desert

That part of the Eastern Desert north of the massive Roman quarries at Gebel Abu Dukhan (ancient Mons Porphyrites) has been little surveyed and, not surprisingly, much less is known about the ancient remains in this region than in the areas to the south between Mons Porphyrites and Berenike. Other archaeologists and our own surveys have recorded a few other ancient settlements in northern parts of the Eastern Desert including some copper mines in Wadi Dara. Moreover, our survey investigated one particularly strange and undatable ancient copper mining site in August 1997 in Wadi al-Missara. Here, in addition to the usual array of workers' huts, our survey located several odd parallel straight lines of stones laid on the ground that do not appear to have been roads; until now we have no idea of their purposes.

About fifty kilometers south of the modern Red Sea town of Ras Gharib at Gebel Zeit a few prehistoric sites have been noted where investigators found lithic tools and other implements from the Paleolithic period and later. Furthermore there were some Twelfth Dynasty (Middle Kingdom, 1991–1783 BC) to late New Kingdom period galena mines, the latter of which were carefully investigated by teams from the *Institut français d'Archéologie Orientale* in the 1980s. In the Roman period an ancient petroleum seep at Gebel Zeit provided bitumen (Pl. 3.4).

Abu Sha'r

One major site in this northern portion of the Eastern Desert that is probably best known is the late Roman fort at Abu Sha'r. When our expedition excavated there between 1987 and 1993 it lay about twenty kilometers north of the center of Hurghada. Today it is completely surrounded by a tourist resort, construction of which began in late 1989 or 1990. The earliest modern European visitors to the fort at Abu Sha'r to record their observations were the British travelers J.G. Wilkinson and his companion James Burton in the 1820s, both of whom drew plans of the site (Fig. 3.5). From that time on many scholars identified the remains at Abu Sha'r with the Ptolemaic and Roman Red Sea port of Myos Hormos. Superficial comparisons of the site and its surroundings with ancient descriptions in the texts of Strabo *(Geography)* and Pliny the Elder *(Natural History)* confirmed in the minds of many nineteenth- and twentieth-century savants that the ruins at Abu Sha'r had to be the port of Myos Hormos. This association continued in some scholarly circles into the late 1980s despite evidence produced by our excavations conclusively demonstrating that the ruins at Abu Sha'r could not possibly be those of ancient Myos Hormos.

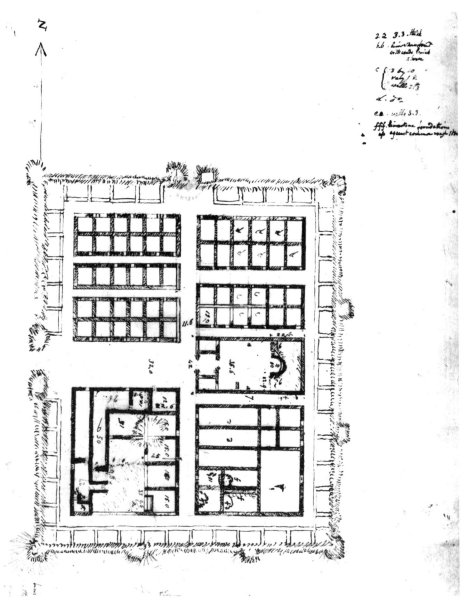

Fig. 3.5: Plan of Abu Sha'r, drawn by Richard Burton in the 1820s. Courtesy of the British Library, London.

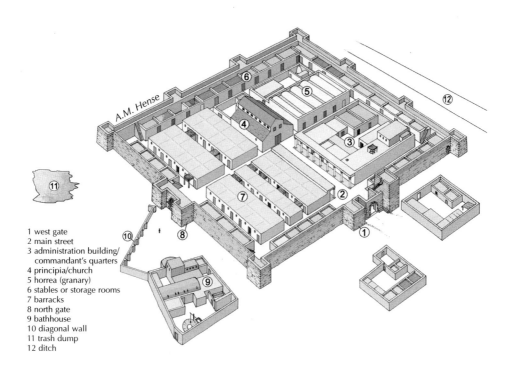

1 west gate
2 main street
3 administration building/
   commandant's quarters
4 principia/church
5 horrea (granary)
6 stables or storage rooms
7 barracks
8 north gate
9 bathhouse
10 diagonal wall
11 trash dump
12 ditch

Fig. 3.6: Reconstruction of the Roman fort at Abu Sha'r.

Our excavations at Abu Sha'r identified the remains not of a walled port town, but rather of a late Roman military garrison (Fig. 3.6). The typical Roman fort here enclosed an area 77.5 meters by 64 meters. The enceinte was originally probably 3.5 to 5 meters high and made of stacked hard stone cobbles and small boulders transported from the mountains and wadis some kilometers west of the fort. The walls were built on sand and had, surprisingly, virtually no foundations. Along the outer enceinte were twelve or, less likely, thirteen rectilinear shaped towers made of relatively soft, brilliant white gypsum blocks that had been carefully hewn. There were two primary gates, the main and largest one lay on the west wall and another slightly smaller one on the north (Fig. 3.7). We also discovered a smaller portal at the southern end of the western wall that had been blocked sometime in antiquity for unknown reasons. The interior of the fort contained a kitchen, food storage areas (called *horrea* by the Romans), a headquarters building

S. E. Sidebotham

Fig. 3.7: North gate of the fort at Abu Sha'r. Scale = one meter.

(*principia* in Latin), fifty-four barracks rooms (called *centuriae* by Roman soldiers) plus a larger building of unknown function—perhaps an administrative building or commandant's quarters—in the southwest. There were also numerous rooms abutting the interior faces of the fort's defensive wall. We recovered catapult balls (Fig. 3.8), made of white gypsum in one of the towers and in a few of the rooms abutting the main fort wall. Outside the fort's north gate lay the largest Roman bath building ever discovered in the Eastern Desert plus an extensive trash dump. The former preserved the hot bath (*caldarium* in Latin) complete with elevated floor beneath which heat circulated to warm the water, as well as the stoke hole for the furnace. We found windowpane glass suggesting that part of the bath had windows.

Excavation of the large extramural trash dump north of the fort and east of the bath produced abundant finds that told us a great deal about the daily life of the troops stationed here. These included many fish hooks made of copper, bronze, and iron, fishing nets, net weights, and fish remains. Clearly marine fauna comprised an important element of the garrison's diet and fishing probably also provided a pastime that relieved a great deal of boredom in this remote desert outpost. The narrow weave on the fishing nets and examination of the bones of the fish and of the remains of mollusks revealed that the troops caught mainly species that dwelt on or

S.E. Sidebotham

Fig. 3.8: Catapult balls in the south tower flanking the west gate of the fort at Abu Sha'r.

near the reef and in shallow waters and seldom ventured far from shore to catch larger pelagic fish. In the fort we also found large numbers of gaming boards and gaming pieces (Fig. 3.9) suggesting that this was another amusement to keep the troops busy during their off-duty hours. The boards tended to be incised on discarded pieces of gypsum blocks used in the fort's construction and the gaming pieces were most often shards of pottery shaped into round counters.

We were also very lucky to recover large fragments of Latin inscriptions when excavating the western gate in June 1990 (Fig. 3.10); we also found two inscriptions in Greek plus numerous graffiti at the northern gate in summer 1992. The contents of these ancient texts were very exciting and provided far more information about the fort and the troops stationed here than we could have reasonably expected. The Latin inscriptions announced that the fort's garrison was called the *Ala Nova Maximiana* and that it was a mounted unit of either cavalry or dromedaries. From the number of barracks preserved inside the fort we estimated the unit comprised about 150 to 200 men. According to the Latin texts, which are fragmentary—we did not recover them all—the fort had been founded (or perhaps refounded) during the joint reigns of four emperors: Constantine I, Licinius I, Galerius,

S.E. Sidebotham

Fig. 3.9: Fragments of game boards found at Abu Sha'r. Scale = ten centimeters.

S.E. Sidebotham

Fig. 3.10: Fragments of monumental Latin inscription over the west gate at Abu Sha'r. Scale = one meter.

and Maximinus II; at the time Aurelius Maximinus was Roman governor of this part of Egypt. The periods that these various emperors and the governor ruled allow us to date the inscription to the years AD 309–310. The fragmentary text further alluded to the fort at Abu Sha'r as part of the Roman *limes*, an administrative zone, by the sea. The mention in the text of the Latin term for merchants and traders *(mercatores)* suggests that one of the fort's functions was to promote or protect commerce.

The inscriptions we excavated at the north gate told a very different story and provided insights into the history of the installation late in its existence. All the texts that we recovered here were written in Greek and were Christian ecclesiastical in nature. The two most impressive texts were carved into the arch over the entrance to the north gate. In addition, numerous graffiti scoured the northern gate area in the form of personal names, all written in Greek, and Christian crosses. One graffito mentioned "Andreas who sailed to India." At the point when the north gate received all this Christian graffiti, almost none appeared at the west gate. This indicates that the west gate, so important during the earlier military occupation, had been abandoned and had collapsed by the time of the Christian ecclesiastical use of the fort. What happened to the Roman military garrison and why and how did a Christian group move into the fort?

The information from our excavations indicates that sometime in the late fourth or early fifth century the military peacefully abandoned the fort. There is no evidence at all that the installation was attacked or sacked or otherwise subject to violence. We are not certain why the army withdrew, but it seems to have been part of a broader trend that is evident elsewhere in the eastern Roman Empire at the same time. The military seems to have abandoned a number of forts in the eastern Roman Empire during the late fourth and early fifth centuries AD. At Abu Sha'r there was, then, a period—whose length we could not determine—of non-use followed by the arrival of the Christians. Fleeing the crowded Nile Valley for a variety of reasons in the late third, fourth, and fifth centuries, one lucky group of Christians would have found the fort an ideal place to live and worship with its ready-made defenses. These people seem to have been fewer in number than the military garrison that had preceded them as there is no evidence that they used the barracks or some of the other interior buildings at all. They converted the military headquarters into a church and, possibly into a *martyrium,* a place where the bones of some martyr were interred and worshiped. Yet, Abu Sha'r was not unique in its transformation from a Roman military installation into a Christian ecclesiastical center. This happened on several occasions in the neighboring province of Judea. We are not certain when or why the Christians finally abandoned Abu Sha'r. We found pottery at Abu Sha'r that might date into the sixth and seventh centuries and an unidentifiable 'Byzantine' coin that was minted after AD 498, but we recovered nothing that would allow us to date definitively when the fort was finally abandoned in antiquity by these Christian desert dwellers.

Shrines, Bathtubs, and Stone Quarries
How the Stone was Quarried and Moved
Along the Desert Roads to the Nile

E arlier chapters referred briefly to the presence of stone quarries in the Eastern Desert (Fig. 4.1). The oldest date from the Late Predynastic period shortly before the unification of Upper and Lower Egypt by Menes/Narmer in about 3000 BC. Smaller stone objects including cups, bowls, and cosmetic palettes seem to have been the main products deriving from the quarries at this early date. Graffiti and inscriptions found in long-abandoned stone workings attest the activities of quarrymen and masons from Early Dynastic times approximately five thousand years ago. While we cannot examine all the quarries that were exploited during the millennia of our interest in the Eastern Desert, we will discuss a number that are especially well preserved or suitably well studied. These occur especially in the Ptolemaic and Roman eras. We can, by looking at these, provide some insights into the great effort in time, money, organization, and suffering that went into finding, quarrying, and dragging the stones from these remote desert lairs to the Nile.

In the pharaonic period, anyway, the ultimate destinations of these stones were the temples and other structures erected for the deities and to the glory of the god-kings along or near the Nile. In later Roman times, however, most of the stone deriving from Eastern Desert quarries was built into huge imperial structures well beyond Egypt's shores. We can only stand in awe of a civilization that was capable of conducting such huge quarrying endeavors in remote desert regions and successfully hauling the stones, which were

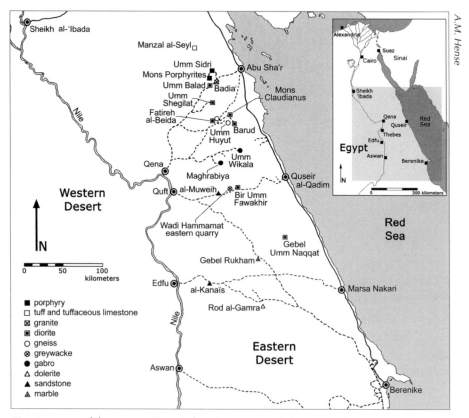

Fig. 4.1: Map of the Eastern Desert showing important stone quarries.

often giant monoliths, to destinations sometimes thousands of kilometers away in the far reaches of the Roman Empire.

Stone Quarries in the Late Predynastic to Late Pharaonic/Late Dynastic Periods
Gebel Umm Naqqat

A University of Toledo survey recently discovered a diorite quarry dating to the Late Predynastic period at Gebel Umm Naqqat. The quarry, lying seventy kilometers southwest of Quseir, consists of two sloping, discontinuous, trench-like excavations. Since no tool marks or other indications appear on the quarry walls showing what methods were used to extract the two varieties of pegmatitic diorite, quarrymen likely exploited the natural fractures within the rock. Through a combination of pounding and levering they were probably able to dislodge blocks between fractures. Given the close fracture spacing, however, the largest blocks obtainable would have been less than one meter across.

The Toledo survey found only one manufactured stone tool, a twenty-seven-centimeter-long pounder that had been crudely notched at one end to take a wooden handle. Instead of using manufactured stone tools to quarry the diorite, workers likely used large, heavy, natural well-rounded cobbles made of the local gabbro. Once loosened, the blocks of diorite were shaped into vessel blanks with the aid of smaller pounders. These vessel blanks were the ultimate product of the quarry. In addition to the quarry, other discoveries at Gebel Umm Naqqat included seven stone rings forming remains of a Late Predynastic cemetery, and an early Roman settlement, consisting of eleven well-preserved stone huts.

Nearby, west of the quarry at Gebel Umm Naqqat, is Wadi Sutra and this is the likely route by which the quarried diorite was taken away. This wadi runs northwest and joins Wadi Miya ten kilometers from the quarry. From there it leads to the Nile Valley.

Gebel Manzal al-Seyl

In the Early Dynastic period volcanic tuff and tuffaceous limestone were quarried at Gebel Manzal al-Seyl in the central Eastern Desert (Pl. 4.1). Like the diorite at Gebel Umm Naqqat, this material was used for the production of stone vessels, mainly for funerary purposes, which reached the level of mass production in this period.

Wadi Hammamat

From the Predynastic period onward extensive mining and quarrying activities took place in or near Wadi Hammamat (Valley of Baths), one of the dry canyons in the rugged mountains of the Eastern Desert (Fig. 4.2). Wadi Hammamat, which led to a major source of gold exploited at Bir Umm Fawakhir, lies about halfway between Quseir on the Red Sea and Quft (ancient Coptos) on the Nile and constitutes the shortest and one of the most important routes across the Eastern Desert. Within Wadi Hammamat itself are quarries for both the so-called *breccia verde antica*, a variegated green stone, and for the famous *bekhen* stone, known to geologists as a type

S.E. Sidebotham

Fig. 4.2: Wadi Hammamat (Valley of Baths), one of the dry canyons in the rugged mountains of the Eastern Desert.

of graywacke that does not occur anywhere else in Egypt, and which was highly prized by the ancient Egyptians. The *breccia verde antica* was used mainly for royal sarcophagi in late New Kingdom to Late Period pharaonic times (thirteenth to fourth centuries BC) while in the Roman era it was shaped into columns, basins, and wall and floor inlays.

The most striking reference to Wadi Hammamat is the so-called Turin Mining Papyrus, an ancient vividly colored map drawn on a scroll of papyrus during the reign of Ramesses IV (1163–1156 BC) of the Twentieth Dynasty (Fig. 4.3). The map came from a private tomb in the ancient village of Deir al-Medina near Luxor and is now housed in a museum in the northern Italian city of Torino. It was discovered between 1814 and 1821 by agents of Bernardino Drovetti, the French consul general in Egypt. It is the earliest surviving topographical map known from ancient Egypt and one of the earliest maps in the world with real geological content as it incorporates color-coded geological zones.

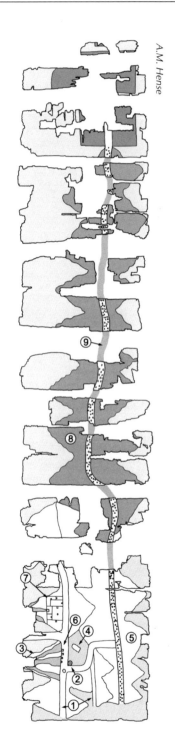

A.M. Hense

1 road to the sea
2 well
3 mountain with gold-containing quartz veins
4 stele of Seti I
5 mountains with gold
6 settlement of the gold miners
7 shrine dedicated to Amun
8 mountains
9 main route through the Wadi Hammamat

Fig. 4.3: The Turin Mining Papyrus.

The map illustrates a region of wadis and hills along with the locations of some mines and quarries, three roads, and some trees in the main wadi. Written on it are numerous short texts in hieratic script. On the largest and best preserved fragment of the papyrus are several cultural features, including a commemorative stela from the time of Seti I (1306–1290 BC) of the Nineteenth Dynasty, a cistern (or 'water-reservoir'), four houses forming a gold working settlement, a shrine dedicated to 'Amun of the pure mountain,' and a well. The main wadi is marked by colored spots, while the hills are shown as stylized conical forms with wavy flanks laid out flat on both sides of the wadi.

Although there has been some debate about which region the map represents (some scholars assert that portions of the auriferous regions of Wadi 'Allaqi, southeast of Aswan, are depicted), it is likely that it records a fifteen kilometer stretch of Wadi Hammamat. Located here were, as we have already noted, the ancient gold-working settlement at Bir Umm Fawakhir and the famous *bekhen* stone quarry, to which Ramesses IV alone sent at least three major quarrying expeditions, one involving no fewer than 8,362 men! The top of the map is oriented toward the south with west on the right side and east to the left. There is no constant scale, but by comparison with the actual distances in Wadi Hammamat it is evident that the scale varies between fifty and one hundred meters for each one centimeter on the map.

The papyrus map was probably drawn as an aid to or a record of Ramesses IV's *bekhen* stone quarrying expedition to Wadi Hammamat late in the third year of his reign. The author of the map might be Amenakhte, son of Ipuy, 'Scribe of the tomb,' who worked as the chief administrative officer in the village of Deir al-Medina, where builders of the royal tombs in the Valley of the Kings lived.

Rock faces surrounding the quarries at Wadi Hammamat as well as east and west of the quarries are covered with prehistoric petroglyphs depicting animals and hunters and more than four hundred inscriptions, which date from the Old Kingdom to the end of the Roman period (Figs. 4.4–4.5). The hieroglyphic and hieratic inscriptions record the activities of expeditions sent to obtain the precious stone from this area. On the north side of the wadi, remains of ancient quarrying activity include debris and a split, abandoned stone sarcophagus halfway up the cliff face.

H.M. Nouwens

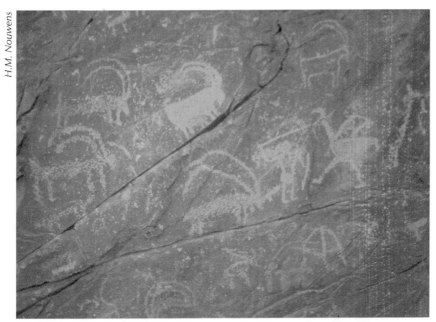

Fig. 4.4: Petroglyphs in Wadi Hammamat, depicting animals and hunters.

H.M. Nouwens

Fig. 4.5: Hieroglyphic inscriptions in Wadi Hammamat.

The inscriptions in Wadi Hammamat typically include a dedication to the Coptos divine triad of Isis, Horus, and Harpocrates or to Min, the ithyphallic fertility god who served as the protector of mining areas in the Eastern Desert. Min, who was already worshiped in the late Predynastic period, was first associated with Coptos and later with Akhmim, known as Panopolis in the Ptolemaic period, because of the Greeks' association of Min with the god Pan. Surmounting some of the inscriptions is an offering scene or an image of the god(s) mentioned above.

Furthermore, most of the inscriptions, which are historical records of royal activities, provide the name of the expedition leader and his titles, as well as the name of the pharaoh who ordered the quarrying activities. In other cases details of the expeditions are given, such as the labor force employed or the number of blocks quarried. It is from these reports of special achievements or events that we learn about the workings of the expeditions in the Wadi Hammamat. These include the methods used for quarrying, and the problems the quarrymen encountered in finding, selecting, and transporting the required material.

Although the first hieroglyphic inscriptions recording quarrying expeditions date to the great pyramid builders of the Old Kingdom (2649–2152 BC), the Middle Kingdom inscriptions (2040–1640 BC) are among the fullest and most informative. Especially noteworthy are the lengthy accounts of pharaoh Mentuhotep IV of the Eleventh Dynasty; they report his dispatch of ten thousand men and ample provisions for them to bring back some suitable stone to use for the king's sarcophagus and lid. According to the texts no fewer than two miracles happened during this expedition. A fleeing gazelle gave birth on the very block that was chosen for the king, and a rare flash flood revealed a well of clean water, all-important in this hyper-arid region. Another Middle Kingdom inscription, carved during the reign of Senwosret I (1971–1926 BC), tells of seventeen thousand men sent to obtain stone for sixty sphinxes and 150 statues, while an inscription, dating to the reign of Amenemhat III (1844–1797 BC), vividly illustrates the technical difficulties encountered in fulfilling the king's orders to secure certain materials.

The New Kingdom pharaohs (1550–1070 BC) are poorly attested in Wadi Hammamat before the Ramesside period; those few inscriptions provide little more than some royal names. The last hieroglyphic inscriptions date to

ROCK ART

The history of the Wadi Hammamat extends much further back than pharaonic times. Artifacts from the Badarian period (about 5500–about 4000 BC) and numerous Predynastic petroglyphs (rock carvings), found immediately northeast of the *bekhen* stone quarries, attest its early importance.

From before the era of writing, humans scratched depictions of animals and themselves on rock faces throughout the Eastern Desert. In the prehistoric era, in addition to representations of gazelles, long-horned cattle, giraffes, elephants, ostriches, and other animals, the artists who produced these images also carved sickle-shaped boats, animal traps, and human hunters. This art may represent game that they stalked for food or may embody more magical or religious meanings; we simply do not know. The richness of wildlife, however, is a strong indication that the Eastern Desert was more abundantly watered in late prehistory than it is today. The style in which these carvings were made, by comparison to designs painted on pottery, allows us to date them to sometime before the late fourth millennium BC.

the reign of Nectanebo II (360–343 BC) of the Thirtieth Dynasty. Thereafter, the record continues in a nearby shrine to Pan where there are demotic and Greek texts, dating to the Ptolemaic and Roman periods.

Rod al-Gamra

An excellent example of a late pharaonic (Thirtieth Dynasty) quarry was only recently discovered at Rod al-Gamra (Fig. 4.6). The dolerite porphyry stone pried from the desert terrain there using iron tools was employed to produce *naoi*. These were stone boxes in which relatively small cult statues might be placed. Five of the *naoi* quarried there remain on the site, abandoned for reasons we can only imagine. Rod al-Gamra lies not far south of the ancient route linking Berenike on the Red Sea to the Nile at Edfu (ancient Apollonopolis Magna), a road used extensively between the third century BC and early Roman times and one we will discuss in a later chapter. Yet, there is little or no indication that the people traversing this highway during those later times knew of the quarry.

ARTHUR E.P. WEIGALL

Arthur Edward Pearce Brome Weigall was born in November 1880. He left Oxford to join the Egypt Exploration Society Fund as an assistant to Sir Flinders Petrie. Between 1905 and 1914 he was the Egyptian Government's Inspector-General of Upper Egypt, Department of Antiquities. After he left Egypt in 1914 he became a designer for London theaters and a film critic for the *Daily Mail*. He wrote about Howard Carter's excavation of Tutankhamun's tomb for that newspaper in 1922 and 1923. He published extensively in several genres (novels and history) and on a variety of topics: Greek and Roman history, modern Egyptian history, the history of ancient Egypt, and Egyptian archaeology. Of his prolific publications on ancient Egypt the most relevant for our purposes is *Travels in the Upper Egyptian Deserts*. He died in a London hospital in January 1934 at the age of fifty-three.

A few stone huts or buildings—made of local cobblestones stacked forming walls built with little or no use of mortar or binding—that might have accommodated workers or administrative officials survive, so we can only hypothesize that activities at Rod al-Gamra were not conducted over extended periods. Perhaps only a few dozen people ever labored here at any one time and they may well have lived in tents. The sizes of the *naoi* preserved on the site are not substantial; the largest is less than 1.5 meters long by 82 centimeters wide by 80 centimeters deep, so their conveyance to the Nile would not have been overly difficult. We assume they were hauled there on small wagons pulled by teams of donkeys or horses. Examples of these *naoi* can still be seen at Egyptian religious sites and in museums in Europe; a fine specimen, which dates to the Thirtieth Dynasty, complete with a small cult statue inside, may be viewed in the Kunsthistorische Museum in Vienna, though we cannot be certain that this particular example came from Rod al-Gamra.

Stone Quarries in the Roman Period

The best-known and largest quarries in the Eastern Desert are, however, Roman in date and the extent of the work and the logistical complexities entailed in their ongoing operation dwarf anything that preceded them. Most Roman quarrying operations sought the various beautiful hard stones, mainly granites, diorites, porphyries, and others, available in the Red Sea Mountains that form the watershed between the Nile and the Red Sea. There was even a marble quarry, exploited in Roman times at least, located at Gebel Rukham just north of the modern highway joining Marsa 'Alam on the Red Sea with Edfu on the Nile. Some 'soft' stones (especially limestone and sandstone) also came from the Eastern Desert, mainly nearer the Nile. There was also a very soft talc or schist (called *baram* in Arabic) quarried and used locally in the Eastern Desert in a number of locations at various times; small bowls, beads, jewelry including bangles, and children's toys were the main products.

There are many facilities surviving from the Roman era that allow us to reconstruct how the quarrymen accessed the stone, removed it from high peaks to wadi floors below, and then transported it to the Nile. First they chiseled wedge holes along the line between the block they sought to extract from the quarry and the bedrock in which it lay. They then inserted metal wedges which they continued to hammer, thereby cracking the rock. The block could be further worked into the rough shape desired before being shipped to the Nile. No stones were ever carved and worked to their final finished appearance in the quarries for by doing so the item stood a good chance of being damaged during transport to its final destination. Thus, a thin protective 'coating' of stone was left on each product, which would be removed, and the final desired appearance achieved only at the point of destination.

There is evidence in at least one quarry, in Wadi Umm Shegilat, which lies south of Mons Porphyrites and northwest of Mons Claudianus, that the Romans occasionally sawed the stones to desired proportions after they were removed from the quarry and prior to shipment to the Nile.

There are dozens of Roman period quarries known from the Eastern Desert, but the largest and most important ones and those that have been excavated and best-studied lie in the central portion of the region. From north to south they include the massive operations at Mons Porphyrites, those at Mons Claudianus and the ones in Wadi Umm Wikala (ancient Mons Ophiates). There were others, too, some clearly satellite operations affiliated with the larger ones especially at Mons Porphyrites and Mons Claudianus (Pl. 4.2) and we will briefly look at those as well.

Mons Porphyrites

The expansive quarrying operations at Mons Porphyrites, in and around Gebel Abu Dukhan (Mountain of Smoke/Smoky Mountain) lay northwest of the modern Red Sea city of Hurghada. The site was first rediscovered by James Burton in 1822, but aside from a brief article he wrote for a British newspaper the following year it was really the intrepid and indefatigable J.G. Wilkinson who presented a paper on his and Burton's findings in 1830 and then published the first lengthy account of the site in 1832. A number of European and American visitors followed as well as many published reports of their journeys. Between 1994 and 1998 a British team undertook a detailed study that included surveying and mapping the remains and excavating portions of the site. Theirs is the fullest record we have of the ancient settlements and quarries at Mons Porphyrites.

The quarrying operations at Mons Porphyrites seem to have been confined to the Roman period, from the first into the fifth centuries AD. Study of the pottery, coins, ostraca, papyri, and inscriptions found at Mons Porphyrites does not indicate any earlier exploitation of the site, though in the 1920s the British surveyor and cartographer G.W. Murray noted some evidence for an Early Dynastic presence in this region. Early Christian hermits seem to have lived in the area during the latest phases of quarry activity and also, apparently, after the quarries were abandoned. They had a cemetery near some of the ruins, which has preserved tombstones inscribed in Greek from their time. There were, however, no Islamic quarrying endeavors at Mons Porphyrites. Briefly between the 1880s and 1990s there were various projects that sought to obtain the much coveted 'imperial' purple porphyry of Mons Porphyrites, but none was large nor, ultimately, successful in the long run.

The quarries at Mons Porphyrites (Pl. 4.3) are scattered over a large area and there were several settlements built to accommodate the workers and administrators responsible for operations. As with all human activities in the desert, the primary concern was the acquisition, storage, and distribution of adequate supplies of water and food. The large and impressive remains of hydraulic installations throughout the quarry and residential areas indicate that most if not all water was obtained from digging wells in surrounding wadi floors. Water from the wells was then channeled into storage facilities or flowed into troughs for consumption by the numerous

GEORGE WILLIAM MURRAY

George William Murray was a Scotsman born in 1885. He was educated at Westminster School and joined the Survey of Egypt in 1907 where he served as political officer for the northern Red Sea region during the First World War. He was appointed Director of Desert Surveys in 1932. An avid mountaineer, he worked for the Survey of Egypt for forty-five years drawing maps of Sinai and the Eastern and Western Deserts. His breadth of knowledge of the land and the people of the Eastern Desert is unsurpassed. He also exhibited great curiosity about the ancient remains and reported these in a number of articles and in his book *Dare Me to the Desert*. Murray died in Aberdeen, Scotland in 1966 and was survived by his wife Edith.

draft animals required to haul supplies to and stone from the site to the Nile Valley. Water from one such well north and below the main fort *(prae-sidium)* in Wadi Ma'mal was probably laboriously transported by porters in leather bags or amphoras up the hill and poured into a large cistern (known as a *lakkos* in Greek or *laccus* in Latin) inside the Roman *praesidium*, which was the largest building at Mons Porphyrites. Nearby were a small bath and several temples. One settlement in the quarries has the remnants of a broken tub or sarcophagus made of purple porphyry (Pl. 4.4) while British archaeologists found a spectacular Roman-era inscription written in Greek at another quarry village. This engraved stone, which depicts an image of the Egyptian god Min/Greek deity Pan, records on July 23, AD 18 (early in the reign of the emperor Tiberius) that Gaius Cominius Leugas discovered Mons Porphyrites and the various types of stone it provided. It goes on to state that he dedicated a sanctuary to (the gods) Pan and Serapis for the well-being of his children. The Greek deity Pan was associated with the pharaonic ithyphallic fertility god Min, who served as a protector of mining areas in the Eastern Desert and was also guardian of desert travelers. Serapis was a hybrid of the Egyptian god Osiris and the Apis Bull, with the attributes of a number of other Hellenistic deities.

S.E. Sidebotham

Fig. 4.6: The late pharaonic
(Thirtieth Dynasty) quarry at
Rod al-Gamra.

The most sought after stone from Mons Porphyrites was the 'imperial' purple porphyry used in structures such as columns, sculpture, and sarcophagi, especially those of the Roman emperors and their families. Spectacular examples survive. The famous statue of the Tetrarchs, four Roman emperors who ruled jointly between AD 293 and 305, built into one corner of the Basilica San Marco in Venice is carved from the purple porphyry of Mons Porphyrites. The impressive and intricately carved and highly polished sarcophagi of Helena, the mother of the emperor Constantine the Great (AD 306–337) and of his daughter Constantia, now in the Vatican Museum in Rome, are perhaps the finest examples of sculpted art from the Mons Porphyrites quarries. Black porphyry was also sought. These stones, especially the purple variety, were in demand long after quarrying operations ceased. Although work at Mons Porphyrites came to a halt in the fifth century AD, 'imperial' purple porphyry columns, clearly recycled from other earlier structures, appear in the church of Hagia Sophia built in the early sixth century by Justinian I (AD 527–565) at Constantinople.

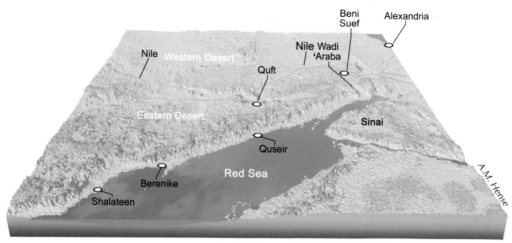

Pl. 2.1: Map of Egypt, the Eastern Desert, and the northern end of the Red Sea.

Pl. 2.2: View of Egypt's Red Sea coast.

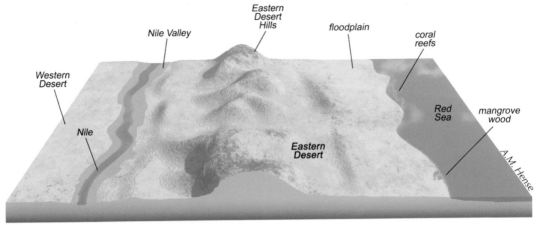

Pl. 2.3: Cross-section of the Nile Valley and the Red Sea area.

Pl. 2.4: The multi-hued red-and-black granite mountains in the Eastern Desert that form the watershed between the Red Sea and the Nile.

Pl. 3.1: The Via Nova Hadriana near Antinoopolis.

Pl. 3.2: Remains at Makhareg, about forty kilometers east of Antinoopolis, comprising a few buildings and a large well.

Pl. 3.3: The early Roman fort in Wadi Safaga, about fifteen kilometers southwest of Safaga.

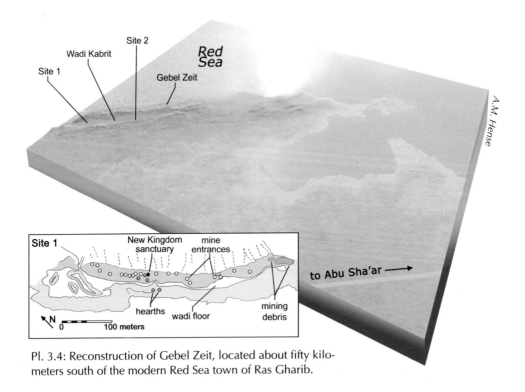

Site 2

Wadi Kabrit

Site 1

Red
Sea

Gebel Zeit

Site 1

New Kingdom
sanctuary

mine
entrances

to Abu Sha'ar →

hearths   wadi floor

mining
debris

N

0   100 meters

Pl. 3.4: Reconstruction of Gebel Zeit, located about fifty kilometers south of the modern Red Sea town of Ras Gharib.

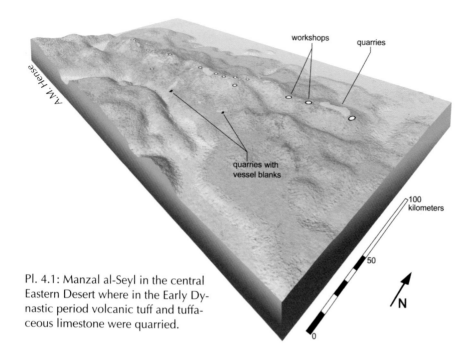

workshops

quarries

quarries with
vessel blanks

A.M. Hense

100
kilometers

50

0

N

Pl. 4.1: Manzal al-Seyl in the central
Eastern Desert where in the Early Dynastic period volcanic tuff and tuffaceous limestone were quarried.

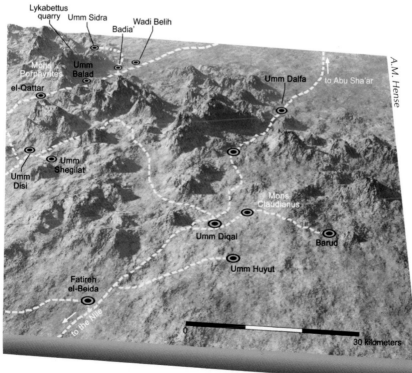

Lykabettus
quarry   Umm Sidra

Badia'

Wadi Belih

Mons
Porphyrites

Umm
Balad

Umm Dalfa

to Abu Sha'ar

A.M. Hense

el-Qattar

Umm
Shegilat

Umm
Disi

Mons
Claudianus

Umm Diqal

Barud

Umm Huyut

Fatireh
el-Beida

to the Nile

0

30 kilometers

Pl. 4.2: The area of Mons Claudianus and Mons Porphyrites.

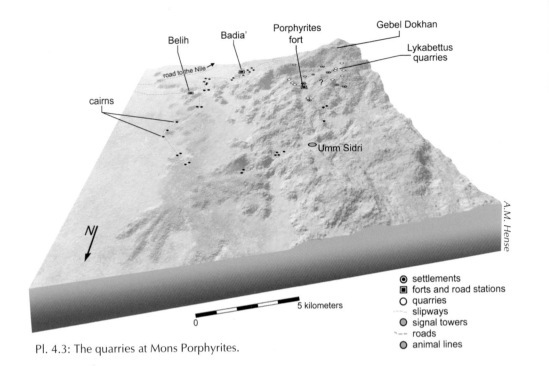

cairns

Belih   Badia'   Porphyrites fort   Gebel Dokhan

Lykabettus quarries

road to the Nile

Umm Sidri

N

A.M. Hense

5 kilometers

0

- ◉ settlements
- ▣ forts and road stations
- ○ quarries
- --- slipways
- ◉ signal towers
- --- roads
- ◉ animal lines

Pl. 4.3: The quarries at Mons Porphyrites.

S.E. Sidebotham

Pl. 4.4: Mons Porphyrites bathtub or sarcophagus in Northwest Village.

Pl. 4.5: Ramp of 1,700 meters length connecting the Lykabettus quarries at Mons Porphyrites to the wadi floor below.

Pl. 4.6: The Serapis temple at Mons Porphyrites.

Pl. 4.7: The well-preserved *praesidium* at Umm Balad (ancient Domitiane/Kaine Latomia).

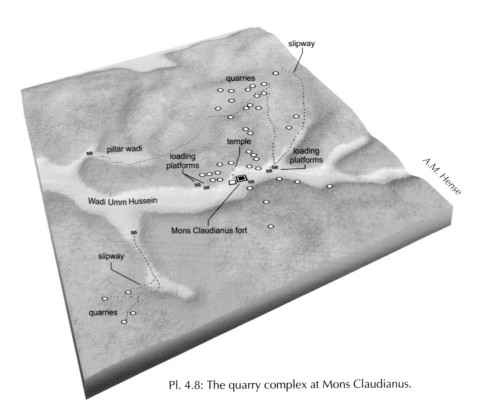

Pl. 4.8: The quarry complex at Mons Claudianus.

Pl. 4.9: Unfinished tub or basin in quarry at Mons Claudianus

Pl. 4.10: The large fort at Mons Claudianus.

Pl. 4.11: Small fort and tower near Mons Claudianus.

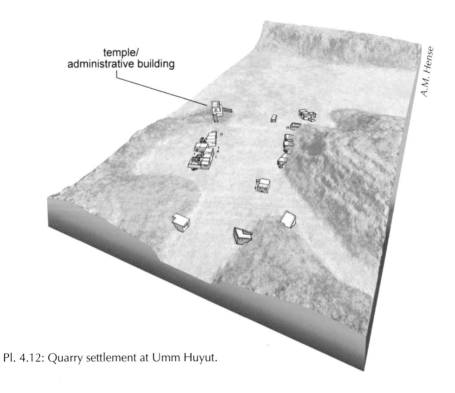

temple/
administrative building

Pl. 4.12: Quarry settlement at Umm Huyut.

Pl. 4.13: Possible shrine or administrative building at Umm Huyut.

Pl. 4.14: The fort at Badia'.

Pl. 4.15: Deir al-Atrash: gate with flanking towers made of mud brick.

Pl. 4.16: Deir al-Atrash: corner tower made of stacked stone.

Pl. 4.17: The lower fort at al-Heita with mud-brick superstructure, including nice examples of round towers flanking the main south-facing gate. Unfinished hilltop fort center and above.

Pl. 4.18: Signal tower on the Quseir–Nile road.

Pl. 4.19: Reconstruction of signal tower on the Quseir–Nile road.

Pl. 4.20: *Praesidium* at al-Zarqa (ancient Maximianon).

Pl. 4.21: Interior stairway in the *praesidium* at al-Zarqa (ancient Maximianon).

Pl. 6.1: The temple at al-Kanaïs, built by Seti I of the Nineteenth Dynasty.

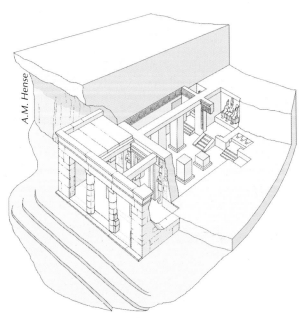

Pl. 6.2: Drawing of the temple at al-Kanaïs

Pl. 6.3: Bedouin guides in front of the Ptolemaic-era temple at Bir Abu Safa.

Once the stone was actually cut free from the basement rock in which it had lain and had been shaped, it had to be removed, often from quarries near the peaks of mountains. To move the stone artificial ramps—often of impressive dimensions—were constructed that wound down the sides of mountains. In the Mons Porphyrites complex, for example, the stone was laboriously, yet carefully dragged, we assume manhandled on wooden sledges and slowly lowered using a series of ropes and pulleys operated by quarrymen themselves or using horses or donkeys. Several of these slip-ways survive in excellent states of preservation, especially the lengthy one connecting the so-called Lykabettus quarries at Mons Porphyrites (Fig. 4.7) to the wadi floor below which was over 1,700 meters long (Pl. 4.5). Ramps like this one reveal the great expenditure of effort and the incredible infrastructure needed to remove the stone. Numerous footpaths along which workmen moved between quarries and settlements appear in a spider web-like manner throughout the region.

S.E. Sidebotham

Fig 4.7: Part of Lykabettus quarry, village, and ramp at Mons Porphyrites.

Leading from the quarries at Mons Porphyrites was a road and elaborate infrastructure to ensure the successful conveyance of the stones to the Nile Valley. One way station at Umm Sidri near the quarries preserves animal tethering lines and hydraulic facilities designed to handle the hordes of pack and draft animals moving the stone out of the quarry on its long journey to the Nile. Another nearby site has a massive loading platform. Clearly stones were dragged up a ramp leading to the top of the platform from which they were wrestled into the beds of awaiting wagons that would then haul them to the Nile. All quarry facilities were built of local cobblestones and small boulders stacked to form walls. On the other hand, hydraulic installations including tanks, channels, troughs, and so on were sometimes made of kiln-fired bricks as well as local cobblestones. Whether of kiln-fired bricks or stacked stone, those features directly exposed to water were then coated with a waterproof lime plaster. These hydraulic features often survive in remarkable states of preservation.

Study of the ancient written documents from the quarry settlements and analysis of the human bones from the badly looted ancient cemeteries at Mons Porphyrites clearly identify men, women, and children who lived and died there. They appear to have been free labor, toiling at the quarry of their own volition, and not slaves. Wages paid to those working at Mons Porphyrites in the mid-second century AD were probably similar to those earned by their counterparts at nearby quarrying operations at Mons Claudianus, which was a maximum of about forty-seven drachmas a month for a highly skilled man regardless of his profession. Apparently, top pay depended on experience more than upon the type of work performed. Forty-seven drachmas was about twice what a skilled laborer earned working in the Nile Valley, but only about half of what a Roman legionary received each month in the second century AD.

The residents of Mons Porphyrites had an abiding interest in religion; the remains of several impressive temples survive attesting their devotion. Aside from the sanctuary in one of the outlying quarry villages dedicated by Gaius Cominius Leugas to the deities Pan and Serapis that we noted above, there are, near the large fort in Wadi Ma'mal and not far from the base of the long ramp leading to the Lykabettus quarries discussed above, temples built to Isis, Isis Myrionomos, and Serapis (Pl. 4.6). Detailed inscriptions carved in Greek on large finely wrought local stone, some still

surviving on the site, indicate that these temples were erected and flourished beginning in the reigns of the Roman emperors Trajan (AD 98–117)
and his successor Hadrian (AD 117–138). It was in these years that activities at Mons Porphyrites seem to have peaked.

Satellite Settlements of Mons Porphyrites

Satellite quarries of Mons Porphyrites also produced stones for export to
the Nile; those at Umm Towat and Umm Balad (the ancient Domitiane,
later Kaine Latomia, which means 'New Quarry' in Greek) are good examples. The latter quarry, which operated in the late first and second centuries
AD, has a well preserved *praesidium* guarding it (Pl. 4.7) and was joined by
an excellent example of a cleared desert road linking it to the main thoroughfare between Mons Porphyrites and the Nile. French archaeologists
have only just undertaken work here and among their discoveries were
numerous ostraca that provide the ancient name of the settlement and
quarry and the dates of its operation.

Mons Claudianus

The quarry complex at Mons Claudianus (Pl. 4.8) is perhaps even more
spectacular than that at Mons Porphyrites. Mons Claudianus lies south-
southeast of Mons Porphyrites and the stone obtained here was hard
grandiorite/tonalite gneiss. Though the quarries at Mons Claudianus appear
to have operated for a shorter time than those at their more northerly neighbor, that is, from the first to third centuries AD, the sizes of the stones
quarried from Mons Claudianus were, in general, substantially larger than
those pried from Mons Porphyrites. They were also apparently used more
frequently in gargantuan Roman imperial building projects throughout the
ancient Mediterranean. For example, large monolithic columns from the
quarries at Mons Claudianus decorate the front porch of the Pantheon in
Rome and the Basilica of Trajan in his forum, the largest one of its kind, also
in Rome. Columns made of Mons Claudianus stone can be seen in the Flavian Palace (first century AD) on the Palatine Hill and in the Baths of
Caracalla (an emperor who ruled AD 211–217) at Rome. Mons Claudianus
columns also appear in the emperor Hadrian's villa at Tivoli just east of
Rome and at the retirement palace of the emperor Diocletian (AD 284–305)
at Split on the Adriatic coast of Croatia (Fig. 4.8).

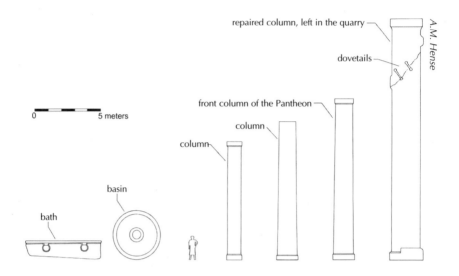

Fig. 4.8: The products of the stone quarries of Mons Porphyrites and Mons Claudianus.

The massive dimensions and weights of some of the quarried objects found at Mons Claudianus are truly staggering. Numerous columns, tubs, and other rupestral products can still be seen now silently reclining in abandoned workings around the area. One giant monolithic column now broken and discarded in a quarry behind the main settlement measures in excess of eighteen meters long with an estimated weight of 207 tons (Fig. 4.9). A huge unfinished tub or basin 5.8 meters long by 2.98 meters wide lies derelict and unfinished in another hilltop quarry (Pl. 4.9). It must weigh dozens of tons. We assume that these monolithic monstrosities would not have been quarried in the first place if some means of transporting them to the Nile were not available. We can only imagine the size and appearance of the vehicles, and the number of draft animals and people used to haul these giant blocks across the desert to the Nile (Fig. 4.10).

Though there are several impressive Roman period settlements in the region, the main focal point for activities at Mons Claudianus was clearly the large fort (Pl. 4.10 and Fig. 4.11) and associated bath, temple of Serapis, and animal tethering lines. The surprisingly well-preserved temple

S.E. Sidebotham

Fig 4.9: Eighteen-meter-long monolithic column now broken and abandoned in a quarry behind the main settlement of Mons Claudianus.

A.M. Hense

Fig. 4.10: Reconstruction of a transport wagon with column.

Fig. 4.11: Somewhat fanciful view of the large fort at Mons Claudianus, drawn by G.A. Schweinfurth. From G. Schweinfurth, *Auf unbetretenen Wegen in Aegypten* (Hamburg-Berlin: Hoffmann und Campe Verlag, 1922).

and its elaborate inscription lie within a stone's throw of the fort and the extramural bath. The latter was not large and probably could accommodate only a handful of bathers at one time. Parts of the hypocaust system—the elevated floor beneath which heat circulated—for the *caldarium* (the hot baths) can still be seen beneath the broken floor. Archaeological surveys and excavations conducted here and in the environs by an international team lead by the *Institut français d'Archéologie Orientale* between 1987 and 1993 produced the largest single cache of ostraca ever excavated anywhere in the ancient Greco-Roman world. Approximately 9,200 ostraca, written predominantly in Greek, some in Latin, detail many aspects of the lives of the men, women, and children who made Mons Claudianus their home. In addition to precise pay records showing top salaries of forty-seven drachmas per month, and the usual requests for various foods to be sent from the Nile Valley to supplement what must have been a rather monotonous diet, there are also remains of school practice exercises undertaken by the children whose parents lived and worked in this remote desert outpost.

Close by the main fort, bath, temple, and animal tethering lines is another concentration of buildings that includes a fine example of a large hydraulic

S.E. Sidebotham

Fig. 4.12: *Praesidium* at Barud (ancient Tiberiane) that guarded a nearby quarry.

tank. This settlement is, in turn, joined to yet another small fort with large
guard tower (Pl. 4.11). A large modern water tank constructed by a unit of
the New Zealand army during the Second World War near this small fort
and tower attests the keen and ongoing interest in securing and protecting
water in this hyper-arid region throughout history.

Nearby satellite quarries of Mons Claudianus boast interesting if not
huge remains. One of these was at Barud, whose ancient name was Tiberiane, where there is a fine example of a *praesidium* with internal cisterns
(lakkoi/lacci) that guarded the quarry. There is an excellent view of this
structure from the nearby mountaintop southwest of the fort (Fig. 4.12).
Despite the name that would seem to imply a connection with the emperor
Tiberius (AD 14–37), the pottery from Tiberiane dates to the second and
possibly into the third century AD suggesting that no activity took place
here in the first century AD.

Another quarry, with four areas of excavation complete with *skop*eloi
(watch or signal towers) and a nicely made stone hut, at Umm Huyut (Pl.
4.12) was also clearly a satellite operation of Mons Claudianus. Our survey only discovered this site when our Ma'aza Bedouin friend and guide

Salah 'Ali Suwelim showed it to us in June 1993. He claims that he first found it in 1981. Only small stone products including pedestals (possibly for use as altars), small columns, and other items were obtained here and some can still be seen abandoned between the quarries and the small settlement. Comprising fourteen buildings of dry laid stone, one edifice was particularly large, prominent, and well built (Pl. 4.13). We have not been able to identify with any certainty what function this building served. It perches on a small natural rise approached by two staircases, one on the northwest and the other on the southwest, with a rectangular shaped niche at the southeastern end and benches abutting the southern and western interior walls. Clearly, it must have played an important administrative role and perhaps religious, but we found no inscription or other artifacts that provided any clue. Pottery we collected from the surface at Umm Huyut for study was early Roman (that is, first to second centuries AD) in date. The geographical and chronological proximity of Umm Huyut to Mons Claudianus and the similarity in appearance in the types of stones taken from both locations can be explained by the differences in the sizes of the products that these respective places produced. Mons Claudianus clearly provided and shipped huge stone pieces while those extracted from Umm Huyut were quite diminutive by comparison. Our survey could find no ancient road leading from Umm Huyut, but there must have been one and it undoubtedly headed west where at some point it joined up with the main road leading from Mons Claudianus toward the Nile; there must have also been one that linked it to Mons Claudianus.

Wadi Umm Wikala (Mons Ophiates)

The third set of quarries that have been studied, though not in as great detail as those of Mons Porphyrites and Mons Claudianus, are those in Wadi Umm Wikala, near Wadi Semna (Fig. 4.13). These lie south–southeast of Mons Claudianus and are substantially smaller than either those or the ones at Mons Porphyrites. The ancient name for the workings here was Mons Ophiates (Snaky Mountain) and its period of operation was confined to early Roman times with the latest evidence for quarrying being possibly in the third century AD. The stone sought was gabbro, mainly from the summits or upper slopes of the surrounding mountains. The mountain peaks also have numerous cairns, *skopeloi* (watch/signal towers), and slipways similar in appearance to those seen at Mons Porphyrites and

S.E. Sidebotham

Fig. 4.13: Wadi Umm
Wikala (Mons Ophiates):
objects from one of the
quarries in foreground and
praesidium in background.

Mons Claudianus, down which the quarried stones were hauled. Our surveys between 1997 and 2000 found thirteen quarry excavations and a
number of places where someone had prospected for useable stone in the
early Roman period. Many of the partly finished products extracted here
lay abandoned only a few dozen meters away from one of the main buildings on the site, a *praesidium* enclosing a cistern *(lakkos/laccus)*. Many of
the stones destined for export were small comprising, for the most part,
columns, basins, pedestals, cornices, and wall and floor tiles. A few semi-
finished products that lie abandoned in a more remote working some
distance from the *praesidium* are quite large, and include column bases. We
found these gathered near the end of a loading platform; for some reason
these pieces were never placed on wagons and hauled out of the quarry
area. Yet, even the largest stones quarried from Mons Ophiates were
nowhere near the dimensions of the behemoths obtained from Mons

Claudianus. Their transport to the Nile probably seldom caused many problems though our survey once found some larger Mons Ophiates stones dumped along an ancient track some distance from the site suggesting, perhaps, that they had been abandoned when the vehicle carrying them had broken down. Stone from Mons Ophiates has been found in a number of Roman structures outside Egypt and was so highly valued that it was later stripped from them and recycled. Good examples of recycling appear in the Basilica of St. Lorenzo in Rome and also in the Basilica of St. Peter in the Vatican where Mons Ophiates stone was used as a base for a bronze statue of St. Peter.

Just across the wadi from the *praesidium* at Mons Ophiates are the remains of a multi-roomed structure built of locally available cobblestones and boulders. A little dilapidated, but with some walls still standing to a height of 5.4 meters in one corner and preserving some windows, it was in or near this structure that F.W. Green discovered an important Roman period inscription written in Greek. He published this stone in 1909, which several later visitors and scholars have republished over the years. This important text records in the fortieth year of the emperor Augustus (May 26, AD 11 to be exact) that an official, styled *archimetallarchos* in Greek, named Popilius Iuventius Rufus, who was overseer of the emerald and topaz mines, pearl fisheries, and quarrying operations in the Eastern Desert, dedicated a sanctuary to (the god) Pan. The text also mentions by name the architects Mersis and Soter who designed the building. Other lesser structures lay nearby, probably the remnants of quarters for some of the personnel living and working here; heavy flooding in this part of the wadi has clearly carried away a number of these edifices; small cemeteries and individual graves, all of ancient date, lay scattered in various locations around the quarrying operations. A few kilometers away to the south near a modern railway lay the remains of another impressive fort. Though now badly destroyed, our survey was fortunate to have studied this now lost treasure before its untimely destruction by a front-end loader for reasons and by persons unknown between late August 1998 and June 1999.

Quarry Roads, Water Stops, and Forts

Though substantially closer to the Red Sea than the Nile Valley, it is clear that the stone quarried at Mons Porphyrites was, like that from Mons Claudianus and Wadi Umm Wikala and their satellite operations, transported to the Nile and not to the Red Sea. All indications from detailed study of the roads joining the quarries to the Nile and the Red Sea show this (Fig. 4.14).

Numerous roads of various sizes and importance crisscross this central portion of the Eastern Desert, which was clearly a busy area in the early and middle Roman periods as well as in later Roman times. The three major thoroughfares we will examine include the one leading from the fort at Abu Sha'r and its nearby satellite installation at Abu Sha'r al-Qibli and that passed by the Mons Porphyrites, Umm Balad, and Umm Towat quarries on its way to the Nile. The second led from the Mons Claudianus area west-southwestward to the Nile. At Abu Zawal this route bifurcated with a more northerly route sharing the one from Mons Porphyrites from the station at al-Saqqia onward to the Nile. The more southerly one passed by the major Roman watering point with extensive animal tethering lines in Wadi Abu Shuwehat, then via the large stop with a pair of stations and animal tethering lines at Abu Greiya, which lies just north of the modern paved highway linking Safaga to Qena on the Nile. The third road led from Quseir and

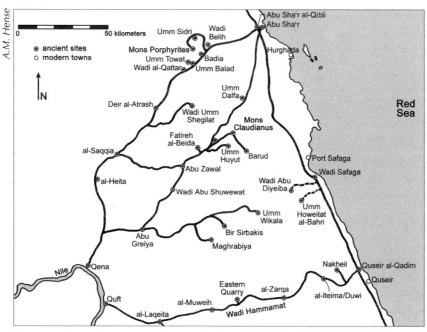

Fig. 4.14: Map of quarry road network.

Quseir al-Qadim (ancient Red Sea port of Myos Hormos) to Quft (Coptos) on the Nile via the Wadi Hammamat and the Mons Basanites quarries.

As we noted in Chapter 3, the Via Nova Hadriana was merely a smoothed track and such, too, was the case with the other ancient Eastern Desert highways in the Roman era. Those few areas that preserve paving made of small boulders and cobblestones appear in very sandy areas and were undoubtedly created in the early twentieth century to facilitate vehicular transport between Mons Porphyrites and the Nile. The major ancient Roman roads leading to the Nile from the quarries had dotted along their lengths water points, often *praesidia* with wells *(hydreumata)* and cisterns *(lakkoi/lacci)*. In the Roman period the cisterns, and usually the wells, lay inside the protective walls of the *praesidia*. Most *praesidia* between Mons Porphyrites, Mons Claudianus, and the Nile also had outside their walls tethering lines and drinking troughs to accommodate the many draft and pack animals hauling supplies to and large stone products from the quarries. Some stone conveyed from Mons Porphyrites could conceivably have been hauled by pack animals, perhaps camels and donkeys, though some of the larger items would have required sledges or wheeled vehicles pulled by large teams of beasts. Virtually all those stone products conveyed from Mons Claudianus would have required massive wheeled transports to haul them to the Nile approximately 120 kilometers away. The impressions made by some of these huge wheeled contraptions can still be seen on the flat desert floor near the station at Deir al-Atrash and closer to the Nile in the Naq al-Teir plain in the region of the *praesidia* at al-Saqqia, al-Heita, and near the unfortified road station at Bir Salah. Our surveys in this area in 1989 and 1996 noted, measured, and photographed many of these wagon ruts (Fig. 4.15) as did earlier British visitors including George W. Murray and our late friend Leo Tregenza. The gauges of these wheeled vehicles range from as narrow as 2.13 meters to as wide as 4 meters. The latter seems to have been a wagon or cart with three sets of wheels. We might guess that the narrow gauges represent vehicles bearing the generally smaller stones from Mons Porphyrites while the larger sets reflect the substantially huge and heavy stone cargoes transported from Mons Claudianus. Both quarries used the road from the station at al-Saqqia onward to the Nile, but we will never be certain which tracks came from which quarry.

S. E. Sidebotham

Fig. 4.15: Roman wagon ruts on the Abu Sha'r–Nile road.

The crews traveling between Mons Claudianus and the Nile also had another route option available to them that ran farther south via several watering points including those in Wadi Abu Shuwehat and Abu Greiya, before arriving, like its more northerly counterpart, at the Nile city of Kainepolis (modern Qena). Abu Greiya is especially impressive as there are two *praesidia*, one of which is partly covered by the modern paved highway linking Safaga on the Red Sea to Qena on the Nile about forty-one or forty-two kilometers away. Between the two forts are the remains of large and well-preserved animal tethering lines. J.G. Wilkinson was the first to draw a sketch plan of this site and our survey drew a detailed measured one in summer 1998.

Sections of these roads have route-marking cairns, though not as numerous as those found on the Via Nova Hadriana. There are also signal towers, which are especially numerous and well preserved on the Quseir–Quft road. On the other two highways, however, signal and watchtowers are not frequent and tend to appear in the more mountainous areas through which the roads pass. A few cleared sections, as on the Via Nova Hadriana, and portions preserving the ruts of Roman wagons (as noted above) also survive. The two northerly roads also have watering and resting points for the draft, pack animals, and crews. The ones on the Mons Porphyrites–Nile road are the most numerous and best preserved. Some of these *praesidia* were so well located and important that they were repaired in the twentieth century for continued use. Surprisingly, no animal tethering lines exist on the Quseir–Nile road to support quarrying operations in the Roman period in Wadi Hammamat/Mons Basanites. We do not know why this was the case.

Good examples of these Roman rest stops, especially those that are large and fortified and have extensive animal tethering lines on the Abu Sha'r/Mons Porphyrites-Kainepolis road, include those at Badia' near Mons Porphyrites, Umm Balad that protected a small satellite quarry, Deir al-Atrash (Monastery of the Deaf One), al-Saqqia, and al-Heita. These clearly accommodated traffic coming from the quarries of Mons Porphyrites and its environs and some—those at al-Saqqia, al-Heita, and one other—also serviced traffic from Mons Claudianus. A smaller fort at Wadi Belih is too far from Mons Porphyrites to have been associated with operations there, but it is also too early to have been affiliated with the late Roman activities on the Red Sea coast at Abu Sha'r. Its function remains a tantalizing mystery. Likely the fort at Wadi Belih was a stop on the road leading from the Red Sea coast at Abu Sha'r al-Qibli to the Nile in the period during the initial use of the Via Nova Hadriana in the early second century AD.

It is clear that some of these installations, like that at Deir al-Atrash, had wells inside their protective walls while others depended on extramural sources of water, which were then conveyed and stored inside the adjacent forts, like those at Badia' and Umm Balad. What all these *praesidia* had in common, however, was extensive animal tethering lines that, together with the forts themselves, were built of locally available cobblestones and small boulders. The animal tethering lines often lie some distance from the water troughs; it is clear that the strategy was to water the animals and move them quickly away from the troughs to the tethering lines so that they would not foul the water and so that they could rest and eat elsewhere. In this manner large numbers of animals could be quickly circulated into the watering area and just as rapidly moved away to allow the next batch to be watered, as we discuss further in Chapter 13. Such facilities are found only between the quarries and the Nile; none appear between the quarries and the Red Sea. This clearly demonstrates, despite the greater distances, that the stones from the quarries were transported to the Nile and not to the Red Sea ports.

Badia' was unusual; near the fort (Pl. 4.14) and animal lines lies a huge rock outcrop which has a large, thick oval shaped fortification wall around it, again, made of locally obtained small boulders and cobbles (Fig. 4.16). The reason for this strange feature in such close proximity to the nearby *praesidium* remains a mystery.

The small fort protecting the quarries at Umm Balad (ancient Domitiane/Kaine Latomia) is exceptionally well preserved with an intramural cistern and an ancient trash dump in front of its gate; this was only recently excavated by a French team. Deir al-Atrash, about halfway along the road between the Red Sea and the Nile, preserves fine examples of extramural animal tethering lines and associated water troughs as well as channels that piped water from the intramural well to those exterior troughs. Remains of a large well lined with stones and part of a barrel-vaulted building made of mud brick grace the interior of the fort. The stones lining the well may have been a feature common to many of the large *hydreumata* in the desert though few of these linings remain visible. Such stone linings would have facilitated deeper well excavation and would have minimized their collapse and the resultant pollution of the water. There is also a large tower made of mud brick near the well. This enigmatic structure, which has only one parallel in the Eastern Desert that we have ever seen (at al-Heita, discussed below), may have contained a device known as a *shaduf* used to lift water

S.E. Sidebotham

Fig. 4.16: Rock outcrop surrounded by an oval wall, near the fortification at Badia'.

from the well to the internal channels that then conveyed it to exterior troughs for consumption by the draft animals. The front gate of Deir al-Atrash preserves an exquisite example of mud-brick architecture as one of the two square towers protecting that entrance stands to a height of about 2.5 meters (Pl. 4.15) while an excellent example of a tapering stone tower at the southwestern corner of this fort has recently, unfortunately, been destroyed by vandals (Pl. 4.16).

Although the fort at al-Saqqia is small, it was clearly important as the find of painted wall plaster from inside one of the rooms suggests. It may have accommodated an important administrative official in charge of water distribution to the numerous convoys that passed by. It was near al-Saqqia that the roads from both Mons Claudianus and Mons Porphyrites met and it is, thus, no surprise that the watering and animal tethering facilities here are quite sizeable.

The penultimate installation on the Mons Porphyrites road before reaching the Nile was that at al-Heita (which means 'the wall' in Arabic). There are badly looted animal tethering lines and at least one animal-watering trough together with a cistern, which lay south of the main entrance of the fort on lower ground. This lower fort has much of its mud-brick superstructure, built atop cobble walls, intact, including nice examples of round towers flanking the main south-facing gate (Pl. 4.17). Mud-brick edifices comprise some internal structures that were built with barrel vaulting; at one point part of the outer perimeter wall was heightened in mud brick which resulted in the blockage of an earlier stone staircase. A mud-brick tower similar in appearance to that at Deir al-Atrash survives, though no well is visible that it might have served. There is also a fort atop a hill north of the lower *praesidium*. This installation, built except for its foundations entirely of mud brick, some sections of which are over four meters high, appears never to have been completed. Its purpose atop the hill remains unknown. It is a rare, though not unique, example of a fort built on a hilltop in Roman times in the Eastern Desert.

The third Roman highway we will examine is that connecting Quseir and Quseir al-Qadim on the Red Sea with Quft (Coptos) on the Nile. Probably the best known and most studied of the three ancient routes we have examined, it was also the shortest of the Roman roads joining the Red Sea with the Nile. It was, thus, heavily traveled in antiquity. Certainly the quarry about midway along this road, in Wadi Hammamat, had been exploited from Predynastic times on. There were also nearby quarries at Mons Basanites, which were active in the Roman era. The eight surviving *praesidia* dotting the course of the highway are, in their current appearance, Roman in date. Surveys over the years have recorded their presence, appearance, and dates of construction and use, and the most recent work conducted by a French team has included excavations at several of these *praesidia*. They were built between Flavian times (AD 69–96) and the reigns of the emperors Trajan (AD 98–117) and Hadrian (AD 117–138). Apparently before the Flavian emperors the region was peaceful enough that only unfortified water points were needed. Translations of ostraca excavated at some of these *praesidia* indicate that barbarian/Bedouin attacks became frequent enough that forts had to be constructed between the late first and early second centuries AD. In addition to accommodating traffic between the quarries in Wadi Hammamat and the Nile, these forts also assisted civilian commercial caravans bearing merchandise arriving from India and southern Arabia at the Red Sea emporium of Myos Hormos. Ostraca from these desert *praesidia* indicate that one of the functions of the garrisons was to escort these caravans.

The ostraca also show that the majority of the troops garrisoning these forts were Egyptian. Most written communications, including official orders, however, were conveyed in Greek with very little Latin being used. Some of these forts continued in late Roman times to provide logistical support to the gold mining operations at Bir Umm Fawakhir in the fifth and sixth centuries AD. Later, Muslim *hajj* traffic between the Nile and Quseir also made use of some of these forts as the presence of a small mosque inside one of the *praesidia* (that at Bir Hammamat) indicates.

Between the various *praesidia* on the Quseir–Nile road were approximately sixty-five to seventy *skopeloi*. These watch/guard/signal towers (Pl. 4.18–4.19) lay in a variety of locations either on mountaintops, or part way down their slopes or on flat ground in the wadis below. They are inter-visible with each other and with the forts. Manned in rotation by groups of two or four men, presumably sent out from the nearest *praesidium*, signals would most often have been sent only locally and seldom along the entire length of the road between the Red Sea and the Nile. Fire signals would rarely, if ever, have been used. There was little flammable material available in the desert and flames would have been difficult to see in the daylight hours due to the

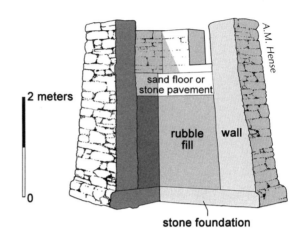

A.M. Hense

2 meters

sand floor or
stone pavement

rubble
fill

wall

0

stone foundation

Fig. 4.17: Cross-section
of a signal tower on the
Quseir–Nile road.

bright sun, haze, and dust. In any case, there is no evidence of burning
inside any of the towers. Our hypothesis is that prearranged signals were
sent using reflective surfaces such as mirrors or highly polished metal plates
or waving signal flags, perhaps of varying sizes, shapes, and colors.

Three of the better-preserved *praesidia* on the Quseir–Nile road can still
be seen at al-Iteima (also known as Duwi or Hammad), closer to the Nile at
al-Zarqa (ancient Maximianon) (Pls. 4.20–4.21) and at al-Muweih (ancient
Krokodilo). The last two are the best known from recent French excavations
which recovered numerous ostraca detailing many aspects of the lives of
those who lived in these remote desert outposts. Maximianon actually
boasted a small bath inside the fort. It is clear from the ostraca found in
these desert forts along the Quseir–Nile road that most food, wine, and
other commodities were imported from the Nile Valley. Yet, some vegetables were locally cultivated, as were chickens and pigs. There is even slight
indication that beer may have been brewed in some of these remote desert
forts. According to the ostraca found in them, terms of service in these *praesidia* ranged from at least three to seven months; they may have been longer
for some of the soldiers.

Most *praesidia* on these three roads, and on other routes in the Eastern
Desert, lay on low ground. In fact of the three thoroughfares examined here,
only the fort at al-Heita noted above, lay on higher ground. Common sense
and basic defensive military tactics in normal circumstances would dictate
their location on high ground. Yet, most are placed immediately at the base

of a mountain or hill. If the mission of these *praesidia* had been to protect large swaths of territory then their location on elevated terrain would have been a *sine qua non*. Clearly this was not the case. It was unrealistic to attempt to control the entire Eastern Desert; this would have required a huge expenditure of money and troops. The forts had much more limited and realistic objectives; they were carefully situated along regularly and frequently used routes and guarded precious water supplies. They were also designed to control nodes of mineral wealth, lines of communication and travel, and monitor wayfarers.

The Joys and Sorrows
of the Desert Survey

When many people think of archaeologists they picture them on excavations scratching away in the dirt, removing the soil in minute increments with trowels, small brushes, and dustpans, and in extreme cases, using dental tools to clean objects embedded in the ground. While this image is partially true, there is another important dimension in which the archaeologist plays a critical role in understanding our human past, one that involves little or no excavation whatsoever.

After all, how do archaeologists find ancient sites and how do they know where on those sites they should excavate, should they decide to do so? What about sites that, for whatever reason, will never be excavated, but nevertheless, should be as accurately recorded as possible? How should they be documented for posterity? Most archaeologists are acutely aware of the great value that surveying plays in our overall study of the material remains of the ancient past. Surveying is a relatively quick and highly cost-effective method of obtaining a vast amount of information. This is a very attractive prospect to most archaeologists who are almost always desperately short of funds to conduct their fieldwork. Our teams over the years have divided survey efforts in the Eastern Desert into two major types. We call them 'site extensive' and 'site intensive' surveys. They are not mutually exclusive and overlap each other to some extent in the results they achieve.

Site Extensive Surveying

A site extensive survey, at least the way we conduct one in the Eastern Desert, involves a small team usually comprising no more than two of us, ideally accompanied by a very capable Bedouin guide, searching for ancient remains. The guide also acts as the cook, sometimes driver, and, hopefully when needed, vehicle mechanic. Many of these guides have become close friends over the years and are fonts of wisdom not only about the locations of ancient sites, but about desert flora, fauna, and Bedouin lore. The ancient sites we seek might be roads, unfortified road stations, or other remains such as *praesidia*, villages, quarrying and mining communities, cemeteries, and ports. Usually this type of surveying involves investigating a fairly wide geographical area with immediate objectives that include checking Bedouin reports about the existence of ancient sites and, if found, noting their existence by plotting them on a map using global positioning system (GPS) technology.

In addition to plotting the site's location using GPS, during a 'site extensive' survey we also estimate the approximate number of buildings and size of a site, its age (usually from potshards we collect, but occasionally, when lucky, from inscriptions and coins), and its function; the latter is not always possible. We usually take many photographs and also make quick sketches of architectural remains. This method of site extensive surveying has the advantage of being relatively inexpensive to conduct and allows us to develop an archaeological and historical picture of a number of sites spread across a relatively broad expanse of terrain in a rather short amount of time.

Global Positioning System Technology

GPS is an ingenious invention that became available and affordable to the general public worldwide in the late 1980s. Basically this is how it functions: the United States Department of Defense launched twenty-four satellites into orbit around the earth. 'Spare' satellites are occasionally launched to replace older ones, which sometimes results in more than two dozen in earth orbit at one time. Orbiting at about 20,200 kilometers in space, these satellites continuously emit specially coded signals, twenty-four hours a day, year in and year out. At least four satellites are visible above the horizon at any point on the earth's surface at any one time. Triangulating three or more of the satellites using a rather inexpensive hand-held receiver allows the operator to determine, with a fair degree of precision, his point on the surface of the earth. The more satellites' signals one can obtain with the GPS receiver, the more accurate the reading, up to within a few meters or better. The reading is then digitally displayed on the screen of the receiver in the form of latitude and longitude. This method of site location is quick and usually very accurate and dispenses with the old fashioned compass bearings that may be extremely inaccurate. Also, if there are no obvious geographical landmarks, such as distinctive mountain peaks, in the area from which to take compass bearings, it is impossible to obtain accurate coordinates for site location; such a situation makes GPS even more attractive. The Russians have a similar system, called Glosnass, as do the Europeans; theirs is called Galileo and is currently being integrated with the GPS. In theory, GPS can also provide measurements of elevations above sea level, but we have never found the results very reliable.

Site Intensive Surveying

Site intensive survey work involves more labor than the site extensive variety. A site intensive survey usually comprises a slightly larger team than a site extensive one. These team members remain at one site for a relatively extended period, depending upon the size and complexity of the archaeological remains. During this type of survey we draw detailed measured plans and, often, architects' elevation drawings of the more important or better preserved buildings. We undertake site intensive surveying when we deem the ancient remains to be of particular importance, for example in cases where future excavations are planned, or when we consider that they might be under threat from vandals or endangered by development. The latter includes the natural growth of Red Sea towns and cities, modern mining and quarrying, and construction of tourist facilities. We require somewhat more gear for this kind of surveying. To draw accurate plans we previously used tape measures and compasses. This method was quite tedious and prone to errors as we became fatigued. Later we could afford to purchase a theodolite (Fig. 5.1), a rather simple piece of surveying equipment, from which we took elevation, and distance measurements of the buildings we sought to draw plans of, or, most recently, we borrowed a total station (Fig. 5.2).

The total station is an expensive piece of gear with a built-in computer and laser range-finding system. While one person operates the total station,

H.M. Nouwens

Fig. 5.1: Working with the theodolite at Berenike.

one or more additional team members hold reflective prisms attached to poles over the points that must be measured. The laser beam emitted from the total station, which is set at a known and fixed point on the site, reflects off the prism and back to the total station, which records precise distance and elevation. All the thousands of 'points' taken during a site intensive survey are then downloaded into a computer which 'draws' a plan or map of the site. We can also add contour lines. Unfortunately, we have been unable to use the full power of the total station on our surveys. Since this device runs on batteries that must be recharged every four to eight hours, and our surveys are out in the desert far from any electrical grid for days or weeks at a time, we hook it up to a portable solar panel to provide—adequate sunlight and lack of cloud cover permitting—electrical current to the total station. Unfortunately, the solar panel while hooked up to the total station, cannot, at the same time, run the data notebook, which, ideally, would simultaneously record the various points for subsequent quick downloading onto a computer. Thus, we must write down by hand all the points (usually

S.E. Sidebotham

Fig. 5.2: Working with the total station at Sikait.

at least three sets of numbers per point) in a notebook; this is a laborious, time-consuming, and error-prone method. Still, this is more accurate and faster than using tape measures and compasses or a theodolite.

Another very useful technique that one can use in a site intensive survey to determine what walls or other features might lay below ground surface is ground penetrating radar, which is also known as magnetic surveying. This method is used when we want to have some idea of the features beneath our feet to determine where we might optimally place our excavation trenches to achieve the best results. This technique involves laying out a grid over a portion of a site and traversing it at fixed distances with special equipment. The radar sends back signals of varying strength depending upon the density of the material from which it is reflected; walls and other potentially man-made features built of stone or brick appear differently on the screen than does the looser and less dense soil that has accumulated around them over the centuries. Drawbacks to using magnetic surveying in the Eastern

Desert are that most commercially available gear cannot penetrate beneath the ground surface deeper than about a meter or a meter and a half. If the site had a long history of habitation and numerous structures were built atop one another, then the radar will send back a very jumbled image of the various features off which it has been reflected. This frequently causes more confusion than clarification.

Of course, both intensive and extensive surveys might be combined into a single project, as we have done on a number of occasions. It is often a good strategy to maintain peak efficiency in a survey crew to take a break from one type of surveying and switch to the other.

Surveying in Actual Practice

The surveys we conduct in the winter are usually less exhausting than those we undertake in the summer. During winter surveys we can also stay out in the field longer as we need to carry and use far less water than in the summer, when we drink an average of four to six liters per person per day. If you add water for cooking and occasional minimal bathing then this equates to about ten liters per person per day. A liter of water weighs one kilogram. Thus, three of us on a two week survey consume about 420 liters of water or twenty-one jerry cans. The water, plus gasoline, food, and other gear completely fills up the back of a Toyota Hilux pickup truck, the most ubiquitous vehicle in the Eastern Desert and the one that we have used for the majority of our desert survey work over the years.

Refueling the truck is simple. We insert a siphon into one of the gasoline jerry cans, which has been placed on the top of the truck, and suck on it as if using a large straw. Once the flow of gasoline starts (you always get a little fuel in your mouth with this technique) you place the other end of the siphon hose in the gas tank. If you are not feeling up to tasting a little eighty or ninety octane gasoline, you can always use our alternate method of refueling: pour the contents of the jerry can directly into the tank. This is best done by cutting off the top of one of those commercial plastic bottles containing drinking water and using it as a funnel to facilitate pouring the fuel into the tank. We have found this technique quite effective and in so doing, have discovered yet another one of the many uses for an empty plastic water bottle. It is interesting that while we foreigners prefer the latter technique, most of the Bedouin prefer the siphon method.

If the survey is a site extensive one our small team does not use tents in either the summer or winter. We sleep on small rollup mattresses, using sheets in the summer, and sleeping bags and blankets in the winter. In both summer and winter we cook over an open fire. If we are conducting a site intensive survey and are not more than about one hundred kilometers' round trip from a town, then the vehicle can make forays to bring water, food, and other items as needed. In this situation we often cook on a small gas stove and in winter we will pitch tents, since it can be incredibly cold at night. On one survey farther north in the Eastern Desert in winter 1995 it was so cold one night that the water on the tops of our canteens froze. In the summer we will store our gear out of the sun, often in tents with flaps open to allow some air circulation. As long as the sun is up, we pitch shade tents, which look like giant beach umbrellas, under which we eat, do our paperwork, and study our finds. In the summer we sleep out in the open as it is simply too hot to be inside a tent.

On our surveys, if we are lucky, our Bedouin guides will make us fresh bread. Most prefer to make *gurs/gaburi* though if we are very lucky, they will make *rudaf/marduf*. Both types are unleavened and simply produced using only flour, salt, and water. *Gurs* is easier and faster to make. Mixing the flour with salt and water and working the dough on top of a piece of cloth, the resulting pizza-shaped concoction is then placed atop burning embers (the best are of acacia wood, but any flammable dried branches will do), which have been placed in a slight depression in the sand. The entire concoction is then covered in sand and embers and 'bakes' for about fifteen minutes after which it is turned over to bake for another quarter of an hour. The bread is then taken from the sand, beaten, and scraped to remove as much sand as possible and eaten. We love this bread and it is very tasty with cheese (feta) or peanut butter. Those Bedouin who are not as adept at making *gurs* tend to leave too much sand on or large pebbles in the bread. This can have serious consequences for your dental work. Another type of desert bread that we do not eat as often is *rudaf* (the 'Ababda Bedouin term) or *marduf* (the Ma'aza Bedouin word). This is more time-consuming to prepare and is usually produced for celebrations and special occasions. It is made in a similar fashion as *gurs*, but is somewhat chewier as there is a higher ratio of water to flour in the dough. This pizza-shaped dough is also deposited in a hole in the sand at the bottom of which are large pebbles or small cobbles that have been heated by fire placed above them. The dough is slapped directly atop these hot stones, covered with sand and baked.

Some of the More 'Interesting' Surveys

We will relate here a sampling of some of the more interesting surveys we have conducted over the years between 1987 and 2004. As might be imagined, many of our desert forays have had their share of problems. Occasionally 'guides' have gotten us lost and failed to find the sites for which we were searching. Frequently our survey vehicles became stuck in the sand for periods ranging from half an hour up to three days. Often critical parts of vehicles fell off or were seriously damaged and on one of our early surveys fire consumed our vehicle. Broken windshields, defective engine parts, non-functioning gasoline gauges, more flat tires than we had spares for, intense heat and cold, and other 'inconveniences' have also hampered our efforts. In addition, we have had moments when we realized that the fancy total station we brought out did not work and had to scramble to save the survey from being a total loss. Other issues such as spoiled food or running low on food, while critical, were not dire; we simply adopted the Eastern Desert diet plan: we didn't eat!

Many of these incidents required lengthy hikes on foot back out to the nearest paved road to seek help or led to ingenious and, in some cases, probably previously untried methods to solve particular problems or make vehicle repairs. Fortunately, none of these problems caused injuries to any of us.

The Burning Land Rover Survey, January 1989

This was one of our earlier surveys in the Eastern Desert and the one that came the closest to total disaster of any of the dozens of surveys we have conducted. The Land Rover we had obtained in Cairo from the American Research Center in Egypt was notorious, among those of us who knew it, for being extremely unreliable and temperamental, but it was readily available and extremely affordable to rent. Invariably it had to be pushed by several people to get it started, something not easily done in the desert; while in the desert we often parked it facing downhill to make the ignition process easier. On the morning of January 24, 1989 we were surveying along the ancient Roman road joining Abu Sha'r on the Red Sea and the nearby Roman quarries at Mons Porphyrites on the one hand with the Nile on the

LEO A. TREGENZA

Leo A. Tregenza, born in the small Cornish fishing village of Mousehole, near the larger and better known town of Penzance, came to Egypt to teach school in the Upper Egyptian town of Qena in the 1920s. During his summer vacations in the late 1940s he made extensive trips lasting several months each into the Eastern Desert on foot and camel. He lovingly recorded his experiences in two books, *The Red Sea Mountains of Egypt* and *Egyptian Years*. He also published a number of articles on ancient remains, inscriptions, and birds of the Eastern Desert. He was the last of this generation of travelers to the region prior to 1960. Born the year Queen Victoria died, 1901, Leo himself passed away in 1998.

other. We were just west of the Roman *praesidium* at al-Heita when we stopped to examine a length of Roman road and some route-marking cairns. The three of us climbed back into the vehicle. The driver (Sidebotham) started the engine; bare wires beneath the dashboard started to glow red and ignited. The flames spread quickly and, realizing that it was an electrical fire, we disconnected the battery cables beneath the hood in an attempt to stall the fire, but all to no avail. We jumped out of the vehicle and tried to save as much of our gear as possible. We also threw jerry cans of gasoline, kerosene, and motor oil together with food and our water supplies out of the back of the blazing Land Rover. We then ran from the vehicle fearing that it might explode. It did not, but it burned furiously, creating an especially impressive black smoky fire when the spare tire attached to the hood ignited.

The survey architect stayed behind to gather and protect the gear we had salvaged while the Ma'aza Bedouin guide and the other team member (Sidebotham) started the long walk out—as it happened we later measured it to be thirty-seven kilometers—to the paved road that links Safaga on the Red Sea to Qena on the Nile. The two of us each carried about four liters of water, which we had completely consumed long before we reached the highway. Hitching a ride to Qena, we headed to the police station to file a report and to seek help. The police took the report, but they were not interested in helping; they indicated, despite the possession of all the required permits, that we should not have been out there in the first place. Thus, we looked around the garage and vehicle repair district of Qena and we eventually found and hired a driver with his large truck to go back into the desert to haul out the burned hulk; this was no easy task as we had to lie to the driver about how close to the paved road the Land Rover was; he did not want to drive deep into the desert. If it had been up to us we would have abandoned the Land Rover in the desert where it had burned, but we had been told by the American Research Center in Egypt, when we phoned them from Qena about the accident, that we had to tow it to Qena as the vehicle had special 'customs' license plates on it and had to be accounted for. We spent parts of two days hauling the burned remains out of the desert and back to Qena. Steering it while being pulled by the larger truck was daunting as an incredible amount of ash blew back into the windowless cab. The driver (Sidebotham) wearing a knit hat pulled down over his eyes to limit the amount of ash hitting his face allowed him, with extremely limited vision, to steer the Land Rover, which was tethered close behind the larger truck. The tow rope periodically broke and with each repair, it became shorter and the towing more difficult. At one point the large back bumper of the truck around which the tow rope was attached fell off. We had to find another portion of the truck to attach the rope. In addition, clouds of sand and dust further limited visibility and made the ride one from hell.

One might rightly ask why we did not have two vehicles on survey as a safety feature precisely for such an eventuality. As always, our funds were extremely limited and we could not afford a second vehicle. This is frequently the case with many of the surveys we conduct.

The upshot of this particular incident, once we coaxed the truck driver to haul the incinerated skeletal remains into Qena, was removal of the remnants of the Land Rover onto a second vehicle, a large flatbed truck, which conveyed it to Alexandria. The Land Rover was then placed on a boat, taken out into the Mediterranean to Egypt's recognized national maritime boundary, and unceremoniously dumped into the sea. Apparently this type of disposal of vehicles is common and as we understand it, a large artificial reef has formed in this part of the Mediterranean as a result.

After the fire, we recovered what we could of our gear that we had wisely chucked out of the back of the Land Rover, hired another Ma'aza Bedouin

A DESERT SURVEY WITH NO WINDSHIELD: JULY 1991

Sometimes problems develop before a survey, but one tries to minimize them and continue on. This happened in July 1991, as Sidebotham's diary entry recounts:

"While we were excavating at the late Roman fort and early Christian site of Abu Sha'ar north of Hurghada, I gave everyone a mid-dig break of about a week. Some staff opted for a trip into Luxor to see the sites, others stayed in our small fly-blown and frequently waterless hotel in Hurghada to rest and catch up on paperwork. I headed out for a survey of some of the ancient sites farther south, especially those along the ancient Berenike–Nile road. Departing Hurghada after a full excavation day I topped off the gas tank of the project's Land Rover, this one rented from the Canadian Institute in Cairo, at Quseir and drove south on the coast road. Not far south of Quseir a passing truck, probably carrying gravel, drove by and a stone hit the driver's side of the Land Rover shattering the windshield. I was unharmed, and after stopping to inspect the damage, drove on to Marsa 'Alam where I would rendezvous with a second vehicle with driver and a guide. I tried to get the windshield replaced in Marsa 'Alam, but Land Rovers are not that common in Egypt and the nearest place I was told I could get a replacement was in Cairo. Clearly the survey would go forward in the desert without the windshield.

Throughout the desert survey, the broken windshield proved more of a problem than I had anticipated. I had to wear ski goggles or sunglasses to minimize the wind, dust, and sand that got into my eyes; my nose, ears, hair and everything else were caked in sweat mixed with sand and dust at the end of each day. Driving the Land Rover was miserable. Exacerbating the problem was the force of the wind coming through the broken windshield. It was so great that it broke the interior door latch so the door on the driver's side was constantly blowing open when I drove the vehicle even at minimal speeds. To solve this problem I tied a rope around part of the door near the handle and ran it over to the other door on the passenger's side and tied it there. It was not only uncomfortable to lean back into the seat with this rope running across my back, but every time I wanted to get out of the vehicle to do survey work, I had to untie the elaborate knot system I employed to keep the door shut. Despite these problems, the five- day survey was a great success and I saw a number of sites that we would return to in later years to study in some detail. It was some weeks, however, before we managed to get a replacement windshield from Cairo."

and his trusty Toyota Hilux pickup truck, and continued our survey. About a year and a half later when we were once again in the vicinity of the fire, we drove over to the spot. There, still lying melted into the sand, were aluminum bits of the Land Rover; we collected some pieces as souvenirs.

Stuck in the Sand for Three Days: The Aborted January 1999 Survey

In addition to problems with the survey vehicles themselves, there is the omnipresent danger of the survey vehicle becoming stuck in soft sand. This can and does occur with some regularity even to the most experienced Bedouin driver who knows the desert well. To us non-Bedouin working in the area, this happens frequently, but we can often extricate the vehicle after pushing and digging around the tires. Usually we are stuck for no more than half an hour to a few hours at most. A scheduled three-day survey involving four of us in January 1999 would be one that none of us would ever forget, but not for any reasons we had anticipated at the time.

We were conducting excavations at Berenike on the Red Sea coast that winter and always used days off to conduct surveys. This particular survey had as its objective to study and record more accurately some of the ancient *praesidia* that lay along the Ptolemaic and Roman routes linking Berenike to the Nile. Since three of the participants had never seen the fascinating ancient settlement of Ka'b Marfu', we decided that a brief visit might be a good idea; it was right on the way to the other sites we planned to study. We tried to drive our heavily loaded, but underpowered, Toyota Hilux pickup truck up a hill to reach Ka'b Marfu', but became mired in the sand with the vehicle facing uphill. We did not think much about it, and we went ahead and walked the short distance to the ruins at Ka'b Marfu' where we had a nice visit; we returned to the vehicle at about noon.

Try as we might, we could not get the Toyota out of the sand; we dug, placed stones under the wheels so that they could gain traction, and even unloaded everything from the back to lighten the vehicle and make it easier to move. Nothing worked. We realized by the end of that first day that we would be lucky to get the truck down to flat ground by the next day.

We spent all of day two cajoling the vehicle down the hill to flat, but also very sandy ground. By this time our gear including jerry cans of gasoline, water, food, sleeping bags, and camera equipment was scattered all over the place and we spent a miserable day from about 7:30 in the morning until sunset trying every trick we had collectively learned over the years to get the vehicle out of the sand. At one point in the afternoon large black ravens or crows began to circle overhead, an ominous sign we thought, and then out of nowhere a little 'Ababda Bedouin girl wearing a bright lime green dress, carrying orange flowers and herding four goats walked by. She did not have much to say and continued on her way. Her appearance was surreal.

It was fast becoming clear to us that using smaller stones to provide traction for the mired Toyota was not working so we looked for larger ones. These could be found only some considerable distance from the truck and required that we use ropes to haul them; we were so desperate that we even dismantled nearby ancient, but fortunately previously robbed, graves to use their stones. We assuaged our guilt, however, by photographing the tombs before 'borrowing' parts of them. But even portions of these funerary monuments failed to free the vehicle from the sand. So day two ended in frustration and disappointment with the realization that our water and food supply was running dangerously low. We had not planned on undertaking heavy manual labor from sunrise to sunset, which resulted in a much greater consumption of our drinking water than we had planned to use in the course of our normal winter survey work.

That night was cold and damp and more or less reflected our spirits. We had the car on flat ground, but we still had to turn it at least ninety degrees so that it faced away from the hill on which we had been initially stuck. On the third day of our ordeal, we had to turn the truck around somehow. The only way we could accomplish this was by digging massive holes around the truck, elevating it up using the car jack and then pushing it off the jack (Fig. 5.3). In this way we slowly turned the Toyota around. This we did all day: digging, elevating, and pushing it off the jack. It was exhausting. At about 10:45 AM an 'Ababda Bedouin man accompanied by a donkey and a dog appeared. We do not know if he was related to the girl we had encountered on the previous day and we really did not care. He was quite free with his advice on how to get the truck unstuck, but not inclined to help otherwise; we were not impressed as we had already tried and failed using the methods he proposed. He wandered off. Finally, we managed to turn the vehicle so that it faced toward flat ground. We then built a lengthy and elaborate road of stones and boulders that was slightly wider than the width of the truck. Many of the stones and boulders we lifted from areas where we had used them on the two previous days; others we dragged from farther afield. By building this road, which, we thought, closely resembled one of its Roman ancestors in Europe, we had constructed in our eyes, an engineering marvel, but one that required all our energy. With one last effort, three of us pushed as hard as we could while the fourth drove along the length of our stone highway. We built up enough speed and finally we were free! It was 3:20 PM of the third day, January 20, 1999. We loaded the gear, which we had to carry several hundred meters to the Toyota, and headed back to Berenike. Upon arrival sometime after 8 PM that night the rest of the staff at the dig asked about the survey. One can imagine what we had to tell them. We discovered only later that the constant strain of elevating of the truck and pushing it off the car jack had resulted in a serious fracture to one of the main struts of the vehicle. If this had broken while we were attempting to extricate ourselves from the sand we would have been in dire trouble. It is a good thing that we did not know this while we were still stuck in the sand as this knowledge would only have added to our worries.

We passed by the area where we had been stuck about a year later and portions of the huge holes we had dug in the sand to free our vehicle could

S.E. Sidebotham

Fig. 5.3 Stuck in deep sand near the ancient settlement of Ka'b Marfu'.

still be seen. Needless to say, subsequently we found and bought a pair of 'sand ladders.' These are long pieces of corrugated steel with large round holes punched through them at fixed intervals. They proved very useful in later incidents in extricating us relatively quickly and easily from the sand.

The Hottest Survey We Ever Had: Summer 2001

In July and August 2001 we continued a site intensive survey that two of our team members had started in winter 2000: drawing a detailed plan of the large and impressive Roman emerald mining settlement in Wadi Sikait. The goal was to complete drawing a plan of the site and check what had been drawn in winter 2000 for accuracy; we also hoped to draw architect's elevations of several of the larger and better preserved structures, including two rock-cut temples. We then intended to move our camp north up the wadi to draw plans of two other emerald mining settlements, which we named Middle Sikait and North Sikait. The team started off with five people, two of whom had spent about forty days in winter 2000 drawing a site plan of the main settlement in Wadi Sikait, which they did not finish. We had no illusions about the nature of the survey and anticipated the usual summer desert heat, but we were not prepared for what we in fact had to face: the most grueling survey any of us had ever endured.

The ancient settlement in Wadi Sikait nestles in a relatively narrow defile surrounded by mountains. This not only prevents much, if any, wind or breeze from entering the wadi, but it also retains the heat very efficiently, more so than in a flatter, more open place. In addition, the heat soaked up by the ground and surrounding mountains then radiates off them at night making the wadi miserably hot twenty-four hours a day. Our normal routine was to awaken at sunrise—which was about 6 AM—eat, and move out quickly with the total station, solar panels, and prisms and survey as much as possible before the incredible heat built up, which was usually sometime between 11 AM and noon. We would then retire to our shade tent, eat, rest, attempt to read, and vegetate during the hottest part of the day until about 3 PM. During those listless hours the heat was unbearable. The bindings in our paperback books became so dry that the pages fell out. The glue holding the nozzles on our camping shower bags (which were kept in the shade during daylight hours because of the intense heat caused by direct sunlight) melted and the nozzles and hoses fell off.

None of us had a normal weather thermometer, but someone brought a thermometer used to measure human fevers. We will never know how hot it actually got during those blistering afternoons because the thermometer did not register above 42°C (108°F), but we were able to measure the coolest temperatures. The air temperature never got below about 34°C (94°F) and that was at 2 or 3 AM. The ground temperature was much hotter and it was on the ground that we slept, or tried to. Sleeping was difficult. Usually we hauled our sleeping mattresses out from under the shade tent soon after the sun went behind the mountains, at about 6:00 PM. It was then that we ate dinner and bathed, if there was enough water. We usually rested on the mattresses for about thirty to sixty minutes and then had to move them as the heat radiating off the wadi floor was retained beneath the mattresses while the surrounding wadi floor became cooler. Thus, a good part of the night was spent moving mattresses every hour or so to try to find ever cooler spots.

When we had adequate water we looked forward to showers, again, only after the sun went behind the mountains at the end of the day and the scalding water in the shower bags had cooled down somewhat. One of us proudly rigged a shower bag on one of the tripods we used to mount the total station. The others went behind nearby boulders to wash. We drank so much that we could hear the water sloshing in our stomachs, but we were always thirsty. The *esprit de corps* was wonderful and although two team members had to leave before the end of the survey, we are all understandably very proud of the work we did over those three weeks or so; we formed a bond that will last a long time. We can also never thank our 'Ababda Bedouin friend enough for bringing out to us every three or four days desperately needed water, food, and the occasional surprise snacks.

There are many other stories we could recount about our desert surveys, but these four should provide some insight into the trials and tribulations that might occur while conducting this important archaeological work. Not all surveys were as plagued as the ones described above; some have actually taken place without a hitch, but you must be prepared for anything to happen in the Eastern Desert and try to accommodate the best way possible.

Gods of the Desert
The Temples and Shrines of the Eastern Desert

As one might imagine, over the long history of human activity in the Eastern Desert, many of those who dared to travel, work, and live in this hostile environment came from the Nile Valley and beyond. They brought with them their cultural baggage including, of course, their languages and religious beliefs. The latter must have been of special interest and concern in the alien and potentially deadly arid desert landscape. Prayers to a number of deities for good luck, safe travel, and good health appear on a wide variety of written documents including ostraca, papyri, and formal inscriptions as well as graffiti carved on the rock outcrops lining desert routes and around the all-important wells. The desire to appease and secure the good will of the gods is also obvious from a number of shrines and temples that have been found and studied. Who were the deities of special interest to those in the desert and how were they honored?

A wide range of evidence, including written as well as sculptural and architectural, survives in the Eastern Desert spanning the many millennia between pharaonic and late Roman times. Major centers of human habitation including some of the desert forts, the Red Sea ports and the quarries and mines, where carefully surveyed or excavated, preserve evidence of shrines, relatively elaborate temples and, later, churches. We cannot examine them all, but we will highlight the more interesting and better preserved of these remains.

Pharaonic Temples and Shrines

One of the oldest pharaonic religious monuments in the Eastern Desert survives in Wadi Gawasis on the Red Sea coast, between Safaga and Quseir. This Middle Kingdom (2040–1640 BC) shrine, comprising a number of stone anchors, was dedicated to sailors. French excavators found other places of worship at Gebel Zeit, north of Hurghada on the Red Sea coast. These pharaonic era sanctuaries were dedicated to Hathor "Mistress of Galena," Horus "Lord of the Desert," Min, and Ptah.

One of the most unusual pharaonic shrines in the Eastern Desert, however, survives at al-Kanaïs (Pls. 6.1–6.2), which ironically means 'the churches' in Arabic, though there is nothing notably Christian on the site. Located just south of the modern paved highway connecting Edfu on the Nile with Marsa 'Alam on the Red Sea coast, and lying only about forty-six or forty-seven kilometers east of the former, there survives a Ptolemaic-Roman *praesidium* just north of a rock outcrop on which appear hundreds of inscriptions from many different eras. Just southwest of the *praesidium* and west of the bulk of the rupestral graffiti and inscriptions stand the well-preserved remains of a rock-cut temple built by Seti I (1306–1290 BC), father of Ramesses II (the Great) of the Nineteenth Dynasty. The door leading to the interior of this New Kingdom period temple has been blocked, sometime in the modern era, presumably to protect it from vandals, but the portico, comprising a colonnade with a roof, juts from the rock face and marks a grand façade for the now inaccessible interior. Affiliated and contemporary inscriptions indicate that Seti I ordered the small temple built together with a water station, a settlement, and a well. Presumably these structures, and the well, assisted those traveling across the region to exploit gold in the farther reaches of the desert.

Ptolemaic Sanctuaries

From the Late Period (the Achaemenid Persian occupation: 525–404 BC and 343–332 BC) and Ptolemaic eras (late fourth century BC–30 BC) there survive few recognizable religious edifices in the Eastern Desert. There are two shrines dating from the reign of Ptolemy III Euergetes (246–221 BC). One located at Umm Fawakhir on the Quseir–Quft road no longer exists. The second is a façade at Bir Abu Safa, deep in the southern reaches of the Eastern Desert.

Bir Abu Safa

Local Bisharin Bedouin indicated to our survey team that an ancient spring at Bir Abu Safa, together with a well, was one of several stops on an ancient track that connected Abraq to the Nile and that this putative trans-desert route terminated somewhere near Aswan. At some point in the late third century BC a small structure, now weatherworn, was cut into the lower mountain face immediately above the point where the spring surfaces. This small façade lies about one hundred kilometers southwest of the Ptolemaic-Roman port ruins of Berenike, some thirteen kilometers south of Abraq as the bird flies and about twenty-two kilometers via Wadis Hodein and Abraq south of the Ptolemaic and early Roman fort at Abraq.

In March 1832 Linant de Bellefonds visited and briefly described this small shrine-like structure at Bir Abu Safa. His is the first recorded Western account of this feature. He also drew a picture of it and the immediate sur-roundings (Fig. 6.1), which he published, together with a map mislocating the site, in his book *L'Etbaye, pays habité par les Arabes Bicharieh. Géographie, ethnologie, mines d'or.* He noted an inscription above the false door and

Fig. 6.1: L.M.A. Linant de Bellefonds' drawing of the Ptolemaic-era temple at Bir Abu Safa, which he visited in March 1832. From L. de Bellefonds, *L'Etbaye pays habité par les Arabes Bicharieh, géographie, Ethnologie, mines d'or* (Paris: A. Bertrand, 1868).

believed it to be of Ptolemy III Euergetes (246–221 BC). Yet he made no copy of the text so, until recently, we could not be certain that he was correct. If he was, year nineteen of Ptolemy III's reign would equate to 228/227 BC. Bellefonds believed that the square holes in the architrave/entablature were to accommodate some type of roof or awning to protect the water. The water, however, pools too far from the façade for such a putative sunshade to have been effective. More likely, if there was an awning, it was to protect any visitors standing immediately before the structure.

Our survey in September 2002 observed that the soft stone carving does, indeed, represent a building façade, measuring a mere 5 meters high by 4.6 meters wide, but lacking an interior. Although completely carved from the sandstone bedrock, lines have been scored into its façade to resemble quarried building blocks (Pl. 6.3). The faint traces of a four-line inscription in Greek survive above the main 'opening.' Our recent studies confirm Bellefonds' conclusion that the structure was, indeed, dedicated by Ptolemy III in 228/227 BC.

This is the only structure of its type currently known from the Eastern Desert. Other rock-cut temples exist in the region, for example that of Seti I (1306–1290 BC) of the Nineteenth Dynasty at al-Kanaïs noted above, and those of various Egyptian-Greco-Roman deities from the Roman period, if not earlier, at the emerald mines at Sikait. Yet, the Sikait structures have interiors and their functions, though religious, seem to have nothing to do with water. Although the third century AD inscription on the smaller temple at Sikait records the construction of a well nearby, there is no indication that the temple itself had any religious affiliation with this hydraulic feature. Inscriptions associated with the temple of Seti I at al-Kanaïs indicate that the erection of a settlement and the excavation of a well were part of the same building project.

There was a long classical Greek and Roman tradition throughout the Mediterranean and elsewhere among peoples of the Near East, like the Nabataeans, of monumentalizing both water sources and terminal points for their conveyance in the form of fountains and *nymphaea*. The façade at Bir Abu Safa is clearly Ptolemaic, but in an Egyptian setting and connected with water. One might note that classical Greco-Roman associations of nymphs (who were guardian spirits of sources of pure water) with Pan are well known. Pan was often identified with the Egyptian deity Min in desert regions. His worship is readily apparent in the numerous *Paneia* (areas of worship dedicated to Pan) in the Eastern Desert. Thus, Pan would have been an appropriate guardian and focal point of devotion at the small shrine at Bir Abu Safa in the midst of the barren landscape of the Eastern Desert.

A small trickle of water, part of a geological syncline carrying rainwater through the mountain, emits just below the western side of the façade and runs downhill where it pools beneath an acacia tree. Today Bisharin Bedouin water their sheep, goats, donkeys, and camels at a nearby well about one hundred meters west of this 'temple.'

We have also discovered small enclosed structures at gold and amethyst mines of Ptolemaic and early Roman date that appear to be religious in nature. We have found these at the putative Christian *laura* community at Bir Handosi, at the gold mining center of Bokari, and at the amethyst mining settlement in Wadi Abu Diyeiba.

Wadi Abu Diyeiba

During a survey we conducted in June 2004 at the amethyst mining area of Wadi Abu Diyeiba, southwest of the modern Red Sea port of Safaga, we found fragments of half a dozen inscriptions in Greek that record religious activities. Add these new discoveries to texts found previously in the area and a picture develops of Ptolemaic religious preferences of miners and administrators from at least the second century BC if not earlier. Pan, Harpocrates, Isis, and Serapis were popular. At least one of the inscription fragments we found joined with and completed a text recovered and published many decades ago dating to the reign of Ptolemy VI and his wife Cleopatra II (175–145 BC). Some of the sandstone bedrock as well as looser stones around the main settlement, which must have been the administrative center for the mining operations, had carved on them representations of dozens of human feet and hash marks (Fig. 6.2). Found in other areas of Egypt and in the Nile Valley as well as other regions of the classical Mediterranean, such carved feet are sacred to Isis; the hash marks were elongated abrasions produced by deliberate rubbing made by pious pilgrims.

In conjunction with the Greek inscriptions we also recovered a small altar made from the locally available sandstone and two pictorial reliefs. One of the fragmentary reliefs preserves a portion of a female facing the viewer and

S. E. Sidebotham

Fig. 6.2: Carved representations of human feet and hash marks at the amethyst quarries at Wadi Abu Diyeiba. Scale = twenty centimeters.

wearing a headdress; this may be a representation of Isis. The second relief, which we reconstructed from numerous shattered pieces of sandstone, depicts a canopied structure supported by two simple columns. Beneath the canopy walking toward the left is a man holding what appears to be a flail or fly whisk. He may be a priest or other important official (Fig. 6.3).

About a kilometer from the main settlement our survey found a small building atop a low ridge at the base of a mountain, approached by a series of steps, now destroyed, and a long narrow defined path (Fig. 6.4). Built of locally available granite with a small interior, this building resembles a small temple with surrounding precinct wall *(temenos)*. The covered part of the structure is small and could not have been entered by a person standing upright; perhaps the interior originally held a cult image that has long since disappeared. Though our survey could not date the building, its association with the amethyst mining activities all around suggests that it also belongs to the Ptolemaic era, or, less likely, to early Roman times.

Fig. 6.3: Relief found at the amethyst quarries at Wadi Abu Diyeiba, probably dating to the second century BC. Scale = twenty centimeters.

Fig. 6.4: Small temple at amethyst quarries at Wadi Abu Diyeiba.

LOUIS MAURICE LINANT DE BELLEFONDS

Born in Lorient, France, on 23 November 1799, Louis Maurice Linant de Belle-fonds, the son of a naval officer, was destined for a career at sea. After finishing his exams at age fifteen, Louis participated in a surveying and charting opera-tion along the coasts of Canada and the USA. Three years later, during an expedition through several countries in the Near East, he was invited to pro-ceed to Egypt to make maps and illustrations for several savants working there. After a year in Cairo, in 1818 he accompanied a team on an expedition as far south as Dongola. Being a brilliant artist and draftsman, he subsequently joined many expeditions in Egypt, Sudan, and Arabia. As he was asked to perform and lead new travels himself, he became the first European to see many ancient sites in Egypt's deep south and in Sudan. He explored Sudan and the White Nile in 1827, and searched for gold in the Eastern Desert under commission of Muhammad 'Ali, the ruler of Egypt. In 1831 his wife died of cholera in their home in Cairo. He had produced by that time a large number of drawings and notes on countless monuments, many of which are now lost or severely dam-aged. After 1835 the time of his long exploratory travels was over, and he then focused on engineering work for irrigation projects. He also played an impor-tant part in designing the Suez Canal. Louis Linant de Bellefonds became Egyptian Minister of Public Works in 1869 and earned the title of Pasha in 1873. He died in Cairo on July 19, 1883.

Roman and Early Christian Sanctuaries

The most numerous, and best preserved surviving religious shrines in the Eastern Desert, however, appear in the latest period of ancient use of the region: the Roman and early Christian. Let us look at several of the more spectacular Roman period temples and other evidence of worship before engaging in an overview of some of the Christian remains.

The large quarry settlements noted in Chapter 4 at Mons Porphyrites, Mons Claudianus, and Wadi Umm Wikala (ancient Mons Ophiates) preserve some excellent examples of temples dating from the first and second cen-turies AD, but there are also equally fascinating examples as well at some other desert sites. We will look at the beryl/emerald mining settlements at Sikait and Nugrus, which also preserve impressive architectural and written remains of the hoary cults practiced by peoples residing in these remote locales. There are also a few others in the general vicinity of the quarries and emerald mines.

Sanctuaries at the Hard Stone Quarry Settlements

Mons Porphyrites

Studied off and on since the early nineteenth century, the quarry complex at Mons Porphyrites preserves, in the main settlement in Wadi Ma'mal, at least three temples with accompanying inscriptions that leave their identification in no doubt. There is also a recently discovered inscription found in one of the satellite villages near Wadi Ma'mal that appeals directly to two deities who were quite popular throughout the region in the Roman period. All the texts relating to the religious facilities at Mons Porphyrites date to the first and second centuries AD and all were written in Greek, the *lingua franca* of the Eastern Roman Empire. In the main settlement in Wadi Ma'mal, where the large fort can be seen, lies undoubtedly the most spectacular religious structure at the site. Although dilapidated, this architectural gem of a temple to Serapis, who represents the conjoining of Osiris and the Apis Bull, and who was popular from Ptolemaic times on, rests atop a small rise on the eastern side of the wadi and south of the main fort we examined in Chapter 4. Although tumbled down, most of the blocks, columns, column capitals, entablature, and the dedicatory inscription survive more or less intact, fallen near their original position. This allows for a fairly complete picture of the ancient appearance of the building. J.G. Wilkinson, the British traveler, was so impressed by what he saw that he drew a detailed sketch of the tumbled remains on his visit in the early nineteenth century (Fig. 6.5). Access to the shrine was via a staircase on the north. Originally the temple itself faced west and had four monolithic columns made of local stone that graced its entrance. The inscription that once stood over the entrance above the columns indicates that the temple was erected early in the reign of the Roman emperor Hadrian during the tenure of the governor Rammius Martialis (AD 117–119).

Nearer to and immediately south of the small bathhouse is a more ruinous temple dedicated to Isis. Isis was a goddess who epitomized the archetypical Egyptian wife and mother; she was extremely popular in Ptolemaic and

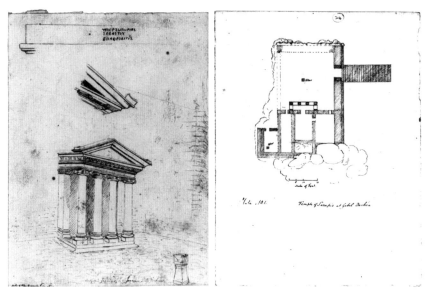

Fig. 6.5: The Serapis temple at Mons Porphyrites, drawn by J.G. Wilkinson (Ms. G. Wilkinson XLV. D169.V; Gardner Wilkinson papers from Calke Abbey, Bodleian Library, Oxford; courtesy of the National Trust).

Roman times and was often associated (syncretized) with a number of other deities. Worship of Isis would not be at all unusual in this desert environment. First discovered in the early twentieth century at the base of one of the ramps leading to a quarry in the mountains to the east, the identification was confirmed by the find of a beautiful four-line inscription precisely dated to January 28, AD 113, late in the reign of the emperor Trajan (AD 98–117). Fortunately, the inscription was studied and photographed by the British excavators prior to its theft by unknown persons using, to judge by the substantial tire tracks, a large truck in the winter of 1997/1998.

Farthest from the main fort and on the west side of the wadi at the base of the impressive 1,700 meter-long ramp that led to the Lykabettus quarries (mentioned in Chapter 4) are the remnants of the temple of Isis Myrionomos (Isis of the Many Names) (Fig. 6.6). Although in better condition than the Isis temple located near the fort, the temple of Isis Myrionomos is not as well preserved as that of Serapis on the other side of the wadi and about 360 meters away. James Burton and J.G. Wilkinson first saw the inscription associated with the Isis Myrionomos temple and published what remained in 1832. The text dates to year 22 of the Roman emperor Hadrian

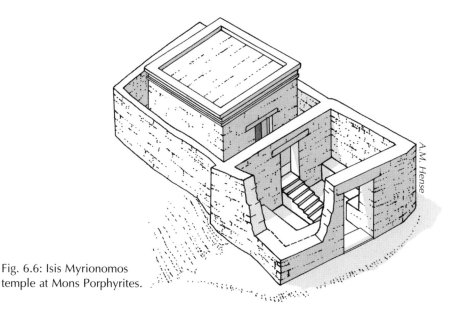

Fig. 6.6: Isis Myrionomos
temple at Mons Porphyrites.

A.M. Hense

(AD 117–138). A number of subsequent European visitors noted the
inscription thereafter, but it has, unfortunately, since disappeared.

The erection of three temples in relatively close proximity to each other
within about a twenty-five year period early in the second century AD probably indicates the intense level of activity at the quarries at that time.
Surprisingly, British archaeologists working in one of the satellite quarry
and village complexes, named the Bradford Quarry after the man who discovered it, north of the main fort in Wadi Maʿmal and the temples we just
described, found another inscription. Recovered inside a building that must
be a shrine or temple, the text in Greek records in fascinating detail that a
man named Gaius Cominius Leugas discovered the Mons Porphyrites
quarries and the multi-colored varieties of 'marble' that could be found
there. It also mentions that he dedicated a sanctuary to Pan and Serapis for
the well-being of his children on July 23, AD 18, that is, early in the reign of
the Roman emperor Tiberius (AD 14–37). A large image of Pan/Min graces
the stone standing left of the inscription. Pliny the Elder notes during the
reigns of Augustus and Tiberius that varieties of colored marbles were first
discovered in the Eastern Desert. This newly found inscription would be
some confirmation of Pliny's claim.

Mons Claudianus

Lying south–southwest of Mons Porphyrites, the Mons Claudianus quarries also boast the remains of an extremely well-preserved temple (Fig. 6.7)
located only a short distance from the large and impressive main fort and
bath building that we discussed in Chapter 4. The temple comprises multiple rooms indicating, no doubt, that each was the preserve of one of the
gods worshiped there. The rooms have niches and alcoves and with some
walls preserved to heights of several meters complete with intact doors and
windows. A once impressive staircase leads up to the complex from the
south, from the direction of the main fort. Approached by multiple doors,
excellently preserved niches, some with their mud wall plaster intact, column capitals and at least three inscriptions in Greek, this is arguably the
best-preserved Roman-era religious structure in the entire Eastern Desert.
The temple was sacred, as the main inscription tells us, to "Zeus Helios
Great Serapis" and other gods who shared his temple. Thus, the building
might be called a Roman 'Pantheon' in the desert. While there is no absolute
proof of the date of this building, all the evidence suggests that it was
erected during the reign of Trajan (AD 98–117). A nearby altar preserving
a datable text suggests that was sometime in AD 108–109. J.G. Wilkinson
records finding a terra-cotta head of Isis in the environs of the temple during his visit in the earlier part of the nineteenth century, which may suggest
one of the many deities venerated here.

S.E. Sidebotham

Fig. 6.7: The temple at Mons Claudianus, sacred to 'Zeus Helios Great Serapis' and
other gods who shared his temple.

Umm Huyut

Our survey work in June 1993, March 1995, and August 1997 found, with
the help of a Ma'aza Bedouin friend, the ancient quarry and settlement at
Umm Huyut. Located very near and just south of Mons Claudianus, the
stone from Umm Huyut was similar in appearance to that from Mons Claudianus, but was used, as we noted in Chapter 4, for smaller items than were
produced at Mons Claudianus. The small settlement at Umm Huyut had
rather nondescript and unimpressive buildings with the exception of one
(Pl. 4.13). It stood atop a small rise, was nicely constructed with benches in
the interior and approached by two staircases. The southeastern end of the
structure preserved a square 'niche.' It was clearly the most important building in the settlement. Was it for administrative or religious purposes or could
it have combined both functions? No inscription or other evidence provided
any indication of what activities took place here in the early Roman period.

Fatireh al-Beida

Southwest of Mons Claudianus and on the road that joined it to the Nile at
Kaineopolis/Maximianopolis (modern Qena) is a small quarry located at a
place called Fatireh al-Beida. Though long known to scholars, the site was
only first carefully examined by our small survey team in August 1997.
Amid the rather unremarkable remains of workers' huts our small three-per-
son survey noted a relatively impressive structure that appears to have had
a cultic-religious function. Unfortunately, we found no accompanying
inscription to indicate the deity that might have been worshiped here.

Mons Ophiates

At the Mons Ophiates quarries, which lay generally south of those at Mons
Claudianus, travelers earlier in the twentieth century reported seeing several
inscriptions. One of these was clearly religious in content and suggested the
presence of a shrine or temple. In fact, the building in question lies on the
opposite side of the narrow wadi from what must have been the main
administrative complex on the site, a walled enclosure containing a water
cistern. Comprising two separate rooms connected originally by a doorway
that was blocked sometime in antiquity, portions of this religious structure
have been washed away over the centuries by floods passing through the
adjacent wadi. Nevertheless, segments of the walls preserve impressive

doors and windows with one corner wall still standing to a height of 5.4 meters. As we noted in Chapter 4, the lengthy inscription in Greek found here in the early twentieth century and first published in 1909, indicates that this edifice was erected late in the reign of the emperor Augustus (on May 26, AD 11) to the popular desert deity Pan/Min. In one of the rare examples where the names of architects are mentioned, this text, which also boasts an image of Pan/Min similar to that found on the Mons Porphyrites stone we noted above from the Bradford Quarry, records that Mersis and Soter, who are otherwise unknown, designed the building.

Sanctuaries at the Emerald Mining Settlements
Sikait

Deeper in the southern reaches of the Eastern Desert in a region the Romans knew as Mons Smaragdus, the only sources of beryl/emeralds to be found anywhere inside the Roman empire were exploited from at least the first century AD until the sixth. This area was also mined in Islamic and modern times. Hundreds if not thousands of shafts and pits honeycomb this region in which our surveys over the years have identified and studied nine principal mining settlements. While some of these preserve few edifices, several of the other ancient communities are Pompeii-like in the preservation of some buildings. Two of the largest and most impressive of these desert emerald mining communities are those in Wadi Sikait and the adjacent Wadi Nugrus. Wadi Sikait has, in fact, three settlements, which our project has named Sikait, Middle Sikait and North Sikait.

The French goldsmith and metallurgist Frédéric Cailliaud first discovered Sikait in 1816 and made a follow-up visit in 1817. He was in the employ of Muhammad 'Ali Pasha, Egypt's ruler at the time, and had been commissioned to search for the lost emerald mines with a view to reopening them. Muhammad 'Ali, however, never did reopen the area to extensive exploitation. The gemstones from the Sikait area were low grade and the mines were remote and difficult to access. There were also much higher quality and more easily accessible emeralds available from the mines in Columbia, South America. These various factors meant that while some modern mining in the Sikait region has been undertaken, it was never extensive. Cailliaud made several impressive, but fanciful, drawings of two of the more alluring features at Sikait: the larger and smaller rock-cut temples (Pls. 6.4–6.5).

Sikait, the southernmost of the three settlements and by far the most impressive, preserves at least two identifiable rock-cut temples. Hewn directly into the sides of the mountain, the larger of the two has attracted the most attention from visitors over the past two centuries (Pl. 6.6 and Fig. 6.8). This large three-chambered temple at one time had an extensive—up to 4.5 meters long—three or four line inscription over the front entrance. Our survey found just a few letters of the beginning and end of the text in Greek. The rest may well lay fragmented and buried in the tumble beneath the entrance. It would be fascinating to uncover these broken stones to determine who carved this structure and to which deities it was dedicated. It is noteworthy that none of the earlier visitors to this temple mention the existence of these texts, which can only really be clearly seen at certain times of day and in particular types of light. Graffiti (carved) and dipinti (painted) from ancient to modern times emblazon the interior walls of the temple and include some from the nineteenth-century travelers. At the back in the third room on the altar we only recently noticed a large Christian cross carved over the badly worn remnants of a hieroglyphic text (Fig. 6.9).

S.E. Sidebotham

Fig. 6.8: The large rock-cut temple at Sikait with side chambers north and south of the main entrance.

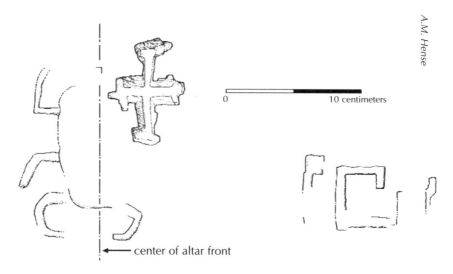

A.M. Hense

0   10 centimeters

center of altar front

Fig. 6.9: Remains of hieroglyphs and a Christian cross found on the altar in the large rock-cut temple at Sikait.

This tantalizing evidence suggests use of the temple before the arrival of the Romans, perhaps during the Ptolemaic era, as well as by the later Christians. We hope to excavate here someday in conjunction with conservation and restoration measures to help preserve this wonderful antiquity for future generations. We have undertaken some consolidation work inside this building as well; we erected a support pillar in place of its ancient and now broken and fallen antecedent and have also shored up some of the walls (Pl. 6.7 and Fig. 6.10). In the course of excavating to install the temporary support we recovered a beautifully preserved tetradrachm (four-drachma coin) of the emperor Nero (AD 54–68) on the reverse of which is depicted the bust of the deified emperor Tiberius (AD 14–37). We also found a small, highly stylized statuette of Isis (Fig. 6.11) that is very similar in appearance to depictions of Isis in artwork from the ancient Kingdom of Meroë in what is today Sudan. Perhaps this latter discovery provides some evidence for one of the deities worshiped in this impressive shrine cut into the face of the mountain.

The second, smaller and less impressive rock-cut temple (Fig. 6.12) farther south in the same wadi as the larger structure preserves still today, and in its original position, portions of a lengthy inscription in Greek (Pl. 6.8

H.M. Nouwens

Fig. 6.10: Large rock-cut
temple at Sikait. Temporary
conservation/consolidation
measure to shore up the
sagging interior roof. The
column was erected in the
position of the original one.

A.M. Hense

Fig. 6.11: Small metal stylized figurine of
Isis from the large rock-cut temple at Sikait.

0   2 centimeters

S.E. Sidebotham

Fig. 6.12: Small rock-cut temple at Sikait.

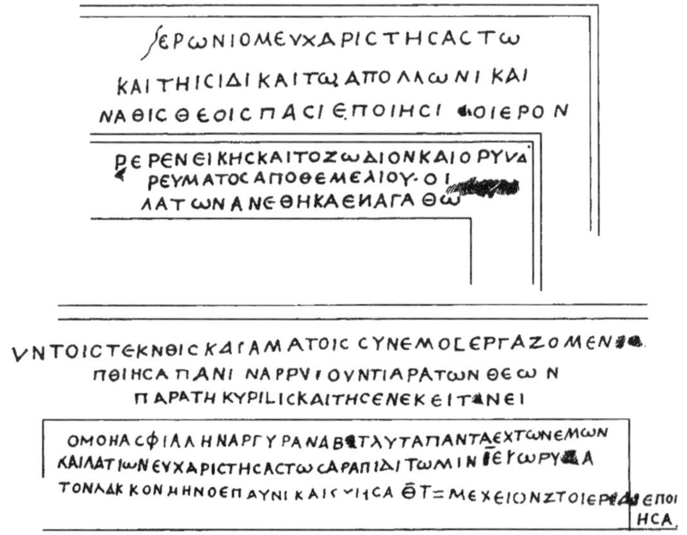

Fig. 6.13: Inscription in Greek over the entrance of the small rock-cut temple at Sikait, drawn by N. L'Hôte (J. Letronne ND, *Recueil des inscriptions grecques et latines de l'Égypte*. Atlas. Paris: Imprimerie royale, PL. XVI).

and Fig. 6.13). Various nineteenth-century visitors including Wilkinson and
the Frenchman Nestor L'Hôte undertook the transcription of this text. That
inscription, carved over the entrance of the small shrine, is extremely
informative. It relates that the Roman emperor Gallienus (AD 260–268)
dedicated the small rupsetral temple to Serapis, Isis of Senskis (the ancient
name of Sikait), Apollo, and other gods on the 20th of February of an
unknown year during his reign. It also mentions the excavation of a nearby
well on June 15. Much of the text has disappeared and even fragments we
saw lying on the ground in front of the temple on our first visit in 1991 have
since been stolen. It is possible, indeed likely, that this temple was in use long
before Gallienus and that his inscription is merely the latest period of
recorded activity at this petite shrine. During our winter 2002/2003 field
season we erected three pillars made of pieces of locally available stone at
the entrance of this structure as temporary support to prevent collapse until
we can conduct more careful consolidation and conservation (Fig. 6.14).
There are other rock-cut structures at Sikait as well as several additional
well-preserved and impressive freestanding edifices that may also have been
temples, but we do not know this for certain.

H.M. Nouwens

Fig. 6.14: Small rock-cut temple at Sikait after consolidation.

Nugrus

In a large wadi southwest of Sikait is the ancient emerald and beryl mining settlement of Nugrus. Here are the remains of several hundred structures approximately twenty of which survive in spectacular condition. One building, part way up a hill southeast of the main site, is most certainly a temple (Figs. 6.15–6.16). Approached by a long and elaborate set of stairs, the multi-roomed shrine rests atop a well-built artificial platform. The thick walls are built of carefully stacked locally quarried stone. Several doors with their lintels, as well as niches survive in excellent condition. Amid the ruins our survey recovered the lower portion of a seated cult statue. Only the legs and throne, the sides of which are much worn, but seem to preserve hieroglyphs, survive to a height of less than twenty-five centimeters (Fig. 6.17). Yet, we could not establish which deity was honored in this finely wrought building.

S.E. Sidebotham

Fig 6.15: Nugrus, part of the temple on the east side of the Roman-era beryl/emerald mining community.

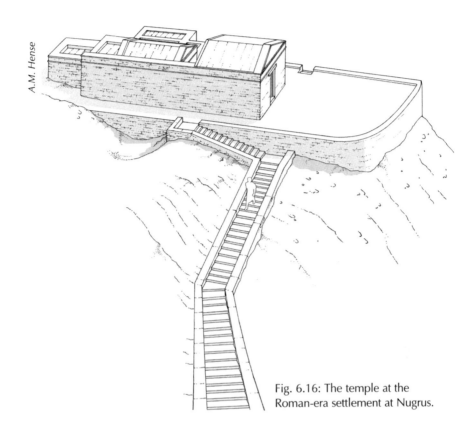

A.M. Hense

Fig. 6.16: The temple at the Roman-era settlement at Nugrus.

Ka'b Marfu'

At Ka'b Marfu', in the emerald mining district of the Eastern Desert, an impressive structure built halfway up the side of a mountain immediately draws the visitor's attention. Nestled atop a massive four-meter high artificial platform and approached by an impressive flight of stairs from a major cluster of buildings in the wadi below, this structure must have been a temple (Figs. 6.18–6.19). Doors provided access from two sides, a main one from the south and a smaller one from the east. Our survey found no inscription indicating the purpose of this noteworthy edifice, but its prominence and elevation well above the rest of the settlement strongly suggests that it was for religious activities.

A.M. Hense

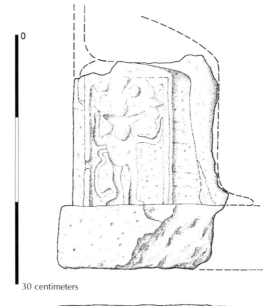

0

30 centimeters

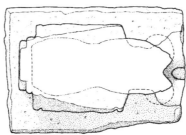

Fig. 6.17: Statue fragment
from the temple at Nugrus

Sanctuary at a Settlement of Unknown Function
Bir Kareim

Lying thirty to thirty-five kilometers southwest of the Red Sea port of
Quseir are the extensive remains at Bir Kareim. Long believed to have been
one of the sources of potable water to the Red Sea port of Quseir al-Qadim
(ancient Myos Hormos), brief and incomplete surveys were conducted here
in the winters of 1978 and 1980 by a team from the Oriental Institute of the
University of Chicago, the same group that excavated Quseir al-Qadim.
They believed that Bir Kareim was also a Roman gold mining settlement.
Yet, a brief return visit to Bir Kareim by our survey team in August 1998
located none of the telltale gold grinding stones that are ubiquitous at other
Ptolemaic and Roman gold mining settlements in the Eastern Desert. Thus,

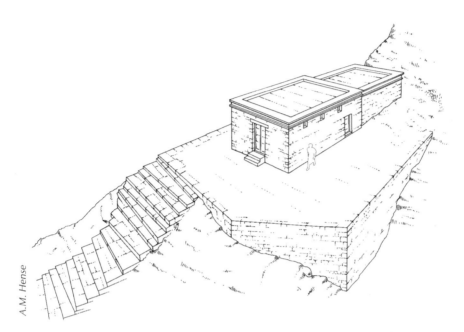

A.M. Hense

Fig. 6.18: Drawing of the temple at the Roman-era settlement at Ka'b Marfu'.

S.E. Sidebotham

Fig. 6.19: The temple at the Roman-era settlement at Ka'b Marfu'.

until we undertake more detailed work here, we cannot be certain of the purpose of this sizeable and apparently early Roman settlement. In any case one of the more prominent edifices on the site is a temple or rather a structure that closely resembles in plan a temple; it is built of a purple-red stone very different from that used in the other buildings in the settlement. It has two courts and a tripartite *cella* (enclosed cult area) near the rear wall. This architectural arrangement would suggest that the building had a religious function. We do not know to whom the putative temple was dedicated or who erected it. The structure sits at the base of a prominent mountain. In 1980 the survey team found a fragment of a pictorial relief with part of a *uraeus* (cobra) decoration on it in the vicinity of the building. This may or may not have any bearing on the identification of the edifice as a temple.

Sanctuaries in *Praesidia*

Temples and cult centers in the Eastern Desert were not confined only to quarries and mines. Recent French excavations of Roman-era *praesidia* along the road joining the ancient Red Sea port of Myos Hormos to the Nile at Coptos (Quft) noted that each seems to have had its own protective patron deity. While worship of Pan is evident from the many small *Paneia* scattered throughout the desert, especially along the various trans-desert routes, he was also honored in at least one of the desert *praesidia*. Ostraca indicate that other apotropaic deities venerated at the forts included Apollo, Athena, the Dioscuri (the twins Castor and Polydeuces/Pollux), Serapis, and Philotera, the deified sister of Ptolemy II Philadelphus 285–246 BC). Yet, it is very rare to be able to identify a particular area inside any of these forts that was set aside specifically for the worship of these deities.

Sanctuaries in Red Sea Ports
Myos Hormos and Marsa Nakari

Though portions of the Red Sea ports of Myos Hormos and Marsa Nakari (perhaps to be associated with the ancient Nechesia and which lies about 150 kilometers south of Myos Hormos) have been excavated, no recognizably religious structures have been found. Archaeologists from the University of Southampton excavating at Myos Hormos in 1999–2003 believe they may have unearthed a temple or synagogue, though they are very tentative about this identification.

Berenike

At the Red Sea port of Berenike (which lies about three hundred kilometers south of Myos Hormos and approximately 150 kilometers south of Marsa Nakari), on the other hand, we have excavated several temples, sanctuaries, and a church. We have also found inscriptions indicating the existence of other cults whose buildings now lie silently somewhere amid the buried ruins of the city.

The best-known temple at Berenike is undoubtedly that dedicated to Serapis and other deities (Figs. 6.20–6.21); it dominates the highest part of the city and its remains were somewhat visible as early as 1818 when Giovanni Belzoni first rediscovered the site. In fact, he made a drawing of what he saw at the time. Built for the most part of brilliant white locally obtainable gypsum, the temple blocks that compose the walls were joined together with clamps made of wood. This structure has fared badly over the centuries. It was the focal point of attention of many of the nineteenth century visitors who spent time 'clearing' the building and recovering inscriptions and pieces of statuary that once graced the structure's interior. Even then, the inscriptions, mainly in hieroglyphs, that covered the walls were in extremely fragile condition. They were so delicate that one visitor passing his hand over the walls noted pieces of the inscriptions falling off. The ancient texts that emblazoned the interior walls of the temple are mainly Roman in date, first and second century AD, though there are some from the Ptolemaic period reported to have come from the temple interior. We have to assume that this temple, or a predecessor, existed here after the foundation of Berenike by Ptolemy II Philadelphus in about 275 BC. We do not know when it ceased to be used as a religious sanctuary. More has been written about this Serapis temple prior to our excavations than any other structure at Berenike.

Between 1994 and 2001 our project uncovered several other buildings having religious functions. In addition, dedicatory inscriptions surviving on stone demonstrate that men and women, both civilian and military, paid homage to a number of deities worshiped in the port. We found three inscriptions inside the same building during the 2001 season at Berenike while excavating in the late Roman quarter. Here were located multistoried edifices that served both a commercial and residential function. A wealthy woman named Philotera honored Zeus on two inscribed stone slabs carved during Nero's reign (AD 54–68) (Pl. 6.9), while a man whose name is lost

Fig 6.20: The Serapis temple at Berenike.

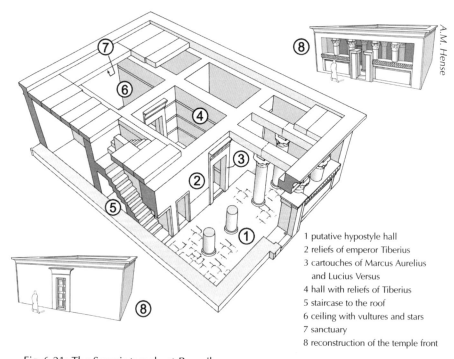

1 putative hypostyle hall
2 reliefs of emperor Tiberius
3 cartouches of Marcus Aurelius
  and Lucius Versus
4 hall with reliefs of Tiberius
5 staircase to the roof
6 ceiling with vultures and stars
7 sanctuary
8 reconstruction of the temple front

Fig. 6.21: The Serapis temple at Berenike.

to us, but who was an interpreter and secretary and the son of Papiris, made a dedication to Isis during the reign of the emperor Trajan (AD 98–117).

A diminutive shrine, in a small narrow structure built of coral heads and cut blocks of gypsum and anhydrite, lay west and down the hill from the Serapis temple. Though small, it contained the most spectacular finds found at any time during our excavations (Fig. 6.22). We collected fragments that comprised about sixty percent of a nearly life-sized bronze statue of a female holding either a snake or a cornucopia (Pl. 6.10). The statue originally rested on an inscribed stone base dedicated by a Roman auxiliary soldier from the Syrian Desert caravan city of Palmyra (Fig. 6.23). Serving as an archer in the Roman army stationed at Berenike, this man, whose name was Marcus Aurelius Mokimos son of Abdaeus, offered the inscription and statue to the emperor Caracalla and his mother Julia Domna as part of the Roman imperial cult. Worship of Roman monarchs and their relatives was especially popular in the Eastern portions of the Roman world where deification of rulers had a long tradition, especially in Egypt. Mokimos' precisely dated offering of September 8, AD 215 was one of a number of important religious objects found in this relatively tiny and compact cult center.

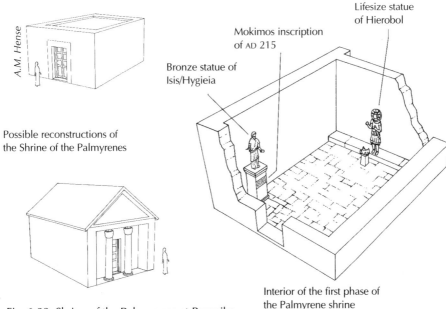

Possible reconstructions of the Shrine of the Palmyrenes

A.M. Hense

Lifesize statue of Hierobol

Mokimos inscription of AD 215

Bronze statue of Isis/Hygieia

Interior of the first phase of the Palmyrene shrine

Fig. 6.22: Shrine of the Palmyrenes at Berenike.

A.M. Hense

Fig. 6.23: Reconstruction of statue base, inscription, and statue fragment from the shrine of the Palmyrenes at Berenike.

Another inscription, found in the same shrine by our camp guard after a particularly heavy rain washed it from the surrounding area into the same trench as the Mokimos dedication, proved even more exciting (Figs. 6.24). It was a bilingual text carved in both Palmyrene and in Greek with the Greek text being longer and more informative. It records several Roman soldiers plus the Roman governor of Berenike by name and rank and the dedication of a statue of the Palmyrene god Yarhibol/Hierobol. Most fascinating is the mention of Berichei, the sculptor who crafted the image of the god. His name suggests that he, too, was probably from Palmyra. Though undated, the names on the inscription indicate that it was carved sometime between about AD 180 and 212.

Our excavations in the same trench that produced the Mokimos and Berichei inscriptions also unearthed a large monolithic block in its original position with two carved indentations for fixing a standing statue into it. We also found fragments of lead, which would have been used to seal the statue

Pl. 6.4: Drawing by F. Cailliaud of the larger rock-cut temple at Sikait. From F. Cailliaud, *Voyage à l'oasis Thèbes et dans les déserts situés à l'orient et l'occident de la Thébaïde* (Paris: 1821).

Fig 6.5: Drawing by F. Cailliaud of the smaller rock-cut temple at Sikait. From F. Cailliaud, *Voyage à l'oasis Thèbes et dans les déserts situés à l'orient et l'occident de la Thébaïde* (Paris: 1821).

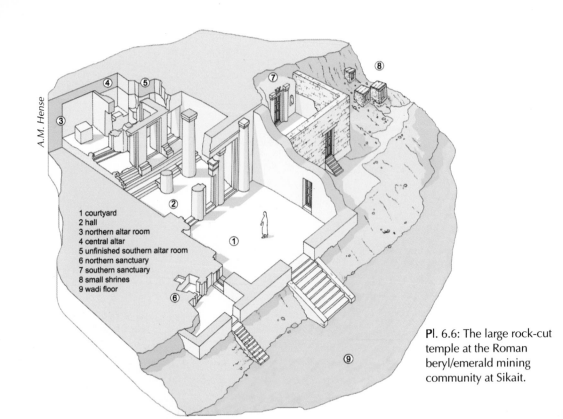

A.M. Hense

1 courtyard
2 hall
3 northern altar room
4 central altar
5 unfinished southern altar room
6 northern sanctuary
7 southern sanctuary
8 small shrines
9 wadi floor

Pl. 6.6: The large rock-cut temple at the Roman beryl/emerald mining community at Sikait.

Pl. 6.7: Interior of the large rock-cut temple at Sikait with broken column.

Pl. 6.8: Fragment of the inscription in Greek over the entrance of the small rock-cut temple at Sikait.

Pl. 6.9: Berenike, inscribed stone slab carved during Nero's reign (AD 54–68). Dedication by Philotera to Zeus found in the courtyard of a house in the late Roman residential/commercial quarter.

S.E. Sidebotham

Pl. 6.10: Bronze statue originally set on an inscribed stone base dedicated by a Roman auxiliary soldier from the Syrian Desert caravan city of Palmyra. Scale = fifty centimeters.

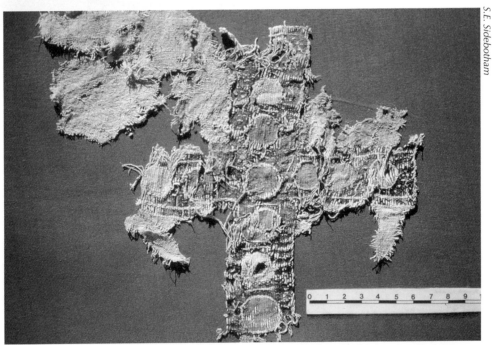

S.E. Sidebotham

Pl. 6.11: Textile cross found in the principia/church at Abu Sha'r. Scale = ten centimeters.

Pl. 6.12: Inscription from the north gate of the fort at Abu Sha'r, carved in Greek, which reads: "There is one God only, Christ." Each black-and-white increment on the scale = twenty centimeters.

Pl. 6.13: Oil lamps with Christian symbols and a bronze cross-shaped handle from a lamp found in the large ecclesiastical complex at Berenike.

Pl. 7.1: Remains of Myos Hormos.

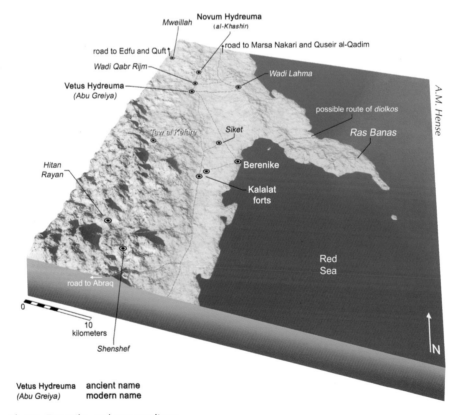

Pl. 7.2: Berenike and surroundings.

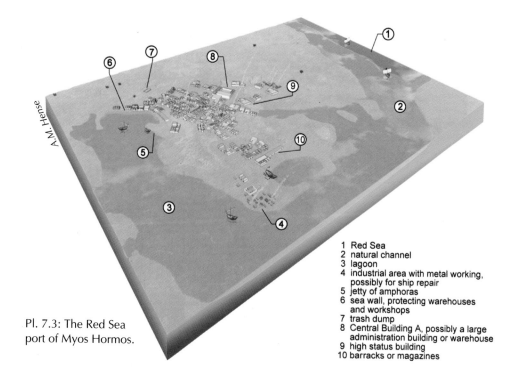

Pl. 7.3: The Red Sea
port of Myos Hormos.

1 Red Sea
2 natural channel
3 lagoon
4 industrial area with metal working,
  possibly for ship repair
5 jetty of amphoras
6 sea wall, protecting warehouses
  and workshops
7 trash dump
8 Central Building A, possibly a large
  administration building or warehouse
9 high status building
10 barracks or magazines

Pl. 7.4: Berenike, large round-bottomed clay jars made in India. Scale = twenty centimeters.

Pl. 7.5: Peppercorns found in Indian-made jar embedded in the courtyard floor of the Serapis Temple at Berenike.

Pl. 7.8: Bead from Jatim, Eastern Java found at Berenike. Each black-and-white increment on the scale = one centimeter.

Pl. 7.6: Warehouse in Berenike with amphorae from about AD 400.

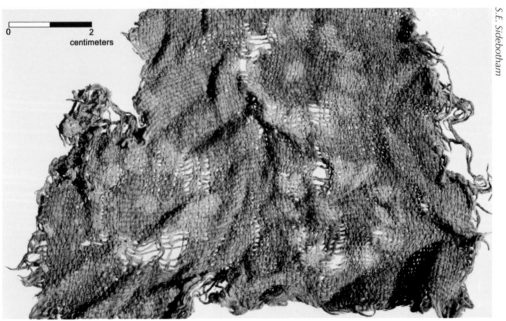

0   2
centimeters

Pl. 7.7: Fifth century AD cotton resist-dyed Indian textile found at Berenike. Very similar textiles were excavated at two sites along the Silk Road in western China. Each black-and-white increment on the scale = two centimeters.

Pl. 7.9: Stamped plaster amphora stopper found at Berenike. Scale = ten centimeters.

Pl. 7.11: First century AD Tamil-Brahmi graffito carved on a Roman amphora fragment. Scale = ten centimeters.

Pl. 7.10: Fragments of terra sigillata bowls with makers' marks. Scale = five centimeters.

Pl. 7.12: Ostraca found at Berenike in the early Roman trash dump. Each black and white increment = one centimeter.

Pl. 7.13: Ostracon, inkwell, and reed writing pen found at Berenike. Scale = five centimeters.

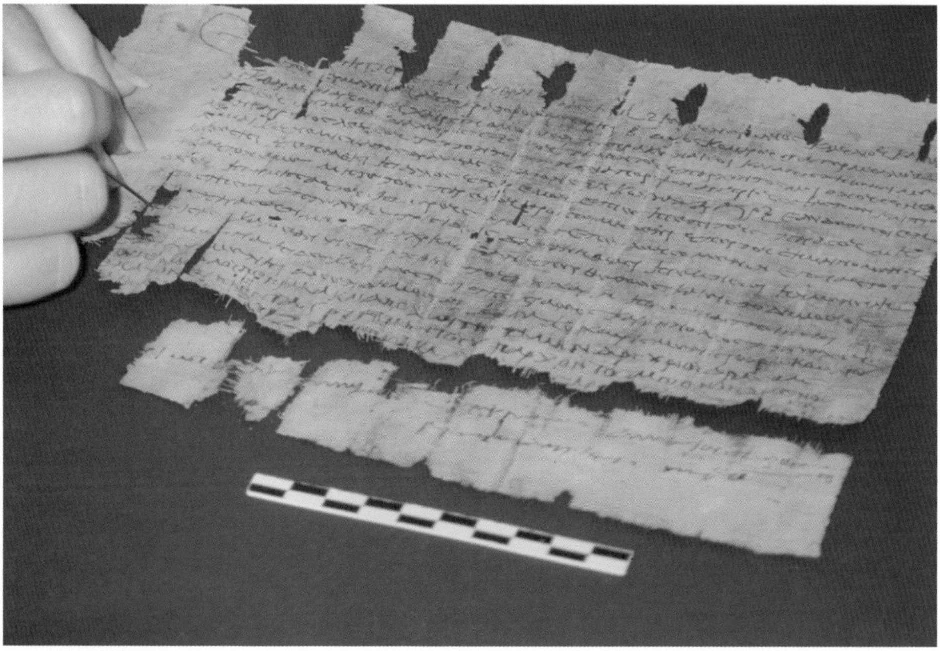

Pl. 7.14: Berenike, papyrus: bill of sale for a white male donkey and a packsaddle for 160 drachmas, dating to 26 July, AD 60 (during the reign of Nero AD 54–68). Scale = ten centimeters.

0   5 centimeters

Pl. 7.15: Eastern Desert ware.

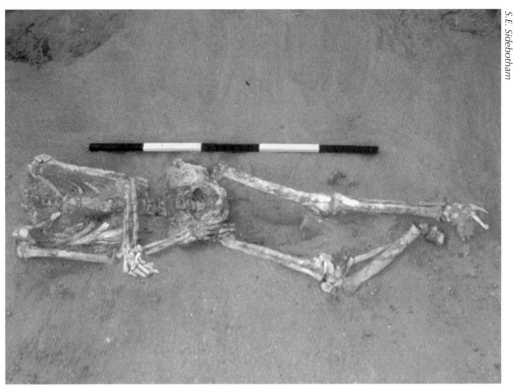

Pl. 8.1: Berenike, skeleton missing its head deposited at an unknown date in the abandoned Ptolemaic industrial area. Scale = one meter.

Pl. 8.2: Grave in the large cemetery at Taw al-Kefare, used in the fifth century AD and later.

Pl. 9.1: Large circular ore-grinding facilities at the site of Daghbag.

Pl. 9.2: Large circular ore-grinding facilities at the site of Daghbag. (Detail of Fig. 9.1).

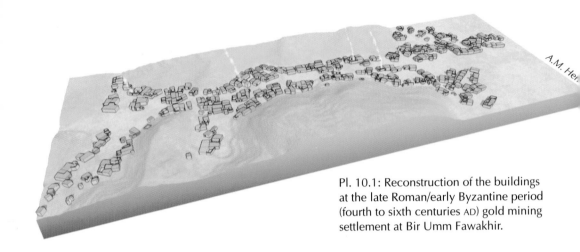

Pl. 10.1: Reconstruction of the buildings at the late Roman/early Byzantine period (fourth to sixth centuries AD) gold mining settlement at Bir Umm Fawakhir.

Pl. 10.2: Well-preserved structure (called 'Three Windows') at the Roman-era mining community at Sikait.

Pl. 10.3: Barracks blocks in the late Roman fort at Abu Sha'r.

Pl. 10.4: View of interior of late Roman fort at Abu Sha'r looking northwest.

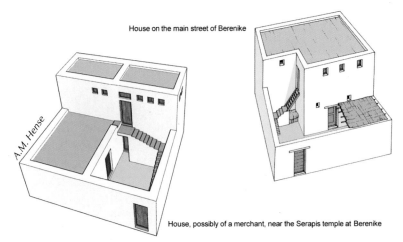

House on the main street of Berenike

House, possibly of a merchant, near the Serapis temple at Berenike

Pl. 10.5: Reconstruction of two houses at Berenike from the late Roman (late fourth–fifth century AD) commercial-residential quarter.

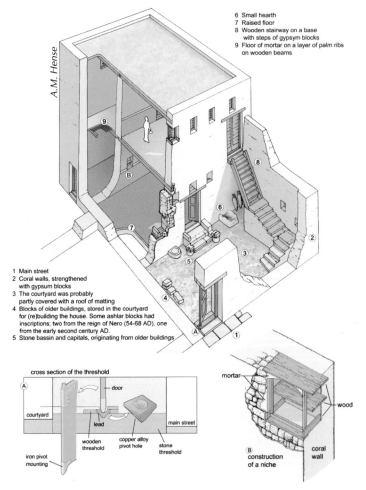

6 Small hearth
7 Raised floor
8 Wooden stairway on a base
  with steps of gypsym blocks
9 Floor of mortar on a layer of palm ribs
  on wooden beams

1 Main street
2 Coral walls, strengthened
  with gypsum blocks
3 The courtyard was probably
  partly covered with a roof of matting
4 Blocks of older buildings, stored in the courtyard
  for (re)building the house. Some ashlar blocks had
  inscriptions; two from the reign of Nero (54-68 AD), one
  from the early second century AD.
5 Stone bassin and capitals, originating from older buildings

cross section of the threshold

door

courtyard

main street

lead

wooden
threshold

copper alloy
pivot hole

stone
threshold

iron pivot
mounting

mortar

wood

construction
of a niche

coral
wall

Pl. 10.6: Reconstruction of a multiple-storied house near the Serapis temple at Berenike.

S.E. Sidebotham

Fig. 6.24: Bedouin excavator holding a Greek-Palmyrene bilingual inscription (left). The Greek-Palmyrene bilingual inscription containing a dedication to the Palmyrene god Hierobol/Yarhibol. Scale = ten centimeters (right).

to the base. Unfortunately, aside from a single bronze hand (Fig. 6.25), nothing else of Berichei's masterpiece survives. Other evidence of religious activity included a small stone altar with burning on the top, cultic bowls made of terra cotta, and about one hundred bowls made of wood, a small statue of a sphinx (Figs. 6.26–6.27), which had been rebuilt into one of the later walls of the shrine, and a small stone head of the Egyptian deity Harpocrates. Clearly, this shrine was extremely active in the late second to early third centuries AD and later. It also suggests that Palmyrene troops helped to patrol the desert road joining Berenike to the Nile emporium of Coptos, where interestingly, another inscription dated to AD 216 also mentions a Palmyrene mounted unit stationed there. That these men had ample funds to make such elaborate dedications, something they probably could not

Fig. 6.25: Statue base with two holes in it for the feet of a bronze statue (likely of Yarhibol). Scale = fifty centimeters.

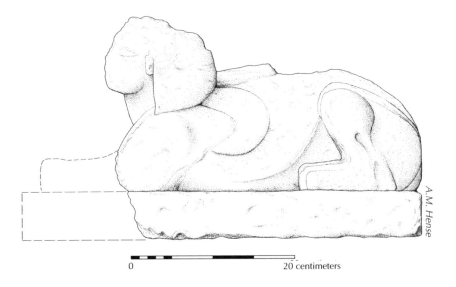

0   20 centimeters

Fig. 6.26: Sphinx statue of local gypsum rock from the shrine of the Palmyrenes.

S.E. Sidebotham

Fig. 6.27: Sphinx statue *in situ* in the Palmyrene shrine.

have accomplished on their military pay alone, might indicate that they made extra income participating at some level in the lucrative commerce that passed through the port.

Elsewhere at Berenike our excavations recovered a statuette of Aphrodite sculpted in local stone from the early Roman trash dump and a nicely carved Aphrodite wringing her hair decorating the top of a wooden jewelry box (Fig. 6.28) from about AD 400. Both indicate that deity's popularity at the port. We also recovered a small representation of Bes, a minor Egyptian god associated with love, marriage, and the warding off of evil.

Only about eighty meters north of the Serapis temple our excavations uncovered another small, perhaps vaulted, cult center with a single narrow entrance at its eastern end. Unlike the sanctuary with the inscriptions and remains of the two bronze statues, this one had a short life at the turn of the fourth and fifth centuries AD. During two phases this shrine honored some deity whose identity remains uncertain; though this may have been a mystery cult (Figs. 6.29–6.30). Mystery cults in the Greco-Roman world were those with limited membership and special initiation rites. Often times, the initiation process was a closely guarded secret and one the inductees swore never to reveal. Isis was possibly worshiped here as she was quite popular elsewhere in the Eastern Desert and, as noted above, we recovered a second-century inscription in another trench at Berenike dedicated to her. The small enclosure contained a columnar shaped altar at the back (western) end, the top of which had been heavily burned. This altar had been used during both phases of the life of the building. Adjacent to it were four stone-carved temple-pools, items commonly found throughout the pharaonic period and later in many sanctuaries throughout Egypt (Fig. 6.31). We also recovered an intact ostrich egg painted in hues of red, a small bronze statuette, a number of terra-cotta oil lamps, and about fifty amphora toes which had been reused as torches; clearly artificial lighting was necessary. Inside and parallel to the long walls of the building were two benches. In the latest phase, reused stones served as bench tops. One of these, unfortunately very fragmentary, was a relief depicting two figures. One figure to the right stood on an elevated dais and the other stood at a lower level to the left. We do not know if this relief was an original part of this building or if it had been recycled from some other part of town. Nor do we know what to make of the scene. Could it be that the figure on the dais was a deity and that below and to our left was a priest or devotee, or could the scene be secular in nature?

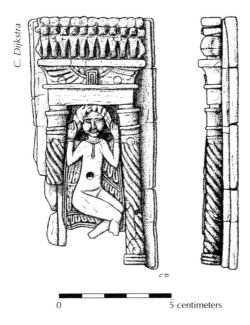

C. Dijkstra

0   5 centimeters

Fig. 6.28: Decorated wooden panel depicting Aphrodite. Likely the lid of a jewelry box.

Fig. 6.29: Small sanctuary north of the Serapis temple at Berenike, possibly used for a mystery cult. Scale = fifty centimeters.

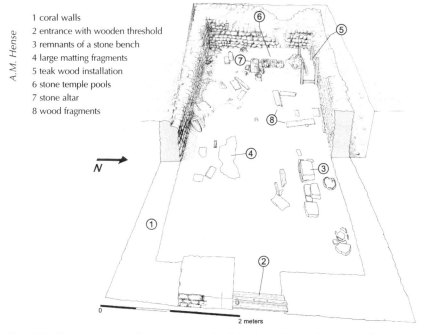

1 coral walls
2 entrance with wooden threshold
3 remnants of a stone bench
4 large matting fragments
5 teak wood installation
6 stone temple pools
7 stone altar
8 wood fragments

N

0   2 meters

Fig. 6.30: Drawing of small sanctuary north of the Serapis temple at Berenike, possibly used for a mystery cult.

H.M. Nouwens

Fig. 6.31: Stone altar, ostrich egg, and four temple pools *in situ* in the small mystery cult sanctuary at Berenike. Scale = twenty centimeters.

Christian Remains in the Eastern Desert

Ancient written sources, especially those of the early Christian church fathers, recount that many people from all walks of life, both men and women, fled to the desert areas to escape persecution or to worship without the quotidian distractions encountered while living in crowded villages in the Nile Valley. This process of departing the cultivated areas adjacent to the river for the desert was known as *anachorsis* and it was practiced not only because of religious motivation, but also by those seeking to evade taxes, escape the long arm of the law, and for a host of other reasons. In fact, the desert was long the haunt of bandits who preyed on those passing along the roads that threaded through the desiccated landscape; the bolder among them occasionally also attacked villages closer to the Nile.

Several excellent examples of monasteries in the Eastern Desert, established in the third or fourth centuries and which continue to operate today, can be found in the northern areas. The flourishing monasteries of St. Antony and St. Paul lay not far from one another. Yet little can now be seen of ancient date at these sites. Several churches from the later fourth to fifth centuries survive in the region, however, as do other material remains attesting the presence of Christian desert dwellers.

The late Roman fort at Abu Sha'r, which we discussed in Chapter 3 in conjunction with the Via Nova Hadriana, had, after its abandonment by the Roman military sometime in the late fourth or early fifth century, been reoccupied by a group of Christian squatters. Clearly less numerous than the earlier Roman garrison, as can be seen from their non-use of many of the buildings inside the fort's enceinte, they confined most of their activity to the large former headquarters which they converted into a church. Our survey and excavations at Abu Sha'r between 1987 and 1993 noted large crosses carved on some of the white gypsum stones used to construct the building. In 1991 we also recovered a beautiful polychrome cloth-embroidered Christian cross (Pl. 6.11) that must have been part of an altar decoration or monk's or priest's vestment.

Another spectacular find was an almost complete papyrus, which we discovered rolled up and placed adjacent to one of the piers that supported the roof of the headquarters/church. This twenty-seven-line-long Greek text, probably written in the fifth century, is nearly complete and refers to Slamo, the wife of a man named John, and his daughter Sarah. The papyrus had a note on the front requesting delivery to "Father John from Apollonios," which implies that the letter itself was written by a man named Apollonios to Abba (father) John. After the usual formulaic greetings Apollonios writes, "The Lord testifies for me that I was deeply grieved about the capture of your city, and again we heard that the Lord God had saved you and all your dependents." Needless to say, we would very much like to know the details of this part of the epistle, but we can only hypothesize. John's wife's name, Slamo, which is Semitic, may point to some place in the Sinai as being the city in question. Were John and his family here at Abu Sha'r as refugees after the capture of their city or were they visiting pilgrims who only received news of the fate of their city while at Abu Sha'r?

Also immediately in front of the apse of the military headquarters/church we recovered part of an adult human leg bone wrapped in cloth. We believe this was the remains of a venerated individual, perhaps a local saint or martyr, some of whose bones had been placed here. Worship of saints and martyrs was particularly in vogue among the early Coptic Christians of Egypt and the bones we found may well be those of a holy man whose name has long since been lost to us. To reinforce our interpretation of this building being converted to a martyr shrine (a *martyrium*), we found the shoulder of an amphora in the extra-mural baths at Abu Sha'r that had *mart*[—-?] written on it in Greek. These are the first letters of the words martyrium, martyr, and their cognates.

At the time these Christians were using the fort at Abu Sha'r as a place of refuge, they were entering and exiting mainly via the surviving north gate; the principal western gate used earlier by the military had apparently collapsed and been abandoned by the period of Christian use. The arch, part of the fort wall and even portions of the crenellated battlements that had originally stood over the north gate, had fallen forward and away from the fort; we excavated and reassembled these in summer 1992. In so doing, we found cut into some of the blocks of the toppled arch two inscriptions carved in Greek, clearly Christian religious in content. One merely noted, "There is one God only, Christ," accompanied by a palm branch, a typical symbol of victory in both pagan and early Christian art (Pl. 6.12). The second text was far longer and called upon the Lord God, 'our' fathers Abraham, Isaac, and Jacob, all the saints and Mary 'Mother of God' to have mercy upon those who carved the inscription, but whose names do not appear. Both texts were likely written in the fifth century. The north gate area itself preserved numerous graffiti from the Christian period of the fort's use as the appearance of numerous crosses indicates.

West of Abu Sha'r in the quarry area of Mons Porphyrites various expeditions over the years, including ours, found ample evidence that Christians in the fourth, fifth, and sixth centuries had lived and died in this barren wasteland. Christian cemeteries have been found in the region with a particularly noteworthy one located not far from the small village toward the top of the mountain near the so-called Lykabettus quarries. In 1989 our survey recovered the remains of a tombstone preserving a text in Greek of the deceased. His name was John and he originally hailed from the Nile city of Hermopolis; there are several cities of that name so we cannot be certain which one was John's home. Nor can we be certain that John was here voluntarily. While it is likely he was one of those fleeing the Nile Valley for the solitude of the desert, it is also possible that he was here under duress as forced labor work-ing the quarries, a situation which some ancient written sources indicate was a fairly common punishment for criminals or political undesirables.

In Wadi Nagat, a small offshoot of Wadi Qattar, are remains of a building; there Wilkinson, Murray, and Tregenza had noted a Christian inscription indicating the presence of an *anchorite* community. Murray says he removed the inscription for safe-keeping to Luxor in 1949.

The other major Christian building in the Eastern Desert is the large ecclesiastical complex we excavated at Berenike between 1996 and 2001 (Figs. 6.32–6.33). When we first began excavations in this structure, located in the extreme eastern part of Berenike, we did not recognize that it was Christian, only that it was late Roman. However, after the recovery of a large bronze cross, that was probably part of a decorated handle of an oil lamp used for illumination that we found nearby, as well as three other terra-cotta oil lamps, two of which bore crosses and the third an aphorism in the Cop-tic language that translates "Jesus, forgive me," (Pl. 6.13) we were fairly certain that the large structure was, indeed, a church. The orientation of the

S.E. Sidebotham

Fig. 6.32: Berenike: large ecclesiastical complex. Scale = one meter.

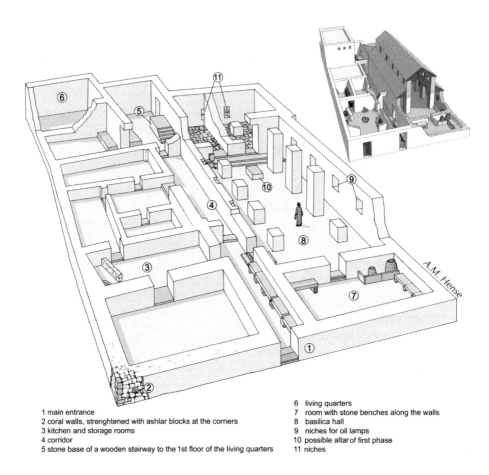

1 main entrance
2 coral walls, strenghtened with ashlar blocks at the corners
3 kitchen and storage rooms
4 corridor
5 stone base of a wooden stairway to the 1st floor of the living quarters

6 living quarters
7 room with stone benches along the walls
8 basilica hall
9 niches for oil lamps
10 possible altar of first phase
11 niches

Fig 6.33: Reconstruction of the large ecclesiastical complex at Berenike.

building toward the southeast also fit with what we know about early Christian churches in Egypt. In size, the Berenike church dwarfed any of the 'pagan' temples we uncovered in the city. Yet, the near contemporary use of the church with the two smaller pagan cult centers noted above suggests that various religions, including Christianity, coexisted in some degree of harmony at the entrepôt in the late Roman period.

Other remains of possible Christian hermit communities can be found throughout the Eastern Desert. During our surveys we have located over a dozen villages ranging in size from 47 to 190 structures and more. These settlements were located off the main roads, but usually not more than a day's walk to some other settlement or from the Red Sea coast. Clearly they were not situated to attract a great deal of attention. Mainly circular, oval to roughly rectilinear in plan and comprising usually one room, but also occasionally two, three or even, rarely, up to four rooms, the buildings found in these settlements have a number of features in common. The walls of all structures are usually not much higher than a meter or so and invariably have wall faces comprising larger cobbles or small boulders with the fill between consisting of smaller pebbles. Upper wall portions must have been made of mats, animal hides, or tent-like structures, which have left no traces. Some of these rooms have raised benches or *mastaba*s inside for sleeping and small alcoves, storage facilities, patios, or areas that seem to have been animal pens.

Pottery found at these sites was invariably made in the late fourth to the sixth or seventh centuries AD. Most of the shards are from amphoras (storage and shipment containers) with a significant proportion imported from southern Asia Minor or Cyprus. Palladius, a Christian writer from the fifth century, reports that Cilician amphoras were used in these desert settlements and that is precisely one of the places, on the south coast of Turkey, where the amphoras we have found in such profusion at these enigmatic Eastern Desert sites were made. A number of the necks and shoulders of these amphoras bear *dipinti* (writing in ink) in red paint, but these are, for the most part, completely illegible; they must indicate the volume or nature of the contents of the jars. At several of these desert sites our surveys noticed larger buildings, which may have served as communal gathering spots. For example, the ancient community, which we call Umm Howeitat al-Bahari, has one larger building with an entrance on the south; it preserves an apse-like structure at its eastern end and a bench at its western. Could this have been a small chapel or church? We do not know for certain. If it was, it could only have accommodated a small number of people at one time from this relatively large settlement.

Judaism

Little evidence has come to light in the Eastern Desert for the presence of Jews though we did find a graffito in Hebrew from the late Roman period at Berenike plus some ostraca written in Greek that refer to 'Jewish' delicacies, an otherwise unidentifiable food no doubt.

As mentioned before, recent British excavations at the Red Sea port of Myos Hormos have found a structure that might have been a temple or, more likely a synagogue. Whatever function it served, it seems to have fallen out of use early in the life of the port.

Islam

There is also, of course, evidence for Muslim presence in the Eastern Desert. We have found early Islamic pottery at some of the *praesidia* and there was a small mosque inside one of the *praesidia* on the road linking Myos Hormos to Quft. Undoubtedly associated with *hajjis* traveling between the Nile Valley and Mecca by sea between Quseir and Jeddah, these remains lay outside our period of interest. There was a concerted Muslim presence at Quseir al-Qadim from the late eleventh/early twelfth to the fifteenth centuries. Thereafter the port was abandoned and the new city of Quseir about eight kilometers to the south replaced it. There are also Islamic remains at 'Aidhab (Abu Ramada), about 250 kilometers south of Berenike, that facilitated the movement of *hajjis* by sea between Egypt and the Arabian port of Jeddah.

Continued exploration of the Eastern Desert in the future should reveal more about the religious activities of the people who passed through or called the region home even if for only brief periods of time.

The Horn of Plenty
International Trade

F rom earliest recorded times Egypt traded with regions beyond her frontiers (Fig. 7.1). The land the fifth century BC Greek historian Herodotus called "the Gift of the Nile" possessed many natural resources, as we know from the large and impressive ancient remains, the artifacts recovered during extensive archaeological investigations, and from the decipherment of numerous ancient written documents. Egypt's geological wealth included soft and hard stones used for constructing temples, tombs, and secular structures both inside Egypt and abroad. Rupestral products coming from Egyptian quarries were used for statues, sarcophagi, columns, and other architectural elements that have been found all over the ancient Mediterranean world in the Roman period. Materials such as sandstone, limestone, granites, porphyries, marble, basalt, metals such as copper, tin, iron and gold, and precious and semiprecious stones like turquoise, beryls/emeralds, amethysts, carnelian, and so on were all pried from the mines and quarries of Egypt throughout antiquity for thousands of years from the earliest period of the pharaohs until late Roman times. Some of these mineral products were gleaned more easily than others; large columns and other architectural elements made of hard stone and quarried from sites deep in the desert were the most difficult and costly of all to obtain as we discussed in Chapter 4.

Yet, despite being blessed with all manner of natural resources, Egypt lacked some key assets. She did not possess adequate supplies of long-beam

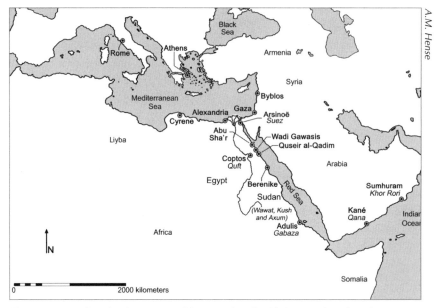

Fig. 7.1: Map showing important sites associated with international trade.

timber with which to build a variety of objects including large seafaring ships. In pharaonic times Egypt sought mainly the famous cedars from Lebanon, probably shipped via Byblos. Later, in the Ptolemaic era Egypt controlled regions of the Aegean, southern Asia Minor, and Cyprus, which supplied much of what she needed to construct and maintain her massive fleets in the Mediterranean.

Pharaonic Period

In the pharaonic period Egypt's insatiable desire for gold led to massive exploitation not only of her own sources, but also of mines in the ancient lands of Wawat and Kush, in what is today Sudan. Intense exploitation of auriferous bearing regions of the Eastern Desert and Nubia continued and perhaps accelerated in Ptolemaic times and persisted in Egypt throughout the Roman and Byzantine occupation (see Chapter 9).

Although examples of silver artifacts have been found in Egypt dating as early as the Predynastic period, ancient texts indicate that the metal was mined elsewhere; silver was more valuable than gold until the end of the Middle Kingdom (2040–1640 BC). Virtually all silver used in Egypt in pharaonic times was imported—probably from Syria, Asia Minor, and per-haps from as far away as Armenia. In the fifth century BC, and later, the Egyptians may have obtained silver from mines in Greece, especially those in the Laurion district near Athens.

Egypt also lacked other commodities deemed essential. Religious and funerary customs demanded aromatics and incense, which were used in the mummification process and for burning on altars in temples. These were available only from the farther reaches of the Red Sea and northern Indian Ocean, mainly southern Arabia (Yemen and Oman) and also from the Horn of Africa, in Somalia today. The dates for the earliest appearance of this com-merce in aromatics and incense with Egypt have been debated, but the exchange appears to have begun sometime during the pharaonic period, likely during the New Kingdom (1550–1070 BC), when Queen Hatshepsut (1473–1458 BC) sent her famous expedition to Punt (somewhere in the region of the Horn of Africa and/or southern Arabia). These easily trans-ported, but relatively valuable products could have come either by sea to Egypt or via desert caravans from southern Arabia to Palestine and, thence, overland across Sinai to Egypt. Ivory, exotic animals, slaves, and other com-modities also trickled in from more southerly African regions; these probably came overland mainly via the Nile Valley or were imported along an age-old route in Egypt's Western Desert called the *Darb al-Arba'in* (Route of Forty Days) (Fig. 7.2).

One major avenue for Egypt's international trade passed across the East-ern Desert. Surviving written sources from as early as the Old Kingdom period (that is, from the Third Dynasty on: 2649–2152 BC) note harbors on the Red Sea coast. Despite what ancient written records report, however, there has been surprisingly little archaeological evidence found for any pharaonic port or roadstead along Egypt's Red Sea coast. Archaeologists have not discovered remains of any Old Kingdom Red Sea harbors. From the Middle Kingdom (2040–1640 BC) and early New Kingdom (1550–1070 BC), a single port has been identified and partially excavated at the mouth of Wadi Gawasis (Fig. 7.3), which lies about twenty-two kilo-meters south of the modern port of Safaga. Excavations by the University of Alexandria there in the 1970s unearthed a few completely effaced stones that once bore inscriptions and stone anchors (Fig. 7.4), some of which originally formed parts of a religious altar.

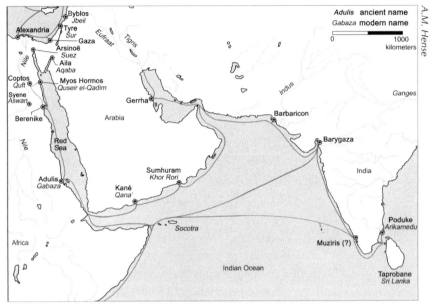

Fig. 7.2: Map with long-distance trade routes.

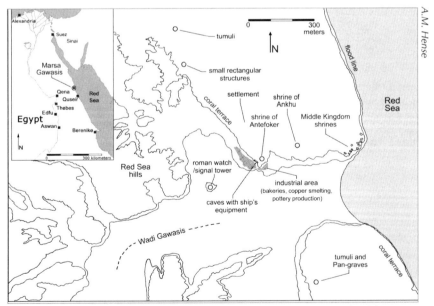

Fig. 7.3: Map of Gawasis, located about twenty-two kilometers south of the modern port of Safaga.

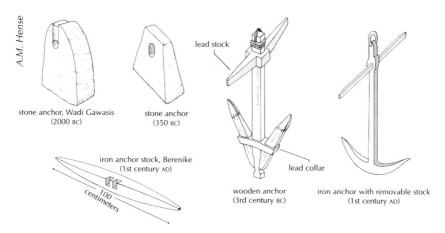

Fig. 7.4: Stone anchors from the Middle Kingdom to the Roman period.

More recently a joint Italian-American team of archaeologists has found caves containing cedar ship planking and ropes. It may be that the remains found in Wadi Gawasis were not those of a formal port at all, but simply a roadstead that allowed ships to be pulled up onto the beach or, alternatively, a place where larger ships anchored offshore and smaller coastal lighters ferried between the ships and the beach. Some of the inscriptions found at Wadi Gawasis during the course of excavations have been removed to safety. They record activities by the pharaohs Senwosret I (1971–1926 BC), Amenemhat II (1929–1892 BC), and Senwosret II (1897–1878 BC). Until at least 1992 other steles could still be seen on the site though whatever inscriptions they may have originally borne have long since been worn away by wind and sun.

One would think that the famous expedition to Punt launched by pharaoh Hatshepsut (1473–1458 BC) in the Eighteenth Dynasty, and recounted in her funerary temple of Deir al-Bahari near the famous Valley of the Kings, would have been launched with much fanfare from a port on the Red Sea coast (Fig. 7.5). Yet, aside from a few traces at Wadi Gawasis, archaeologists have found no evidence for a New Kingdom port anywhere on Egypt's Red Sea shore. Could Wadi Gawasis have been the port used during Hatshepsut's expedition? A number of forays to Punt are reported in Egyptian records throughout the pharaonic period and we have little reason to doubt that they actually occurred. These would have had to start in the Nile Valley, traverse

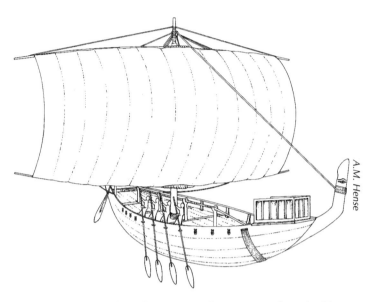

Fig. 7.5: One of the ships of the famous expedition to Punt launched by
Pharaoh Hatshepsut.

the Eastern Desert, and leave from some point on the Red Sea coast. The
regions around Quseir, or farther south near Berenike, were likely areas of
departure and arrival. The former is the nearest point on the Red Sea from
the Nile Valley, while sailing to the latter would have minimized tacking
against the fierce and almost constantly blowing north winds in the Red
Sea. Nothing of pharaonic date has, however, been found at or near either
of these ancient Ptolemaic-Roman ports or anywhere else along the Red
Sea coast that archaeologists have been allowed to examine.

Ptolemaic Era

The earliest evidence we have of a permanent presence on Egypt's Red Sea
coast comes relatively late in history, from the Ptolemaic period (late fourth
century BC–30 BC). As we noted in Chapter 2, Ptolemy II Philadelphus
(285–246 BC) and his immediate successors from the third century BC on
sought to systematize trade and communications in the region. These
activities included the acquisition of war elephants from more southerly
regions of the Red Sea, which necessitated construction of a number of
ports (Fig. 7.6). The aromatics trade also seems to have grown during

these last centuries before our era, as did first-time diplomatic relations with India and continued political dealings with states in the southern Arabian Peninsula, and Africa south of Egypt. Many of the contacts with these lands would have been by sea via the Red Sea ports in Egypt.

Much of this trade from southern Arabia never entailed voyages by sea whatsoever as it passed along age-old terrestrial caravan routes (Fig. 7.7). These lay east of and parallel to the Red Sea coast and stretched from frank-incense and myrrh production areas in the southern Arabian peninsula winding their way north. Aromatics transshipped by sea from the Horn of Africa via southern Arabia may also have made the same caravan journeys. Eventually these routes terminated at various points on the Mediterranean Sea, especially near Gaza (Palestine). A number of documents, particularly

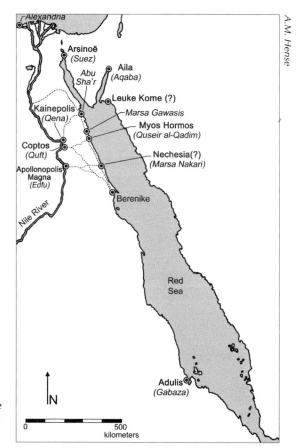

Fig. 7.6: Map showing the important ancient harbors on the Red Sea coast.

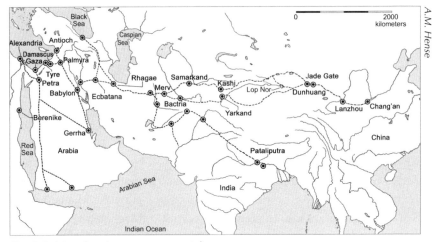

Fig. 7.7: Map showing some terrestrial caravan routes.

from the Archive of Zenon, a collection of papyri of Ptolemy II's chief minister Apollonius dating to the middle of the third century BC, deal with this commerce. Later Roman era authors including Strabo, in his *Geography*, and Pliny the Elder, in his *Natural History*, report caravan journeys of sixty-five to seventy days that carried frankincense and myrrh between southern Arabia and the areas of Aqaba and Petra (in Jordan). The duration of similar treks earlier in pharaonic times is unrecorded, but these may well have been close to those reported by Strabo and Pliny.

Ptolemaic Ports in Egypt
Port construction at the northern end of the Red Sea was widespread from the time of Ptolemy II Philadelphus and later. Red Sea emporia founded by Philadelphus or his immediate successors included Arsinoë/Clysma/Cleopatris, called Qolzum in Islamic times, near modern Suez, which was partially excavated by French archaeologists in the 1930s. Off and on between 1978 and 2003 American and British teams excavated at Myos Hormos, which is today called Quseir al-Qadim about eight kilometers north of the center of modern Quseir. Myos Hormos also appears to have been a Ptolemaic foundation though little of that period has so far actually been excavated; most of what has been uncovered there is early Roman and medieval Islamic in date (Figs. 7.8 and Pl. 7.1).

S.E. Sidebotham

Fig. 7.8: Remains of Myos Hormos.

Berenike

The southernmost Ptolemaic port in Egyptian territory was Berenike (Pl. 7.2), which is approximately 825 kilometers south of Suez, about three hundred kilometers south of Myos Hormos, and on about the same latitude as Aswan. It was founded sometime before the middle of the third century BC. The site is located south of Ras (Cape) Banas, and near an Egyptian military base. Several travelers since the sixteenth century searched for the ancient port without success. The Portuguese sea captain Dom João de Castro missed finding the remains in April 1541 while patrolling the Red Sea. The French cartographer J.B.B. D'Anville failed to locate the site in the eighteenth century. The honor of finally pinpointing the ancient city fell to the intrepid Italian adventurer G.B. Belzoni in 1818. Thereafter numerous European travelers explored the heavily sanded up remains. In 1826 J.G. Wilkinson drew the first plan of any architectural structures visible above ground (Fig. 7.9). He and later visitors even conducted limited and unscientific 'clearing' operations of some of the ancient ruins with the Serapis temple being their main interest. Sustained scientific survey and excavations, however, did not commence until our project initiated them in winter 1994.

GIOVANNI BATTISTA BELZONI

Giovanni Battista Belzoni (1778–1823) left his hometown of Padua in 1798 to travel to Rome. There he claims to have studied hydraulics. By about 1800, however, being six feet and seven inches tall, he had become a circus strongman in an English theater where he was known as the 'Patagonian Samson' or 'The Great Belzoni.' The highlight of his act was to lift an iron frame with twelve people sitting on it, and then walk across the stage. In 1814 he came to Egypt initially seeking employment at the court of Muhammad 'Ali Pasha, in his case as a hydraulic engineer. Fortunately for those studying the archaeology of Egypt he failed to interest the Egyptian government in his waterwheel, which would have increased efficiency dramatically. He soon drifted into what we would call today 'contract' archaeology. Bankrolled by the British savant and government representative Mr. Henry Salt, Belzoni ventured far and wide both in the Nile valley and in the Eastern Desert to discover new sites and carry off those antiquities he deemed worthy of Salt's attention; those he could not sell to Salt, he sold to others. In the years following his appointment as an antiquities surveyor, he visited many sites including Luxor, Fayyum, Aswan, and he followed close behind Jean Louis Burckhardt (Sheikh Ibrahim) to the great temples at Abu Simbel. He was the first to enter the Pyramid of Khafra, and in the Valley of Kings he discovered six royal tombs, including that of Ramesses I, the founder of the Nineteenth Dynasty, and that of Seti I, one of the finest tombs in the Valley of the Kings. He also ranged throughout the Eastern Desert, visiting the emerald mines in Wadi Sikait soon after their discovery by Cailliaud. It was Belzoni who discovered the ruins of the famous Ptolemaic-Roman Red Sea port of Berenike in 1818 and reported them in his book *Narrative of Operations and Recent Discoveries within the Pyramids, Temples, Tombs, and Excavations in Egypt and Nubia* in 1820. He published accounts of his journeys, which go some way to mitigating his often heavy-handed approach to many of the antiquities he found. In 1823, only five years after his discovery of Berenike, he died of dysentery in a small village in what is now Nigeria during an expedition to discover the source of the Niger River.

Fig. 7.9: J.G. Wilkinson's plan of the central area of ruins at Berenike, drawn in 1826 (Ms. G. Wilkinson XLV. D.11 K.6 (c. 1823-6) MS. Wilkinson dep. a. 15, fol. 52; Gardner Wilkinson papers from Calke Abbey, Bodleian Library, Oxford; courtesy of the National Trust).

Our archaeological excavations over an eight-year period between 1994 and 2001 began to document the history of Berenike and the critical role it played in Ptolemaic and Roman commerce with lands in the Red Sea and Indian Ocean. Ruins of the metropolis cover an area that stretches about seven hundred meters from north to south by approximately five hundred meters from east to west. The highest point rises about seven meters above sea level and includes the remains of a temple dedicated to Serapis.

According to Pliny the Elder, Ptolemy II Philadelphus (285–246 BC) founded Berenike in about 275 BC and named it after his mother. The creation of a port at Berenike was part of a broader project initiated by Philadelphus and his immediate successors to exploit the Eastern Desert and Red Sea coast not only of Egypt, but also of Sudan and other regions of the African littoral.

Our excavations have shown that Berenike was, indeed, founded by the middle of the third century BC, or earlier, thereby confirming the date Pliny indicates for the city's creation. Our excavations demonstrate habitation until sometime before about AD 550 (Fig. 7.10). After that the city was abandoned except for the rare visitor who camped there briefly as attested by the occasional remains of temporary campfires.

Our excavations indicate that Berenike enjoyed three peak periods of activity. The first immediately followed its foundation (in the mid-third to mid-second century BC) when elephants destined for use in the Ptolemaic army were in transit through the city en route from more southerly Red Sea ports to points along the Nile. Depictions of these pachyderms can still be seen along several of the roads radiating from Berenike (Figs. 7.11–7.12); all we have found at Berenike itself associated with this trade is a single elephant tooth and a 'V'-shaped ditch (Fig. 7.13) where elephants might have been corralled. We also assume that ivory passed through Berenike along

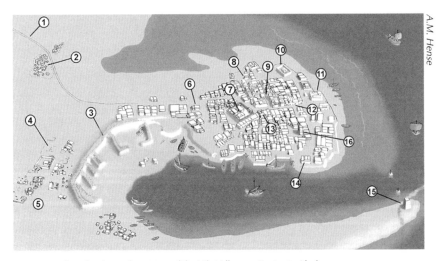

A.M. Hense

1 road to the northwest toward the Nile Valley	9 street with shops
2 late Roman cemetery	10 possible temple
3 possible Ptolemaic quay	11 Christian ecclesiastical complex
4 Ptolemaic industrial zone	12 main street
5 demolished Ptolemaic building	13 house with monumental entrance
6 Palmyrene sanctuary	14 late Roman warehouse
7 Serapis temple	15 possible harbor monument
8 mystery cult center	16 possible lighthouse

Fig. 7.10: Berenike in fifth century AD.

Fig. 7.11: Elephant graffito from Abraq.

Fig. 7.12: Elephant graffito from al-Kanaïs.

S. E. Sidebotham

Fig. 7.13: V-shaped ditch at Berenike where elephants might have been corralled. Scale = one meter.

with the elephants and we have found some ivory, though mainly from the Roman period. This peculiar commerce in elephants and their ivory lasted from the third into about the middle of the second century BC after which time there seems to have been a decline in the fortunes of the port.

The terrifying appearance and huge size, loud trumpeting, and unusual odor of elephants were anathema to horses of enemy cavalry and hugely intimidating to any but the boldest infantry. The impetus to secure the pachyderms in sufficient numbers to compete with those Indian species of their Seleucid adversaries in the Eastern Mediterranean led the Ptolemies to found numerous ports along not only the Red Sea coast of Egypt itself, such as the one at Berenike, but also dotting the littoral south to the Bab al-Mandab and even beyond into the Horn of Africa, what is Somalia today.

The beasts were moved to Egypt by sea in specially designed transport ships called *elephantegoi*. Ports on Egypt's Red Sea coast, especially the southernmost at Berenike, had to accommodate these large vessels and other ships associated with the aromatics and spice trade as well as Ptolemaic naval units.

Despite the more diminutive size of the African pachyderms, probably the Forest elephant variety, compared to the Indian elephants fielded by their Seleucid opponents in the Near East, all evidence suggests that the elephant gathering expeditions continued until the reign of Ptolemy IV Philopator (221–205 BC) or, possibly, as late as Ptolemy VI Philometor (180–145 BC). After investing so heavily in operations to capture elephants we can only surmise why these activities came to a sudden halt. Perhaps by the second century BC the Ptolemies had established a successful elephant-breeding program in Egypt and no longer needed to import the beasts by sea at such great cost and effort. Possibly, too, the Seleucids no longer had access to their sources of Indian pachyderms due to the loss of the eastern portions of their realm to the Parthian state in the late third century BC. If so, the Ptolemies may no longer have felt compelled to continue an elephant-arms race with their Seleucid rivals.

Ivory, deliberately and separately harvested or the by-product of elephant gathering operations that had gone badly, together with gold, also helped finance the Ptolemaic diplomatic and military machine, which was a hugely expensive endeavor. Much of this, too, would have arrived by sea at the Egyptian Red Sea ports for transport across the desert to the Nile. Ivory apparently flooded the market, for an inscription found on the Aegean mercantile island of Delos indicates that its price dropped precipitously during the reign of Ptolemy II.

The bulk of the Ptolemaic remains we have uncovered at Berenike are those of an industrial zone in the western part of the site. Here metals including iron and copper alloy nails, tacks and fittings, lead sheets and bricks were made. The metals would have been used in building activities, furniture making, and ship repair. Lead was commonly used in antiquity to sheath the hulls of merchant ships to protect them from the deleterious effects of boring marine creatures. It could also be used to make brailing rings. When attached to sails, ropes passed through the brailing rings allowed sails to be raised and lowered. Thus far, however, we have recovered no lead brailing rings at Berenike though we have found a large number made of animal horn and wood. The kiln-fired bricks would have been used, of course, in building activities, especially of hydraulic structures.

Marsa Nakari

Other Red Sea ports of likely Ptolemaic foundation include Nechesia, which may be tentatively identified with the ruins recently excavated at Marsa Nakari (Figs. 7.14–7.15), about nineteen kilometers south of Marsa 'Alam. Archaeological excavations in 1999, 2001, and 2002 by a team from Northern Arizona University recovered substantial evidence for early and late Roman activity at this small port. However, little of Ptolemaic date, aside from a terra-cotta oil lamp and a gold grinding stone, was found. The diminutive size and presence of a fortification wall around much of the site suggests that it was not a major player in long distance maritime commerce. It may well have served as a safe haven for ships sailing between Berenike, about 150 kilometers to the south, and Myos Hormos, about 150 kilometers to the north, and, likely, other more northerly Red Sea ports as well.

Our archaeological surveys in winter 1997 and summer 2000 identified an ancient road linking Marsa Nakari to Edfu (ancient Apollonopolis Magna) on the Nile. Various stations we found along this highway, for example the one at Bir 'Iayyan and other mining communities that it served, date from Ptolemaic times and later. This suggests that the route catered to traffic in that period including those journeying between Marsa Nakari and points in the hinterland or on the Nile.

S. E. Sidebotham

Fig. 7.14: Remains of the Red Sea site at Marsa Nakari (perhaps the ancient port of Nechesia).

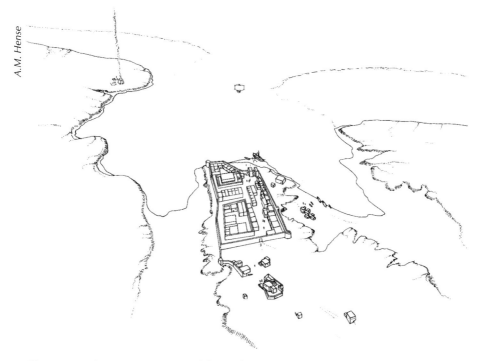

A.M. Hense

Fig. 7.15: Artist's reconstruction of the Red Sea port at Marsa Nakari

Other Ptolemaic Red Sea Ports

Although the Ptolemies established about a dozen ports farther south beyond Egypt's frontiers, along what are today the Red Sea coasts of Sudan and Eritrea, and may have even built one somewhere in the Horn of Africa on the Indian Ocean, only the remains of one in the general region of Adobona in Sudan have possibly been identified on the ground. Once investigated, these may prove to be the ancient Ptolemais Theron (Ptolemais of the Hunts), a port referred to by several ancient authors, including Strabo, writing at the turn of the Christian era. A famous Ptolemaic inscription called the Pithom Stele, found in the Egyptian Nile Delta, and associated with Ptolemy II's Nile–Red Sea canal building activities in that area, narrows the date of the foundation of Ptolemais Theron to sometime between 270 and 264 BC. The Pithom Stele indicates that Ptolemais Theron was a major colonizing effort involving farming and animal husbandry, but its main purpose was to support elephant gathering operations for the

Ptolemaic government. Elephants were shipped by sea through Ptolemais Theron north to Berenike. Ptolemais Theron seems to have declined dramatically after the Ptolemies lost interest in the elephants, but in the early first century AD the *Periplus of the Erythraean Sea* reports that the emporium still exported turtle shell and small amounts of ivory. By that time, however, its halcyon days had long since passed.

Philoteras/Aenum

Another Egyptian Red Sea port whose name survives, but which has thus far eluded detection and identification by archaeologists, is Philoteras, also known as Aenum. Philoteras is reported in several ancient texts including those of Strabo, Pliny the Elder, and by Claudius Ptolemy, the mid-second-century AD scholar, in his *Geography*. One lesser known Roman writer, Pomponius Mela, also records Philoteras in the early first century AD. Named after one of Ptolemy II's sisters, Pliny and Claudius Ptolemy disagree on the relative location of Philoteras vis-à-vis other Red Sea ports, but the general consensus among archaeologists today is that it lies somewhere in the vicinity of the modern port of Safaga; its location and identification remain to be determined. That Roman authors from the late first century BC through mid-second century AD refer to the port, however, suggests its operation well into Roman times.

Roman Period

Leukos Limen

In addition to more northerly Egyptian Red Sea ports active in the Roman period such as Arsinoë/Clysma/Cleopatris, which we do not consider here, there was, besides Philoteras, another emporium whose identification and location have eluded archaeologists for many years. Claudius Ptolemy mentions the port of Leukos Limen, known also as Albus Portus in Latin ('White Harbor'). Ptolemy places this harbor between Myos Hormos and Nechesia. The site remains unlocated today and, indeed, Ptolemy is the only ancient source to mention its existence. Is it possible that he has somehow confused Leuke Kome (somewhere on the eastern side of the Red Sea in Saudi Arabia) with another location, calling it Leukos Limen and mistakenly placing it on the Egyptian Red Sea coast? We cannot be certain.

Leuke Kome

Leuke Kome, although more prominent in Roman times, may have figured in Red Sea commerce earlier as one of the few ports on the Arabian coast of the northern end of the Red Sea that was likely not under Ptolemaic control. At a certain point in its history, the Nabataeans dominated this harbor town. They were a nomadic Arab people first mentioned in Assyrian texts of the mid seventh century BC. Once they settled down, probably by the late fourth century BC initially in southern Jordan, parts of Sinai, and north-western Saudi Arabia, they became deeply involved in the overland caravan trade between southern Arabia and the Mediterranean described above. Surviving Ptolemaic sources suggest that the Nabataeans were also involved in maritime activities, ranging from trade to piracy. They may well have been privateers or otherwise in the 'official' or 'unofficial' employ of the Nabataean government. Whatever their status, the Ptolemies viewed Nabataean activities as dangerous to their own interests and took measures to minimize or at least control Nabataean depredations.

It may have been from Leuke Kome that the Nabataeans raided Ptolemaic merchant ships. Although the precise location of Leuke Kome is unknown, archaeological surveys conducted in the late 1970s suggested that the area around Khuraybah/'Aynunah in northwestern Saudi Arabia near the Straits of Tiran opposite the southern tip of Sinai, is a likely location for the port. One ancient author writes that a frequently used caravan route joined Leuke Kome with Petra, the capital of the Nabataeans.

The *Periplus of the Erythraean Sea* also describes how Leuke Kome catered to smaller Arab vessels, but it was clearly large enough to accommodate a sizeable fleet of about 130 warships sent from Egypt by the Romans in 26–25 BC. Strabo recounts this expedition in some detail as it was commanded by a friend of his and former governor of Egypt, Aelius Gallus. Gallus' fleet landed about ten thousand Roman and allied Nabataean and Jewish troops from the Kingdom of Herod the Great to attack southern Arabia overland. The stated objective of this expedition was to suborn those wealthy incense-producing lands to Roman control. While the expedition seems to have reached as far as the city of Marib in Yemen today, it was a military failure; the army was forced to withdraw and the Romans never permanently occupied southern Arabia. The Roman emperor Augustus (27 BC–AD 14) reports this campaign in his autobiography (the *Res Gestae Divi*

Augusti), however, which suggests that he viewed the results of the operation in a positive light. Indeed, soon thereafter several south Arabian and Indian states sent embassies to Rome, an indication that the diplomatic consequences of the 'failed' military campaign were probably quite favorable to Rome.

By the time of the *Periplus*, Leuke Kome was clearly important enough that a fort with a centurion (a high ranking enlisted soldier in the Roman army) and a garrison were located there. No doubt part of their function was to ensure that the government official collected a 25 percent tax on goods passing through the emporium. Both the Roman and Nabataean armies used the military term 'centurion,' so the presence of a man bearing this rank does not in itself solve the scholarly debate about who controlled Leuke Kome in the first half of the first century AD. The same passage in the *Periplus* also mentions an overland track connecting Leuke Kome to Petra and to Malichus, King of the Nabataeans, but this does not tell us the 'nationality' of the centurion or the garrison either.

Archaeological Remains of Ports

What remains of the ancient Red Sea harbor works? Surprisingly little has come to light that provides much information about the physical appearance of harbors and wharfs at the Red Sea ports. Myos Hormos and Berenike provide what data we do possess.

Myos Hormos

Extensive excavations at Myos Hormos by American and British archaeologists between 1978 and 2003 brought to light substantial remains. Myos Hormos may have been a Ptolemaic foundation, but the vast preponderance of the ancient structures and documents found there is early Roman through the third century AD when the port ceased to operate. These indicate a thriving harbor catering to international trade between the Mediterranean world and the littorals of the southern Red Sea and Indian Ocean (Pl. 7.3). The port lay abandoned for about a millennium until it was revived in the Medieval Islamic era during the Ayubbid and Mamluk dynasties. By the fifteenth century the site was, once again, deserted. Thereafter, activities moved to Quseir, about eight kilometers south of the ruins of Myos Hormos.

British excavations at Myos Hormos uncovered a pier, jetty or artificial
extension of the coast comprising many thousands of recycled early Roman
amphoras (Fig. 7.16). Unfortunately, this does not give us much information
about the overall appearance of the early Roman harbor works at Myos Hormos. It does indicate a rather jerry-rigged and *ad hoc* approach to harbor
construction, which is more or less consistent with the overall appearance of
the port, built as it was of coral chunks, sea shells, readily available stones,
and mud brick. The emphasis in the construction of most structures at Myos
Hormos and Berenike, as we shall see later in this chapter, was on basic, util-
itarian architecture. The objective was clearly to keep overhead costs minimal
in order to maximize profits.

Berenike
Following the early Ptolemaic period, the next era of prosperity at Berenike
was the early Roman (first century AD). This was the zenith of commercial
activity at the emporium with abundant evidence for extensive long-distance
commerce reaching as far west as Spain and at least as far east as India.

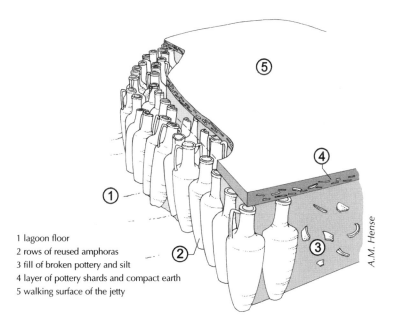

1 lagoon floor
2 rows of reused amphoras
3 fill of broken pottery and silt
4 layer of pottery shards and compact earth
5 walking surface of the jetty

A.M. Hense

Fig. 7.16: Artist's reconstruction of a pier, jetty, or artificial extension of the coast in
the harbor of Myos Hormos.

Mercantile contacts with India, southern Arabia, and other regions of the Red Sea and Indian Ocean were at their peak and many products passed through the port from the East and from the Mediterranean. At that time Berenike was home to a population of great ethnic and social diversity. Peoples from throughout the Roman world, from India and from other Eastern lands resided at Berenike in this era of great economic growth.

Surprisingly, despite the abundance of artifacts of early Roman date that we have recovered, few of early Roman Berenike's buildings have thus far been excavated. These include some scattered structures in the center of the city near the Serapis temple, the Serapis temple itself (which our project has not excavated), some trash dumps north of town and a few piers, wharfs, or sea walls (Fig. 7.17) in the eastern part of the port. In 1999 our excavations reached what we believe to be the early Roman courtyard floor of the Serapis temple. Embedded in this surface were two large round-bottomed clay jars made in India (Pl. 7.4). One preserved the remains of its original wooden lid while the other contained, much to our amazement, 7.55 kilograms of black peppercorns (Pl. 7.5). Imported from southern India during the acme of Roman maritime contacts with that area in the first century AD, the peppercorns were, perhaps, temple property and may have been des-

S.E. Sidebotham

Fig. 7.17: Berenike, early Roman sea wall on the northeastern side of the site. Scale = fifty centimeters.

tined for religious rituals. This is the largest cache of peppercorns ever found within the boundaries of the Roman Empire.

At Berenike we have located some architectural features that either are or appear to be harbor facilities. One is a large lunate-shaped berm from the concave side of which extend mounds of earth resembling spokes of a wheel. Their location immediately southeast of the Ptolemaic industrial area may suggest a date for construction and use. Found in scattered piles atop the berms were concentrations of vesicular basalt. Not found in naturally occurring geological features anywhere in Egypt, but imported, the vesicular basalt found at Berenike was—we estimate from chemical analysis—from Qana, an ancient port on the Indian Ocean coast of southern Arabia. This basalt was used for a variety of purposes including ballast for ships and as grinding stones for grain. These basalt stones may have been discarded from the holds of ships that had arrived at Berenike. While they remain unexcavated, the location and shape of the berms and the discovery of the basalt here suggests that this part of Berenike may well have been the Ptolemaic, and perhaps also some of the early Roman, harbor facilities (Fig. 7.18).

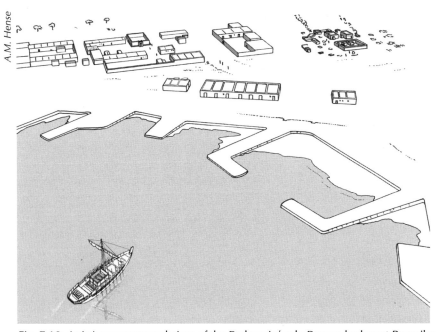

Fig. 7.18: Artist's reconstructed view of the Ptolemaic/early Roman harbor at Berenike.

Aside from this putative Ptolemaic, and possibly early Roman, harbor works at Berenike, the only other maritime-related features that we have found are scattered along the eastern edge of the visible ancient remains. At the northeastern end of the site we discovered a sea wall from early Roman times that seems to be associated with a small harbor or inlet. Farther south, beneath the fifth-century church, we found another feature that appeared to be a pier or sea wall, and in yet a third location immediately south of the church we discovered a large early Roman sea wall made of huge limestone boulders. While these structures provide some indication of the location of the ancient shoreline at different periods in the city's history, they reveal no overall picture of the harbor itself.

The third and last era of commercial prosperity at Berenike began about the middle of the fourth century and carried over into the fifth. We have found no recognizable harbor structures from this time. Temples and smaller religious shrines to a variety of Greco-Roman, Egyptian, and Semitic deities, a large church (see Chapter 6), a number of private dwellings which also served as centers of commercial activity (Fig. 7.19), warehouses (Pl. 7.6), small-scale industrial areas, and a late Roman cemetery (see Chapter 8) have, however, been unearthed from this final era of the port's greatness. At that time the cult center where we found the inscriptions mentioning a Palmyrene archer and the god Yarhibol (see Chapter 6) was revived, another shrine to an unknown deity—possibly Isis—was built, and a Christian ecclesiastical center was also constructed. A new residential and commercial quarter was created just east of the Serapis temple and a huge layer of potshards was laid down to extend the late Roman city toward the receding coastline to the east. We found few ancient texts of any kind, but ample evidence of extensive trade with India and Sri Lanka in this period.

The latest ancient written reference to Berenike appears in the sixth century. It is the *Sancti Martyrium Arethae,* which records in AD 524–525 that Timothy, bishop of Alexandria, under orders from emperor Justin I (AD 518–527), sent ships to assist the Christian kingdom of Axum (in Ethiopia and Eritrea) in its war with the Himyarites in southern Arabia. Two ships loaded with troops were to depart from Berenike in support of this operation; we do not know, in fact, whether the troops were ever dispatched.

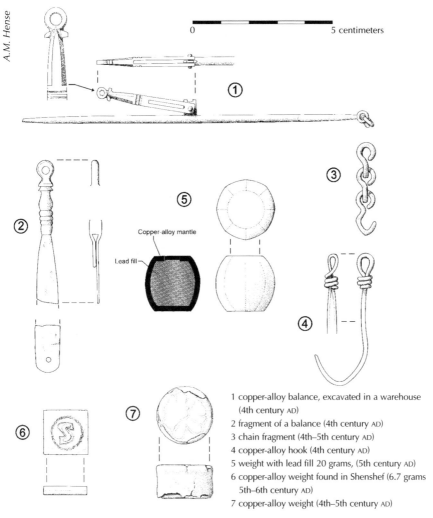

A.M. Hense

0   5 centimeters

Copper-alloy mantle

Lead fill

1 copper-alloy balance, excavated in a warehouse
  (4th century AD)
2 fragment of a balance (4th century AD)
3 chain fragment (4th–5th century AD)
4 copper-alloy hook (4th century AD)
5 weight with lead fill 20 grams, (5th century AD)
6 copper-alloy weight found in Shenshef (6.7 grams
  5th–6th century AD)
7 copper-alloy weight (4th–5th century AD)

Fig. 7.19: Weights and scales found in structures in the late Roman
commercial/industrial area of Berenike and Shenshef.

Yet, between these peaks in Berenike's halcyon days were nadirs. We have,
for example, little evidence of activity at the port in the late Ptolemaic period
(second–first centuries BC) or in Roman times from the late second or early
third to about the middle of the fourth century AD. The port slid into its final
decline later in the fifth century and lay completely abandoned except for
the occasional passerby before the middle of the sixth century AD.

Causes of Death of the Harbors

At both Myos Hormos and Berenike, the harbor works and associated geological examinations have shown that the ancient residents confronted
serious problems of harbor silting. Huge quantities of waterborne sediments
washed into the harbors from inland wadis and this siltation process had to
be confronted. There was also a rise in sea level of between one and two
meters over the last two thousand years or so. The choices facing residents
of both Myos Hormos and Berenike were to dredge the harbors, which they
may have attempted at Myos Hormos, or move the town and harbor facilities as the harbor silted up and the seashore receded. While migration of the
settlement may have taken place at Myos Hormos as a concomitant to
dredging, there is no evidence of any dredging attempts at Berenike; there
the town simply moved eastward and somewhat southward toward an ever-
receding coastline. Despite this, Myos Hormos seems to have been
abandoned by the third century while Berenike continued to operate until
the sixth. Silting alone may not have doomed these emporia. In the third
century, acute political, economic, and military crises throughout much of
the Roman world would have adversely impacted the commerce through
these ports. In the sixth century, competition from Axumite and Arab middlemen and a severe bubonic plague may also have played a key role in
Berenike's demise.

Extent and Nature of the Trade

Ptolemaic Era

Ancient authors are clear that the Ptolemaic monarchs had a number of
items they deemed to be high priority. Many of these passed through Red
Sea emporia south of Egypt's frontiers. Perhaps the strangest were elephants, as already noted, but also ivory. As we pointed out, the Ptolemies
considered pachyderms essential to the military campaigns they waged
against their Seleucid adversaries in the Near East. Although smaller than
the Indian counterparts used by the Seleucids, the Ptolemies clearly
believed that they had to possess a source of elephants of their own and they
expended a tremendous amount of time, effort, and money to guarantee
their own exclusive source as close to Egypt as possible.

Much of the international commerce passing across the Eastern Desert in
the Ptolemaic period initially seems to have been state sponsored or tightly

controlled by the government. In later Ptolemaic times the initiative passed more to private entrepreneurs. It is very difficult to determine whether it was an important source of revenue to the private sector or directly, or indirectly through taxation to the Ptolemaic government itself. Some merchandise passing through the Ptolemaic domains from the East had tariffs levied on it that varied from twenty to fifty percent. While onerous, the government clearly felt it could do this, which suggests that whatever trade passed this way must have been extremely lucrative. Did these tolls, however, more than offset the high costs the Ptolemaic government incurred in its extensive Red Sea port foundations, Eastern Desert road and station construction and maintenance, and elephant gathering activities? Clearly Ptolemaic endeavors on the Red Sea and in the Eastern Desert were deemed of strategic importance whether they were financially profitable or not. The Ptolemaic navy had a presence to protect their interests and to ensure the safety of the Egyptian-bound merchantmen and elephant transport ships plying the Red Sea.

Roman Era

The annexation of Egypt as a province of the Roman Empire in 30 BC dramatically changed the nature and scope of the international commerce that landed at the Red Sea ports and traversed the Eastern Desert. Red Sea ports founded in the Ptolemaic era were enlarged and reinvigorated by the Romans whose trade in and via the Red Sea with more distant lands in the Indian Ocean dwarfed in size that of their Ptolemaic predecessors. In addition to a larger volume, a greater variety of goods also now passed along the trade routes leading to and from the Egyptian Red Sea ports during Roman times.

The lands in contact with these emporia in the Roman period were among the same as had piqued Ptolemaic interests, but included some that the Ptolemies seem not to have known. Unlike Ptolemaic times when Egyptian contacts with India appear to have been very limited and quite sporadic, during the Roman period, especially in the first century AD and later, there was extensive interaction between the Egyptian Red Sea ports of Myos Hormos and Berenike on the one hand and India on the other. Clearly, based upon the types of pottery found and the quantities of black peppercorns recovered in excavations at Myos Hormos and Berenike, favored ports in India were those of the south, along the Kerala (southwestern) and Coromandel (southeastern) coasts. There is a little evidence in the form of woven matting (used perhaps as awnings or sails), some semiprecious stones and beads, banded agate cameo blanks, and a single coin found in our excavations that Berenike, at least, was also in direct or indirect contact with some of the more northerly ports on India's west coast.

The *Periplus* and ostraca from our excavations indicate that wines were exported to various areas of the Red Sea and Indian Ocean via Berenike from the Mediterranean; we discuss these later in this chapter. Our archaeological record at Berenike confirms many ancient written sources that list items imported and exported via Berenike such as black pepper from southern India, but has failed to confirm others, such as frankincense and myrrh from southern Arabia or the Horn of Africa—though we have found peripheral evidence of the passage and use of these aromatics at Berenike. There is also no indication of the transport of exotic animals through Berenike in the Roman era.

Pliny tells us how Romans coveted pearls from India. He even reports that the emperor Caligula's (AD 37–41) spouse Caesonia owned a garment decorated with forty million sesterces (ten million denarii) worth of pearls! Aside from a few small samples, including some surviving on a gold earring, however, we have found no pearls in our excavations. Pliny, the *Periplus of the Erythraean Sea*, and an Indian compilation entitled the *Kauṭilīya Arthasâstra*, note the fascination that Indians had for red coral imported from the Mediterranean. Yet we have not found any in our excavations, although we have unearthed quantities of the poorer quality Red Sea variety.

Contacts between Egypt and Sri Lanka are also evident especially in late Roman times, from the fourth and fifth centuries particularly, in the form of large numbers of beads. We have found thousands of these beads at Berenike, at Marsa Nakari, and in our excavations at the emerald mining center at Sikait. These tiny monochrome glass beads appear in a number of colors, especially yellow, green, turquoise-blue, and orange-red. They have close affinities with ones made in Sri Lanka/Ceylon, known to the Romans as Taprobane or Serendip, and excavated at the site of Mantai at the northern end of that island. The occasional finds of sapphires both at Berenike and at Shenshef, an outlying desert site with close ties to Berenike and discussed further in Chapter 15, also indicate contact either with India or Sri Lanka.

There were certain restrictions on this vibrant trade. For example, in the later second century AD a Roman law specifically forbade the export of iron. This prohibition may have been due to the fear that enemies of Rome might make use of the metal for military purposes. Of course, iron had been known to much of Eastern Hemisphere for some time and, consequently, such a restriction would have had little or no effect.

Extended accounts in numerous ancient authors, surviving papyri, ostraca, and inscriptions from the Roman world as well as references in ancient, but imprecisely dated, Tamil Sangam (south Indian) poems detail many aspects of this lively commerce and how much more extensive it was in the Roman period than in Ptolemaic times. In a famous passage, written in the last decades of the first century BC following the Roman annexation of Egypt, Strabo recounts how in his day as many as 120 ships per annum sailed from Egyptian ports into the Indian Ocean for trade whereas earlier (in Ptolemaic times) barely twenty did so. We do not know where Strabo obtained these statistics, but the archaeological record suggests that the zenith of this commerce was several decades after Strabo wrote, during the period from the 40s to the 70s AD and later into the early second century.

Pliny the Elder recounts an interesting tale the truth of which can, of course, never be proven. Pliny relates the story of Lysas, the freed slave of a wealthy Roman citizen, who was shipwrecked on Ceylon/Sri Lanka. Lysas learned the Sinhalese language and impressed the local ruler with the high quality of a Roman silver coin he possessed. This, we are told, so enthused the local potentate that he is said to have desired trade relations with the Romans.

The Tamil poems recount how the *Yavanas* (westerners, including Romans) brought gold to India and sought sacks of pepper. These poems also report that Tamil rulers imported palace guards and maidens from the *Yavanas,* and were especially fond of wines from the Mediterranean and Aegean. Interestingly, the *Periplus of the Erythraean Sea* notes that the south Arabian and Indian rulers especially liked wines from Laodicea (in Syria) and the Aminaean variety (a very expensive brand originally from Italy) and in our excavations at Berenike the ostraca we found from the city's customs house archives, dating from the same period as the composition of the *Periplus,* also record the export of Laodicean and Aminaean wines. Ostraca we have uncovered at Berenike also list other types of wines exported to the east. These included vintages from the Aegean islands of Rhodes and Euboea, and from Ephesus and Kolophon on the west coast of Asia Minor. In some cases Mediterranean wines with a high salt content dominated the export market; though these were not the best varieties, the salt helped to preserve them on their long voyages to the East.

Many years ago a hoard of ostraca was found recording the trading activities of the Nikanor family from the Nile city of Coptos. Spanning the period from the late first century BC into the 60s AD, these documents reflect this Egyptian family's interest over several generations, especially in trade between the Nile emporium of Coptos and the two largest Egyptian Red Sea ports at the time, Myos Hormos and Berenike. In fact, a few of the ostraca that we have excavated in the trash dumps at Berenike preserve some of the same Nikanor family names as appear on the earlier-discovered documents. The Nikanor ostraca reflect mainly mundane cargoes for consumption by residents of Myos Hormos, Berenike and by ships' crews rather than expensive items destined for export to southern Arabia, India, or other locales.

While ancient authors, ostraca, and to a lesser extent papyri, record many of the items involved in this booming international commerce in early Roman times, they fail to list all of them. Few of these ancient authorities whose writings survive, aside from the anonymous author of the *Periplus*, would have had an intimate firsthand knowledge of this trade as they themselves did not engage in it. Thus, they can be forgiven for discussing only the items that were 'high profile' and costly such as incense and aromatics, pepper, and other spices, textiles (Pl. 7.7), precious and semiprecious gem stones, pearls, ivory, turtle shell, exotic unguents, and woods; they paid little or no attention to what they deemed more prosaic merchandise. Their readers would be fascinated about these 'exotic' imports, but not in more quotidian items.

Imports we have found in our excavations at Berenike include some that are nowhere recorded by any ancient texts. We must ask ourselves, then, were these items, unreported by the ancient authors, really imports destined for profitable resale, or did they have other significance? Rice, sorghum, job's tear (a grass seed), bamboo, coconut, and teakwood, among other commodities, all seem to be nowhere reported as imports to the Roman world from the Indian Ocean basin, yet all appear at Berenike. As noted above, we have also recovered thousands of beads, many of which were

made in India and Sri Lanka, plus a very few from Vietnam or possibly
Thailand and one even from Jatim in Eastern Java (Pl. 7.8). The presence of
these beads does not necessarily indicate direct commercial contact with
Berenike; small items such as beads and coins could easily be transported by
second or third parties and lost while visiting the port. Also found in our
excavations at Berenike, but unreported by ancient authors, are banded
agate cameo blanks used to make the beautiful Roman cameos. The latter
clearly came from India as our excavations at the Indo-Roman trading station at Arikamedu on the Coromandel (southeastern) coast of India between
1989 and 1992 found many of these, probably intended for export to the
west. Such cameo blanks likely originated from sources in northwestern
India as excavations from Kamrej (ancient Kammoni), near the important
port of Barygaza, suggest. Perhaps the profits to be made from some of
these unreported items were paltry and unworthy of the attentions of
Roman writers or they were items brought by ships' crews, traveling friends,
or relatives of those residing at Berenike for their own personal use and were
not meant to be sold at all. These objects probably never appeared on any
ship's manifest as they were not intended for formal sale; perhaps some were
smuggled in to avoid the high tariffs. We will probably never know.

Quantities of Indian-made pottery, including large storage and shipment
containers, fine table ceramics, and coarse cooking wares also appeared in
our excavations at Berenike; some of these same types of Indian ceramics
have also been excavated at Myos Hormos. Unrecorded in any surviving
ancient written sources, these items were either for the personal use of residents of Myos Hormos and Berenike or were employed to ship
commodities; it was, after all, the contents of the containers that customers
valued and not the containers themselves.

We have found teak, quantitatively the dominant wood recovered in our
excavations at Berenike and, very surprisingly, even more abundant than
indigenous species such as acacia, mangrove, and tamarisk. Teak derives
from South Asia and those samples recovered from our Berenike excavations
survive mainly in the form of sizeable wooden beams, in one instance over
three meters long. These beams were mostly recycled as architectural supports for walls in the buildings of the late Roman city. From the intricate
dowel holes cut in these timbers and the presence of iron nails in some
beams, it is clear that their original use was not as wall supports. As a hard

wood, teak would have been ideal for use in shipbuilding and repair; we know
from written sources that this was one of its uses. Perhaps the teakwood
beams we have found in the walls of structures at Berenike were originally
parts of ships, which had been dismantled or repaired upon arrival in port
after a long and arduous sea voyage from the subcontinent. In a wood-poor
environment like the Eastern Desert, such beams would have been too valuable to be discarded as trash or to be burned as fuel. That would have been
very wasteful and these timbers would, instead, have been recycled.

Also in the late Roman period there were continued commercial contacts
between Egypt's Red Sea ports, and other emporia at the northern end of
the Red Sea, and an apparent increase in trade with the African kingdom of
Axum, located in Ethiopia and Eritrea today. Axum's major port on the Red
Sea was at Adulis. Italian archaeologists early in the twentieth century, and
more recently a British team, have worked at late Roman era Adulis; the Ital-
ians conducted limited excavations there. The British team only recently
discovered the location of the earlier port reported in the *Periplus*; the presence of land mines in the area, however, prevents any work there in the near
future. Axumite pottery and a coin found in our work at Berenike (Fig 7.20)
and pre-Axumite and Axumite pottery found in excavations at the Red Sea
ports of Myos Hormos and Aila (modern Aqaba) in Jordan attest this commerce. Even in the early Roman period the *Periplus* notes that Adulis

S.E. Sidebotham

0   1
                        centimeter

Fig. 7.20: Axumite coin of the
last pre-Christian king Aphilas
(AD 270/290–before 330).

exported ivory, but the zenith of Adulis and of the Kingdom of Axum was from the late third to fourth century AD and later when it, together with some of its south Arabian rival kingdoms across the Red Sea, competed with and even surpassed the Egyptian Red Sea ports as major trade centers. The accounts of the sixth-century Christian monk Cosmas Indicopleustes, which survive in his book entitled *Christian Topography*, clearly demonstrate the prominence of Adulis at that time.

Recent study of pottery shards from both early and late Roman times excavated at Berenike, Myos Hormos, and Aila indicates the presence of ceramics from southern Arabia thereby confirming what many ancient authors say was a robust trade between that region and the northern Red Sea ports. Certainly Russian and French excavations at the southern Arabian port of Qana in Yemen, and American and Italian excavations at the Omani port of Khor Rori (ancient Sumhuram, perhaps equated with the site of Moscha Limen mentioned in the *Periplus*) have recovered extensive evidence of trade with the Roman ports on the Red Sea coast of Egypt as well as with India, Axum and elsewhere (Fig. 7.21). The excavation at Berenike, Myos Hormos, and Aila of pottery shards made in southern Arabia also bespeaks the important incense and aromatics commerce from that region that passed through the northern Red Sea ports. A study of this pottery made in southern Arabia and appearing in the excavations of northern Red Sea ports in the Roman period has just begun in earnest so we have much yet to learn about this trade and what goods other than frankincense and myrrh may have been exported from southern Arabia to the Mediterranean world.

We have found none of the fabled frankincense and myrrh at Berenike, but we have recovered tantalizing circumstantial evidence of its passage through or use at the port. Our botanical specialist identified very hard, small, brilliantly hued black and red seeds from our excavations, which are called *Abrus precatorius* L. Highly poisonous if consumed, this particular species of seed was used until quite recently in India as a gold weight in jewelry stores and is also mixed with frankincense and myrrh. Perhaps it had such a function in antiquity and, once the valuable aromatics had been burned, the only trace of their existence was these toxic seeds that had originally been mixed with them. The find of incense altars with burned residues preserved on their tops at Berenike and at a number of other sites in Egypt may also provide indirect evidence of the presence and use of these or similar aromatics.

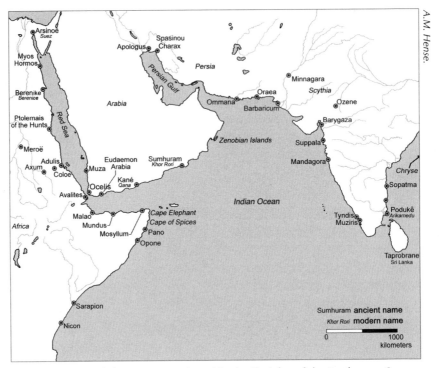

Fig. 7.21: Map with locations mentioned in the *Periplus of the Erythraean Sea*.

Of less importance to the Red Sea ports at any time of their history was contact with the Persian Gulf. Most of the commerce from the Persian Gulf to the Mediterranean passed via camel caravans that plodded across the wastes of the Arabian Peninsula or followed the Euphrates before crossing over to the Levantine coast at several points. One of the most important, but by no means only, routes between the Euphrates and the Mediterranean was via the Syrian Desert oasis kingdom of Palmyra. It was clearly deemed safer, more cost effective and, in some instances, perhaps faster to use various desert caravan routes than to transport goods by sea from the Persian Gulf to the Red Sea ports. We have found a few potshards at Berenike that seem to have been from vessels made in the Persian Gulf, but there was no regular contact with that area and the *Periplus of the Erythraean Sea* somewhat corroborates this; it does not suggest that much if any trade passed between the Persian Gulf and the Red Sea, at least in early Roman times. The Persian Gulf's major trading partners would have been the west coast of India, other points in the Indian Ocean and with the Mediterranean via the overland trade routes just noted. We have recovered nothing identifiable from China or central Asia at Berenike though such artifacts have been excavated elsewhere in the ancient Mediterranean world, especially Chinese silk found in tombs in Palmyra, Syria dating to the early centuries AD.

Other items from throughout the Mediterranean basin passed through Berenike from as far west as Spain and Gaul, from Italy and North Africa and, especially in late Roman times, from the eastern Mediterranean. The bulk of the pottery shards we have recovered at Berenike were Egyptian-made, mainly at different centers in the Nile Valley. Certainly much of our knowledge of other regions of the Roman world, which were in contact with Berenike, derives from examination of the pottery, especially the ubiquitous amphoras (Pl. 7.9). A study of the fired clays from which these vessels were made and their shapes provide information on when and where they were manufactured. These terra-cotta storage and shipment containers of varying sizes and shapes held a wide array of liquids including olive oil, fish sauce, and wine as well as other commodities. By quantifying the large number of amphora shards recovered from Berenike, we can form a picture of commercial trading patterns over centuries of the port's existence with other areas of the ancient world.

Study of fine tablewares, the equivalent of today's quality dinner china, also indicates regions in touch with Berenike and, likely, where people came from who used this dinnerware at the port. Most interesting are the so-called terra sigillata wares, which are fine highly glossed orangish-red bowls, cups and plates made in Italy, and elsewhere in the western and eastern Mediterranean (Pl. 7.10). These were popular just before the turn of the Christian era and throughout the first and, less so, into the second centuries AD. Many of these terra sigillata wares have the names of the makers stamped on the bottom inside faces of the vessels. At about the same time the Mediterranean-made terra sigillata appeared at Berenike, another type of fine dinnerware from India was also in use. Made in the shape of large flat plates with rims, and bowls, these wares were invariably black glossed, sometimes with reddish colored rims. The inside bottoms of the plates had a type of rouletted decoration while many of the bowls had impressed designs on their interiors. Well-to-do Indian entrepreneurs resident at Berenike may have used this 'china.'

Costs of the Trade in Roman Times

We indicated earlier that Ptolemaic authorities levied a twenty to fifty percent tax or toll on many items imported from the East. From the Roman period we have several ancient documents that indicate Roman customs rates. The *Periplus of the Erythraean Sea* reports that a twenty-five percent tax (called a *tetarte*) was levied on the value of the cargo by a government official at Leuke Kome. A papyrus dating to the middle of the second century AD, purchased in Egypt in about 1980, and now housed in a museum in Vienna, Austria, has been extensively studied by those interested in this international commerce in Roman times. This document confirms the levy of a 25 percent tax on merchandise landing somewhere on the Red Sea coast of Egypt that came from Muziris, a port on the southwestern coast of India. The *tetarte* mentioned in the Vienna papyrus was to be collected at Alexandria. The text on the papyrus continues by noting the transport of merchandise by camel across the desert to Coptos and thence down river to Alexandria. Therefore, it stands to reason that the cargo had to be carefully watched between the time of its disembarkation at a Red Sea port and its arrival at Alexandria; both the merchants and the government, through its tax collectors, stood to lose immense profits if any of the cargo were to go astray.

This amazing papyrus document then lists the nature of the cargo, its quantity and its value. The contents include nard (an aromatic root used for perfume, medicine, and in cuisine) from the Ganges, ivory, and bales of cloth. Paying this customs duty was, of course, only part of the expense that merchants had to absorb. To transport the commodities across the desert to the Nile required renting camels and donkeys. Since the Roman state had a virtual monopoly on the requisition of these animals it is likely that the government as well as the animals' owners made a tidy profit at this point in the shipment process as well. It seems that desert convoys transporting valuable imports like the ones mentioned in the Vienna papyrus were distinct from those hauling more prosaic items such as were conveyed by the Nikanor family business. These high status caravans rated protection from troops stationed in *praesidia* dotting the roads between the Red Sea ports and the Nile. In fact, ostraca from recent French excavations at some of the desert garrisons on the highway between Myos Hormos and Coptos report the use of escort troops to guard such caravans.

One wonders where in the Nile Valley those operating the caravans obtained the myriads of donkeys and camels required to haul merchandise both directions across the Eastern Desert. Such beasts of burden were also needed by the large quarrying operations we recounted in Chapter 4 and would also have been critical to carrying grain from the fields to collection points on the Nile just before the seasonal flood. Thus, at certain times of year there would have been huge demands placed on the animal transport system in Egypt; this would have caused a scarcity in animal availability and would have resulted in a sharp rise in rental prices for those used in caravans between the Red Sea ports and the Nile.

There were other fees to pay including those of commercial agents, and salaries for the ships' captains and crews. How did the merchants pay the maritime shippers, ship owners, the ships' crews? What were the going rates? We cannot be sure; perhaps the rates were not fixed, but negotiated for each voyage depending upon the cargoes and the destinations. It may be that the salaries were calculated as a percentage of the value of the cargo or bonuses were offered; this would have increased the crews' incentives to make every effort to arrive back in Egypt in a timely manner with cargoes intact. While we have figures and percentages for these activities along the Nile, we can be certain that the amounts were substantially higher when dealing with the exceptionally long and dangerous voyages in the Red Sea and Indian Ocean to transport these commodities.

As if all these expenses were not enough, one also had to pay tolls to cross the desert, as we know from the contents of the so-called Coptos Tariff, an inscription carved on stone in Greek and dated May, AD 90. This document itemizes tolls levied on people, wagons, animals, and various goods so that they could cross between the Nile and the Red Sea ports. Not all human travelers paid the same amounts. A guard, a sailor, or a shipbuilder's servant, for example, had to pay five drachmas each to travel along the desert roads. Ability to pay, or at least the perception that this was the case, increased the toll rates. An artisan had to pay eight drachmas, a woman arriving by ship or a woman of a soldier paid twenty drachmas; a prostitute had to pay 108 drachmas! In some cases lower toll rates of one obol (1/6 of a drachma) on a ticket for a camel may indicate a rather high volume of traffic. An ass was assessed two obols, a covered wagon paid four obols, and a ship's mast was charged twenty drachmas. Even the dead had to pay: a funeral procession was levied the relatively modest sum of one drachma and four obols.

Yet, in calculating the value of the merchandise listed on the Vienna papyrus, and this was likely only a fraction of the ship's total cargo, the staggering sum of 1,154 talents, or 6,924,000 drachmas (a month's pay for a Roman soldier at this time was about one hundred drachmas) makes it clear that merchants could reap immense profits even after deducting the tariffs, transport costs, salaries, and other expenses. Multiply this amount by Strabo's figure of 120 ships a year trading in his day, and undoubtedly more during the zenith of this mercantile activity later in the first and early second centuries, and we have a very rough idea of the value of this commerce both to the private entrepreneurs and to the government's coffers.

One of the major issues that has engendered much debate among those studying this commerce is how merchandise was paid for and how were the huge sums noted above in the case of the items reported in the Vienna papyrus acquired? Much has been written about this and the debate comes down to several issues, one of which is whether this was mainly a monetary buy-sell type of commerce or one based heavily on barter. Clearly, as the *Periplus of the Erythraean Sea* suggests, both methods were used, at least in early Roman times. In either case large sums were involved. Lending banks in our sense of the word for large commercial ventures barely existed. Most capital for these expensive, but potentially lucrative, journeys was raised from private sources. Financiers, perhaps mainly merchants themselves, formed *ad hoc* associations to underwrite specific trade ventures. Following a successful voyage the group would often break up and new associations would be formed to undertake other business opportunities. These would include providing bottomry loans to the ship owners and captains, and funds to buy the products in foreign ports or purchase items in the Roman world to be used as barter or for sale overseas.

Clearly, it must have been only the most daring individuals who engaged in this trade. The price of failure in the form of pirate attacks or shipwreck meant loss of everything—including one's life. Not only were initial outlays of capital necessarily very high, but the risks of shipwreck, piracy, and problems at the various ports of call while dealing with merchants and officials there made every voyage an adventure. This was not an activity for the faint of heart.

The Periplus of the Erythraean Sea

While we have repeatedly mentioned a manuscript entitled *The Periplus of the Erythraean Sea* (the *Periplus*) here and in previous chapters, it is worth raising the question whether this was a unique document in its day or whether it was merely one of many similar types of guides and handbooks available to merchants and sea captains. Could the *Periplus* simply have been compiled by one individual based upon his personal experiences and those of others he may have known and questioned about their own activities in the same regions? The *Periplus* was written by a keen observer in the common *(koine)* Greek spoken at that time in Egypt and the eastern part of the Roman Empire. Unfortunately, the author remains anonymous to us. As we noted in Chapter 2, he must have been a ship captain, navigator, or merchant who made numerous voyages from several of the Egyptian Red Sea ports into the southerly reaches of the Red Sea into the Indian Ocean. This amazing guidebook discusses the political situations at various ports of call, the items available and in demand at those ports, and the navigational difficulties of sailing to and from the various emporia. It also lists the optimal times of year to leave from the Red Sea ports when sailing to India and to coastal sub-Saharan Africa. On the other hand, the *Periplus* has little to say about the Persian Gulf. Clearly, as noted above, it was not an important destination for ships plying the Red Sea–India–Africa route.

Individuals Involved in the Commerce

While no individual names of entrepreneurs, sailors, or others involved in this commerce, aside from a few monarchs, are mentioned in the *Periplus*, other documents do preserve some of this information along with ethnic origins and social standings. In addition to the previously mentioned Nikanor Ostraca we also have those ostraca, papyri, and a few inscriptions carved in stone found at Myos Hormos and Berenike. Those from our excavations at Berenike list the names of men of Egyptian, Greek, and Latin origin as well as a few Semitic ones. The men are mainly military: soldiers, lancers, officials in charge of markets, and so on. One of these individuals was Andouros who was a *quintanensis* (a market official). Another was a soldier possibly attached to the freed imperial slave Tiberius Claudius Dorion; there are also merchants, customs officials, and camel drivers. Frustratingly few of the ostraca detail the actual titles or functions of these individuals, no doubt because their official status was well known to all concerned parties.

Several archives have been found including those of Sosibios, Rhobaos, Andouros, Gaius Julius Epaphroditus, Sarapion, and Claudius Philetos. Men like Satornilos, the official or merchant Germanos, the centurion Julius Marinus, the cavalryman Nonnius Abaskantos, and others also appear on the ostraca from our early Roman trash deposit found north of the city. All are related in one way or another to goods passing through the customs port at Berenike and, therefore, have a connection to the passage of merchandise onto the ships.

The international and cosmopolitan nature of Berenike is evident not only from the many imported items we have examined, but also from the different ethnic groups residing at the port. So far excavations at Berenike have recovered evidence of eleven different ancient languages preserved as written texts. Most of these come from the early Roman period, some from the late Ptolemaic and late Roman. These include hieroglyphs decorating the walls of the Serapis temple, Greek on coins, ostraca, papyri, and stone, Latin on coins, ostraca, papyri, and stone, Demotic on ostraca, Palmyrene on stone and possibly on some ostraca, Hebrew as graffiti on potshards, Aramaic also on ostraca, Coptic on a terra-cotta oil lamp, Tamil-Brahmi (a south Indian language) carved on the neck of a Roman amphora (Pl. 7.11), a combination of Prakrit and Sanskrit on a fourth century AD silver coin from India (Fig. 7.22) and one unknown text either of North or South Arabian or Ethiopic origin painted on a shard dating about AD 400. Most documents we have excavated are written in Greek, the *lingua franca* of both Ptolemaic Egypt and the eastern portions of the Roman Empire. These documents, together with the excavation of a plethora of finds clearly imported through Berenike or destined for export from the city, attest a robust mercantile life of truly international stature.

The bulk, though not all, of the written documents we have excavated from Berenike, which includes several hundred ostraca, papyri, and inscriptions on stone, come from the early Roman era and provide a bonanza of information on the personal names and activities of soldiers and civilians involved in the trade. In fact, we have recovered a large number of ostraca from the early Roman rubbish dumps north of the city (Pls. 7.12–7.13).

Fig. 7.22: Indian silver coin of
Rudrasena III (minted AD 362)
found in the church at Berenike.

0   1
                                           centimeter

Most of these are public records that reveal customs house documents and
official passes allowing people and goods to proceed onboard waiting ships.
Some objects appear to be merchandise while other goods seem to be for
use by the crews. The dozens of papyri we have unearthed from the same
trash deposits tend to be more private in nature and record items such as a
bill of sale for a white male donkey and a packsaddle for 160 drachmas concluded on July 26, AD 60, during the reign of Nero (AD 54–68) (Pl. 7.14).
Other papyri include a land register, an inventory of equipment, and private
letters. The inventory seems to be for nautical equipment while one of the
private letters is from Hikane to her son Isidorus. In it Hikane complains
that she has not received a letter from him in some time. These documents
from the early Roman trash deposit date mainly in the period of the 40s to
the 70s AD, though some appear from the reigns of Augustus (27 BC–AD 14)
and Tiberius (AD 14–37).

   The names of several soldiers from Palmyra appear on elaborate and
costly dedications they made at Berenike in the late second to early third
centuries AD. Found inside a small religious area dedicated to a number of
cults including the worship of the Roman emperor, veneration of the
Palmyrene deity Yarhibol/Hierobol, and that of the Egyptian deity Harpocrates, some of these dedications were beyond the abilities of those

offering them to afford on modest army salaries. We discussed this in some detail in Chapter 6. These fancy inscriptions and accompanying bronze statues suggest that some of these troops also had a hand in and, legally or otherwise, made a profit from some aspect of the lucrative commerce passing through Berenike.

Other individuals residing at Berenike remain anonymous to us, their presence, status, and ethnicity known only as the result of the survival of some of their belongings: a gold and pearl earring, remains of escargot as a culinary delicacy imported from the Mediterranean, marble slabs originating from the Sea of Marmora in Turkey for use as wall or floor decoration in their homes, elaborately woven floor carpets, furniture covers or wall hangings, fancy beads, and ring bevels carved with incised decoration made of semiprecious stones. These items and the discovery of beloved pets buried with their collars tell us of the elite positions held by some residents of the city, but not, unfortunately, their ethnicities. The remains of late Roman tombs from a high status cemetery at the northwestern edge of town, however, suggest a desert origin for some of its occupants.

Written Evidence from the Desert Roads

In addition to these ostraca, papyri, and inscriptions we have another fascinating source for the personal names of some of these intrepid travelers. Along the roads crisscrossing the Eastern Desert between the Nile and the various Red Sea ports travelers rested, frequently in the same places because of the safety, shade, or water available to them. Often these locales were not officially sanctioned forts or wells, but might be conveniently located natural rock outcrops or small caves or grottos that offered protection from the scorching sun and frequently howling winds and blowing sand. Here, while spending time waiting for the cooler hours of the day in which to travel, many individuals scratched their names and some provided fairly detailed accounts of their reasons for being in the desert.

One small natural grotto near Menih al-Heir, on the northern half of the route linking Berenike to Coptos, contains dozens of such messages in a variety of languages (Fig. 7.23). One man named Gaius Numidius Eros left graffiti here on two different visits, one of which dated to sometime between late February and late March AD 2. He specifically says that he was returning from India. Another man named Lysas states in bilingual graffiti in Latin

S.E. Sidebotham

Fig. 7.23: Graffiti in a variety of languages from the small natural grotto near Menih al-Heir, on the northern half of the route linking Berenike to Coptos.

and Greek that he was the freed slave of the Roman Popilius Annius Plocamus and dates his visit to the grotto to July 5, 6 BC. The Annii Plocami were a well known mercantile family from Puteoli, a major Roman port on the northern side of the Bay of Naples in Italy. The Lysas who left his graffiti in this grotto may be the same man (or a close relative) who Pliny the Elder recounts as arriving in Sri Lanka after having been blown off course by the monsoon winds and who impressed the local monarch with the high quality of Roman coinage that we noted above. Euphemos, freed slave of the Roman Lucius Attius Felix visited the same grotto on April 29, AD 44, while Primus, freed slave of the Roman centurion Sextus Mevus Celer of the XXII legion, also left his mark sometime between 4 BC and AD 6. The status of many of the travelers seems to be that of a freed slave. We know that freedmen, as the Romans called freed slaves, often undertook commercial dealings for their former masters and these desert graffiti corroborate that this was also the case with the lucrative Red Sea–Indian Ocean commerce.

We have few if any personal names preserved from Berenike's latest period of existence. We do have, however, some indication that different ethnic groups continued to live side by side in the late Roman port. We recovered residues of camel, goat, and sheep remains concentrated in certain parts of late Roman Berenike from the middle of the fourth century AD on. These together with analysis of weaving patterns of textiles and matting and the find of an unusual handmade and burnished pottery called Eastern Desert Ware (Pl. 7.15), all of which were associated with the faunal remains, suggest that a group originating from the desert was living in Berenike at that time. Other areas of the community contemporary with these finds have produced remains overwhelmingly of marine life: fish bones and shells. These hint that part of Berenike's late Roman population was oriented more toward the sea. Together, the faunal record suggests that several disparate groups resided at Berenike at that late period in the life of the city and that these peoples may well have lived in separate quarters.

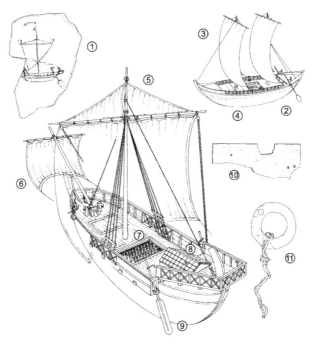

A.M. Hense.

1 ship graffito (AD 50–70)
2 Indian merchant ship (second century AD)
3 an Indian sail fragment was found in Berenike
4 hull of teak wood
5 Roman merchant ship (first century AD)
6 artemon sail
7 hold with cargo
8 galley with a roof covered with pottery tiles
9 hull beneath the waterline covered with protective lead sheets, held in place with copper-alloy nails
10 lead sheet (length 20 centimeters)
11 bone brailing ring (diameter 47 millimeters, first century AD)

Fig. 7.24: Indian, Arab, and Roman trade ships (with ship graffito).

SHIPS

What did the ships hauling these fabulously valuable cargoes look like (Fig. 7.24)? What evidence do we have of their sizes, the materials and methods of their construction, and the sizes of their crews? The scant remains of several Roman-era shipwrecks have been found in the Red Sea, three in Egyptian waters, and one off the coast of Eritrea, but the former three have never been excavated and the latter only partially so. Therefore, they provide no useful evidence for the sizes, appearances or materials from which ancient merchantmen were made. The *Periplus* suggests that merchant ships plying the Egypt–India and Egypt–Africa routes were quite large and well built. They would have to be to withstand the rigors of sailing in those regions and to convey sizeable cargoes to maximize profits on each journey. Of course, ships sailing more locally or regionally need not have been that large.

We also have the representation of a ship in the form of a graffito. One striking example scratched on a broken piece of pottery excavated at Berenike and dating about AD 50–60/70 shows a sailing ship at anchor with sails furled (Fig. 7.24). One of the early Roman ostraca from a trash dump excavated at Berenike actually preserves the name of one of the ships that came into harbor there, the Gymnasiarchis. At both Berenike and Myos Hormos excavators have found wooden and horn brailing rings which were tied to Indian-made cotton sails to facilitate raising and lowering them on the masts and nets, perhaps used to lift cargoes onto and off of the ships. Also unearthed were wooden pulleys, ropes, and lead hull sheathing noted earlier in the chapter. Teak timbers, possibly from dismantled ships and recycled into walls of late Roman buildings at Berenike were described above. Matting found in the early Roman trash dumps at Berenike was woven in a north Indian style; this may have been used aboard the large ocean-going merchantmen as awnings or sails.

Burying the Dead in the
Eastern Desert

he Eastern Desert must have been a bustling place throughout much
of its history, but especially in the Ptolemaic and Roman periods.
Many people—men, women, and children—from various walks of
life and from a number of places in Egypt and the wider Mediterranean
world traveled between the Nile and the quarries, mines, other civilian settlements, and military installations of the Eastern Desert. Individuals and
groups from the Red Sea and Indian Ocean basins also journeyed between
the Nile and ports along the Red Sea coast. Many people, of course, resided
for various lengths of time in the region and it follows that a number ended
their days here especially in the Roman era. While some of the deceased
were transported back to the Nile for burial, as we shall see below, most people probably could not afford this expense and would have been laid to rest
near where they expired.

Though ubiquitous, ancient burials in the Eastern Desert have been little-
studied by archaeologists. This is an unfortunate oversight as there are many
hundreds if not thousands of graves and tombs from throughout antiquity
scattered about the region. Most burials that we see today are quite modest
and can be found especially near the settlements and along the roads that
crisscrossed the region. Unfortunately, most of these graves, usually shallow
cist burials marked by modest piles of stones or slightly larger cairn graves,
have been badly looted over the centuries; thieves engaged in one of the oldest professions in the world, grave robbing, have desecrated the last resting

places of their distant ancestors looking for valuable burial goods. We cannot know with any certainty who the culprits were, but it is likely that they recovered little of any intrinsic value. Their depredations, though, have in most instances, destroyed or badly damaged the archaeological evidence that might have told us more about the deceased who were buried in this hostile and arid environment. In many instances on our surveys we have seen the bones and broken pots that have been scattered close to their graves by looters. Evidence from all eras of antiquity indicates that bodies were inhumed and not cremated. This would have been in keeping with historic Egyptian practices of preserving the mortal remains for the afterlife. There would have also been practical reasons for inhuming the dead: the fuel to cremate would have been in very short supply, indeed, in this hyper-arid and relatively treeless region.

What did the desert graves look like and what type of funerary goods might have been found in most of these poor sepulchers? Many of these final resting places were no more than simple and sometimes rather shallow holes dug in the ground in which the body had been deposited in a crouched, fetal position. Crowning a typical example was a pile of stones. In some cases, a single course of smaller stones outlined by larger ones lay immediately on the surface of the ground (Fig. 8.1) beneath which the bones and artifacts accompanying them had been deposited.

The slight information from the very few graves that have been found intact and that have been scientifically excavated suggests that personal possessions including beads, some pottery and, occasionally, some nicer jewelry were interred with the deceased; sometimes, there were no grave goods placed with the most destitute. In most instances, however, the bones from the robbed graves have been so badly disturbed and scattered, and so few archaeologically investigated graves have been quantified, that it is impossible to determine much at all about the demographics of those buried here. Were those interred in the Eastern Desert predominantly male adults or were there sizeable numbers of females and children also laid to rest there? What were their social statuses and ethnicities, if these can be determined?

The graves themselves tell us little, but a surprising source for who might have been deposited in these last resting places, in Roman times anyway, comes from the documents written by and about those living and traveling in the region that have turned up in excavations at some of the ancient

S.E. Sidebotham

Fig. 8.1: Example of a small oval-shaped grave, likely for a single individual, near the Via Nova Hadriana.

quarries, forts, and ports. We can extrapolate from these that, indeed, in addition to the adult males, there were numbers of women and children who resided here as well. If they lived here, some certainly died here, too.

Written sources abound, which provide us with insights on the official and daily lives of men, women, and children and, therefore, give some indication of a cross section of those people who would have died in the region. These include thousands of ostraca from the Roman quarries at Mons Claudianus and from Roman *praesidia* excavated by French archaeologists along the road linking Myos Hormos to Coptos. There are hundreds of documents written on ostraca, papyri, and stone from Berenike and others from Myos Hormos. The quarries at Mons Porphyrites as well as inscriptions carved on stone and letters preserved in papyri from the Eastern Desert also add to our knowledge.

Most of those who appear in these documents hailed from the Nile Valley or beyond. Of course, indigenous desert peoples, the predecessors of today's Bedouin, would have appeared only obliquely, if at all, in the written sources—such as references in ostraca to *barbaroi*/raiders attacking the stations on the Myos Hormos–Nile road—but would certainly have been buried in the desert. How different the burial customs and appearance of graves of the indigenous peoples were from those originating from the Nile Valley and beyond remains to be determined though we make some general observations about this below.

Bir Asele

The earliest intact graves we have seen during our desert surveys were in a large Predynastic (before about 3000 BC) cemetery at Bir Asele in the deep south, which we visited in June 2002 (Fig. 8.2). This burial ground seems to consist of several groups of tombs, built within short intervals of time. This is the largest, the most complete, and the oldest necropolis ever identified in the Eastern Desert. The vast majority of graves appear to contain inhumation burials. Small piles of stones mark the last resting places of individuals and the entire Bir Asele graveyard was enclosed by a low boundary wall made of larger stones and boulders. It is clear that there were two separate cemeteries in close proximity to one another that eventually grew together. The overall size of this necropolis is quite impressive: 137 by 53.5 meters. The few graves that were robbed here prior to our visit revealed scraps of ostrich egg shells, probably originally used as beads or other forms of jewelry, and some handmade Nubian-style pottery; these lay scattered around the looted burials. We are not certain why such a large cemetery appears at Bir Asele, as our survey did not locate any habitation centers,

S. E. Sidebotham

Fig. 8.2: The Predynastic or early Dynastic cemetery near Bir Asele.

mines, or quarries in the immediate environs. The nearest area of human activity that we know of is a gold working site of later date seventeen kilometers to the north. The closest known contemporary mine lies even farther away, about 105 kilometers to the north. Necropoleis similar in appearance to the one at Bir Asele have been identified in the Sinai.

We cannot determine what percentage of those dying in the Eastern Desert in the vicinity of Bir Asele was interred in the necropolis here, and what numbers may have been transported back to the Nile for final burial. Thousands of years later, the Coptos Tariff, a Roman period inscription of the late first century AD (discussed in Chapter 7), records that bodies were transported from the Eastern Desert to the Nile and that a toll was levied on them. The amount was small, one drachma and four obols. A month's pay for a skilled workman at the Roman quarries at Mons Claudianus was forty-seven drachmas (as we noted in Chapter 4), so the toll levied on the funeral procession "going up and down," as the inscription indicates, was, in this context, rather modest. "Going up and down" may well refer to the initial funeral procession of friends and relatives who were traveling from the Nile Valley to retrieve the deceased's remains from the desert and accompany them back to the Nile for burial. That there is a special category for this round trip in the Coptos Tariff suggests that it was probably a fairly frequent occurrence, at least in the Roman era.

There is no indication in the Coptos Tariff of who these deceased individuals were, but we might speculate that when alive they were financially well enough off that they could stipulate in their wills or to surviving friends and relatives that they were to be taken home, that is, back to their villages in the Nile Valley, for burial. This may help explain why various archaeological surveys have noted so few apparently well-to-do tombs and graves in the Eastern Desert. Nothing resembling the famous painted and very realistic Fayyum mummy portraits that are so ubiquitous in Fayyum and some cities of the Nile Valley especially in the first, second, and into the third centuries AD, has been found in the Eastern Desert thus far. As these portraits seem to have been associated mainly with relatively prosperous mid-level ranking individuals one would expect far fewer of them to have been in the Eastern Desert in the first place. Those that were may, in many instances, have been returned to their homes along the Nile for burial. As we noted above, perhaps it is this group, especially, that is noted in the Coptos Tariff. A parallel situation suggested by the Coptos Tariff may have existed in earlier periods in the Eastern Desert as well, with those of higher status being returned to the Nile for burial and those of lesser means having their mortal remains laid to rest near where they died.

We have also noted another type of burial in the Eastern Desert, one in which large circular tombs many meters in diameter and often a meter or more high contained the remains of several individuals. Where we have examined these tumuli-like structures containing multiple burials associated with nearby sites, they seem to be late Roman in date. These have also been found and studied in the Eastern Desert of southern Egypt and northern Sudan. Nothing like these tombs survive in the Nile Valley suggesting that they were built by and contained the mortal remains of desert dwellers, but we cannot be certain. In the late Roman examples we have investigated in the Eastern Desert, individual compartments made of large flat upright stones appear within these round sepulchers. The bodies would have been placed on their sides in a crouched, fetal position and the chambers then covered by one or more large flat stones. We assume that funerary goods would have accompanied the bodies though we have not seen any in our surveys. Large cobbles and small boulders then topped the entire round structure in which these compartments were situated. The exterior edges of these round tombs often comprised large upright stones, which corralled the cobbles and boulders surrounding the individual chambers.

Berenike and Environs

At Berenike we located and excavated, in part, a late Roman era cemetery. Found during our excavations in winter 2000–2001, this necropolis lay at the extreme northwestern edge of the city flanking the road that led to the Nile (Fig. 8.3). Though we excavated only a small portion of this cemetery, we noted two types of burials. The more high-status tombs were built of the omnipresent coral heads that comprised all late Roman buildings at Berenike. Inside the variously shaped mausolea had been placed, in some instances, wooden coffins fastened together using iron and copper alloy nails (Figs. 8.4–8.5). All but the smallest scraps of these wooden sarcophagi had long since disappeared and from our excavations only paltry evidence survives indicating that this was the mode of interment. These burials all seem to have been of adults, but they had been thoroughly looted and the bones

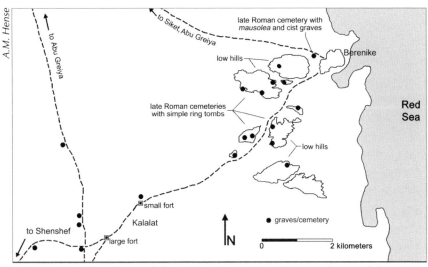

Fig. 8.3: Berenike, plan with late Roman-era cemeteries in and around the city.

Fig. 8.4: Berenike, late Roman cemetery with bones scattered by looters inside mausoleum. Scale = twenty centimeters.

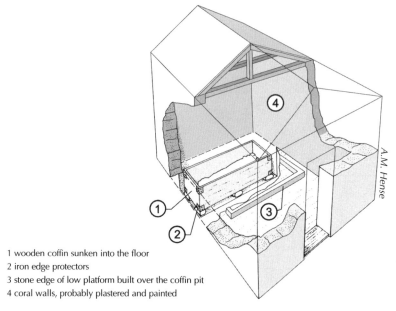

A.M. Hense

1 wooden coffin sunken into the floor
2 iron edge protectors
3 stone edge of low platform built over the coffin pit
4 coral walls, probably plastered and painted

Fig. 8.5: Berenike, reconstruction of late Roman mausoleum.

unceremoniously thrown out of the graves or tossed to one end of the cubi-
cles in which we found them. The decoration of the exterior tops of some of
these graves, small black pebbles mixed with small pieces of broken white
coral, resembles burial decorations from other areas of the Eastern Desert of
southern Upper Egypt and Lower Nubia. In fact, just south of Berenike we
noted a concentration of small black and white stones and tiny chunks of
coral on a low mound. It remains to be determined if this was a tomb.

The second type of burial we found in our limited area of excavation in
the late Roman necropolis at the northwestern corner of Berenike consisted
of cist graves. These intermingled with the fancier mausolea and were not
spatially segregated from them. The cist graves were merely cuts in the surrounding ground into which human remains were then placed and covered
with stones. One contained a complete skeleton of a small girl who we estimate died at about the age of two. She had been deposited lovingly in a small,
shallow oval-shaped hole laid in a fetal position (Fig. 8.6). Her head had
been covered with a large broken potsherd the underside of which had fragments of some textile, clearly the remains of a burial shroud. Accompanying
the little girl were a few beads. The burial, potsherd, and beads had been

topped by largish pieces of coral placed in such a way as to cover the burial pit completely. Another cist grave was substantially larger and contained the prone remains of what appeared to be an adolescent whose gender we could not determine. The body had also been deposited in a long shallow hole though we did not find either the covering of corals for the final resting place as we did for the little girl nor did we find any grave goods.

Elsewhere around Berenike we found other human remains. Some were digits—fingers, toes, and so on—found in the trash dumps, perhaps amputations due to medical procedures or accidents. We also found the remains of a prematurely born infant or fetus elsewhere on site from a Roman context. In the Ptolemaic area atop the mound beneath which we found the Ptolemaic-era brick factory in 1996 we excavated the remains of a woman lying on her back (Fig. 8.7). A large potshard covered her pelvic area. Her estimated height was 1.61 meters and she was between forty and fifty years old when she died. We found no grave goods with her and we could not determine precisely when she was buried, but it was certainly long after the kiln had fallen out of use.

Another skeleton found during that same excavation season appeared near the eastern end of the site and in a late Roman context. This one was of an adult male with an estimated height of 1.71 meters who died when he was between thirty and forty years old; he was found on his right side, facing west, next to a wall. Study of his bones indicated that he had been a very robust and muscular individual suggesting that he may have performed heavy manual labor. Perhaps he had been a stevedore. His skull and pelvis were crushed, but the position of his head, with the neck bent backward, would not have been one a living person could have maintained. He seems not to have been buried so much as discarded here and his presence in this location remains a mystery. He may have died in an accident or he may have been murdered. Whatever the circumstances of his death, his final placement inside a building was very unusual, at least at Berenike.

Two other skeletons found at Berenike are also worthy of our attention. We excavated both in areas of the Ptolemaic industrial area. In fact, both had clearly been placed here long after the region had been abandoned. Yet, we could not determine when this might have been. Neither individual seems to have been buried properly so much as thrown out. We found no grave goods and scavengers had gnawed at one foot suggesting a period of

S.E. Sidebotham

Fig. 8.6: Late Roman-era burial site of a two-year-old girl at Berenike. Scale = ten centimeters.

S.E. Sidebotham

Fig 8.7: Berenike, remains of an approximately forty-year-old woman with a large potshard covering her pelvic area. Scale = fifty centimeters.

exposure before being covered by sand. Both skeletons, lying on their backs, lacked heads (Pl. 8.1). Whether these individuals had suffered some very traumatic accident that caused death by decapitation, or they had been executed by decapitation is uncertain. Another skeleton we found in the same area was complete. We excavated yet another skeleton that we found placed in a fetal position inside the broken portions of an earlier Ptolemaic cistern. It was so fragile, however, that we could not determine its gender or estimate its age at death.

West of Berenike in the region of some modern military bunkers erected in the 1970s, and southwest of the city atop the low hills flanking the route leading between Berenike and the Roman *praesidia* in Wadi Kalalat, about 8.5 kilometers away, are numerous doughnut-shaped ring tombs. Like the other burials we have described in the region, the vast majority of these have been looted, in some cases the bones and some paltry grave goods, usually broken pottery, have been left scattered near their final resting places. Ceramic evidence suggests that these were all late Roman in date. We are then left with the unanswered question of where the Ptolemaic and early Roman cemeteries of Berenike were located.

Our surveys throughout the 1980s, 1990s, and into the new millennium also noted graves near the main early Roman quarry settlement in Wadi Umm Wikala (ancient Mons Ophiates) and scattered throughout the area near the various locations associated with the main settlement there. We have also noted graves near the late Roman fort at Abu Sha'r and in the vicinity of the early Roman port of Myos Hormos. In addition, we have seen a few of them, and all of these have long since been robbed, immediately west of the coastal remains at Marsa Nakari (perhaps the ancient Nechesia).

Other burials, some rather fancy by Eastern Desert standards, can also be seen at the settlements of Shenshef and Hitan Rayan. Both of these were late Roman communities that lay southwest of Berenike. Although close physical proximity to Berenike prompted numerous contacts between these two desert settlements and the port and between each other, the precise functions of both Shenshef and Hitan Rayan remain mysterious.

Hundreds of ring tombs surround the town at Shenshef and these, like Berenike itself, are overwhelmingly late Roman (predominantly late fourth–fifth–sixth century) in date. Several dozen late Roman ring tombs, similar to those at Shenshef, also appear near the entrance (eastern end) of the site at Hitan Rayan. While approximately nine hundred meters east of the narrow entrance leading into Hitan Rayan, our survey in winter 1995 found the remains of what appears to be an early Roman cemetery. A thin topping of pebbles and small cobbles bordered by larger cobbles covered the dozens of graves that we noted there. Floods had clearly washed many graves away over the years; pottery allowed dating of this cemetery. We found no early Roman settlement associated with this graveyard and, as noted above, Hitan Rayan itself was a late Roman community with its own small ring cairn cemetery.

We also found a huge late Roman cemetery at Taw al-Kefare (Pl. 8.2) during a survey in winter 1997 that lay on a secondary route linking Berenike to the five forts in Wadi Abu Greiya (ancient Vetus Hydreuma). This large necropolis was not related to any apparent nearby settlement and its location here remains a mystery to us. It is possible that people who died while traveling on this road between Berenike and Vetus Hydreuma were buried at Taw al-Kefare, but if so, why are, apparently, only late Roman graves found here? The interments were small cairn types though we also noted some larger tumuli with wide cleared areas surrounding them, which were, in turn delineated by a circle of stones. As this second-ary route debouched into the main Wadi Abu Greiya, but south of the ancient forts there, we found another substantial necropolis that preserved both the larger ring type graves and the smaller cairn graves. Most had been badly robbed.

Our survey of the region around Berenike also discovered a small late Roman cemetery comprising perhaps only two dozen robbed graves located just off the main ancient route linking Berenike, via Wadi Abu Greiya and Wadi Khashir, to the Nile. This small graveyard at Bint Abu Greiya was, likely, the last resting place of those expiring at or near Vetus Hydreuma, which was the first major stop on the road from Berenike to the Nile. Again, as in the case of the necropolis at Taw al-Kefare, we do not understand why the buri-als there were late Roman in date. Where were early Roman-era travelers buried who had died during their journey between the Nile and Berenike?

Our extensive surveys of the emerald mining areas around Wadi Sikait and Wadi Nugrus, a region the Romans called Mons Smaragdus, have detected hundreds of small cist- and cairn-type burials, virtually all of which have been thoroughly looted. Some bones and a few broken potshards are

JAMES BURTON

James Burton was born in London in 1788 and educated at Trinity College, Cambridge. After receiving his master's degree in 1815, he worked several years for the architect Sir John Soane. Traveling in Italy with Sir John, he met Egyptologists like Wilkinson and Lane. In 1822 Muhammad 'Ali Pasha invited Burton to search for coal in the Egyptian deserts. Not happy with his role as mineralogist, Burton shifted his attention to the ancient monuments in Egypt. He traveled south to Aswan, during which expedition he spent several months in Luxor. There he excavated at Medinet Habu, Karnak, and the Valley of Kings. A volume of hieroglyphic texts Burton recorded during his travels was published in 1828. In 1834 he returned to England, bringing a whole cortège of servants and animals. His family did not seem to be pleased, especially after they found out his wife-to-be was a former Greek slave girl, purchased in Egypt some years before. Acting swiftly, they disowned James shortly after his return.

During his years in Egypt Burton had collected quite a few antiquities, but most of these were auctioned off in 1836 to repay his debts. He died in 1862 in Edinburgh as a "zealous investigator in Egypt of its language and antiquities." Burton, unfortunately, appears rarely to have published any of his observations on the Eastern Desert, but his notes, plans, and drawings stored in the British Library in London—donated after his death by his brother Decimius—are, in contrast to Wilkinson's, extremely clear and legible and in some cases he records observations not made by his more famous travel companion.

all that survive of these once extensive cemeteries. This is extremely unfortunate. We know that the basement rocks of this rich beryl and emerald-bearing region emit low-level radiation. It would be most interesting, indeed, if some complete skeletons could be found. We could then determine gender, ages at death, and perform experiments to see what effects long-term exposure to this radiation might have had on the health of these individuals. We might also be able to measure the deletrious impact on those consuming food and water obtained from this area, so heavily polluted by residues from the huge mine tailings (spoil heaps).

The French-led expedition at Mons Claudianus between 1987 and 1993 located a cemetery about 320 meters west of the settlement's main fort. Many of the simple inhumation graves there had been badly looted and the team conducted only a cursory survey of the necropolis. Previous visitors, including James Burton in the early nineteenth century, and Leo Tregenza in the late 1940s, found tombstones either known or suspected to have come from this graveyard. Burton noted one that recorded the epitaph of a Roman cavalryman named Gaius Luconius. We know Luconius was active during the reign of the emperor Trajan (AD 98–117) from the excavation of an ostracon near the Mons Claudianus fort that also bears his name.

At Mons Porphyrites a Christian cemetery has long been known and inscribed tombstones have been found there. Our survey in January 1989 located a large tombstone, now broken in two, with a short inscription carved in Greek on a piece of the ubiquitous purple porphyry (Fig. 8.8); it indicated that a man named John from the city of Hermopolis had been buried here. We are not sure which Hermopolis as there were at least two cities that bore this name in the Nile Valley. This same tombstone had on its back side other carvings that appeared to be upside down in relation to the "John" epithet.

British archaeologists discovered other burials and skeletal remains during their work at Mons Porphyrites between 1994 and 1998. Pit burials and cairn graves were studied with the former being by far the most prevalent. Examination of skeletal remains from some graves corroborates the thousands of ostraca exhumed and translated from the nearby quarry settlement at Mons Claudianus that women and children lived in these desert communities along with their spouses or other male relatives. Residents in these desert communities apparently had a fairly healthy diet, yet were particularly subject to gastrointestinal and eye disorders (as indicated in ostraca from elsewhere in the Eastern Desert, especially from military installations along the Myos Hormos–Nile road where women and children were also living). Examination of the skeletal remains shows, not surprisingly, that some individuals, especially the males, exhibited a high incidence of damage or strain to vertebrae, indicative of constant and long-term lifting of heavy objects, an occupational hazard for many men working at such a site.

S.E. Sidebotham

Fig. 8.8: Detail of the tombstone of John the Christian of Hermopolis (on the Nile) from a cemetery near the Lykabettus quarries at Mons Porphyrites. Scale = ten centimeters.

The only other probable tombstone our survey has found over the years in the Eastern Desert came to light along the southern portion of the Via Nova Hadriana in winter 1998. One day an 'Ababda man living in the region of Hammata, a coastal community about forty kilometers north of Berenike, reported seeing a stone with writing on it near the 'ancient' road. Following the end of one excavation day at Berenike two of us drove out from camp with the 'Abadi guide to see this stone. It proved to be a small boulder that had been scratched on in Greek recording a man named Adidos from Pharan, a town in the Sinai. A Christian staurogram (cross) was scratched above Adidos' name and a small but unidentifiable quadruped animal had been carved running to the left beneath the inscription "PHARANITES" (Fig. 8.9). A second, smaller stone also bore what appeared to be a cross inside a square or rectangle; on the other side of this smaller stone were two other crosses.

S.E. Sidebotham

Fig. 8.9: Tombstone of Adidos from Pharan (in the Sinai) found along the Via Nova Hadriana north of Berenike. Scale = twenty centimeters.

The 'Abadi had hidden both stones in a small gully east of, but not far from, the Via Nova Hadriana. He claimed that he had found them next to an unusually large tomb just a few meters west of the Roman highway and we had no reason to doubt him. Our epigrapher finally worked out from the forms in which the Greek letters were scratched that the text had, most likely, been carved in the sixth century. We will never know what Adidos was doing this far from home, but his burial close to the road and not far from Berenike tells us that he was probably en route between Berenike and some point farther north; it also indicates that this stretch of the Via Nova Hadriana was still in use at that late date.

Conclusion

At some point in the near future archaeologists should undertake a more systematic study of the ancient graves and burials in the Eastern Desert. This investigation should begin with the creation of categories of the various types of graves and burials, a quantification of the numbers, locations, and where possible, their dates. Excavation of a cross section of the different types should also be part of this study. We could, in fact, learn a great deal about lifestyles, health, and disease from an examination of the skeletal remains of ancient peoples who lived, died, and were buried throughout the Eastern Desert in various periods. This vital information, however, may never be obtained if current rates of pilferage persist and present lack of interest in systematically studying funerary remains in the desert continues.

El Dorado
Gold Mines in the Eastern Desert

The most important and consistently sought-after natural resource available in the Eastern Desert throughout antiquity was gold (Fig. 9.1). We have archaeological and written evidence from at least the Early Dynastic and Old Kingdom periods (2920–2152 BC) that expeditions both large and small ventured forth into the arid regions between the Nile and the Red Sea in search of this valuable metal. There are frequent references, especially in inscriptions associated with the king and his courtiers, throughout the pharaonic period to valuable objects as well as the precious artifacts themselves wrought from or decorated with gold including various types of jewelry, altars, chariots, columns, drinking vessels, death masks, thrones, statues, doors, and even whips. These items indirectly attest the acquisition of gold from regions of the Eastern Desert. The late Predynastic town at Nagada, near the mouth of the Wadi Hammamat at the edge of the Eastern Desert, was known as Nubt ('Gold Town'), perhaps indicating that it grew rich from the gold trade. Interest in and exploitation of gold mines in the Eastern Desert accelerated during the Middle (2040–1640 BC) and New (1550–1070 BC) Kingdoms.

New Kingdom private tombs, such as that of mayor Sobekhotep, sometimes include depictions of Nubians bringing gold as tribute. During the New Kingdom, gold was also obtained from Syria-Palestine by way of tribute, despite the fact that Egypt was already much richer in gold than the Levantine city-states. The Egyptians' wealth in gold made them the envy of

Fig. 9.1: Map showing locations of goldmines in the Eastern Desert mentioned in this chapter.

their neighbors in the Near East. This jealousy is frequently expressed in the so-called Amarna letters, an important cache of documents discovered in 1887 at the city of Tell al-Amarna (ancient Akhetaten) in Middle Egypt that was founded by pharaoh Akhenaten (1353–1335 BC). Almost all of the Amarna letters preserve diplomatic correspondence between Egypt and either the great powers in western Asia, such as Babylonia and Assyria, or the vassal states of Syria and Palestine. In one letter from Tushratta of Mitanni we read, "May my brother send me in very great quantities gold that has not been worked, and may my brother send me much more gold than he did to my father. In my brother's country gold is as plentiful as dirt . . . ."

Gold mining continued in the Late Period (712–332 BC) and in Ptolemaic and Roman times (late fourth century BC–sixth century AD). In some instances mines first opened in the pharaonic era continued to be exploited in later times. In other cases new mines were opened where none had been before. The quest for gold continues to lure large joint foreign-Egyptian ventures today. It would be a fascinating exercise to estimate the quantities of gold extracted from the region throughout history.

The importance attached to the success of the gold mining operations and the potential wealth derived from them necessitated that the government strictly control them throughout Egypt's history. Gold paid for elaborate royal building projects and allowed various Egyptian regimes over the millennia to maintain the military forces and the diplomatic leverage necessary to advance Egypt's political agendas both domestically as well as beyond her borders. In the pharaonic period Egypt's major foreign areas of interest lay along the Nile south of her traditional frontier in Nubia and on the Levantine coast of the Mediterranean, and in Ptolemaic times those spheres expanded to include more southerly areas of the African coast of the Red Sea, Cyprus, parts of southern Asia Minor, and some of the Aegean islands. In the Roman period, of course, Egypt was only one province in a large multi-cultural empire spanning parts of Europe, Asia, and Africa that, at its height, stretched from Scotland to the Persian Gulf and from the eastern shores of the Black Sea to Morocco. While Egypt was an important source of gold for the Romans, other regions of their empire including Wales, Spain, and Dacia (modern Romania) also supplied the imperial government with this precious metal.

The most productive gold-bearing areas in Egypt were those immediately southwest of the modern Red Sea city of Hurghada and reaching to the region west and southwest of Berenike and southeast of Aswan into Wadi 'Allaqi. Some expeditions went even farther afield. Not content with exploitation of Egypt's mines, at several points in her long history, expeditions were mounted into regions well to the south of Egypt's traditional boundaries into areas of the Eastern Desert of what is today northern Sudan. In pharaonic times and later the gold-bearing areas of Egypt and Sudan were divided into three major zones which the Egyptians called, from north to south, the Land of Coptos, the Land of Wawat and the Land of Kush. These stretched between approximately 27° and 18° North latitude and encompassed large swaths of the Eastern Desert. Inscriptions from the time of the Twelfth Dynasty (Middle Kingdom) pharaoh Senwosret III (1878–1841 BC) refer to gold mining expeditions dispatched to regions south of Coptos and inscriptions emblazoned on the temple of Medinet Habu from the reign of Ramesses III (1194–1163 BC) of the Twentieth Dynasty also refer to gold derived from various areas of the Eastern Desert.

This vast realm of the Eastern Desert provided gold to the pharaohs, but interestingly during Roman times the regions exploited seem to have been far more circumscribed and confined primarily to the central and southern areas of Egypt's Eastern Desert. Numerous mines and associated settlements with their ubiquitous grinding stones can still be seen from different periods of Egypt's long history of gold mining. Surprisingly, however, only a small handful of mines has ever been studied through detailed surface surveying and mapping, and only one has been partially excavated and the results published. Numerically, the ancient gold mines of the Eastern Desert far outnumber the hard and soft stone quarries we discussed in Chapter 4. The transport problems surrounding the shipment of stone products, particularly the large columns, basins, and other architectural elements sought in the Roman period from these quarries, would not have existed in the gold mines as the ore or even in some instances the refined product could be removed relatively easily by pack animals such as donkeys and camels. Unlike the stone transported from the quarries, however, security considerations would have been paramount for those convoys hauling gold from the mines to the Nile Valley.

The Turin Papyrus, discussed in Chapter 4, depicts a map drawn in Egypt's New Kingdom period during the reign of the Twentieth Dynasty pharaoh Ramesses IV (1163–1156 BC). The map shows a portion of the Eastern Desert where quarrying and gold mining operations took place at that time. Mining operations ranged, as our various archaeological surveys have shown, from small prospecting type endeavors to huge undertakings involving hundreds of people. We would very much like to know the nature of ancient geological prospecting that took place and the kinds of people who undertook it in order to locate the most promising auriferous veins prior to their exploitation.

Preserved for us are numerous ancient texts that record expeditions launched into the desert to exploit gold deposits. These are from the pharaonic period; most are official and list the names of the expedition leaders and the number of people sent as well as the monarchs who commanded them. We do have, however, one fascinating, but relatively late account (from Ptolemaic times) of the mining methods and wretched conditions experienced by those hapless souls who actually had to ferret out the gold. Probably not much had changed between this account written in the first century BC and the situation as it existed during the preceding several millennia.

Gold Mining Methods

Diodorus Siculus, originally from the island of Sicily as his name implies, visited Egypt sometime between 60 and 56 BC and, apparently, researched his book entitled *Bibliotheke (Library)* at that time. Diodorus drew heavily on his predecessor Agatharchides of Cnidus, who had written a volume in the second century BC entitled *On the Erythraean Sea*, for much of his information. While only about a third of Diodorus' tome survives, his section on gold mining in the Eastern Desert is fascinating and instructive. Debate rages among modern scholars as to which area of Egypt's Eastern Desert Diodorus describes. Some believe it is the Wadi 'Allaqi region of southern Egypt and northern Sudan while others argue that the area described lies farther north. It hardly matters for our immediate purposes.

Diodorus set the grim scene: Egypt's Eastern Desert, he says, contained myriads of gold mines, many of them very large and very old, dating back, perhaps, to pharaonic times.

Overseers began the work by locating quartz veins where the gold was found. As we know from numerous, lengthy modern geological and archaeological studies, gold obtained from the Eastern Desert is almost invariably imbedded in quartz veins that spider web through the igneous basement rocks. Diodorus continues by relating that following these veins and extracting the gold ore from them was extremely expensive and was brutal and hazardous work. Many individuals laboring in these mines had been condemned to them for criminal offenses or as captives in war. Some of those toiling in the mines had been falsely condemned and should not have been there. Bound in chains, the mining activities took place day and night; there was no escape except a cruel death either in the mines or in futile attempts to flee into the vast menacing desert realms. The guards at these mines, Diodorus relates, were foreigners who spoke languages different from the miners so that there was minimal possibility of fraternization or collusion.

Miners kindled fires to heat and crack the gold-bearing quartz veins. Workers then crushed the crumbled bits using sledges and further reduced these fragments into smaller pieces using hammers. Those working in the dark, narrow, and twisting tunnels carried lamps tied to their heads and forced their bodies to twist in contorted forms to negotiate the small spaces.

Small boys entered the mineshafts and carried out the ore while older men took the ore and pulverized it with iron pestles in stone mortars until it was reduced further in size. Old men and women took the resulting residue and put it into mills standing in rows and in groups of two or three they ground it to the consistency of fine flour. These workers, Diodorus tells us, could not take care of themselves and wore no clothing. Anyone seeing them took great pity for their plight. These people worked until they died and many looked forward to the ultimate escape.

The end of the process involved skilled workmen taking the fine powder and distributing it on an inclined board and then pouring water over it. The water washed away the unwanted lighter-weight material leaving only the heavier gold behind. That ore was then placed in measured amounts into terra-cotta jars. The gold ore was mixed with lead, salt, tin, and barley bran and the jars were then closed with lids and sealed with mud. This concoction was baked in a kiln for five days and nights. The jars were then removed and allowed to cool. Subsequent examination of the jars' contents revealed almost pure gold with few impurities.

Diodorus' vivid and heartbreaking description raises many questions. For example, where did the fuel for the kilns come from in these remote desert outposts? Archaeological evidence corroborates the actual mining process: terra-cotta oil lamps have been found in mines used for lighting—during one of our surveys we found such a lamp still in its original position in an alcove carved along a shaft in one of the emerald mines in Middle Sikait—and a sculpted relief now in a mining museum in Bochum, Germany, shows a miner probably carrying a lamp. Those boys conveying the rocks from the mines would have used leather or woven sacks, buckets, or baskets and examples have been found of these in many ancient mines from around the Roman world, especially in Spain; we recently found a woven mat basket discarded in one of the emerald mines in Wadi Sikait. Mortars and grinding stones appear in profusion from Eastern Desert gold mines; we found a particularly well-preserved collection of these during our survey of the

Ptolemaic-era gold mines at Umm Howeitat al-Qibli (Fig. 9.2) about four-teen kilometers west of the Red Sea between Marsa 'Alam and Quseir. The grinding stones seem to have been mainly of the 'saddle' variety in Ptole-maic and earlier times and round in the Roman period, though this was not invariably the case.

Our surveys have also found large circular ore grinding facilities that Diodorus does not describe, at the site of Daghbag (Pls. 9.1–9.2), which may be associated with Compasi, mentioned in a number of ancient accounts as a station on the trans-desert route linking Berenike to Coptos. These novel and industrial-sized circular-shaped ore crushing devices were made of hewn stones carefully fitted together and possessing depressions along their long axes to allow a large vertical grinding wheel to be driven by a draft animal. This technology had come to Egypt in the Ptolemaic period from Attica, the region around Athens. In this area of Greece much silver mining, clearly on an industrial scale, had taken place from the early fifth century BC on. The Ptolemies were well acquainted with Attica as the result of their involvement in the Chremonidean War in the third century BC during the reign of Ptolemy II Philadelphus (285–246 BC) and it was likely in these circumstances that this technology came to their attention.

S.E. Sidebotham

Fig. 9.2: Ptolemaic gold mining site at Umm Howeitat al-Qibli, with mortars and grinding stones used in gold ore processing.

While we ourselves have not seen other large grinding facilities like those at Daghbag, several German scholars reported the existence of similar ones at the more southerly Ptolemaic-Roman gold mining settlements of Bokari and Barramiya. In addition, large washing tables have also been found in the Eastern Desert often constructed of stone and mortar, but these have been seen at only a few gold mines in the region. This may indicate that only the larger operations actually washed and 'prepared' the gold as described in Diodorus' account; alternatively, the dearth of these washing tables may simply be due to insufficient examination of the vast majority of gold mines in the Eastern Desert from any period in its history. Even so, there are references to gold washing that occur in texts from the period of the Nineteenth Dynasty pharaoh Seti I (1306–1290 BC) associated with the rock-cut temple at al-Kanaïs, discussed in Chapter 6. There is another reference to gold washing in the famous Kubban Stele, an important inscription found in a village of the same name dating to the reign of Ramesses II (1290–1224 BC). Thus, it seems clear that Diodorus' description of washing the gold at the mines had a long history. Yet, Diodorus may well have omitted, through oversight or lack of information, the use of water in another aspect of the gold mining process. Once the rock had been heated water may have been poured over it to cool it quickly thereby cracking it and breaking it up. This would have facilitated the mining and processing operations.

Status of Gold Miners

What about Diodorus' assertion of the servile status of the workers? In the pharaonic period mining and quarrying expeditions were carried out under military control and many of the laborers may well have been convicts or prisoners of war. While in Ptolemaic times forced labor may have prevailed in the mines, the picture is not as clear for the Roman period and the evidence is decidedly mixed on this issue. Perhaps slave, forced free (called *corvée*), and voluntary free labor was used at different times and places in the Roman era. Certainly there is no indication from the thousands of ostraca found at the Roman quarry at Mons Claudianus that slaves were used there, but rather skilled free laborers who earned up to twice as much as their counterparts in the Nile Valley. Such may have been the case in the Roman-era gold mines of the Eastern Desert as well. Nevertheless, some ancient Roman written sources refer to use of criminals, slaves, and Christians condemned to mines and quarries as punishment; with the present state of our archaeological evidence, we cannot ascertain, however, which mines might have used them.

Gold Mining Sites in the Eastern Desert

Surveys by German scholars have located scores if not hundreds of gold mining settlements ranging from the Early Dynastic period to the Islamic era. Often the same location continued to be worked over long periods of time, frequently this was done intermittently. Our surveys during the summers of 1996–1999 visited a number of Ptolemaic and Roman gold mines and we drew detailed site plans and maps of the remains of some of the more impressive ones. These included al-Ghuzza, Bir Sirbakis, Bukhalug, Umm Howeitat al-Qibli, and Abu Gerida. We cannot describe all of these, but let us discuss a few investigated by our team and one other excavated by the Oriental Institute of the University of Chicago.

Bir Umm Fawakhir

The only ancient gold mining settlement studied in extensive detail, including limited archaeological excavations, is that at Bir Umm Fawakhir (Fig. 9.3). Located near the famous Wadi Hammamat, surveys and excavations were conducted here by a team from the Oriental Institute of the University of Chicago throughout the 1990s. The large settlement scattered up and down several adjacent wadis dated primarily to the late Roman/early Byzantine period (fourth to sixth centuries AD) and would have been, according to the excavators, an important source of revenues for the central government at that time. Scholars investigating this site estimate that at its peak it had a population of about one thousand. It was certainly one of the larger gold mining operations known from any period in the Eastern Desert. The location of earlier mines and quarries along the well-traveled trans-desert route between Myos Hormos and Coptos meant that transport of metals and stone and their protection was greatly facilitated and it may well be that this particular area of gold acquisition prospered in part due to its location on a major transportation artery.

A surprising aspect that our surveys have noted about the vast majority of these gold mining operations from many different eras, including that at Bir

S. E. Sidebotham

Fig. 9.3: Late Roman-era gold mining community at Bir Umm Fawakhir.

Umm Fawakhir, is the lack of associated fortifications or apparent defenses of any kind. This is extremely odd given the value of the metal mined and the temptation among Bedouins and outlaws to attack and rob the settlements or caravans conveying the ore to the Nile. The route linking Myos Hormos to Coptos—along the course of which lay the gold mines and the large associated settlement at Bir Umm Fawakhir—preserves a number of *praesidia* (forts), but these guarded the caravan route or provided escorts for convoys and important individuals as we know from thousands of ostraca recently excavated by French archaeologists. Most of these defenses, certainly those nearby, had long since fallen out of use by the time the late Roman/early Byzantine mining operations at Bir Umm Fawakhir were booming. Other than the *skopeloi* (lookout/watch towers) that can be found on some of the high points surrounding the mines, what means of defense did these mining settlements possess to prevent marauders or bandits from pilfering the valuable metal? The dearth of forts and other defensive features suggests that there may have been little to fear from outsiders; perhaps troops lived at these mines and since none except Bir Umm Fawakhir has been excavated, evidence of their presence has not yet been discovered.

Abu Gerida

The Ptolemaic and possibly early Roman mining center at Abu Gerida seems to have been extremely important to a number of satellite gold mines. It was clearly much larger than the visible remains now suggest as major portions of the settlement have been washed away by flash floods over t... centuries. This gold mining center is the only one we have noted in our surveys that preserves a walled enclosure, perhaps some kind of fort, atop an adjacent hill (Fig. 9.4). Yet, there is no evidence that any gold mining actually took place at Abu Gerida. Its location, the fragments of statues and inscriptions, and the remains of stone molds used for making and repairing metal tools which our survey discovered, indicate, however, that the settlement at Abu Gerida must have played an important administrative role in gold mining operations conducted in the immediate neighborhood. In addition, there is a granite quarry nearby from which the inhabitants of Abu Gerida obtained the material to make the grinding stones used in the gold mining process.

S.E. Sidebotham

Fig 9.4: Walled enclosure, perhaps some kind of fort, atop a hill adjacent to the Ptolemaic-early Roman gold mining center Abu Gerida.

S. E. Sidebotham

Fig. 9.5: Ptolemaic gold mining settlement at Umm Howeitat al-Qibli. Houses and gold-working facilities on north side of the wadi.

Al-Ghuzza

The gold mining operations at al-Ghuzza, just south of the route linking Mons Porphyrites and Abu Sha'r to the Nile at Qena (ancient Kainepolis/ Maximianopolis), like those at Abu Gerida, also date to Ptolemaic and early Roman times and preserve, in addition to a number of edifices mostly of unknown function, several long, narrow water channels. Our survey could not be certain what function these channels served; they may have been for drinking, irrigation, washing, or gold ore processing as described so vividly by Diodorus. Possibly such channels had multifunctional purposes.

Umm Howeitat al-Qibli

Probably the most informative ancient gold mining operations our archaeological surveys have studied are those at Umm Howeitat al-Qibli (Fig. 9.5). The impressive and sizeable remains at this site appear on both sides of a generally east–west running wadi. On the south side is a large walled enclosure with multiple rooms, which may have had an administrative function (Fig. 9.6). Inside it our survey team recovered portions of a small stone foot

S.E. Sidebotham

Fig 9.6: Large walled enclosure with multiple rooms on the south side of the Ptolemaic gold mining settlement at Umm Howeitat al-Qibli.

from a long-lost statue, probably of a reclining lion or sphinx. Walls of this structure were built of local stone and a number of recycled gold ore grinding stones. On the northern side of the wadi—amid which the 'Ababda still use a well of unknown date for watering their goats, donkeys, and camels— lay scores of dilapidated structures, probably living quarters. Some shafts survive tunneled horizontally into the adjacent mountainside. Nearby was a gold ore processing area complete with grinding stones and fist-sized quartz pounders used, no doubt, in efforts to remove the ore from the surrounding stone—mainly quartz. All the pottery we collected at Umm Howeitat al-Qibli dates to the third and second centuries BC indicating that the mines had not been worked earlier and had been abandoned thereafter.

A little farther north of Umm Howeitat al-Qibli, in the region of Umm Russ, are the scant remains of an early Roman mining operation, now almost entirely obliterated by the presence of a large and still impressive modern British mining camp erected at the turn of the nineteenth and twentieth centuries. A branch of the Via Nova Hadriana, which we found during our survey of that road between 1996 and 1999, leads off to these mines, which attests their importance into at least the early second century AD.

GIOVANNI BATTISTA BROCCHI

Giovanni Battista Brocchi was born in Bassano del Grappa, Italy in 1772. He is best known for his interest in mineralogy and botany, especially in Italy. He studied at the University of Pisa and was eventually appointed professor of botany at Brescia. He published on these subjects as they pertained to Italy. Brocchi's interest in Egypt came relatively late in his life. He sailed there in 1823 to study the geology and was supported in his endeavors, as were many of his European contemporaries, by Muhammad 'Ali Pasha. His *Giornale delle osservazioni fatte ne'viaggi in Egitto, nella Siria e nella Nubia* was published posthumously in two volumes in 1841. Volume II is especially important as in it Brocchi mentions a number of ancient sites in the Eastern Desert noted by no other European travelers until our own surveys. Unfortunately, Brocchi died prematurely in Khartoum, Sudan in 1826 at the age of fifty-four.

Conclusion

While numerous gold mines and settlements from various periods of Egyptian history have been located, few have been investigated in any detail. More effort should be made to study and understand the ancient mining techniques and the methods ancient peoples used to live and work in Egypt's hyper-arid Eastern Desert.

Living in the Desert

I n order to have a better insight into the day-to-day lives of people living in the Eastern Desert we must examine their domestic architecture in both military and civilian contexts. While surviving examples range from the Prehistoric period until early Christian times, we will focus on the Ptolemaic and Roman era when evidence indicates a relatively large population living in the area on a more or less permanent basis.

As a result of extensive survey work throughout the Eastern Desert, archaeologists have found large numbers of architectural remains. Many are immediately recognizable as temples, warehouses, areas of industrial activity (mining and quarrying related processes, metal and glass working, and brick making), fortified and unfortified road stations, as well as other public buildings and domestic structures. There are also thousands of road marking cairns and, especially along the Myos Hormos–Coptos road, about sixty-five to seventy signal and watch towers *(skopeloi)*.

The original or main function of many structures, however, often cannot be determined. Some buildings, clearly, had multiple purposes. We must assume that sizeable numbers of structures, whatever else they might have been, also served as domestic spaces for living, cooking, sleeping, or relaxing. Ptolemaic road stations and mining communities present us with the problem of identification of work as opposed to domestic areas. Since no Ptolemaic-era desert settlements have ever been excavated, we can only hazard a guess as to which rooms, based only on walls visible above ground level, might have served domestic functions.

Some of the most easily identifiable domestic/residential structures, however, can be found inside Roman military installations. The *centuriae* (barracks) of Roman soldiers are canonical in their appearance and general location inside Roman forts throughout the empire; these *centuriae* mimicked in stone, brick, and timber the ground plans of tents that Roman troops pitched while on campaign anywhere in the empire and would, theoretically, have accommodated a group of eight men. The Romans called this small unit a *contubernium*. Rooms in other enigmatic late Roman era settlements also clearly served domestic purposes, as we shall see later in this chapter.

Our investigation of domestic architecture will estimate the size of the populations of some of these ancient desert communities as well. The vast majority of the settlements discussed here—mining, quarrying, military, and those of unknown function—scattered throughout the Eastern Desert, have not been examined to any extent. Some have been surveyed, that is, drawn in plan, but very few have been excavated. Thus, we can only surmise that a substantial percentage of structures in any one of these communities served as areas of domestic activity. Determining the sizes of the ancient populations that dwelt in these various settlements is, thus, very tentative as we cannot be at all certain which structures were places where people lived as opposed to those used for more public activities, storage, or animal pens. Nevertheless, estimates have been made for the quarries at Mons Claudianus, a small nearby satellite quarry at Umm Huyut, at Mons Porphyrites, and at Mons Ophiates. Archaeologists, including ourselves and others, have also calculated numbers of inhabitants for the late Roman gold mining settlement at Bir Umm Fawakhir, for five late Roman desert communities, for the fort at Abu Sha'r, for some of the *praesidia* in the desert, especially those excavated by the French along the Myos Hormos–Coptos road, and for some amethyst and emerald mines. Very approximate estimates have also been made for population numbers at Berenike and Myos Hormos.

The Earliest Inhabitants of the Desert

The Eastern Desert was not always as inhospitable as it is today. Prior to the last Ice Age, about twelve thousand years ago, the region received more precipitation, which resulted in the presence of a larger variety and number of flora and fauna. Stone tools show that already in the Late Paleolithic period (before about 10,000 BC) both the desert and Red Sea coast were inhabited. These people were not isolated from the rest of the population of Egypt; some of the earliest evidence for contact between the Nile Valley and the Red Sea dates to about 10,000 BC.

At Sodmein, some thirty-five kilometers west–northwest of Quseir, a cave part way up a limestone cliff forms the oldest known human shelter in the Eastern Desert (Fig. 10.1). Inside, Belgian archaeologists excavated seven archaeological levels of the Middle and Late Paleolithic period the oldest one of which dates back approximately 115,000 years. This layer contained huge fireplaces and stone tools. In a much later phase, just after 5000 BC, the Belgian team excavated the earliest remains of domestic goats thus far identified in Egypt.

The settlements of the Badarian period (5500–about 4000 BC) along the Nile in Upper Egypt comprised temporary structures. People used the huts, windbreaks and storage pits to support themselves in small-scale agricultural, fishing, and hunting activities. It is likely that they also sent occasional hunting expeditions deep into the Eastern Desert.

S.E. Sidebotham

Fig. 10.1: Sodmein Cave, occupied in the Paleolithic (Old Stone Age) period. Note figure standing at mouth of cave.

Later, some domiciles undoubtedly comprised light structures, like the 3500 BC house excavated in Hierakonpolis, which consisted of a wooden frame covered with reeds and skins atop a wooden wall. Similar types of buildings were still used in the Roman period, when they housed workers of the quarries and goldmines in the Eastern Desert. Temporary structures like the tents of the modern 'Ababda Bedouin, made of wooden skeletons covered with skins and mats may also have been used.

Most domestic architecture in these earlier periods, however, has left no trace in the archaeological record. For example, the Early Dynastic (soon after 3000 BC) quarry at Manzal al-Seyl, located about seventy-five kilometers northwest of Hurghada and south of Ras Gharib (discussed in Chapter 4), preserves few if any huts or other structures, aside from some stone rings. This suggests that tents or other portable and impermanent forms of housing were used to accommodate the workmen. Since no potshards were found either during the initial discovery of the site or when we visited it in 1997, dating is difficult. Nor can the age of Manzal al-Seyl be determined from symbols appearing on the stone vessel blanks left abandoned in the quarries. Since, however, the quarries produced numerous stone vessels made of green tuff and tuffaceous limestone, which were used for burial offerings only in the First–Third Dynasties (2920–2575 BC), they must date to this era.

During the early Twelfth Dynasty (Middle Kingdom) and extending into the early New Kingdom period a coastal settlement came into being on a coral terrace at Marsa Gawasis. An industrial area with kilns for copper working indicates that this settlement was inhabited for longer periods, although the houses were simple structures and, apparently, only for temporary use.

The earliest evidence of domestic architecture that our own fieldwork has revealed thus far was in Wadi Abu Mawad. Many small single, double, triple, and quadruple roomed structures hugged the lower edges of some steep but low mountains along both sides of a relatively narrow and winding wadi. Structures were built of locally available stones in haphazard plans. The shards we gathered for study were not Ptolemaic, Roman, or Islamic so, by default, they had to be pharaonic. We could not determine when in pharaonic times this settlement had been occupied, but a number of pictographs carved onto the walls of rock outcrops survive nearby

DAVID MEREDITH

David Meredith received his PhD at University College London in 1954. In contrast to others who visited and wrote about the Eastern Desert noted throughout this book, Meredith was more of a library scholar. He apparently did not care for the desert all that much. Relying mainly upon the notes and observations of others, he nevertheless produced impressive publications that were quite thorough in their presentation. According to Leo Tregenza, with whom Sidebotham had two interviews, one in 1988 and the last in 1993, Meredith only visited the Eastern Desert twice. Nevertheless, he was incredibly prolific throughout the decade of the 1950s, writing many articles and producing in 1958 an important map of the Greco-Roman antiquities known in the Eastern Desert for the important *Tabula Imperii Romani* series.

including one of a giraffe; whether this rock art was contemporary with the settlement remains uncertain. This conglomeration of structures was probably a mining camp though we could not be certain of this identification. Nearby were numbers of shallow pits on the side of a hill, perhaps the remains of some prospecting activities associated with this community.

Settlements of the Ptolemaic and Roman Period

As noted above, we know much more about later settlements, especially of the Roman era, when activities in the Eastern Desert intensified and logistics were dramatically improved. During this period the functions of these sites are more evident, but not necessarily mutually exclusive. This is especially true at the mines and the quarries, where the bulk of the populations were civilian, but where there was also clearly a military presence.

Stone Quarry Settlements

The forts guarding the quarry sites of Mons Claudianus, Mons Porphyrites, and Mons Ophiates (in Wadi Umm Wikala) also contain rooms, some of which must have served as sleeping and eating areas, though both would not necessarily have been found in the same room, as was the case at Abu Sha'r, which we discuss more below. It is often difficult to determine which activities many of these spaces originally served as functions for a specific room may well have changed over the life of the facility in which it was located and, in some instances, rooms were later abandoned, often cleared of their interior décor, and converted to trash dumps where huge amounts of rubbish were deposited. The latter was true at Mons Claudianus and at Abu Sha'r.

Mons Claudianus

The archaeologists who most recently surveyed and excavated at Mons Claudianus made some population estimates. The smaller fort (the excavators referred to this structure as the "*hydreuma*"), near the large fort, accommodated about fifty men while they calculated that the nearby workers' village housed about 150 persons. This is only a small portion of the site. The few graves found around the settlement and their extremely robbed condition precluded population estimates based on mortality figures gleaned from burials. An interesting ostracon found during the excavations, however, lists the distribution of water to those present on the site on a specific day in about AD 110, an era of intense activity at the site of Mons Claudianus. The text names 917 people of whom at least sixty, maybe more, were soldiers. Of course, these numbers would have fluctuated over the course of any given year and, naturally, as operations at the quarries waxed and waned over the centuries.

Mons Porphyrites

At the Mons Porphyrites quarries British archaeologists found several areas of habitation scattered over a wide area dating from the first through fifth centuries AD. While some ancient burials, mostly badly robbed, were studied (see Chapter 8), the ancient written documents found at the site during British excavations between 1994 and 1998 do not provide, unlike those at Mons Claudianus, any indication of the extent of the population here at any point in antiquity. An approximation of the number of people (excluding nearby support stations in Wadi Umm Sidri, and at Badia') can, nevertheless, be made based upon analysis of seven major areas of habitation in the region of the quarries. The settlements from south to north include: Southwest village, Loading Ramp village, Lykabettus village, Porphyrites fort (and village just to the south), Foot village, Northwest village, and Bradford village.

Southwest village preserves about eighty rooms in a number of structures. Some rooms are large enough to accommodate more than one
person. We estimate eighty to one hundred sixty people lived here. Loading Ramp village was smaller, with about twenty-five to thirty relatively
small rooms that could, we calculate, have accommodated about twenty to
twenty-five people. Lykabettus village seems to have been relatively large
with over sixty-two rooms some of which could have housed more than
one person. We estimate that sixty to one hundred twenty people could
have resided here. The large fort in Wadi Ma'mal, called by the excavators
'Porphyrites fort,' and associated, but very ruined, Workers' village just to
the south, are difficult to calculate as the village is in such ruinous condition. The fort preserves numerous rooms of which we estimate twenty-four
to thirty were for habitation. Thus, the fort itself perhaps accommodated
on a permanent basis thirty to thirty-five people and the ruined village to
the south several dozen. Foot village preserves only sixteen rooms, which
are not large, suggesting a maximum population of ten to fifteen people.
The Northwest village was somewhat larger (with about forty rooms)
capable of housing at least thirty-five to forty people. Bradford village was
by far the smallest and was used for a relatively short period of time. Its
approximately ten potentially inhabitable rooms within seven buildings
suggest a population of eight to ten persons. Thus, the seven villages and
one fort in the Mons Porphyrites area accommodated approximately 267
to 441 more or less 'permanent' inhabitants. If we consider outlying pock-
ets of a few workmen here and there living in temporary shelters or small
rock enclosures, guards at the various watch towers scattered around the
site plus the crews arriving and departing to haul the stone, this would add
another several dozen to perhaps one hundred persons. This would make
the entire operation at Mons Porphyrites about half the size of that at Mons
Claudianus, that is, about four hundred to five hundred persons, when
crews hauling stone to the Nile were present.

Wadi Umm Wikala/Wadi Semna
We conducted survey work between 1997 and 2000 at the first to early third
century AD Roman quarry at Wadi Umm Wikala/Wadi Semna (ancient
Mons Ophiates). After Mons Claudianus and Mons Porphyrites, Mons
Ophiates was the third largest hard stone quarry operating in the Roman

period in the Eastern Desert. Yet, despite this, we determined that the residents in the two main areas of surviving structures, one near the quarries in Wadi Umm Wikala, and the other in a large *praesidium* about 1.8 kilometers to the south in Wadi Semna, numbered only approximately one hundred to two hundred. We calculated that the ninety-three extant rooms accommodated about two persons each with some rooms, of course, used for storage or administrative purposes. These figures do not take into account buildings washed away by desert floods, of which there was good evidence, and they also do not consider the several dozen outlying quarries that were worked at different times, and not simultaneously, throughout the life of the site. Judging from the sizes of the various quarried areas anywhere from a few to perhaps a few dozen worked at each location. Rarely do any structures survive in the more remote quarries suggesting no long term activities took place there; as with some of the other quarries and mines examined in this chapter, it is likely that many workmen lived in tents, which have left no trace. Again, population figures would have fluctuated as work at the quarries waxed and waned and as Nile-based crews came and went to haul stone and bring in supplies.

Umm Huyut

In June 1993 our survey located, based on analysis of the abundant pottery we collected there, a small early Roman (first–second century AD) community and associated quarries at Umm Huyut. Only about six kilometers as the crow flies (about fifteen kilometers by desert track) south of the main center in Mons Claudianus, this diminutive settlement comprised only fourteen buildings made of dry laid stone. One of these was a large public structure approached by two staircases; it would not have served any domestic purpose, but was either religious or administrative. The remainder of the rooms ranged in size from relatively small to sizeable. There was also a lookout post or well-preserved hut above one of the quarries. We estimate that perhaps twenty people resided at Umm Huyut.

Mining Settlements

The various mining settlements—gold, amethyst, and some of the beryl/emerald—usually preserve buildings comprising low walls about one to one and a half meters high consisting of one, two, less often three, and rarely four rooms. We assume, since the walls of the vast majority of these quickly erected edifices are relatively low and there is little tumble surrounding them, that the superstructures were likely made of more perishable materials such as matting tied to upright wooden poles, or some type of tent-like edifices. The rooms are invariably relatively small and are roundish and oval to rectangular in plan. Frequently though not always, one room usually could not be reached from inside an abutting room via a common doorway; those wishing to move from one room to the next often had to go outside and enter the adjacent room by a separate portal.

Some rooms contained a single raised feature made of stone (a *mastaba*) that may have served as a bed. Other rooms attached to those with *mastaba*s, were too small for humans to have occupied and likely served as storerooms or animal pens. In a few rare instances small niches or bins also survived inside some of the rooms. On occasion the fronts of those structures comprising multiple rooms had a small raised courtyard. We have rarely found any evidence of burning (suggesting that there was cooking) in any of these rooms; perhaps much of that type of activity took place out of doors. This would have been especially prudent and necessary if the superstructures of these buildings had been made of highly flammable tent-like material or matting. In addition, heat generated by cooking fires in such small enclosed spaces would have been intense and rather unbearable especially in the summer months.

The presence of very few, or lack of any, structures at some of the mining sites, and in areas that have clearly not been washed away by desert flash floods, suggests that some temporary non-stone made features catered to the needs of the workers. The reasons for dearth of more permanent architectural remains indicate in these instances that the work at such quarries and mines was either of short duration overall or of a brief enough period of time each season that more permanent dwellings were not viewed as necessary.

Gold Mining Settlements
Samut

In a gold mining center at Samut, north of the large fort in the wadi of the same name, situated near the ancient road linking Berenike to Edfu, we located another impressive settlement comprising work areas, ramps and platforms, and several substantial walled buildings including one that resembled a fort. This impressive 'fort' had in its interior a series of large rooms, which must have included residential areas, but if so, they did not resemble, in size anyway, any structures of similar function we have seen elsewhere in the region. Pottery from this site, which included some interesting amphora handles stamped with marks of those who made them, indicated activity here in the late Persian occupation and Ptolemaic eras (fourth century BC into third and perhaps second century BC).

Umm Howeitat al-Qibli

In 1998 our survey spent five days in two separate visits drawing a detailed plan of the large Ptolemaic gold mining settlement at Umm Howeitat al-Qibli. Divided into two sections by a wadi oriented roughly east–west, the south side of the settlement comprised a few small structures, but was dominated by a large walled installation, resembling a fort, which must have been the administrative center of the community. Interestingly, the walls of this fort-like structure, which preserved a large open area with rooms on the southern and eastern sides, included many recycled gold ore grinding stones.

The preponderance of the architectural remains at Umm Howeitat al-Qibli, however, consisted of buildings on the north side of the wadi. These included areas where ore processing took place—the fist-sized quartz hand pounders were still laying in bunches—around a somewhat elevated work platform; saddle-shaped grinding stones lay nearby (Fig. 9.2). Clearly, in addition to working here, many people also lived on this side of the wadi. Most structures on the northern side of the site were in very ruinous condition. The majority had such dilapidated walls that few entrances or other details could be identified. In this area we picked up a small early Ptolemaic bronze coin. Pottery shards were abundant and dated activity at the site in the early to middle Ptolemaic period (third–mid second century BC).

Many of the small to medium-sized rooms inside structures found toward the eastern and western ends of the northern side of the wadi at Umm Howeitat al-Qibli undoubtedly served residential purposes. Many of the structures on the north side of the wadi were too small for public activities involving more than a few people and were also clearly separated, in some cases apparently by long partition walls, from the areas where 'industrial' and work-related functions took place. Those work areas that we readily identified lay more or less in the center of the settlement on the north side of the wadi; smaller structures, in some cases no doubt domestic areas, lay to the east and west of the work areas.

Bir Umm Fawakhir

As mentioned in Chapter 9, a team from the Oriental Institute of the University of Chicago conducted a detailed survey and limited excavations in the 1990s at the late Roman/early Byzantine period (fourth to sixth centuries AD) gold mining settlement at Bir Umm Fawakhir. This site is located in the Wadi Hammamat about halfway along the Myos Hormos–Nile road. The Chicago team counted the number of structures at the site (Pl. 10.1), which were scattered up and down several adjacent wadis, and concluded that, at its zenith, there were approximately one thousand people in residence at Bir Umm Fawakhir. This was certainly an impressive number and the logistics of supplying everyone and the various animals there with adequate food and water must have been considerable.

Amethyst Mining Settlement

Wadi Abu Diyeiba

In June 2004 during our survey of the Ptolemaic and early Roman amethyst mines in the Wadi Abu Diyeiba area, about twenty-five kilometers southwest of Safaga, we were surprised to find so few structures of any kind since we counted about four hundred to five hundred trenches, some up to one hundred meters long by twenty meters deep by three meters wide, where digging for amethysts took place. A potentially sizeable, but unknown number of workmen were employed to remove these semiprecious stones; yet we found in three different locations a combined total of less than about twenty structures and some of these were clearly not for domestic use. Many, if not most, of the stone building remains lay some distance from the areas where the amethysts were mined. We must conclude that the bulk of those working and residing in the Wadi Abu Diyeiba mining area likely lived in tents, which, of course, have left no traces in the archaeological record. How extensive the use of tents might have been and to what degree this hinders estimation of numbers of residents are questions that remain to be answered.

Emerald/Beryl Settlements

Some desert communities were surprisingly large and the buildings well crafted. Among these are the emerald and beryl mining settlements at Sikait and Nugrus (see Chapter 12), for example, which consisted of hundreds of edifices. At these mining centers builders paid much more attention to construction techniques than we find at most sites in the Eastern Desert. This was due primarily to the nature of the locally available building stone which, when quarried, sheered off in thin flat sections that could be easily stacked. This is in great contrast to most desert settlements that were made of locally available cobbles and small boulders picked up off the desert floor in their environs. The thin flat stone slabs allowed construction of thicker and more stable walls. This, in turn, permitted the creation of multiple-storied structures fashioned with great care. The larger edifices at Sikait and Nugrus have substantial walls of some height (up to four meters) and thickness (over a meter) with surviving windows, multiple doors, often of impressive dimensions, many with lintels extant, interior niches and shelves, and other accoutrements (Pl. 10.2). Some clearly had stone roofs intact while others were likely of stone or timber, which has long since disappeared. While these larger structures were likely for public rather than private use, we have excavated several edifices at Sikait that were clearly domestic, at least in their primary functions.

During summer 2002 and winter 2002–2003 we excavated trenches in the lowest areas of the mining community at Sikait on both the eastern and western sides of the wadi that bisects the site. We found well-built structures that had large open, walled-in courtyards in which a range of domestic activities took place. These included cultivation of small gardens (Fig. 10.2). Gardening was evident from the numerous small stone boxes used, no doubt, to contain wooden trellis works for plants, bushes, shrubs, or small trees (see Chapter 12). Several of the open courtyards also preserved evidence of small-scale industrial activities and, likely, limited animal husbandry. These pastimes would have alleviated the boredom and supplemented the diets of those living and working here with some fresh produce. Most of the food consumed here was likely hauled great distances from the Nile Valley and to a lesser extent from the Red Sea.

One high status multiple-storied residence at Sikait had operated from the turn of the Christian era until late antiquity (Figs. 10.3–10.4). In this

S.E. Sidebotham

Fig. 10.2: Remains of stone boxes that contained wooden trellises for plants in a courtyard of one of the houses at Sikait. Scale = twenty centimeters.

building we recovered some of the earliest items found during our excavations: a few possible Nabataean shards and a Nabataean coin, which
arrived on the site sometime at the turn of the Christian era or some
decades thereafter.

We found remains of a few wells in the wadi linking Sikait to two sister settlements, those at Middle Sikait and North Sikait, but most wells and water
sources were long ago buried beneath flood-borne sediments carried
through the wadi by torrential rains (see Chapters 2 and 13). Should we ever
be able to locate these wells using ground penetrating radar and somehow
determine when in the lives of these settlements the various water sources
were used, we could begin to obtain some idea of the population sizes of the
communities that served them. The large numbers of graves surrounding the
settlements in Wadi Sikait and Nugrus have been badly robbed and dates for
their deposition, therefore, cannot, in many instances, be determined. Thus,
attempting to calculate population sizes at different points in the histories of
Nugrus or Sikait (both of which operated at least from the first to the sixth
centuries AD) based upon the associated cemeteries, is not possible.

Fig. 10.3: High-status multiple-storied residence at the Roman-era community at Sikait.

1 reconstruction
2 storage bin
3 courtyard with ovens and hearths
4 storage room
5 narrow passage with a stone roof
6 main entrance
7 central courtyard
8 stone stairway to the second floor

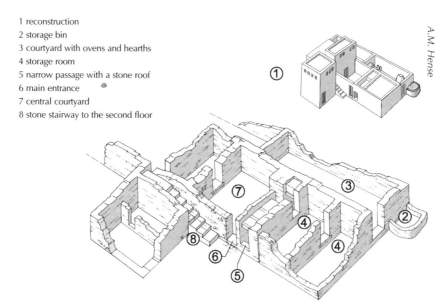

Fig. 10.4: Reconstruction of one of the high-status multiple-storied residences at the Roman-era settlement at Sikait shown in Fig. 10.3.

Praesidia

The numerous *praesidia* (Roman forts) examined during our surveys both along the several ancient trans-desert roads and at quarries, and those sites excavated by other European teams, especially along the Myos Hormos–Coptos road and inside the quarry forts at Mons Claudianus and Mons Porphyrites, suggest that barracks for troops are less easily identified in those cases until excavation provides additional clues. In the *praesidia* many rooms abut the interior faces of the main fort walls. Where excavated, some have proven to be store rooms, baths, and headquarters; others undoubtedly served more domestic purposes.

Abu Sha'r

The best example of domestic quarters for the Roman military in the Eastern Desert appears in the late Roman fort at Abu Sha'r, which we discussed in Chapter 3.

Fifty-four *centuriae* (barracks for troops) are readily apparent in the area between the north gate and the *principia* (headquarters). Some of the additional thirty-eight or thirty-nine rooms found abutting the interior faces of the main enceinte of the fort may also have served as barracks, but we cannot be certain of this as we excavated only a few of the rooms of the *centuriae* and even fewer rooms adjacent to the main fort walls during our expedition between 1987 and 1993. Each barracks room measured only about three by three or three by four meters, a relatively small space that would have accommodated at most three men in very cramped conditions (Pl. 10.3). Thus, there was no room for a *contubernium* (tent group), consisting of eight men. The small living area meant that few domestic activities other than sleeping could have occurred in these *centuriae*. In the southwestern part of the fort, one room where the roof had collapsed subsequently had dumped in it numbers of large skeletons and huge shells of green sea turtles mixed with other types of trash. In this and similar circumstances determining the original function of such rooms is extremely difficult or impossible.

Most dining for troops stationed at Abu Sha'r would likely have been communal and in rotation and would have taken place elsewhere inside the fort. In the southeastern interior part of the fort our excavations in the summers of 1991 and 1992, in fact, uncovered an extensive food preparation

area including a large oven with a floor made of kiln-fired bricks measuring
3.4 meters in diameter (Pl. 10.4). Remains of wood, some pieces of which
were embedded with nails, indicating some previous use, lay nearby. This
was clearly destined for consumption as fuel in the oven. There were also
quantities of ash that had recently been removed from the oven. Located in
the same large, and we assume only partially roofed, room with the oven
were fragments of grinding stones made of vesicular basalt. These would
have been used to grind grain or other foodstuffs. Five long and barrel
vaulted granaries (called *horrea* in Latin) lay immediately west of and adjacent to this kitchen area. We never located any large room, which we could
definitively identify as a mess hall/dining facility. Most extra-curricular
activities involving several men, such as gaming and gambling—as we know
from a number of game boards recovered in our excavations—would in all
probability also have taken place in areas other than the barracks. Due to the
number of gaming boards we found in one room abutting the southern interior fort wall, we surmised that it might have served primarily as an
entertainment area.

Let us estimate the numbers residing at the late Roman fort at Abu Sha'r.
Identifying fifty-four small barracks and probably others abutting the fort
walls and with no more than two or three men per barracks, we arrive at a
rough calculation of approximately 150 to 200 men garrisoning this fort. As
this was a mounted unit (known from the fragmentary Latin inscription we
found tumbled at the west gate—see Chapter 3), probably dromedary
rather than cavalry, the space allotted to each soldier may have been more
generous than for infantry.

Apollonos Fort in Wadi Gemal

Other estimates of population sizes of Roman forts in the desert include
calculations made for the garrison at Apollonos, probably located in Wadi
Gemal. An ostracon that was part of the archive of the Nikanor family,
discussed in Chapter 7, records some grain supplied to the installation
there. Based on this document various modern estimates put the total garrison strength somewhere between sixteen and thirty-six men. Yet, the
structure we see today is one of the largest forts surviving in the entire Eastern Desert. Two huge walls of this fort, though badly damaged and with the
other two completely washed away, measure 119 meters and 78 meters long

respectively. Sixteen to thirty-six men could not possibly have been sufficient to defend such a large installation. The ruined walls we see today, were, in all probability, erected after the Nikanor ostracon was written. In its substantially larger and later manifestation, perhaps over two hundred men garrisoned this 0.92 hectare-large cantonment.

Forts on the Myos Hormos–Coptos Road

French archaeologists made some interesting estimates of garrison sizes of Roman *praesidia* they examined along the Myos Hormos–Coptos road. They based these on space available and notations in ostraca from the excavations of the forts. Ostraca were recovered from the forts of Maximianon and westward toward Coptos on the Nile; none east of Maximianon were found. The garrisons there, along with the ostraca, were primarily from the period of the Flavian emperors (Vespasian and his sons Titus and Domitian, AD 69–96) until those of Trajan (AD 98–117) and Hadrian (AD 117–138)—probably also the era when the large fort in Wadi Gemal, discussed above, was erected. Some of the *praesidia* clearly continued to operate into the later second century AD; there was limited evidence at a few of the stations of late Roman occupation and activity.

One specialist on the Roman military allots 5 to 6 square meters for each legionary, 2.84 to 3.82 square meters for each auxiliary and six square meters for each cavalryman in a typical Roman camp environment, while another scholar suggests between 2 and 4.5 square meters per man. As we know from the ostraca, the *praesidia* on the Myos Hormos–Nile road also accommodated women and children, however, which makes the calculations of these archaeologists somewhat artificial. Nevertheless, in the *praesidium* of Maximianon (which measures overall in its interior space 51.22 by 51.8 meters) estimates range of a garrison strength of 28 to 42 men (a *turma*—unit—of cavalry was 30 to 32 men) to calculations at the low end of 15 to 17 men.

Red Sea Ports

Quseir al-Qadim/Myos Hormos

At the port of Quseir al-Qadim (ancient Myos Hormos) a large multiple-roomed area, excavated by the American team in the late 1970s and early 1980s and dubbed the Indian quarter (Fig. 10.5), preserved evidence suggesting that people often lived, manufactured, and sold wares or conducted their businesses in the same location. Continued excavations by a British team between 1999 and 2003 revealed much additional information about this emporium. The ancient name was definitively proven to be Myos Hormos, thus ending a lengthy scholarly controversy. The British excavators believed that the number of inhabitants varied seasonally, but when ships were in port, there was an estimated population of about one thousand, perhaps somewhat more.

Berenike

At Berenike in the so-called late Roman (late fourth–fifth century AD) commercial-residential quarter, located between the Serapis temple and the church, it was clear that the large multiple-storied structures dominating this portion of the city had a dual function (Figs. 10.6–10.7 and Pls. 10.5–10.6). The ground floors were areas where business was conducted while the upper floor or floors, which had collapsed upon the lower, were rooms where domestic activities took place. Pottery from these upper floors was invariably coarse cooking crockery or finer tablewares used for dining; these types of pottery are prime archaeological indicators of domestic activities. This arrangement of public work and business areas on

S.E. Sidebotham

Fig. 10.5: The large multiple-roomed area at the port of Quseir al-Qadim, dubbed the 'Indian Quarter.' Scale = one meter.

S.E. Sidebotham

Fig. 10.6: Structure in the late Roman (late fourth–fifth century AD) commercial-residential quarter at Berenike. Scale = one meter.

S. E. Sidebotham

Fig. 10.7: Structure in the late Roman (late fourth–fifth century AD) commercial-residential quarter at Berenike. Scale = one meter.

the ground floor and domestic-residential areas on the upper stories of a building was quite common throughout the classical Greek and Roman Mediterranean world and typical of ancient Egyptian town life as well.

Other domestic areas at Berenike included the Christian ecclesiastical building at the eastern edge of the city (Fig. 10.8), which we discussed in Chapter 6. We excavated inside this large structure between 1996 and 2001 uncovering the entire church as well as areas where cooking and other domestic activities took place. The church lay in the southern area of this ecclesiastical compound while a large east–west running corridor separated it from the northern side where a great deal of food preparation took place; one of these rooms preserved an amphora *in situ* with remains of numerous tiny anchovy bones, tell-tale evidence that the jar once contained a pungent fish sauce known to the Romans as *garum*. Although we have not completed excavations in the northern area of the Christian ecclesiastical complex, we suspect that we will also find living and sleeping facilities connected to the food preparation rooms. The amount of space for these putative living and sleeping areas in the unexcavated portions of the complex suggests that a relatively small number of people actually lived here compared to the rather extensive kitchen facilities we have uncovered. Perhaps the food preparation

S.E. Sidebotham

Fig. 10.8: Domestic area of the Christian ecclesiastical building at Berenike (left of photo scale). Scale = fifty centimeters.

areas were not solely for use by those residing here, but also accommodated others living elsewhere in the city who participated in church activities.

Early nineteenth century visitors to the ruins of Berenike attempted to estimate its ancient population. G.B. Belzoni, who discovered the site in 1818, calculated that there were about two thousand houses and arrived at a population of about ten thousand, whereas a few years later J.R. Wellsted figured between 1,000 and 1,500 houses with a population of about five thousand. These figures seem rather too high. There is no way to estimate populations of the Ptolemaic and early Roman communities at Berenike as so little of either has been excavated and no recognizable domestic architecture identified from these early periods. The best known epoch of Berenike's eight-hundred-year-long history is the late Roman, beginning in the middle of the fourth and extending into the fifth century AD. Based upon what we have excavated and calculating the numbers and sizes of rooms enclosed by the tops of walls of unexcavated structures, which are certainly from this late period, we propose a rather modest population for the late Roman city of about five hundred, perhaps upward of one thousand people or somewhat more. Since all the ancient written documents and the limited archaeological evidence we have recovered from Berenike suggest that the port was at its zenith in the early Roman period, that is, the first century AD, the population of the city then, especially when ships were in port during the times of year allowed by the monsoon winds in the Indian Ocean, would have been somewhat greater than in the late Roman city.

Settlements with Unknown Functions

Our surveys have identified over a dozen settlements with an unknown, but possibly Christian ecclesiastical function (Fig. 10.9). We investigated five of these in detail between 1996 and 2000. It was evident that these communities had originally been larger; but floods have washed away an unknown number of structures over the intervening centuries.

Determining population sizes by examining extant ancient cemeteries associated with these settlements proved impossible as we noted very few graves with no assurance that even those were directly affiliated with any of these communities. Determining numbers of residents by available water supplies was also hindered by lack of any visible evidence of sources or quantities of water that would have been accessible to those dwelling there.

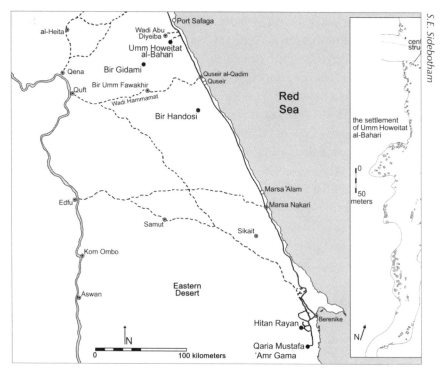

Fig. 10.9: Map of settlements with an unknown, but possibly Christian, ecclesiastical function.

Given all these limitations, however, we estimated the populations of the following: Bir Handosi with 47 structures surviving accommodated perhaps 50 people, Qaryat Mustafa 'Amr Gama with 109 extant structures housed 122 persons, Bir Gidami with 119 structures contained 131 people, Umm Howeitat al-Bahari with 126 structures accommodated 149 souls, and Hitan Rayan with 141 structures housed 176 individuals. Given their sizes, most rooms capable of human habitation could have accommodated one or occasionally two people and we see a rough parity between the number of structures and number of people at each of these sites at 1:1 with slightly more people than structures. This was probably somewhat different at other desert settlements preserving structures similar in appearance and size to those of these putative Christian communities regardless of when these other settlements would have functioned and what activities may have been associated with them. The ratio of buildings to people may have been greater in gold mining areas as they would have consumed more water and used more structures for the various phases of the gold mining process thereby leaving less water and fewer structures for human domestic activities.

Construction of Houses in the Roman Period

Most settlements in the Eastern Desert were difficult to access from the Nile. Although dragging building materials from the Nile Valley to the desert was occasionally undertaken, most structures erected in the Eastern Desert comprised materials available in the immediate neighborhood, especially unshaped cobbles and small boulders dry-laid or erected using mud mortar. The absence of abundant water supplies in the Eastern Desert made large-scale use of bricks, by far the most important building material for houses, palaces, and forts in the Delta and the Nile Valley, a rare phenomenon. We do have, however, a number of examples of mud-brick architecture especially at the fort at Abu Sha'r (Fig. 10.10), and in some of the *praesidia*

S. E. Sidebotham

Fig. 10.10: Mud-brick architecture at the fort at Abu Sha'r. Scale = one meter.

on the Abu Sha'r/Mons Porphyrites–Nile road at Deir al-Atrash and at al-Heita. Fired brick is rather more common than might be expected, used in some quantity in hydraulic installations, especially water catchment basins. These fired bricks were, likely, imported from the Nile Valley.

Some of the Ptolemaic and Early Roman walls of the buildings in Berenike were made of sand bricks and limestone, which were rarely used in late Roman times in the city. The walls of the buildings of late Roman Berenike, on the other hand, were mainly constructed of layers of ancient softball- to basketball-sized coral heads (Fig. 10.11) reinforced with wooden beams. The coral was obtained from nearby fossilized reefs, while most of the wood, much of it teak, likely came from wind- and sea-damaged ships requiring repair. Also used, on a much lesser scale, were cobbles found on the desert plain and blocks of gypsum and anhydrite quarried from nearby Ras Banas. Some of the gypsum/anhydrite blocks were recycled from earlier buildings in the city. These blocks tended to be used as corner stones in buildings or in staircases. In the case of the church at Berenike these blocks were recycled as benches (Fig. 10.12).

In the desert area surrounding Berenike, on the other hand, building materials were very different from those used in the city. The desert installations in Wadi Kalalat, Siket, and Hitan Rayan, for example, were built of naturally occurring hard stone cobbles and small boulders, obtained from the surrounding wadis and nearby mountains. Even deeper in the desert, in the settlements of Shenshef, Sikait, and Nugrus as noted above, walls were almost exclusively made of the stone slabs quarried from the steep hill sides of the wadis. When water was available in reasonable amounts, walls were plastered with mortar or a sandy render.

Windows were usually set high in the rooms. In general elsewhere in the Roman Empire, windows in houses on the ground floor were small and had wooden, terra-cotta, stone, or iron grilles. The smaller ones had wooden shutters. Probably all windows in the Eastern Desert houses had shutters of some sort, to minimize the effects of sun and wind and keep out as much blowing sand and dust as possible. Glass windows were also known. We found window glass associated with the extramural bath at the late Roman fort at Abu Sha'r. There were a few fragments of windowpane glass found at Berenike as well. Other materials might also have been used for windowpanes, as was the case elsewhere in the Roman world.

H.M. Nouwens

Fig. 10.11: Detail of a wall constructed of coral heads in a late Roman building at Berenike.

S.E. Sidebotham

Fig. 10.12: Benches in the fifth-century church at Berenike. Scale = one meter.

Wall niches (Figs. 10.13–10.14) were a common method to create cup-
boards. Some of the niches in the houses of late Roman Berenike were
lined with small gypsum/anhydrite blocks, as was also the case in the fifth-
century church at the eastern end of the town. In other examples in
Berenike in the Late Period the niches had wooden shelves and a wooden
frame, which sometimes supported small wooden doors. In other Eastern
Desert settlements shelves of stone were used to save wood. Good examples of the latter appear at Sikait, Shenshef, Nugrus, and in the recently
destroyed *praesidium* in Wadi Semna near the hard stone quarries in Wadi
Umm Wikala (Mons Ophiates).

We even know what was placed in some of these niches. In one of the
houses of Berenike a wooden box containing large bronze nails was excavated, while those in the church had oil lamps for illumination. Several of
the houses in Berenike had niches associated with the staircases. In these
examples it is very likely that they contained oil lamps as well.

Except for the eastern end of the church, all floors thus far excavated at
Berenike have been made of beaten earth; most houses in desert settlements also had the same type of flooring. Elsewhere in the Eastern Desert
only some of the more important edifices, like the so-called Administration Building and the large rock-cut temple in Sikait, had stone paved
floors. Floors of the upper stories of the houses of Berenike had to be relatively lightweight by necessity, because the supporting walls were not
very stable. These upper floors consisted of a more complex construction,
using timber and matting supported by rows of wooden beams.

Roofs of some buildings in Berenike, Abu Sha'r, and Myos Hormos,
consisted of organic materials, such as wooden beams and layers of palm
ribs, matting, or reeds covered with mud plaster. We excavated large roof
beams approximately four meters long in late Roman houses in Berenike.
We also found wooden roof beams collapsed onto the floors of some of
the buildings in the late Roman fort at Abu Sha'r. As mentioned above,
Sikait, Nugrus, and Mons Claudianus preserve some rooms and buildings
roofed with stone slabs.

Staircases in Berenike consisted of gypsum/anhydrite ashlars, a number
of which had been recycled from earlier buildings. In some cases, these
lower stone stairs likely served as supports for wooden ladders or staircases. Sometimes in the Eastern Desert settlements, complete stone-built

Fig 10.13: Niche in building in late Roman commercial-residential quarter in Berenike. Scale = twenty centimeters.

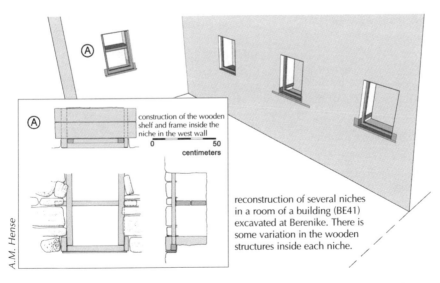

Fig. 10.14: Reconstruction of niches in a building in late Roman commercial-residential quarter in Berenike.

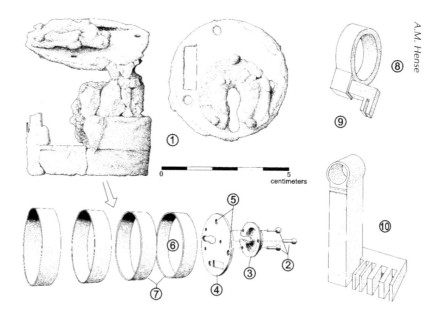

A.M. Hense

1 cyndrical lock with an iron mechanism inside (late 4th century AD)
2 bronze connection pins
3 decorative cover
4 copper-alloy closing plate with rectangular hole for locking pin
5 holes for bronze pins attached to the iron mechanism

6 iron mechanism (only small corroded fragments survive)
7 copper-alloy rings
8 small copper-alloy ring key (early 4th century AD)
9 iron key
10 copper-alloy key (4th–5th century AD)

Fig. 10.15: Keys and locks used at the late Roman Berenike buildings.

stairs survive inside courtyards, while in at least one other location they abut the outer walls of houses. This can be seen in some of the buildings at Ka'b Marfu' near Wadi Gemal.

Doorways leading into the streets had thresholds of ashlars made of gypsum or anhydrite; wooden beams supplemented some of them. One of the late Roman Berenike houses had a threshold with a bronze pivot embedded in it. Bronze facings of locking mechanisms found both at Berenike and Sikait suggest that security of the house was deemed very important. Several doors in late Roman buildings at Berenike were built or strengthened with bronze nails. There were a couple of options for locking the doors, sometimes used in combination. Locks with copper alloy or iron keys (Fig. 10.15) could be supplemented with horizontal bars and wooden props.

Conclusion

It is clear that the study of domestic architecture and the concomitant estimation of population sizes of various settlements in the Eastern Desert and
along the Red Sea coast in antiquity are in their infancy. Additional excavations must take place to identify—more accurately than surface surveying
can accomplish—the layout, construction methods and materials, location,
and numbers of domestic dwellings. Crucial to the problem of estimating
the sizes of ancient populations would be identification and quantification
of available water sources at different periods in history; estimation of population from extant funerary remains, most of which are badly looted
(Chapter 8), is clearly not an approach that, by itself, will achieve any satis-
factory results. If in the future, however, we combine counting structures
and their sizes in each community, estimating water availability and consumption for each, and using the paltry funerary evidence that does survive,
we might begin to arrive at population estimates for some of the Eastern
Desert settlements at different periods.

The Ma'aza, 'Ababda,
and Bisharin Bedouin

The Bedouin comprising the majority of the nomadic groups in the Eastern Desert in our study are, from north to south, the Ma'aza, the 'Ababda, and the Bisharin. The Ma'aza ('Goat People') comprise four clans, each of which is headed by a *sheikh*. They are the most recent of these Bedouin groups to make the Eastern Desert their home. They have their origins in the Arabian Peninsula, something that is still expressed, for instance, in the elaborate masked veils worn by the women of this Bedouin tribe.

Anthropologists include the 'Ababda and Bisharin, who are closely related through marriage, in a large grouping of tribes called the Beja. The name *Beja* derived probably from the Arabic word *badiya*, which means 'plain' or 'desert.' Of Hamitic origin, the Beja comprise perhaps two million people, and extend from southern Egypt through Sudan and into Eritrea. The Beja group also includes the 'Amariin and Hadendowa tribes in Sudan and the Beni 'Amer, mainly in Eritrea. There has been a great deal of scholarly debate about whether the Beja can be associated with desert peoples known as the Medjay who are described in pharaonic texts. There has also been academic controversy as to the relationship between the Beja and the ancient Blemmyes, Nobadae, and other tribes living in the southern part of Egypt's and northern part of Sudan's Eastern Desert in the Roman period (see Chapter 15).

The fifth century AD author Olympiodorus, a native of Thebes in Upper Egypt, reported that by his day the Blemmyes controlled the emerald mines in the Mons Smaragdus region and that one needed permission from the Blemmye king in order to visit the area. Another author named Procopius, writing in the sixth century during the reign of the late Roman Emperor Justinian I (AD 527–565), reported on the activities of the Blemmyes and Nobadae and earlier Roman attempts to play the groups off against one another or, alternatively, the Roman government's bid to co-opt them. These ancient desert peoples have left no written language as far as scholars can determine although a fascinating letter written in Greek on a papyrus from the King of the Blemmyes to his Nobadae counterpart does survive from the fifth century AD. There may also be a few material remains in the form of graves and pottery that can be associated with them.

Boundaries of the Tribes

The boundaries of the Ma'aza, the 'Ababda, and the Bisharin tribes are relatively well defined, but not as meaningful today as they were about a century ago when they were more jealously guarded by each of the groups from any encroachment by outsiders (Fig. 11.1). The Ma'aza can be found generally between the Wadi 'Araba and Wadi Sha'ayb (basically along the line of the current paved road between Za'farana on the coast and al-Krymat opposite Beni Suef on the Nile) in the north to the Quseir–Quft road in the south. Their traditional territory encompasses an area of approximately ninety thousand square kilometers, which is about the size of the US state of Indiana, or the country of Portugal. 'Ababda territory extends traditionally from about the course of the paved Quseir–Quft road in the north to the area around the market town of Shalateen, approximately ninety kilometers south of the ruins of the Greco-Roman site of Berenike. Bisharin territory extends from the Shalateen area south into Sudan. The ranges of these tribes today overlap somewhat and during the years of our survey work in the region from the 1980s into the new millennium we have seen 'Ababda in the southern areas of Ma'aza territory, Ma'aza in the northern areas of 'Ababda territory and the same farther south with the 'Ababda and the Bisharin mingling with each other.

In the nineteenth century the Ma'aza looked down on the 'Ababda because the latter were not 'true' Arabs. Battles were fought between the two groups, usually over territorial boundaries, as a vivid oral tradition

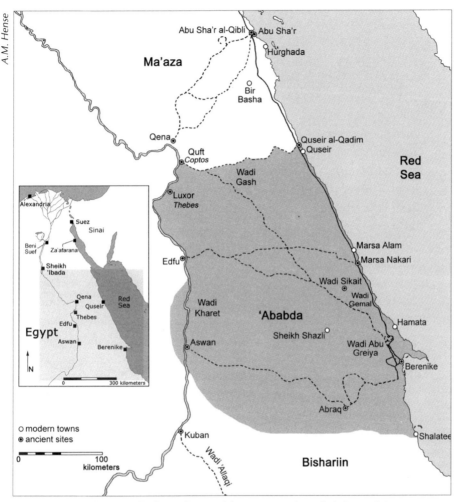

Fig. 11.1: Map showing the boundaries of the Ma'aza, the 'Ababda, and the Bisharin tribes.

recounts. Both tribes also distrusted the central government in Cairo. Wadi Gash, just south of the Quseir–Nile road, was a location where an epic engagement is reported to have taken place between the Ma'aza and Egyptian troops of the central government; according to the Ma'aza account, although greatly outnumbered, they soundly trounced the Egyptian levies. Occasionally the central government played off the various Bedouin tribes against one another with varying degrees of success.

The Ma'aza

According to their oral traditions the Ma'aza arrived only a few centuries ago from Saudi Arabia where they were known as the Beni 'Atiyya. The Swiss explorer Johann Burckhardt, traveling in the early nineteenth century, reported that the Ma'aza arrived in the Eastern Desert sometime in the 1700s having migrated from Arabia after their defeat at the hands of another tribe, the Howeitat. They came by land and by sea though the Howeitat killed many attempting overland migrations to Egypt via Sinai. Both Leo Tregenza, who traveled with the Ma'aza in 1947 and 1949, and Joseph Hobbs, who studied one of their clans in the 1980s, have written about their experiences with a variety of individuals who are members of this tribe.

Our archaeological survey work in the region north of the Quseir–Nile road has been successful due, in large part, to the help of several Ma'aza guides who are also good friends. They have not only taken us to previously known, seldom visited ancient sites that we wanted to investigate, but have also shown us, in several cases, ancient remains that are nowhere recorded by any scholars. These Ma'aza men have provided an oral encyclopaedia of the flora, fauna, geography, geology, and climate of the region as well as the ethnography of their tribe. Unfortunately, Ma'aza customs and life styles are changing rapidly. It is mostly the older men who really know the desert and how to live successfully in it. Many of the younger generation know little about the desert, its flora or fauna. Many, but by no means all, of the younger men have, instead, been lured to take regular jobs and settled life styles in one of the Red Sea coastal towns or along the Nile.

The 'Ababda

The 'Ababda (singular 'Abadi), who have their own language though one rarely hears it spoken these days, have been less affected by modern development than the Ma'aza. Prior to the arrival of the Ma'aza, the 'Ababda occupied most of the Eastern Desert. The 'Ababda trace their ancestry back to 'Abad, the eponymous founder of the tribe, who is buried in Wadi 'Abad near Edfu on the Nile. 'Abad was a descendant of the famous Zubayr ibn al-'Awwam who was a cousin of the Prophet Muhammad and one of the first converts to Islam. The 'Ababda claim to have come from Arabia and believe they arrived in Egypt about twenty-two or twenty-three generations ago, that is, sometime in the thirteenth century. Yet they also trace their descent from 'Azaz and one of his sons Kahil, originally from Kordofan in what is Sudan today. In 1353 the famous Arab traveler Ibn Battuta noted a camp of *Awlad Kahil* ('Children of Kahil') on the Red Sea coast in what is today northern Sudan and southern Egypt, between Suakin (south of Port Sudan) and 'Aidhab (Abu Ramada). James Bruce mentioned the 'Ababda group in his book in 1765 as did L.M.A. Linant de Bellefonds in the early nineteenth century. The German medical doctor C.B. Klunzinger, during his residence at Quseir in 1863–1869 and 1872–1875, also wrote about the 'Ababda, as did the German botanist Ludwig Keimer (1893–1957). The latter, originally educated as a philosopher and a lawyer, became interested in the flora and fauna of Egypt. He settled in Egypt in 1927 and was appointed professor at the University of Cairo in 1936. While searching for a rare palm tree species, he ended up in the 'Ababda territory. In 1950 Keimer collected some personal belongings from this nomadic group and published several booklets in which he drew a picture of the inhabitants between the Nile and the Red Sea in the first half of the twentieth century.

We have established close friendships with a number of 'Ababda in the area of Berenike over the years. Some of these men are extremely knowledgeable about the region and are, therefore, highly desirable as guides when we conduct our desert surveys. Moreover, we hired exclusively 'Ababda workmen for our excavations at both Berenike and also at the emerald mining settlement in Wadi Sikait. Most of the 'Ababda men and boys who work on our excavations come from Arab Saleh or Manazeq, villages near Berenike, but others hail from Hammata, Marsa 'Alam, or even from as far away as Wadi Kharet near Aswan and occasionally from Quseir or Edfu. We even opened a small exhibit in our storage magazine at Berenike that contained 'Ababda cultural artifacts, which was recently moved to a museum constructed in the Wadi Gemal National Park.

The Bisharin

Unlike the Ma'aza and 'Ababda, our projects over the years have had little contact with the Bisharin mainly because most of our work has taken place in areas north of their territory. The Bisharin, like the 'Ababda, possess their own language though Egyptian Arabic is spoken widely. The Bisharin have been impacted far less by the tidal wave of modernity that has engulfed the

more northerly Ma'aza and to some extent the 'Ababda. This is primarily
due to their more remote location, less often visited by westerners than areas
inhabited by the Ma'aza and 'Ababda. The latter have seen their share of
European tourists who flock to Egypt's Red Sea beach resorts in the area
especially between Marsa 'Alam and Hurghada and often take 'Bedouin
safaris' into the desert to meet the 'Ababda and Ma'aza, sample their food
and culture and use them as guides to visit some of the archaeological sites.
It is inevitable that this interaction between Bedouins and foreigners has left
an impression on the former, some of whom are lured by the seeming ben-
efits of a more stable, lucrative, and physically comfortable settled existence.

Bedouin Housing

Given their peripatetic lifestyle, Bedouin housing traditionally has to be easy
to put up and take down. For the Ma'aza this entails tents made of woven
goat wool erected over a wooden frame, which they call *beit sha'r* (house of
hair). With each passing year, however, fewer and fewer such tents remain
in use as more of the Ma'aza opt for a less nomadic existence.

The 'Ababda living arrangements are somewhat different from the
Ma'aza. Traditionally the 'Ababda abode is not a tent in the true sense of the
word, but rather a structure made of woven mats *(burush)*, skins and woven
carpets *(shamlat)* draped over and tied to a framework of wooden stakes or
bifurcated rootstocks and cross beams, connected with rope made of wool
and goat hair (Pl. 11.1). These edifices, which are called *buyut burush* (singular: *beit birsh)*, are still readily evident throughout the region, but
nowadays, modern materials such as discarded metal, plywood, or even
cardboard are increasingly popular, too, as building materials (Fig. 11.2).
We once even saw an 'Ababda structure made entirely of recycled metal
cans. Near the sea, where sufficient driftwood is available, the 'Ababda also
construct wooden houses.

The entrances of the *buyut burush* usually face east to catch the rising sun
and to minimize the effects of prevailing north winds. Most household items
hang from the ceiling to protect them from ravenous goats and provide
more ground space for living. In general, the 'Ababda have no furniture
except floor mats and carpets (Figs. 11.3–11.4). In the last few years, the
government has attempted to settle them by providing concrete and cinder
block housing in places like Arab Saleh, a village fifteen kilometers north of

H.M. Nouwens

Fig. 11.2: 'Ababda house, made of all kinds of materials.

A.M. Hense

Fig. 11.3: Interior of the 'Ababda *beit birsh*.

Fig 11.4: Interior of 'Ababda house: baby in cradle.

Berenike. Even so they often construct *buyut burush* in the courtyards of these buildings. Yet, many 'Ababda have not completely given up the nomadic way of life, since the unpredictable and sporadic rain still dictates where their animals can graze. In dry years, for example, the 'Ababda take their sheep and goats as far south as Gebel 'Elba, where the animals profit from the regular rainfall in this area.

Bisharin dwellings, storage facilities, and animal pens are usually round or rectilinear in plan and comprise a series of upright poles made of long branches of trees. Small numbers of branches are bundled and tied together and placed upright to form the walls of the house. The roofs are also made of wood and can be either conical in shape or flat (Fig. 11.5). Sometimes mud is applied to coat these structures.

Foods

The staple diet of the present-day Bedouin mainly consists of different types of unleavened bread made from a mixture of flour, salt, and water, soups made of lentils, or dried leaves of the *mulukhiya* (a spinach-like vegetable), sugar, tea, and coffee. Traditionally flour was made by grinding

S.E. Sidebotham

Fig. 11.5: Bisharin hut of tree branches.

wheat or sorghum kernels with the aid of small stone rotary querns. Nowadays, however, most foodstuffs mentioned above, including ready-milled flour, are easily obtained in shops and markets.

Originally, _asida,_ a type of porridge, was among the grain-based staples as well. It was traditionally prepared in a stone cooking pot called a _burma_ or _gidur_ made from _barram,_ a soft talc/schist. Some of these _burmas_ can frequently be seen, along with other mementos, at the 'Ababda graves in the Eastern Desert. Today, however, most Bedouin prefer the various types of bread. The latter encompasses primarily _gurs/gaburi, rudaf/marduf_ and _rugag,_ which we introduced briefly in Chapter 5.

Gurs or _gaburi_ is an incredibly tasty, unleavened bread comprising flour, salt, and water. It is made by burning fuel in a small shallow hole dug, optimally, in fine clean sand (Fig. 11.6). Once the flames have subsided, the unleavened, pizza-shaped dough is placed in the hole and covered with embers and sand. The sand retains the heat and bakes the bread, which is turned over once after about fifteen minutes. If the charcoal, for instance derived from the twisted acacia, consists of solid pieces and is handled with care, it is possible to finish the bread with the same charcoal coals. The

H.M. Nouwens

Fig. 11.6: Making *gurs*: placing the pizza-shaped dough.

resulting *gurs* is beaten with a stick and scraped with a stone or a knife to remove clinging sand and burned edges to minimize damage to the teeth. Subsequently, the *gurs* is broken into pieces to cool and then eaten. *Gurs* is extremely heavy and very filling. It is delicious when covered with the Danish-made or Egyptian feta cheese that is readily available in shops and stores in towns on the coast. More recently peanut butter has been a big hit with the Bedouin and with us!

Another type of bread also baked fresh in the desert by all three tribes, though not as frequently as *gurs*, is *rudaf*, also called *marduf*. *Rudaf/marduf* is more labor intensive to make than *gurs*. The dough is produced in a fashion similar to that used to make *gurs*, but the ratio of water to flour is greater in *rudaf*. The bottom of the hole dug in the sand to bake the bread is covered with small stones, often broken, which are heated by the burning fuel that has been placed atop them. The dough is shaped into a pizza-like appearance and placed directly on the heated stones and then covered with sand.

Pl. 11.1: Building the 'Ababda abode: adding mats to the wooden frame.

Pl. 11.2: *Jabana*: a small, narrow-mouthed jug with a handle and some small, handle-less porcelain serving cups.

Pl. 11.3: 'Ababda woman making coffee in *jabana*.

Pl. 11.4: 'Ababda girl with goat.

Pl. 11.5: 'Ababda man traveling with long stick, called *mahjani al-jamal*.

Pl. 11.6: A *mahjani al-jamal* hanging in an acacia tree, held down by a stone while the camel eats from the tree.

H.M. Nouwens

Pl. 11.7: Camels on their way to market.

Pl. 11.8: The use of swords and shields on special occasions.

Pl. 11.9: 'Ababda women in colorful dresses and shawls.

Pl. 11.10: *Loza*, a beautifully decorated container made out of a coconut to keep perfumed sheep's fat.

Pl. 11.11: 'Ababda woman with gold jewelry in nose and on her forehead.

Pl. 12.1: Interior of the so-called Administration Building at Sikait.

Pl. 12.2: Structure at the Roman-era beryl/emerald mining settlement at Nugrus.

Pl. 12.3: Fayyum mummy portrait c. AD 100. Her jewelry is set with amethysts and emeralds © The Trustees of The British Museum

S.E. Sidebotham

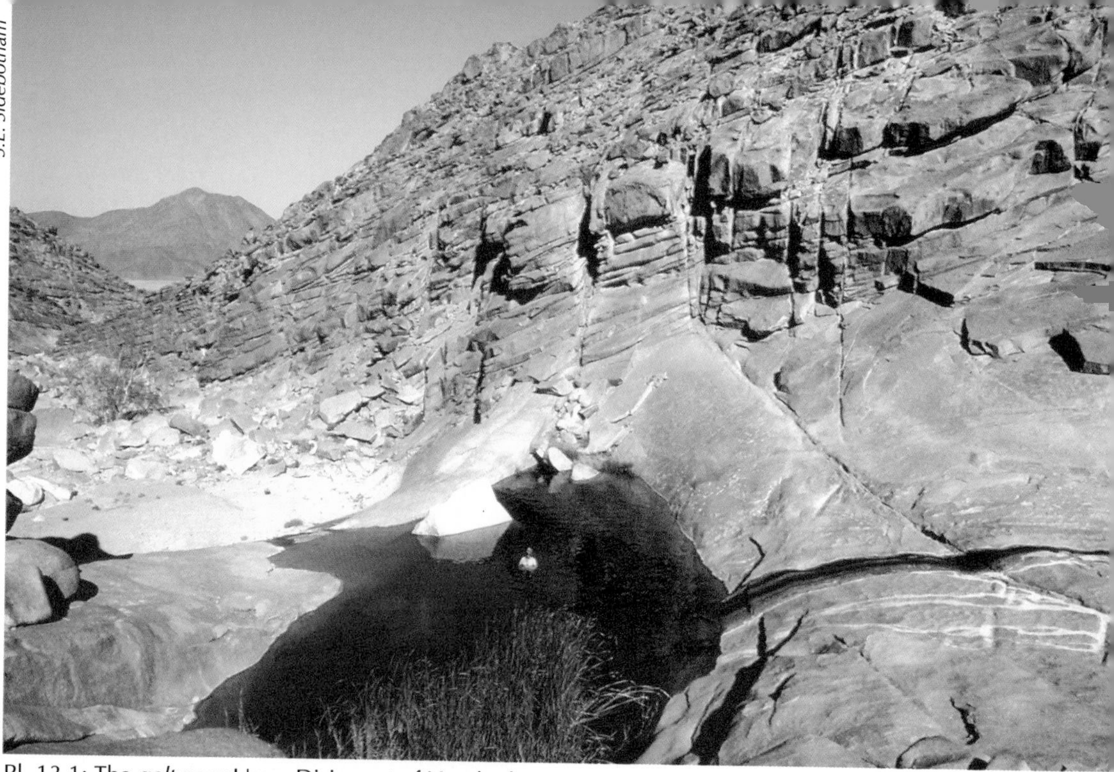

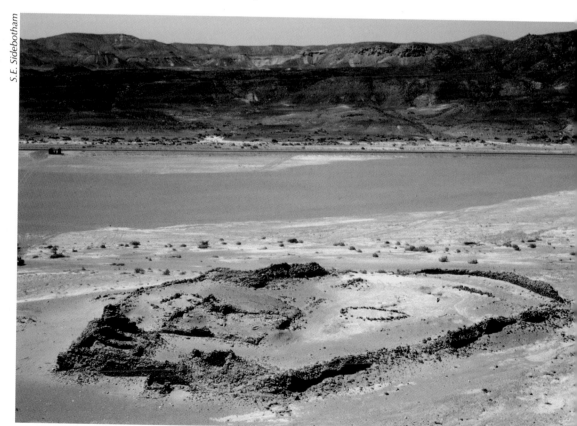

Pl. 13.1: The *qalt* near Umm Disi, west of Hurghada.

S.E. Sidebotham

Pl. 13.2: The Ptolemaic-Roman *praesidium* at al-Kanaïs.

Pl. 13.3: The large *praesidium* in Wadi Kalalat, southwest of Berenike, with well to right.

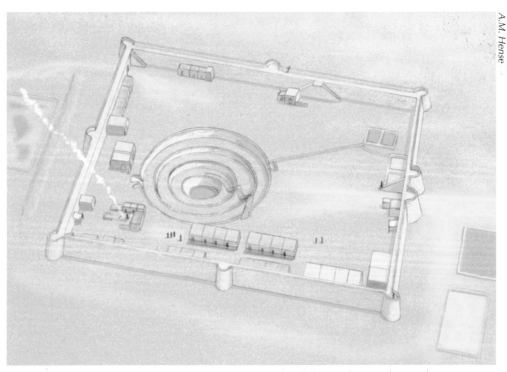

Pl. 13.4: Reconstruction of the large *praesidium* in Wadi Kalalat southwest of Berenike.

S.E. Sidebotham

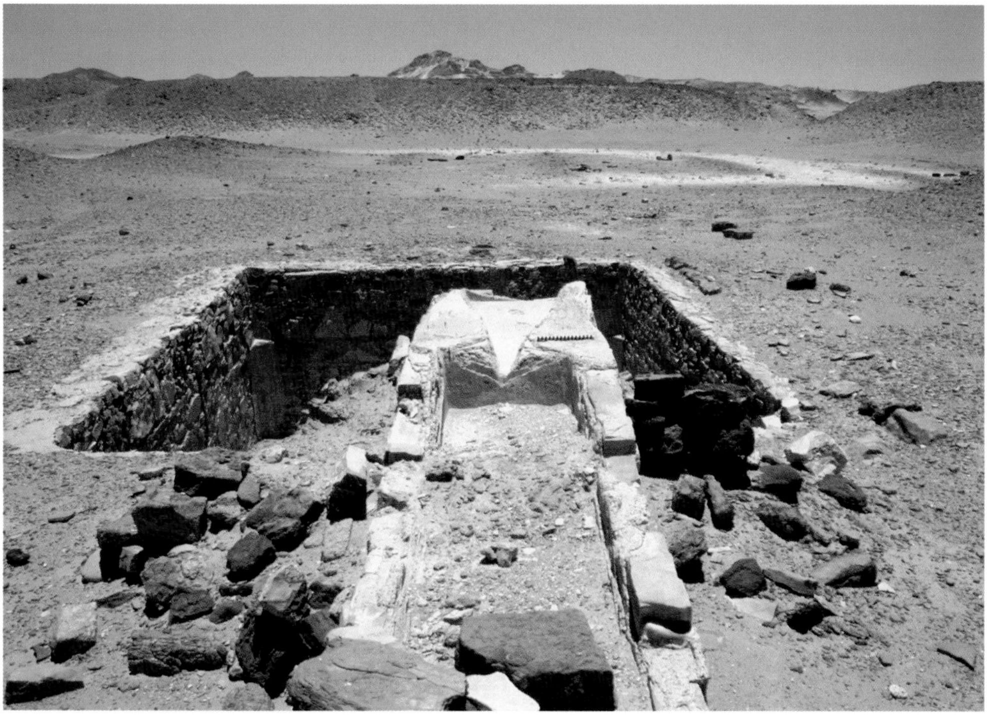

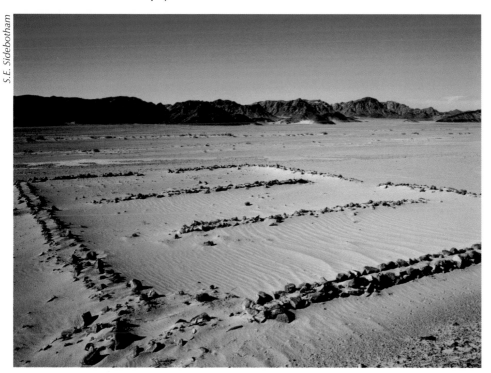

Pl. 13.5: One of the water tanks at the extensive hydraulic facilities at al-Saqqia, a large Roman-era station on the Mons Porphyrites/Mons Claudianus/Abu Sha'r–Nile road.

S.E. Sidebotham

Pl. 13.6: Tethering lines/accommodations for animals at Bab al-Mukhenig. Stone from Mons Porphyrites passed by this stop en route to the Nile.

Pl. 14.1: Samut station on the Berenike–Apollonopolis Magna road.

Pl. 14.2: The *praesidium* of al-Dweig with its fine walls, catwalks, and towers.

Pl. 14.3: The *praesidium* of
al-Dweig with its fine walls,
catwalks, and towers.

Pl. 14.4: Panoramic view of
Vetus Hydreuma (in Wadi
Abu Greiya) with two forts,
when the area was very dry
(top). Panoramic view of
Vetus Hydreuma (in Wadi
Abu Greiya), with abundant
vegetation (bottom).

Pl. 15.1: Overview of the Ptolemaic-early Roman fortress at Abraq.

Pl. 15.2: Aerial view of the hilltop fort of Abraq.

Pl. 15.3: View of the small fort in Wadi Kalalat, about nine hundred meters northeast of the larger *praesidium*. View looking east southeast.

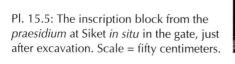
0   5 centimeters

Pl. 15.4: Terra-cotta figurine of a Roman auxiliary soldier found in the early Roman trash dump at Berenike. Scale = five centimeters.

Pl. 15.5: The inscription block from the *praesidium* at Siket *in situ* in the gate, just after excavation. Scale = fifty centimeters.

Pl. 15.6: Artist's reconstructed view of the small *praesidium* at Siket.

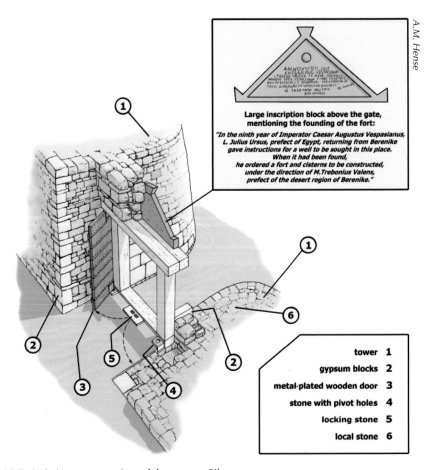

Large inscription block above the gate, mentioning the founding of the fort:

"In the ninth year of Imperator Caesar Augustus Vespasianus, L. Julius Ursus, prefect of Egypt, returning from Berenike gave instructions for a well to be sought in this place. When it had been found, he ordered a fort and cisterns to be constructed, under the direction of M. Trebonius Valens, prefect of the desert region of Berenike."

tower	1
gypsum blocks	2
metal-plated wooden door	3
stone with pivot holes	4
locking stone	5
local stone	6

Pl. 15.7: Artist's reconstruction of the gate at Siket.

Pl. 15.8: View of the late Roman-era settlement in Wadi Shenshef.

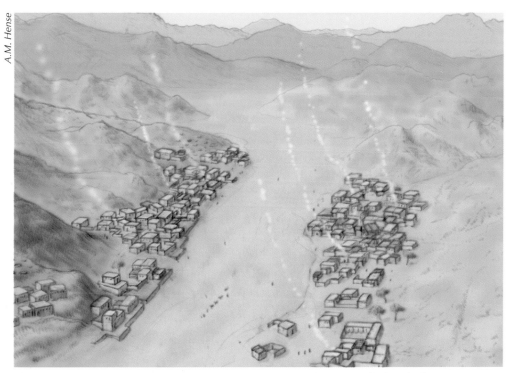

Pl. 15.9: Artist's reconstruction of the late Roman-era settlement in Wadi Shenshef.

Pl. 15.10: The ruins of the first century BC–first century AD hilltop fort at Shenshef, with the older northwestern-most defenses on the opposite hilltop.

Pl. 15.11: Aerial view of the hilltop fort at Shenshef, with the older northwestern-most defenses on the left.

H.M. Nouwens.

Fig. 11.7: Making *rugag* on
top of the lid of an oil drum.

The bread bakes on these stones, which leave an impression in the bottom
of the round pizza-shaped end product. *Rudaf* is chewier than *gurs* and most
people, both Bedouin and certainly we, prefer it to *gurs*. *Rugag* is yet another
type of bread, which is very thin and pancake-like in appearance (Fig. 11.7).
It is made by pouring liquid dough on top of a heated metal surface, such
as the lid of a two hundred liter drum.

The contribution of wild plant species to the Bedouin diet is limited as
only a few of the desert flora are edible (Fig. 11.8). Moreover, the vegetation is directly influenced by the availability of water and is, therefore, scarce
most years. In order to be more self-sufficient some Bedouin produce a few
of their own comestibles. Some permanent and semipermanent settlements
in the Eastern Desert have small kitchen gardens and we have seen these in
both Ma'aza and the 'Ababda territory. Located near more or less reliable
sources of water, such as wells or springs, these small kitchen gardens produce a variety of herbs, fruits, and vegetables, including basil, melons,

S.E. Sidebotham

Fig 11.8: Bedouin with edible *humadth* plant.

tomatoes, cucumber, potatoes, and onions. To prevent poaching by domestic animals, most gardens are surrounded by walls or fences, constructed from spiny branches, such as those from the twisted acacia, wire netting, wood, or sheet iron. Although the productivity of these kitchen gardens is limited, the yield may support a small family. If water is abundant, the kitchen gardens might even produce several yields a year.

Studies have been undertaken of these gardens and it is clear that they have a long history. We have found archaeological evidence of desert cultivation in our own excavations at the Roman emerald mines in Wadi Sikait and in the environs of the *praesidium* at Abu Sha'r al-Qibli. Ostraca and ancient literary sources also report the cultivation of desert gardens at Roman forts along the Myos Hormos–Nile road and in some of the remote Christian hermit communities.

The Bedouin also cultivate various species of trees, such as the twisted and Nile acacia, nabq, date palm, and for instance fig, banana, and henna trees. Although some of these are indigenous to the desert, others originate from the Nile Valley or have been cultivated here from Ptolemaic-Roman times onward. Trees may serve as shade, but are also exploited for their useful (edible) products, while dead branches can be used as firewood.

Small-scale cereal production is also possible in the Eastern Desert. Some Bedouin cultivate fields with cereals, such as wheat, barley, and sorghum. The latter is especially adapted to a desert environment with high temperatures and light intensities. The fields might be irrigated, although rain-fed farming also occurs. Suitable locations for such rain-fed agriculture are shallow depressions in which rainwater accumulates naturally.

Due to the vicinity of the Red Sea, seafood sometimes supplements the Bedouin diet. At certain locations on the Red Sea today fishing is even practiced on a commercial basis.

Fuel

Fuel is indispensable for preparing food and making coffee or tea, and for warmth during cold winter nights. The Bedouin have basically two sources of fuel at their disposal: wood and dung. Because of the sparseness of desert vegetation the Bedouin are extremely cautious in using wood as fuel. They are aware of the possibility of over exploitation and have evolved special rules to prevent this. As a result, for making charcoal or cooking fires most Bedouins mainly use dead wood, the gathering of which occupies an important place in their lives.

When no wood is available, dried camel dung, which when ignited creates great heat, might also be used as fuel. The production of dung cakes, a mixture of dung and threshing remains, is still practiced in some rural areas in present-day Egypt. Dung, however, is only used for making cooking fires to prepare foods and beverages made in containers; it is not used to make bread.

Kindling often comprises dried tumbleweeds of the ubiquitous *zilla* plant which the 'Ababda call *basilli* (the Ma'aza call it *silli*). This bushy annual is trampled down, covered by some branches of a woody plant species, and set on fire. Nowadays matches are used, but traditionally the fire was started by striking a piece of flint on a triangular-shaped bit of steel.

Drinking Coffee

All three Bedouin groups consume coffee in quantity. The process of preparing and serving this beverage is very ritualized. The 'Ababda coffee ceremony begins by roasting coffee beans in a simple recycled tin can with a wire handle over an open fire. The beans, to which some ginger is added as a flavor enhancer, are then ground in a wooden or stone mortar, called a *muhmas,* using a pestle. After that, the ground beans are placed in a *jabana,* which is a small, narrow-mouthed jug with a handle (Pls. 11.2–11.3). In bygone days these were made of stone (usually talc-schist), but more recently of terra cotta or aluminum. A 'filter' *(lefa)* made of plastic or plant mesh prevents the coffee grounds from pouring into the small, handleless porcelain serving cups. To facilitate their transportation, the *jabanas* and serving cups are stored in *kabutahs,* traditionally tightly woven baskets covered by leather. New models are, however, embroidered with plastic, which is often woven in traditional patterns. All equipment is kept in a skin bag.

Livestock

All three tribes herd goats, sheep, and camels (dromedaries) and also use donkeys. Some Bedouin keep chickens as well and use dogs to protect sheep and goats. Goats are by far the most numerous of the charges among the Ma'aza and 'Ababda while the Bisharin raise mainly camels. The Ma'aza and 'Ababda usually leave the goat herding to the women and children (Pl. 11.4). Donkeys and camels are the traditional pack animals, but vehicles, especially the ubiquitous Toyota Hilux pickup truck, are rapidly replacing them. Sheep produce wool, whereas goats are suppliers of milk and hair. Women spin and weave wool and hair and use these fibers to fabricate carpets on looms. Sheep and goats are only slaughtered for their meat on special occasions, such as weddings or to celebrate the end of the Ramadan period. In addition to the meat, the animals provide the Bedouin with skins, which are used for a variety of products, including sandals, amulets, purses, water scoops, and leather bags, to name a few. The shape of the leather bags is often characteristic of their use; some of the smaller bags, used for keeping valuables, are decorated with beads and cowrie shells, whereas the fringes of the bigger examples often have a decoration of printed designs and colored plastic triangles. A lot of leather work, however, is now being replaced by mass-produced items made of imported fabrics, aluminum, plastics, and rubber.

All the tribes allow camels to wander for days on end unattended. Even with their front legs often hobbled, the camels can still travel incredible distances and when someone wants to retrieve his wayward charges he must frequently search for days to locate them.

The Bedouin often actively assist the camels to forage on high branches of the thorny acacia trees that would otherwise be out of their reach. Those caring for the camels use an ingenious long stick with a natural hook on the end, called *mahjani al-jamal,* to reach high up into the trees to snag the verdant branches. They then pull down the branches to within the reach of the camel's mouth. Often the end of the *mahjani al-jamal* will have a rope attached, which can be tied to a large rock to weight the stick and branch so that the camel can eat. These tools are often left hanging in trees by their owners until needed, though occasionally a Bedouin might be seen traveling with one (Pls. 11.5–11.6).

Camels are an important source of income especially for the 'Ababda and Bisharin. Almost daily one sees large trucks traveling north along the Red Sea coastal highway from Shalateen and locations farther south conveying dozens of camels to markets in Aswan, Cairo, and elsewhere (Pl. 11.7). Any visitor to Shalateen in the morning cannot fail to notice the massive camel market. The animals in the truck transports are destined to be eaten while those sold or traded in the camel market serve more traditional Bedouin needs of breeding and cargo haulage. We have also seen large herds of hundreds of camels being driven long distances to market by Bisharin in the Wadi Abu Greiya in the early 1990s. This was a scene we shall never forget for the men leading the camels across the desert also rode camels and brandished shields *(daragat)* and swords *(seyuf).* While fairly common and carried by many adult males, the shields and swords today have a role more as status symbols and are used in ceremonies, especially weddings (Pl. 11.8); they are rarely used these days in martial contests.

Traditionally, the Bedouin use a variety of objects to decorate and harness their camels. In addition to a wooden saddle called a *serj,* which is kept in place by girths made of plaited goat hair, there are leather flaps called *feraya* used to protect the camel's shoulders, and decorative saddlebags called *mukhalayyat,* in which they transport the smallest of their personal belongings.

Appearance

The Bedouin pay a great deal of attention to their appearance. They wear a variety of clothing, depending upon their economic circumstances. At the beginning of the twentieth century 'Ababda men and women wore long white

BEDOUIN GUIDES

One of the Ma'aza who has been our most trusted guide over the years is Salah 'Ali Suwelim. Salah, who was Joe Hobbs' mentor in the 1980s, is not really certain of his age, but he has bragged on several occasions that he misled the authorities issuing national identity cards in his youth thereby escaping the military draft; he is especially happy that he avoided Egypt's involvement in the war in Yemen in the early 1960s. Salah, who in his free time can be found with his friends and relatives in the Bir Basha area near Mons Claudianus, has repeatedly demonstrated his uncanny and unparalleled knowledge of the flora and fauna of the region; he has an incredible memory for the locations of ancient sites, many in very obscure and difficult to reach locations.

Two of the more interesting 'Ababda with whom we have had extensive contact are Hajj Tawfiq 'Ali Muhammad, who died August 1999, and Mansour 'Ali Sa'd from Arab Saleh.

We first met Hajj Tawfiq, so called because he had visited Mecca, which entitled him to bear this proud sobriquet, in the summer of 1991. We had begun conducting an archaeological survey of the Ptolemaic and Roman routes linking Berenike with Coptos and Edfu on the Nile the previous summer using a Ma'aza guide, but the farther south we proceeded into the desert, the less familiar the Ma'aza was with the territory. An Egyptian geologist friend had suggested that we contact Hajj Tawfiq, noting that he had been a great guide for him in earlier years. Hajj Tawfiq had a small shack in Marsa 'Alam where he stayed when not in the desert. We located him and the friendship that developed among us was one that lasted the rest of Hajj Tawfiq's life.

Hajj Tawfiq had an amazing memory and on occasion took us to ancient sites he himself had not visited since the early 1950s. That he could remember their locations over four decades later astounded us. As his eyesight started to fail we encouraged and paid for him to undergo surgery to remove the cataracts that clouded his vision. Hajj Tawfiq was at first reluctant, understandably, to have the surgery, but we pointed out to him that if he could not see, he would hardly be able to continue to guide anyone into the desert. He was convinced by our arguments and underwent successful cataract surgery in a private hospital in Hurghada in July 1993. Thereafter for the rest of his life Hajj's vision was fine as long as he wore his glasses, which had been fitted soon after the surgery.

Hajj Tawfiq, who had two wives, owned an incredibly large and seemingly derelict Soviet-made truck, which he had acquired sometime in the 1950s. When we first saw this vehicle it appeared to be on its last legs and by the mid- to late 1990s Hajj Tawfiq had clearly gotten rid of it or it had completely fallen apart; he never did tell us which. He and Selim Abdel Qadr, also an 'Abadi and friend of Hajj's, and a mechanic for the Egyptian Geological Survey in Marsa 'Alam, made a great survey team. Selim was an excellent mechanic and Hajj a superb guide and *gurs* maker. Both would help measure the remains of ancient structures whenever we asked and also posed in the ruins for our seemingly endless photographs.

Usually at night in the desert when survey work had concluded for the day we would sit eating *gurs* and drinking tea and we would discuss all manner of things including the locations of yet to be visited ancient sites, desert flora, fauna, and stars. One of the most fascinating conversations we once had in winter 1995 involved calculations to estimate the amount of *gurs* Hajj Tawfiq had consumed during his life. Nobody was certain of his age, but for the sake of the calculation, we estimated seventy-five as his ID card recorded his birth in August 1920, a date Hajj assured us was only a guess. Hajj informed us that he ate about one kilogram of *gurs* every day of his life. This works out to 27,375 kilograms or over twenty-seven metric tons in seventy-five years! The ubiquitous Toyota Hilux pickup trucks that are the mainstay of Bedouin transport in the Eastern Desert and which form the backbone of most of our desert surveys, each weigh about 1,500 kilograms, which means that Hajj ate, during the first seventy-five years of his life, the equivalent weight of about eighteen Toyota pickup trucks! Once we had made this calculation and told Hajj we were all extremely impressed. Hajj died in August 1999 of complications from a kidney operation and so ended one of the most incredible relationships we have ever had.

Mansour 'Ali Sa'd we first met in July 1992 at the village of Arab Saleh, which lies about fifteen kilometers north of the ruins of Berenike. While surveying the region around ancient Berenike, Hajj Tawfiq was beyond his geographical range of knowledge so he suggested that we stop at Arab Saleh and ask for some local help in finding the ancient desert settlement of Shenshef. Mansour, who had to be in his fifties or sixties at the time, volunteered to show us and we have known him ever since. Mansour is a very different person than Hajj Tawfiq in that he is more excitable and his *gurs* is not quite as good, but he is generally a great guide and an excellent companion with seemingly endless amusing and bawdy stories. Mansour's Toyota, however, is so dilapidated, breaks down so often, and becomes bogged down in the fine deep sand *(ghars)* so frequently because of its small underpowered engine, that we lovingly refer to it as *karkuba al-jebel* (mountain junk). After a few surveys in this conveyance, we chose to use any other vehicle instead. Mansour has multiple wives, we are not sure how many, and numerous children. One of his sons, Sa'd Mansour, has worked with us over the years excavating and assisting in Berenike and at Sikait. He is incredibly intelligent, curious, and meticulous. Sa'd enjoys drawing and once we realized this, we eagerly supplied him with drawing paper and colored pencils. He then proceeded to produce views of life in the desert with vivid depictions of local flora and fauna, camels, ostriches, Toyota pickup trucks, and Bedouin. We have purchased many of his drawings and have encouraged him to show them to dealers who sell souvenirs to foreign tourists. At the time of writing this chapter we do not know if he has done so.

cotton clothes; nowadays the men wear white cotton trousers, a long garment resembling a nineteenth-century European nightshirt *(gallabiya)* and often a dark colored waist coat. Women wear mostly colorful dresses with a shawl *(khalaga)*, which can be several meters long (Pl. 11.9). Usually the 'Ababda wear sandals; these were originally made of leather, but have been increasingly replaced by slippers made of plastic and other modern materials.

Among the 'Ababda the men wear little jewelry, except for some apotropaic leather amulets around their necks, legs, or upper arms, called *hejabs* (Fig. 11.9). One might see an 'Abadi or Bishari man with a wooden, metal, or plastic comb *(khulal)* left in his hair in what appears to be an absent-minded manner. Previously these combs were made of silver or wood overlaid with silver.

At festivities 'Ababda women plait and decorate their long hair with coins, made of gold or copper, beads, shells, and a ring at their foreheads. They treat their skin and hair using perfumed sheep's fat, which they keep in *lozas*, beautifully decorated containers made out of a coconut or a plant gourd (Pl. 11.10). *Kohl* is used to make up their eyes, whereas henna is sometimes used to decorate the women's hands and feet at wedding ceremonies.

S. E. Sidebotham

Fig 11.9: *Hejab*: apotropaic leather amulet on arm.

In contrast to 'Ababda men, the women wear more body ornaments. These include hair decorations, nose-rings, earrings, necklaces, bracelets, rings, and anklets, made of a variety of materials, ranging from very inexpensive to precious metals such as silver and gold (Pl. 11.11). Some of the jewelry and amulets have hollow areas filled with texts from the *Quran* or curative spices or plants, which serve to protect them. To store the body ornaments the 'Ababda women have leather bags and woven baskets.

Earning a Living
Traditionally the Bedouin engage in animal husbandry. Other ways of making a living include trading goat hair and leather products and making charcoal. All three tribes make charcoal; the best, everyone agrees, comes from the hardwood acacia trees, three types of which are found in the Eastern Desert. In the past, the trees were often wantonly destroyed for fuel; these days most Bedouin are careful to use only the wood from dead trees. We have witnessed this time consuming charcoal-making process in Wadi Gemal. We have also seen many instances of bundles of the finished product in large burlap sacks lying on the ground awaiting transport to

market and donkeys carrying these bundles. The Bedouin also harvest a wide variety of other desert plants and fruits for medicinal and culinary use, for tanning leather and making ropes, mats, and baskets. As an important supplement to their incomes, they frequently sell these plants in large towns on the Nile or the Red Sea coast. Intensive studies of Bedouin exploitation of flora have recently concentrated on the Wadi 'Allaqi, which stretches for approximately 250 kilometers southeast of Aswan before turning northeast where it terminates on the Red Sea coast at 'Aidhab. Other occupations include participation in the tourist industry as drivers, guides, and entertainers.

Religious Beliefs

The 'Ababda, like the Ma'aza and the Bisharin, although devout Muslims, believe in ghosts *(zawal)* and evil spirits *(afrit* and *jinn)*; some Bedouin are ambivalent about the malevolent beings while others are genuinely fearful of them. The 'Ababda celebrate each year for about a month a deceased sheikh named Shazli whose tomb is in a small town of the same name southwest of Marsa 'Alam and northwest of Berenike. One winter while excavating at Sikait several of our workmen requested a number of days off to visit Sheikh Shazli and take part in these celebrations.

Land of Gemstones
Emerald and Amethyst Mines in the Eastern Desert

W e noted previously that Egypt was blessed with great geological wealth. Here we will deal specifically with some of the precious and semiprecious gemstones that were available in the Eastern Desert. Our interest will focus on amethysts and beryls/emeralds. Two regions of the Eastern Desert produced amethysts in antiquity: Wadi al-Hudi and Wadi Abu Diyeiba. The area around Gebel Sikait, Gebel Nugrus, and Umm Kabu, about 120 kilometers northwest of Berenike, were sources for beryls/emeralds (Fig. 12.1).

Amethysts
The earliest gemstones mined in the Eastern Desert were amethysts. From Late Predynastic times (about 3000 BC) onward amethysts were used in jewelry, mainly beads, and small amulets. The ancient Egyptians called amethyst *hesmen*; the English word 'amethyst' derives from the Greek *amethyston*. The fourth-century BC writer Theophrastus in his book *On Stones*, indicates that the term derived from the nomenclature of a wine of the same color.

Wadi al-Hudi
Wadi al-Hudi, an extensive area covering some three hundred square kilometers southeast of Aswan, is geologically diverse with several mining and quarrying sites. The desert hillocks of Wadi al-Hudi have been exploited for their minerals since at least the early second millennium BC; during the

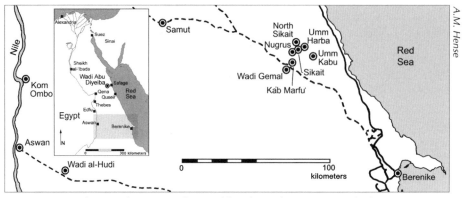

A.M. Hense

Fig. 12.1: Map showing locations of emerald and amethyst mines and other sites in the Eastern Desert.

AMETHYSTS

Amethyst is a translucent violet-colored form of quartz (silicon dioxide) with a glassy sheen. Although the mineral was mined in Egypt from Late Predynastic times onward, the era of its greatest popularity was the Middle Kingdom (2040–1640 BC). In this period amethyst was primarily used in jewelry such as necklaces, girdles, anklets, and multiple-string bracelets. Occasionally amethyst beads were even capped with gold, threaded with gold beads into amulet-case shapes, and carved into various amulet forms including scarabs.

In the New Kingdom (1550–1070 BC), however, amethyst was less commonly used for personal adornment, possibly because it had become very difficult to obtain, as there was a temporary dearth of known sources, although it may be that its strong coloring did not combine easily in the composite inlays popular at the time. Yet, by the Ptolemaic period, the mineral regained its popularity and continued to appear in jewelry, especially in the form of truncated bicon-ical (late Ptolemaic and early Roman period) or pear-shaped beads (sixth and seventh centuries AD). Indeed, Pliny the Elder, writing in the AD 50s–70s in his encyclopedic *Natural History*, referred to Egyptian amethysts, and in about AD 200 Clement of Alexandria wrote that amethysts were among "the stones which silly women wear fastened to chains and set in necklaces."

pharaonic and Greco-Roman periods the Egyptians traveled there to seek barite, gold, mica, and especially amethyst.

The Wadi al-Hudi region was the primary location in Egypt for mining amethyst in the pharaonic period and it appears to have peaked in the Middle Kingdom from the late Eleventh to the Thirteenth Dynasty (2040–1640 BC). At this time the violet hued semiprecious stone was particularly favored in the superb jewelry of the pharaohs, their queens, and princesses. During the Old Kingdom the principal amethyst mines appear to have been located at Toshka in the Western Desert. While there is some evidence for the continued exploitation of Wadi al-Hudi after the Middle Kingdom, the principal amethyst mines of the later Ptolemaic and Roman periods were in Wadi Abu Diyeiba, southwest of the modern Red Sea town of Safaga.

It appears that the mining of amethyst during the Middle Kingdom was on a par with the extraction of turquoise in Sinai, the quarrying of choice stone in Wadi Hammamat, and similar enterprises elsewhere. In the Middle Kingdom, judging from the inscriptions alone, at least thirty-nine expeditions were sent to the turquoise mines in Sinai, fifteen to the Wadi al-Hudi amethyst mines, and thirteen to the Wadi Hammamat region.

Expeditions to the amethyst mines and quarries were dispatched at intervals by royal command. Although the leadership of these expeditions varied from reign to reign, it always fell to representatives of the king and his administration. In addition to the caravan-leaders, the inscriptions at Wadi al-Hudi paint a broad picture of other personnel such as stonemasons, large forces of 'recruits,' 'braves,' 'laborers,' overseers, and certain specialists. The minerals obtained went to the royal and state treasuries, which would enable the king to reward his high officials appropriately. On a symbolic level the campaigns could demonstrate the king's control over the most far-flung regions, while on a political level it seems likely that the mining and quarrying expeditions, like military campaigns, were dispatched to reinforce centralized political control.

The principal landmark of the Wadi al-Hudi area is a prominent rocky hill, Gebel al-Hudi, which is located about halfway along the broad flat floor of the main wadi. Wadi al-Hudi stretches for about twelve kilometers, with a complex network of ridges and smaller wadis. The traces of ancient mining and quarrying expeditions are scattered throughout this adjacent region of smaller valleys rather than on the floor of the main wadi itself.

In the eastern part of the area are five ancient sites all of which are probably Roman or later (Fig. 12.2). From north to south they comprise a barite
mine with a few huts, a small hill fort, and two gold mines with associated
settlement areas, consisting of stone- and mud-brick workers' huts, and
shelters that were partly formed by caves in the rock face.

The amethyst mines at Wadi al-Hudi were rediscovered by the geologist
Labib Nassim in 1923 on the western side of the wadi where several areas
of archaeological interest can be found clustered together amid a succession
of high rocky ridges and valleys. These include two hilltop settlements to
house the miners, one of which dates to the Middle Kingdom. The other,
about three kilometers to the south, can be attributed to the Roman period.

Miners of the Middle Kingdom constructed a substantial settlement
(3,500 square meters) atop an asymmetrical conical-shaped hill, adjoining
an amethyst mine, at the northern end of Wadi al-Hudi. The settlement had
a dry-laid stone enceinte, which provided good defense against attack.

At three corners of the wall are rough protruding piers, each provided
with a crudely constructed platform that enabled the defenders inside the
enclosure to gain a good view around the settlement and maximize their
height above any attackers. Inside the rough stone-fortified enclosure are
about forty dry-laid stone-built workmen's shelters, covering the slopes of
the hill on all sides. At the summit of the hill was a substantial building,
which accommodated successive mining expedition leaders.

S.E. Sidebotham

Fig. 12.2: View from the fortified hilltop settlement into Wadi al-Hudi. Another
fortified installation is visible on lower ground in the middle distance.

South of the Middle Kingdom settlement is a major L-shaped open-pit amethyst mine. The deposits of purple amethyst appear to have been completely worked out in pharaonic times. A low row of stones surrounds the edges of the mine; these apparently acted as a simple demarcation line or boundary. There are also some spoil heaps.

On the wadi floor, about one kilometer from the hilltop settlement described above, is a rectangular stone fort measuring about 70 by 50 meters that likely served as the administrative center and, perhaps, quarters for some of the officials (Figs. 12.3–12.4). It was probably erected in two phases. The installation had two entrances, one on the northern and the other on the eastern side, and some of the perimeter walls of the fortress, with a thickness of about one meter, still stand up to two meters high. This is an unusual if not a unique example of a stone-built fort from the Middle Kingdom; it incorporates features typically seen in the mud brick fortresses of Lower Nubia. The walls, made of unworked pieces of local granite rocks of various sizes, preserve arrow slits, while curved bastions provide a line of fire for the fort's defenders; these project from the perimeter walls and at the corners of the fort.

The interior of the fort, which preserves a number of stone rooms and buildings, can be divided into three main sectors. The most notable and carefully built interior structure is Building A, which might have functioned as the original 'organizational center' of the fort. This building,

S.E. Sidebotham

Fig. 12.3: The Middle Kingdom fort at Wadi al-Hudi. The amethyst quarry was to the left of this structure.

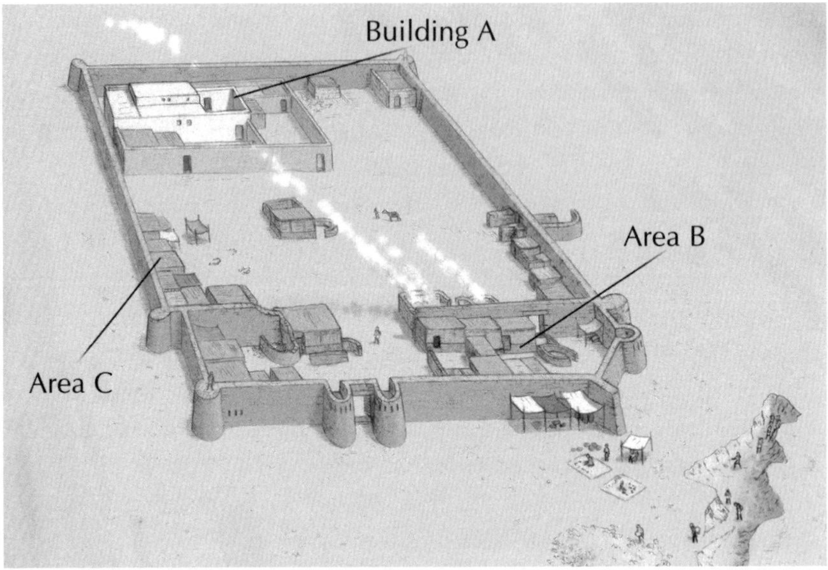

Fig. 12.4: Reconstruction of the Middle Kingdom fort in Wadi al-Hudi.

which is farthest away from either entrance, consists of relatively large and well-defined rooms and has walls that are preserved to about the same height as the perimeter enceinte. It was built, however, well away from this enclosure wall, which created a kind of corridor to allow defenders to man the entire circuit of the main wall quickly in case of attack.

Attached to Building A are adjoining rooms with walls that are lower and less well preserved and which are comparable in quality of workmanship to the rooms built in Area B, in the northeastern sector of the fort. Yet, some of the rooms in Area B were, in contrast to the rooms of Building A, erected directly against the outer wall of the fortification in a way that would have complicated any defensive operation. The third complex of rooms, Area C, is in the southeastern part of the fortified building; its walls are relatively low and of inferior construction.

The Wadi al-Hudi Inscriptions

The area of Wadi al-Hudi preserves numerous inscriptions, freestanding steles, graffiti, and rock-carvings, some of which have been stolen while others have been transferred to the Cairo and Aswan Museums. The Wadi al-Hudi texts provide useful information on the number of gemstone mining expeditions, the caravan-leaders and the personnel working at the site. Although the dated graffiti and steles range from the end of the Eleventh through the Twelfth Dynasty (1991–1783 BC) and into the Thirteenth Dynasty (Sobekhotep IV, 1730–1720 BC), the inscriptions seem to make clear that the amethyst mines were especially exploited in the reign of Senwosret I (1971–1926 BC), as well as frequently in the reigns of Senwosret III (1878–1841 BC) and Amenemhat III (1841–1797 BC).

Many of the larger rocks in the hilltop settlement still bear carved geometric shapes, figures and hieroglyphic inscriptions, particularly near the summit and on the eastern side of the hill. Another hill, with a large number of inscriptions and drawings, is roughly midway between the hilltop settlement and the Middle Kingdom fort.

A large stone stela was originally set up during the beginning of the Twelfth Dynasty on a hill where many other Middle Kingdom inscriptions were carved in the rock. The commissioner of this large inscribed dedication was the royal official Hor, who was sent to Wadi al-Hudi by King Senwosret I:

The majesty of my lord, this chief god of the Two Lands, who has decreed the labor 'beautiful is he in this land'*, has sent me, having assigned to my charge a troop, to do what his ka desires concerning this amethyst of Ta-sety. I have brought a great quantity there from which I have collected like (what I collect) at the door of a granary, been dragged on a sledge and loaded on pallets.

Another stela, commissioned by the steward Hetepu, provides some insight into the number of people involved in the mining operations. It preserves an account of another mining expedition sent by pharaoh Senwosret I:

List of the expedition of the Lord-Life, Prosperity, Health that came to fetch amethyst for the sake of all the wishes of the Lord-Life, Prosperity, Health. General of Troops and Retainer of the South, Resuwi, son of Intef, son of Renesi. Strong troops of recruits of all of the Southern City, 1000 able-bodied men; braves of Elephantine, 200 men; braves of Ombi, 100 men; from the Residence, chief prospectors, 41 men; officers of the Steward Hetepu, 56 men; caravan leaders, 50 men....

---

* The name of the mine or mining project.

Only three years later, the official Mentuhotep proudly recollected his deeds in the Wadi al-Hudi:

I ordered the excavation of new mines. I did not fall behind what others had done. I fetched there from in great quantity, I hewed out lumps of amethyst.

He also reminded travelers of the firm grip the king had on the area:

His dread renown having fallen upon the Hau-nebu, the desert dwellers being fallen to his onset. All lands work for him; the deserts yield to him what is within them. . . .

Wadi Abu Diyeiba

After the cessation of operations in Wadi al-Hudi in the Middle Kingdom there is little evidence that amethyst mining was again undertaken in Egypt until the Ptolemaic period. At that time new areas were exploited in the Wadi Abu Diyeiba region. Our surveys in and around Wadi Abu Diyeiba revealed four hundred to five hundred long narrow trenches covering an area of approximately three square kilometers. The largest of the trenches was about one hundred meters long, twenty meters deep, and three meters wide. We picked up bits and pieces of low grade amethysts on the spoil heaps near some of these trenches. Exposure to the sun over extended periods of time will fade the purple hue and this fact may help explain why our survey recovered so few fragments of these semiprecious gems.

Associated with these mining operations in Wadi Abu Diyeiba were three small areas of building remains. The largest concentration comprised, at most, only ten or twelve badly dilapidated structures. Numerous, apparently modern, robber holes in this location indicate repeated attempts in relatively recent times to loot antiquities and vandalize the remains. We conducted surveys here in June 2000 and June 2004. In our most recent fieldwork we found half a dozen fragments of inscriptions in Greek. Religious in content, the ancient texts indicate the popularity of deities at the settlement including Isis, Pan, Apollo, Serapis, and Harpocrates. One of the inscription fragments we recovered joined with and completed a text discovered and published many decades ago that dated to the reign of Ptolemy VI and his wife Cleopatra II (175–145 BC). We also found scores of representations of human feet carved into the surrounding sandstone. Elsewhere in Egypt and the ancient Mediterranean world such representations of human feet are associated with the worship of the goddess Isis and such is likely the case in the settlement at Wadi Abu Diyeiba as well. Isis, as we have noted in earlier chapters, was an extremely popular deity worshiped in the Eastern Desert.

In conjunction with these Greek inscriptions we also recovered a small altar made from the locally available sandstone and two pictorial reliefs, which we discussed in detail in Chapter 6. The appearance of so many texts, pictorial reliefs, an altar, the representations of human feet and other religious artifacts indicates that this 'main' settlement was probably the administrative as well as religious focal point of the amethyst mining operations in the region.

Only about a kilometer southeast of this main site we found the remains of a small satellite settlement comprising a few crude huts several of which made use of giant boulders for portions of their walls. Also about a kilometer southwest of the main settlement we discovered what appears to be a small temple or shrine, which we discussed in Chapter 6 (Fig. 6.4).

There is no evidence of the existence of small huts near any of the mining trenches, which suggests that the ancient workers lived in tents; these, of course, have left no traces in the archaeological record. The work force was probably never very large; we estimate approximately one hundred individuals. Lack of fortifications suggests that those who worked here felt relatively secure from attack and further indicates that the work force likely comprised free labor, which required no guards, rather than forced slave labor that would have necessitated close supervision. While there is today no evidence of wells in the area from which the work crews would have obtained their water, these were undoubtedly sunk in the various wadis where the work took place and have, over the centuries, been filled in by waterborne sediments carried during the infrequent but torrential rains and resulting flash floods in the region.

Beryl/Emerald Mines

We have far more information about the ancient beryl and emerald mines partly because many more remains survive from these operations and we have studied them in more detail than the amethyst mines. Beryl is a mineral that almost always occurs as elongated crystals with a hexagonal cross-section, and which is colorless in its ordinary form. However, one of the gemstone varieties of beryl is emerald, which has a distinctive green color. True emeralds are bright, uniform medium to dark green, and transparent. Yet, the famous Egyptian emerald mines produced very few of these true emeralds; the Egyptian beryl usually has a cloudy translucency and a light green color.

The beryl/emerald mines lie about 120 kilometers northwest of Berenike and about thirty-five kilometers southwest of Marsa Nakari in a region known to the Romans as Mons Smaragdus (Emerald Mountain). This area is not a single mountain at all, but a series of mountains and wadis covering a zone of about 250 square kilometers in the region of Gebels Sikait, Nugrus, and Umm Kabu. In this area our surveys have located nine major beryl/emerald mining settlements. The terrain is honeycombed with hundreds if not thousands of open pits and vertical and horizontal mining shafts (Fig. 12.5) as well as an abundance of potshards attesting intensive efforts

S.E. Sidebotham

Fig. 12.5: Middle Sikait, entrance to a Roman and Islamic-era beryl/emerald mining shaft.

especially in the early through late Roman periods and, to a lesser extent, in Islamic times. Many ancient authors, including Strabo, Pliny the Elder, and Claudius Ptolemy, report on the mines and the bustling activity surrounding their exploitation. Lesser-known authors writing later in the third and up to the sixth centuries AD also recount the wealth produced from the mines. A local man, Olympiodorus from Thebes on the Nile, recorded in the fifth century AD that one could not visit the emerald mines without the permission of the King of the Blemmyes, a desert tribe that exercised some political power in the region at that time. The latest ancient reference is by Cosmas Indicopleustes, a Christian monk who spent time in the Red Sea and Indian Ocean region in the sixth century.

From the remains of painted letters and numbers surviving above some of the mine entrances and the presence of relatively modern structures, it is evident that emerald mining operations continued, in some places, well into the twentieth century. This is confirmed by reading some of the accounts of earlier twentieth century British geologists who worked in the region. We also have some, though at this point not much, evidence that at least one of these settlements was inhabited and, therefore, the mines worked, in Ptolemaic times.

The Mons Smaragdus area was the only source of beryls/emeralds known to the Romans that lay inside their empire. Other regions mined in antiquity in the Old World could be found in India and possibly Austria though the latter may have been worked only in post-Roman times. Mining in the Islamic period in the Mons Smaragdus area does not seem to have been on as grand a scale as in the Roman era and once the Spanish began to exploit the higher quality emeralds from the mines in Columbia, South America in the sixteenth century and later, most beryl/emerald mining activity in Egypt came to a halt. Today there is some danger that these ancient mines in the Mons Smaragdus region and their related settlements will be damaged or destroyed in the search for beryllium. Used as a highly heat resistant material in the aerospace industry, the great value of beryllium may lead to reopening of the mines in this area with potentially catastrophic consequences for the ancient archaeological remains.

Let us examine a few of the larger and more interesting of these beryl/emerald mining settlements. Our fieldwork has investigated to one degree or another all nine known ancient settlements associated with beryl/emerald mining, but we will discuss here only five of these. The one best known, due to our intensive, detailed survey work and limited excavations, is that in Wadi Sikait, known in antiquity as Senskis or Senskete. Farther north up Wadi Sikait we have examined and surveyed two other related sites. Though their ancient names are unknown, we have simply labeled them Middle Sikait and North Sikait. Two others of great interest, but which we have only examined in a cursory fashion thus far, include one in Wadi Nugrus, just southwest of Sikait and one in Wadi Umm Harba, east of Sikait.

Sikait

Our initial survey work in winter 2000 and summer 2001 drew a detailed site plan of the remains visible above ground in Wadi Sikait and North Sikait. Our survey work continued, but was not completed, at Middle Sikait in summer 2002. While there was a rather sketchy overall plan of the ruins

Fig. 12.6: Roman-era beryl/emerald mining community at Sikait, drawn by J.G. Wilkinson (Ms. G. Wilkinson sect. XXXVIII. 39 page 80; Gardner Wilkinson papers from Calke Abbey, Bodleian Library, Oxford; courtesy of the National Trust).

at Sikait drawn by Wilkinson in the early nineteenth century (Fig. 12.6) and a geological-archaeological one published in 1900 by D.A. MacAlister, surprisingly, ours was the first detailed and precise map ever drawn of the ancient archaeological remains.

The southernmost site in Wadi Sikait preserves the remains of scores if not hundreds of structures that march up the steep slopes of the mountains. The wadi runs more or less north–south thereby dividing the settlement into eastern and western portions (Figs. 12.7–12.8). As mentioned in Chapter 10, many buildings have façades intact and portions of their interiors still standing and include complete doors with lintels, windows, shelves, and other features. Most impressive are two temples on the eastern side of the wadi cut into the mountainsides, which we discussed in Chapter 6. In addition, there is also a large freestanding edifice on the western side of the wadi at the southern end of the settlement, which we called the 'Administration Building' and another, which we called the 'Tripartite Building' located farther up the side of the hill to the north and west of the Administration Building. An amazing architectural façade at the northern end of the site on its eastern side we dubbed 'Six Windows.'

S.E. Sidebotham

Fig. 12.7: Wadi Sikait running more or less north–south, dividing the Roman-era beryl/emerald mining settlement into eastern and western portions. Excavations on the western side of the wadi.

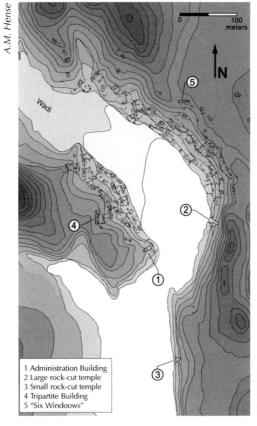

A.M. Hense

1 Administration Building
2 Large rock-cut temple
3 Small rock-cut temple
4 Tripartite Building
5 "Six Windoows"

Fig. 12.8: Plan of the Roman-era emerald mining community at Sikait.

Early European travelers to the southernmost settlement in Wadi Sikait, however, were most attracted to the two rock-cut temples. Frédéric Cailliaud, a French metallurgist and jeweler from Nantes, first discovered the ruins at Sikait in 1816 and made a return trip in 1817. One of many Europeans employed by the Egyptian ruler Muhammad 'Ali Pasha early in the nineteenth century, Cailliaud had been commissioned to search specifically for the lost emerald mines. At that time nobody, except a handful of Bedouins, actually knew where exactly they might be found or if it would be feasible and profitable to reopen them. Cailliaud only had Bedouin tales and the imprecise accounts of ancient Roman authors to guide him. The description he published and the fanciful drawings he made of the two rock-cut temples, which appear in Chapter 6, subsequently piqued the interest of others to visit the remains including the famous Italian adventurer Giovanni Belzoni and British savant J.G. Wilkinson. The larger rock-cut temple lying somewhat farther north up the wadi is far more impressive and is, indeed, the object of attention of the bulk of the tourists who visit the site; most only examine this edifice and rarely venture to other parts of the ancient settlement.

FRÉDÉRIC CAILLIAUD

Of importance to our understanding of the Eastern Desert were the travels of the French goldsmith and metallurgist Frédéric Cailliaud. Born in Nantes in 1787, he studied mineralogy in Paris. He left for Egypt after visiting the Netherlands, Italy, Sicily, Greece, and Asia Minor. There he traveled with Drovetti in 1816 through Nubia as far as Wadi Halfa. Cailliaud became one of several Europeans employed by Muhammad 'Ali Pasha in the early nineteenth century, and he was commissioned to find the lost emerald mines, rumors of which had circulated from various Bedouin and other accounts. He succeeded in discovering them in 1816 and returned the following year for a more extended visit. These sojourns resulted in descriptions and several drawings of the ancient mining settlement in Wadi Sikait which he published in 1821 in a book entitled *Voyage à l'oasis de Thèbes et dans les déserts situées à l'orient et à l'occident de la Thébaïde fait pendant les années 1815, 1816, 1817 et 1818.* While undoubtedly impressive and artistically attractive, these etchings are somewhat fanciful and are not accurate renditions of the remains in Wadi Sikait. Nevertheless, Cailliaud's discoveries attracted others to visit the site to record, often more accurately than he, what was to be seen there. The emeralds from the region proved to be very low grade and while some mining efforts were made thereafter, they were not successful; the gemstones from Columbia, South America were not only vastly superior in quality to those from the Sikait region, but were also cheaper to mine and ship. Cailliaud also traveled to the Khargha and Siwa Oases, and along the Nile as far as Meroë. He returned to France in 1822 with a large collection of objects. Two years later, he was appointed an assistant curator at the Museum of Natural History in Nantes, where he died in 1869.

Opposite this larger rock-cut temple on the western side of the wadi and approached by several staircases and a ramp is by far the most impressive freestanding building anywhere in the ancient settlement and, arguably, in the entire Eastern Desert. Our survey dubbed this impressive structure the Administration Building, though we have little evidence that it served this purpose (Fig. 12.9–12.11 and Pl. 12.1). Cailliaud believed that this structure was a temple, but this identification also lacks any supporting evidence. Cailliaud produced several drawings of this edifice that, although imprecise, are more accurate than those he made of the aforementioned rock-cut temples. Wilkinson also made some plans of this impressive structure. Completely intact, except that portions of the eastern and southern walls lean dangerously at an angle, this three-room building has walls standing to heights of almost four meters, a main portal on the east, and a subsidiary entrance on the south. Two small windows pierce the main walls, one on the north and the other on the south side. The outermost room had been paved in large flat stones carefully fitted together. The wall separating the first and second room has an impressive portal flanked in the wall by niches with shelves topped by pediments. We do not know if these two larger rooms were ever roofed. If so, likely the roof was in timber as the span would have

S. E. Sidebotham

Fig. 12.9: Sikait, panoramic view of the so-called Administration Building.

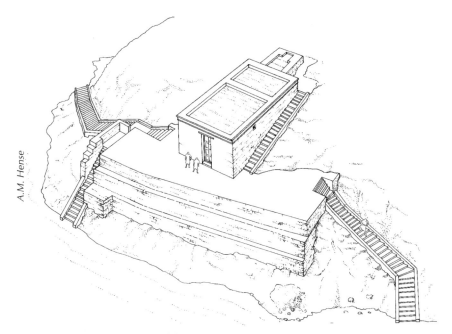

Fig. 12.10: Reconstruction of the so-called Administration Building at Sikait.

Fig. 12.11: Sikait, the so-called Administration Building, roof construction.

been excessively wide and the monolithic stones required would have been too heavy for the walls. A second smaller portal connects the second room to a smaller third room. This latter room is partially cut into the bedrock and is filled with debris including some sizeable tumbled stone roof beams averaging 2.25 meters long; several original stone roofing beams remain intact in their original positions over this third room (Fig. 12.11).

The so-called Tripartite Building (Figs. 12.12–12.13) lies a little north and up the hill from the Administration Building. This impressive structure perches at the upper end of a winding street that leads up from the wadi bottom below. The edifice rests atop an impressive artificial platform that has partially collapsed. Divided into three major rooms, one exterior door and a window survive intact and numerous shelves and interior doors are evident in various states of preservation. Like the Administration Building, the Tripartite Building was also constructed through partial excavation into the surrounding bedrock. We do not know what function this impressive edifice served, but we anticipate that future examination, including excavation and consolidation work, may provide the answer.

S. E. Sidebotham

Fig. 12.12: Sikait, the so-called Tripartite Building.

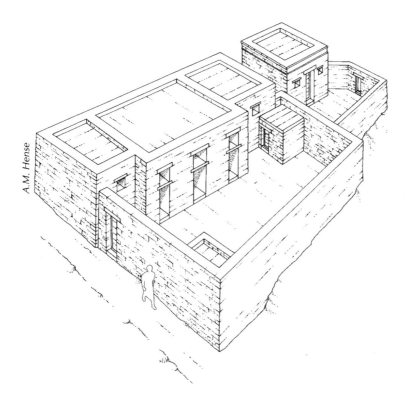

Fig. 12.13: Reconstruction of the so-called Tripartite Building at Sikait.

There are a number of other impressive structures visible at Sikait, unfortunately all serving functions that remain a mystery to us. One of the most haunting is the façade of a structure that we called Six Windows (Fig. 5.2), which we mentioned briefly above. Based upon six surviving windows in its two southern-facing façades, this building was equally alluring to earlier travelers including J.G. Wilkinson who, on his visit to Sikait in the early nineteenth century, drew a panoramic sketch of the settlement with Six Windows shown prominently in the foreground from behind.

Our excavations on the lowest modern visible levels of Sikait on both the eastern and western sides of the settlement revealed extensive activity in late Roman times. Houses dominated this lower part of the settlement. These had large open courtyards in which animal husbandry and some gardening took place (see Chapter 10). Gardening was evident from the numerous small stone boxes used, no doubt, to contain wooden trellis works for plants, bushes, shrubs, or small trees. We even found the remains of a root system intact leading from some of these boxes, but unfortunately the species of the plant could not be identified. Some of the boxes preserved charred remains in their interiors. These small, shallow stone boxes with no stone bottoms were fairly uniform in appearance and size. They survived in areas that would have been directly exposed to the sun as well as in shaded locations, which would have received only indirect sunlight. This suggests that several different species of plants were cultivated. The stone boxes appeared individually or in groups of four to six scattered throughout the courtyards. Several of the open courtyards also preserved evidence of small-scale industrial activities and, likely, limited animal husbandry. These pastimes would have provided a form of entertainment or been hobbies for those dwelling in this forlorn location and would have had the added benefit of supplementing their diets with some fresh produce. Otherwise most of the food consumed here was likely hauled in great distances from the Nile Valley and to a lesser extent from the Red Sea.

We also found a number of locally carved items made from the readily available, very soft, and easily worked schist-talc stone including beads, children's toys such as camels and dolls, bracelets, and loom weights or spindle whorls. Some of the thousands of beryl/emerald fragments we recovered had been pierced to make beads for jewelry for local use. We also retrieved over 2,500 beads many of which appear to have been imported from India and Sri Lanka. Many of these beads were high quality including gilded specimens and ones made from carnelian and quartz, which indicates that at least some of the residents of Sikait had a fair degree of discretionary wealth.

We excavated evidence in the form of a few potshards, possibly, and a coin that there was contact between Sikait and the caravan kingdom of the Nabataeans, whose capital was carved from the mountains at the rose-red city of Petra, in modern Jordan. The archaeological context in which our excavations in winter 2002–2003 recovered these fascinating artifacts suggests that they arrived on the site in the early first century AD, which was the zenith of Nabataean commercial activity throughout the Middle East and the Mediterranean.

Middle Sikait

As we noted above, Sikait was but one of nine emerald mining centers that we have discovered thus far in the region of Mons Smaragdus. A few kilometers farther up the same wadi we found a large site that we named Middle Sikait. Though preserving few buildings, the hundreds of mine shafts and plethora of associated potshards scattered over a wide area indicate a hive of activity here in at least the first, second, and fourth centuries AD. The most impressive single feature of Middle Sikait is a massive artificial ramp or causeway several meters wide that clings to the sides of peaks as it snakes about 1,600 meters up from the wadi floor to a building concentration part way up the mountain side (Fig. 12.14). The large buildings found at the upper end of the ramp appear to have had public functions though given our paltry evidence at this time, we cannot determine what those might have been. Mines and pathways, artificially cut in the mountains and built up of rubble where necessary, cover a large area. Watchtowers and lookout points appear at strategic locations throughout the site. In one particularly alluring example, a rock-cut staircase leads down into a deep shaft that spiderwebs off into many directions no doubt following potentially rich veins. Outside this example is a *tabula rasa* carved beside the entrance (Fig. 12.5). Perhaps at one time this preserved painted letters, or numbers, long since faded away, indicating the mine number and labor force assigned here; surely this would have facilitated the Roman administrators' penchant for keeping accurate records of the lucrative activities conducted in this mine. We can only assume that similar tracking methods were used at many if not all the mineshafts, but we have noted no others.

North Sikait

Somewhat farther north of Middle Sikait, up Wadi Sikait, we have completed a survey of the mining community in a location we named North Sikait. This less impressive settlement comprising scores of structures dates only to late Roman times and may suggest that as earlier more easily accessible and transportable sources of emeralds became exhausted these less accessible sources farther up the wadi were tapped. Many of the mineshafts here have been worked in modern times as the presence of painted numbers and letters indicates and as the existence of clearly modern structures in the nearby wadi attests.

S.E. Sidebotham

Fig. 12.14: Ramp at the Roman-era beryl/emerald mining community at Middle Sikait.

Nugrus

Another impressive mining community nearby and only a few kilometers south and west of the main, southernmost settlement in Wadi Sikait can be found at Nugrus. Our surveys have located one path that linked Sikait to Nugrus over the intervening mountains; there were undoubtedly many others. Strewn along and near the path we noted hundreds of mining shafts and dozens of buildings and graves of those who lived, worked, and perished in these remote mountains in the Eastern Desert. Undoubtedly a thorough archaeological survey of this area would reveal even more. We also marveled at the remains, unique as far as we know, of a bridge-like structure that crosses a steep cliff face along this mountain trail.

Analysis of the potshards we have collected at Nugrus indicates that the community thrived in at least the early and late Roman periods. If we ever excavate the ancient remains, we may well discover that Nugrus had a much longer history than its potshards now suggest.

Nugrus, like Sikait, clings to the relatively steep sides of the wadi of the same name. Our survey of this settlement, which comprises scores of buildings, has only just begun and has concentrated primarily thus far on recording about twenty of the best-preserved structures (Figs. 12.15–12.16 and Pl. 12.2). These contain windows, doors, interior shelves and, in some cases, stone roofs. One impressive structure rests atop a large and elaborate artificial platform. As at Sikait, and despite some excellent preservation, we have no concrete evidence of what purpose most of the buildings served. Somewhat south of the main concentration of structures, our survey located a very nice multi-roomed edifice portions of which preserve doors and stone roofing, which we described in Chapter 6 as a temple.

Wadi Umm Harba

We discovered another mining settlement only in winter 2002–2003 that lay in Wadi Umm Harba, east of Sikait. Approached by a winding narrow path cut through the mountains, which includes rock cut stairways and artificial ramps similar to those we found at Middle Sikait, this mountain track was marked by cairns leading from the southern limits of Middle Sikait to a settlement in Wadi Umm Harba. Comprising about forty-five structures and surrounded by scores if not hundreds of mining adits, pits, and vertical shafts, this quaint community has two distinct areas. One comprises edifices that are relatively well made and built of carefully stacked flat stones (Fig. 12.17) similar in appearance to some of the structures seen in Wadi Sikait, while the other is more cavalierly constructed of whatever cobbles and small boulders were at hand. The cursory evidence we gleaned from surveys in Wadi Umm Harba indicates that the site was active from early until late Roman times. We plan to return here to conduct a more thorough investigation at some point in the future.

Lack of Fortifications

As in the case of Wadi Abu Dieyiba where the absence of fortifications suggests lack of perceived threats and, concomitantly, the presence of a free rather than a servile labor force, the same is true at all of the beryl/emerald mines discussed here. Our surveys have found no forts guarding any of these settlements. Our excavations at Sikait did, however, unearth metal arrowheads and pieces of scale armor indicating the presence of armed guards or soldiers. A large fort does exist in Wadi Gemal, near the southern limits of the beryl mining area. This may be the *praesidium* of Apollonos referred to in a number of ancient texts. The remains of this massive fort of

S.E. Sidebotham

Fig. 12.15: Structure at the Roman-era beryl/emerald mining community at Nugrus.

A.M.Hense

Fig. 12.16: The same structure at Nugrus.

S. E. Sidebotham

Fig 12.17: Structures at the Roman-era beryl/emerald mining settlement in Wadi Umm Harba.

Roman date, one of the largest thus far recorded in the Eastern Desert, covers almost a hectare. It seems by its location, however, not to have served to coerce local labor forces, but more to reassure and provide an important administrative center for regional mining activities. The positioning of this fort on the main route between Berenike and the Nile also indicates that it played a role in the support and monitoring of trans-desert commerce and communications between the Nile emporia of Edfu and Coptos on the one hand and the Red Sea port of Berenike on the other.

Beryls/Emeralds in Jewelry

While we have found amethysts and beryls/emeralds in profusion at the various mining centers, what evidence do we have of their actual use in jewelry from ancient times? There are two valuable sources of information on this. One is, naturally, the jewelry itself. Found in ancient tombs and elsewhere, these gemstones were frequently set in stunning gold necklaces, earrings and bracelets. Numerous examples of these survive and can be seen in museums around the world with particularly fine specimens in the British Museum in London.

Another fascinating source from the ancient world that sheds light on the appearance and use of jewelry set with amethysts and beryls/emeralds survives in the form of painted mummy portraits from Roman Egypt (Pl. 12.3) These so-called Fayyum mummy portraits, used to cover the mummified and wrapped remains of mainly mid-level bureaucrats and their families, survive in large numbers and depict the busts of deceased men, women, and children particularly from the first, second, and third centuries AD. Many of the women appear with elaborate coiffeurs, wearing their finest clothing and donning their most valuable possessions: necklaces and earrings of gold set with a variety of precious and semiprecious stones including pearls, amethysts, and emeralds. These mummy portraits are the prized possessions of several museums and private collections. Some of the finest can be seen in the British Museum and Petrie Museum in London, the Louvre in Paris, the Metropolitan Museum of Art in New York, the Kunsthistorische Museum in Vienna, and the J. Paul Getty Museum in California.

Water, The Desert Elixir

The first consideration of anyone venturing into the Eastern Desert is the availability of adequate quantities of potable water (Figs. 13.1–13.2). Without this primary resource no other activity can take place. Yet precipitation in the Eastern Desert, where measured scientifically in recent times at Quseir on the Red Sea coast, is quite meager, ranging from 4–5 millimeters per annum. Averages were probably much the same in the Ptolemaic-Roman period, though perhaps somewhat greater early in the pharaonic era before the Eastern Desert became increasingly the desiccated region that it is today. Thus, ancient technologies used in the area for finding, storing, managing, and distributing this most basic of all human needs had, by necessity, to be very highly developed.

We understand firsthand the preoccupation with water supplies that ancient peoples had while living in the Eastern Desert. During our numerous desert surveys and archaeological excavations over the years, which we have conducted in both summers and winters, we constantly monitor our large array of twenty-liter plastic jerry cans to ensure that they are not leaking and that we have enough water to carry us until we can be resupplied or until the end of our fieldwork. Since it is basically unavailable to us in the desert, carrying hundreds of liters of water for a survey of several weeks takes up most of the space and weight in our vehicles. This problem is, of course, greatly magnified on an excavation lasting several months and involving scores of people. We do not have the advantage that our ancient

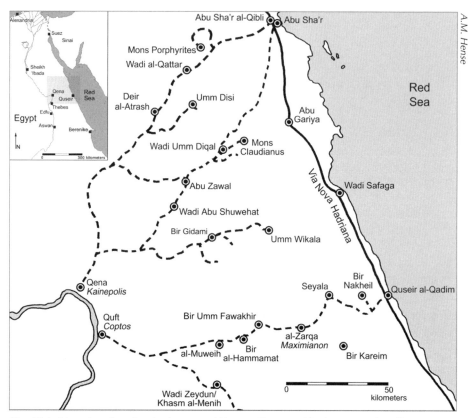

Fig. 13.1: Map showing sites in the central Eastern Desert with cisterns and wells or recipients of water supplies mentioned in this chapter.

forbearers had of obtaining much, if any, of our water from desert wells. These are now few and far between compared at least to the Ptolemaic and Roman periods. Today, those wells that we do encounter are often the preserve of the Bedouin who must water their charges; it would be most inappropriate of us to tap these for our own uses.

As we noted in Chapter 5, our personal experiences have shown that a human, when moderately exerted in the desert, drinks at least four to six liters of water a day in the summer, less in the winter. When we add to this amount additional water consumed for bathing, cooking, and so on, we have found that each human requires an average of ten to fifteen liters per day in the summer, less in the winter.

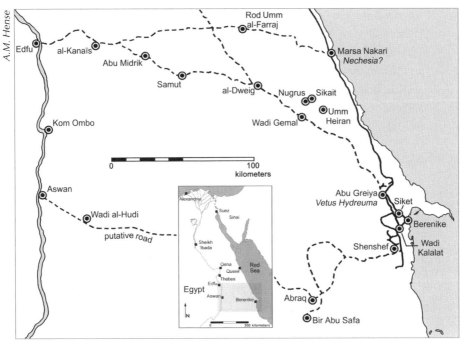

Fig. 13.2: Map showing sites in the southern Eastern Desert with cisterns and wells or recipients of water supplies mentioned in this chapter.

Water used by donkeys and camels, the primary pack animals, would have been critical considerations to those living and traveling through the region. The amounts they consumed would, of course, vary dramatically depending on a whole host of factors including their ages, health, and size, the distances to be traveled, weight of the loads and temperature. On a typical travel day a donkey can carry 70 to 90 kilograms in panniers while a camel averages 200 to 225 kilograms; a camel can carry substantially more than this if transporting over shorter distances, as can a donkey in a non-desert environment. A camel can drink water far more saline than a donkey can tolerate and can, if necessary, go far longer without water than a donkey. A donkey does, however, have the advantage of being able to negotiate stonier ground than a camel.

Based on modern studies in hot weather a pack donkey must drink about ten liters a day while a pack camel averages twenty liters. Stories of great endurance prove exceptions to the rule. In 1926, for example, G.W. Murray, when visiting the Gebel 'Elba area in the extreme southeastern corner of the Eastern Desert, reported that his camels did not drink for an extraordinary 128 days! This, he writes, was due to cool weather, short, easy daily journeys, and the animals' consumption of copious quantities of succulent plants.

Of course, Murray's was a one time visit. How and where exactly did ancient peoples obtain water in the desert on a more or less regular basis for relatively large numbers of humans and animals?

Pharaonic Period
Old Kingdom

We have ample evidence of the prominent role water played for people in the Eastern Desert from the Old Kingdom period (2649–2152 BC) until Roman times (30 BC–seventh century AD). One of the earliest hydraulic features in the Eastern Desert is the remains of an Old Kingdom installation at a location called Sad al-Kafara (Dam of the Infidels), about thirty kilometers east of Cairo. The dam was probably constructed during the reign of Fourth Dynasty pharaoh Khufu (2551–2528 BC), builder of the largest pyramid at Giza. The dam would have measured originally about 113 meters long at its top by about 14 meters high by approximately 98 meters thick at its base. Parts have since been washed away and the structure may never have been completed in antiquity. Its precise purpose remains a mystery.

New Kingdom

Other evidence from the New Kingdom, specifically the Nineteenth and Twentieth Dynasties, also deals with water use in the Eastern Desert. From the Nineteenth Dynasty there are two inscriptions from the reign of Seti I (1306–1290 BC) and one from his more famous son Ramesses II (1290–1224 BC); surviving from the Twentieth Dynasty is a map. The Seti inscriptions, found at the rock-cut temple built by that pharaoh at al-Kanaïs, mentioned in Chapter 6, lie forty-six to forty-seven kilometers east of Edfu. These texts indicate that wells were dug in the proximity of the temple to provide water to those voyaging between the Nile and the desert gold mines. Ramesses' inscription appears on the famous Kubban Stele where he boasts of finding water in a well dug to a depth of only six meters while his father had previously found none. Ramesses' well, like those of his father, was also intended to support gold mining activities in the desert.

The Turin Papyrus map, dating to the reign of Ramesses IV (1163–1156 BC) and described in Chapter 4, shows, among other features, a wall surrounding a well, probably to prevent infilling by flood-borne sediments. There is also a cistern, gold mines, and a *bekhen* stone quarry as well as roads radiating from the map's focal point off to other regions of the desert. The well on the map probably signifies the ready availability of water in the area rather than a single specific well. Water would have been used for human needs—drinking, washing, cooking, irrigation for small gardens—and animal consumption, as well as the industrial processing of gold we describe in Chapter 9. We know that even during his short reign, Ramesses IV sent several expeditions to the region, the last one being huge and comprising 8,362 men. Unless some or all the water these thousands of human beings required was brought from the Nile, about eighty-four kilometers away, which is highly unlikely, they would have obtained what they needed from wells excavated nearby. No trace of these ancient wells would survive, of course, as they were long ago smothered by water- and wind-borne sand.

Ptolemaic and Roman Periods
Times of Year to Travel in the Desert
Ancient graffiti and ostraca dated to Roman times found in the desert, taken together with known sailing seasons to and from the Red Sea ports, indicate that desert travel, quarrying, and mining operations were perennial and not confined only to the cooler winter months. Such was probably also the case in earlier times. Since travel into the desert took place perennially, the pressure on water supplies must have been especially intense during the summer months. Fortunately, we have far more evidence for how water was stored and distributed in the Ptolemaic and Roman periods than any other era of antiquity.

Sources of Water in the Eastern Desert
There were, and are still today, two major sources: surface runoff after rare and heavy rains, and sub-surface water. The former is mainly seasonal, appearing after the rains, when they do fall, usually in November and December; we also include springs in this category. On the other hand, sub-surface water is perennial and, as a result, far more dependable. Let us examine these supplies.

Surface water is, of course, easier to locate and obtain than sub-surface, but its quantity, quality, and dependability are extremely erratic. One method is natural accumulation of rainwater in *qulut*. Another is rainwater run-off flowing from mountains that is deliberately channeled by human action into cisterns, water catchments or perhaps smaller, more portable containers. The last is from springs.

Qulut

Qulut occur naturally in depressions of eroded hard stone, mainly igneous and metamorphic, like granite and other crystalline rocks that are found along wadi beds or at the bases of seasonal waterfalls. They hold vastly varying quantities of water depending, of course, on their sizes, the amount of water that has accumulated in them and their locations in direct sun light or shade. *Qulut* would not have played a major role as regular and reliable sources of water acquisition for consumption by humans or pack animals though the Bedouins might have—as they do today—occasionally watered herds of goats, sheep, donkeys, and camels at such places. Most *qulut* are only useful at certain times of year, immediately following heavy rains. They are often not easily accessible, or large enough along or near the major trans-desert roads in the region for regular and sustained use.

Let us provide some examples of exceptional *qulut* we have seen during our desert surveys. The most impressive must be the one near Umm Disi, west of Hurghada. When we visited it in August 1997 it was large enough to swim in (Pl. 13.1). From reading accounts of earlier visitors to this remote location part way up a mountain slope it is evident that amounts of water there could vary amazingly from one year to the next depending, of course, completely upon rainfall. One visitor wrote that he saw the *qalt* at Umm Disi bone dry while another reported that it brimmed with an estimated one hundred thousand liters of water.

Other *qulut* we have seen on our surveys are much smaller than Umm Disi. The one about 1,550 meters down the wadi southeast of the center of the late Roman-era desert settlement of Wadi Shenshef, 21.3 kilometers in a straight line southwest of Berenike, was quite large when we saw it in winter 1996. There were other pools with varying amounts of water in them between that large *qalt* and the main settlement in Wadi Shenshef. We do not know if this *qalt* and nearby pools supplied the ancient settlement, though they potentially could have done so whenever sufficient amounts of water had accumulated in them.

A French project conducted in the late nineteenth century reported two *qulut* in the region of the ancient Roman beryl/emerald mines at Nugrus and Sikait. Our surveys have not seen these *qulut*, but the French go on to report that one of them was in a small side tributary of "Wadi Nougourans" in a depression in gneiss, a hard 'basement' rock. It must have contained an impressive amount of water, for their report published in 1900 indicates that the source was sufficient for their entire field season for twenty persons. The same French team noted another *qalt* in Wadi Sikait that produced potable water for only a short time. In addition to being easily and quickly fouled by animals, that water remaining in *qulut* becomes increasingly saline as it evaporates. This makes *qulut* even less reliable as sources of potable water.

Springs

Springs (*'ayn* singular/*'uyun* plural in Arabic) were another source of water in the Eastern Desert for ancient travelers. Though these derive from the subsurface, they appear naturally on the surface and so are best discussed in this category. Springs usually produce very pure water, but are rare in the Eastern Desert and generally remote from most areas of substantial habitation or from the major ancient desert roads. They also provide too little water to be important perennial supplies though they are good supplements or sources for very limited numbers of people and animals making infrequent visits. The early twentieth century British geologist F.W. Hume described two of the most noteworthy springs he knew of in the Eastern Desert, one in Wadi Qattar and another in Wadi Dara. One of our surveys in January 1989 visited Qattar, just off the Abu Sha'r/Mons Porphyrites–Nile road, but we found that spring dry.

During our fieldwork in the area of the ancient beryl/emerald mines of Sikait in June 2002 one of our 'Ababda Bedouin workmen showed us a small spring about one kilometer east of the main site. He claimed that it produced about ten liters of potable water per day. Hume also noted a spring near Sikait that produced about fifty liters of "excellent water issuing from a rock drop by drop." He did not, however, indicate where in the Sikait area he saw this spring, but his description suggests that it was not the same one the Bedouin showed us in 2002.

RICHARD POCOCKE

Richard Pococke was born in Southampton in 1704 and studied religion at Oxford. He visited (perhaps in 1737–1741) Egypt, Lebanon, Palestine, Syria, Mesopotamia, Crete, Cyprus, and Greece. The first volume of his *Description of the East and Some Other Countries* was completely devoted to Egypt. His extensive descriptions of the ancient monuments were accompanied by plans, maps, and drawings. Among his maps were the first modern one of the Valley of Kings and the first accurate map of Egypt.

His interest was not restricted to ancient monuments; his book also describes the landscape, flora and fauna, and the habits and material culture of the eighteenth-century Egyptians. Pococke drew a map of Cairo and described Coptic monasteries and Islamic monuments. After his lengthy travels he took up an appointment as bishop of Meath. He died in 1765.

Another example we saw in September 2002 was in the deep south of the Eastern Desert. This is a spring associated with the Ptolemaic temple façade at Bir Abu Safa, which we described in Chapter 6.

Several forts on the Berenike–Nile roads used artificially built channels, apparently in early Roman times, to direct rainwater flow from nearby mountains into the cisterns *(lakkoi)* inside adjacent *praesidia*. We do not know whether this was the sole source of water for these installations or merely supplementary to more traditional methods of acquisition from wells, which were located either inside or outside the forts' walls.

Wells

Subsurface water, mainly obtained from wells (*bir* singular/*abyar* plural in Arabic), was, and remains today, the most common, abundant, and reliable source of water available in the Eastern Desert. While we have descriptions from pharaonic sources about the excavation of wells, none from this period survive in the archaeological record. Our best archaeological source for the physical appearance of wells is from Ptolemaic and especially Roman times. Wells *(hydreumata)* and their partially sanded-up remains survive inside numerous *praesidia* in the Eastern Desert. Most are circular in plan, frequently quite large, and they often dominate the center of these desert forts.

One of the most impressive wells we have ever seen is in the large *praesidium* in Wadi Kalalat only about 8.5 kilometers southwest of Berenike (Figs. 13.3 and Pl. 13.3–13.4). This huge installation provided some of the water supply for Berenike; it, and a small fort only nine hundred meters to the northeast, guarded the southern and western approaches to Berenike in the early Roman period. The larger fort has a stone-lined well in its center that measures about thirty-two meters in diameter, with a stairway leading into the sandy depths, probably originally to the surface of the water. The well is now almost completely filled up with wind-blown sand, but its imposing contours are still visible. The large fort was abandoned in the second century AD for reasons that still remain a mystery; maybe the well water became too saline or the water table had dropped; thereafter a much more modest fort was constructed to the northeast. This smaller installation, also partially buried by shifting sands, may have had an interior well, but if so, it has been completely filled in.

S.E. Sidebotham

Fig. 13.3: Inscription fragments found in the large *praesidium* in Wadi Kalalat from the time of the prefect Servius Sulpicius Similis (AD 109–110), governor during the reign of the Roman emperor Trajan (AD 98–117).

Staircases provided access to many of these wells and remains of staircases can be seen not only in the Wadi Kalalat example, but also at others
in the region. The finely preserved fort at al-Zarqa (ancient Maximianon)
on the Myos Hormos–Nile road (see Chapter 4) has portions of the well
staircase intact. Most ancient wells, where they are at least partially visible, were lined with locally obtainable cobblestones or fired bricks to
minimize internal collapse and maintain some degree of water purity.

In the first part of the twentieth century the Geological Survey under
British supervision re-excavated and relined many of these earlier Roman
wells and added staircases and concrete basins. They did this, like their
ancient predecessors, to facilitate mining and quarrying activities in the
Eastern Desert. These modern repairs may provide some idea of what
their ancient predecessors originally looked like. Examples of modern
reworking can be seen at the Ptolemaic-Roman *praesidium* at al-Kanaïs
(on the Berenike–Edfu and Marsa Nakari–Edfu roads) (Pl. 13.2) where
the modern well and basin are probably not near the original location of
the ancient ones. We have also noted modifications to the station at Qattar on the Abu Sha'r/Mons Porphyrites–Nile road made in the 1920s or
1930s when, as an 'inscription' carved into the wet concrete of one of the
hydraulic tanks indicates, Farouk was Amir of Egypt (1920–1937). Other
sites with modern adaptations or modifications can be seen at Abu Greiya
on the southern portion of the Mons Claudianus–Nile road just north of
the modern asphalt highway about forty-two kilometers from Qena, and
at the *praesidium* at Abu Zawal (Place/Father of Ghosts), a gold mining
camp, also on the Mons Claudianus–Nile road. The cisterns and well
inside the station at Abu Gariya (see Chapter 3) on the Via Nova Hadriana have also been remodeled in modern times as have those at Seyala and
Bir al-Hammamat on the Myos Hormos–Coptos road.

The mid-nineteenth-century German traveler Karl Richard Lepsius
was impressed by the ancient and still functioning well at Bir al-Hamma-
mat noting that it was "broad. . . ., about eighty feet deep, lined with
stones, into which there is a descent by a winding staircase." The Arabs
told Lepsius that Christians had built it and recent archaeological surveys
and excavations at the nearby gold mines at Bir Umm Fawakhir date that
site to the fifth and sixth centuries AD, the Christian period in Egypt. We
would expect traffic between Bir Umm Fawakhir and the Nile to make

frequent use of water facilities en route and the supply at Bir al-Hamma-mat was a natural stopping point, one those responsible for the miners' welfare would have improved to facilitate access to the water. The stop at Bir al-Hammamat, whose ancient name remains unknown, also catered to later Muslim pilgrims making the *hajj* to Mecca from the Nile Valley of Upper Egypt as attested by the remains of a small mosque built into one corner of the *praesidium*. The well itself looks the same today, though clearly the superstructure covering it is a more recent addition of about 1830 or perhaps later.

Roman-era *praesidia* in many instances probably also obtained water supplies from extramural wells. Extensive ground penetrating radar stud-ies of areas around some of these forts and wadis adjacent to the main ancient trans-desert roads should be undertaken to determine if this was the case and extent to which it was practiced.

Civilian or quasi-civilian settlements in the Eastern Desert (see Chapter 10) include those whose exact status remains uncertain. Some of these communities comprise over one hundred buildings and must have had, *a priori*, reliable and perennial sources of water. We have conducted site intensive surveys of six such settlements, which may or may not have been Christian *laura*-hermit communities. These ranged in size from forty-seven to about 190 (at Umm Heiran near Sikait) structures each comprising between one and three relatively small rooms, rarely more. Sometimes there are larger structures on these sites.

Our surveys of these communities found many similarities. The sites, in general, dated from late fourth through sixth centuries AD, sometimes later. All would have acquired water from wells sunk in their environs. We collected large numbers of shards of a type of jar called Late Roman Amphora 1 from these desert settlements and know that these jars were made in Cyprus and Cilicia on the southern coast of Asia Minor. It is surprising to find amphoras imported from such distances at these rela-tively remote and 'low status' sites. Yet, we know from ancient literary sources that some Christian desert settlers consumed imported wine. The Christian writer Palladius writing his *Historia Lausiaca* in AD 419–420 recounted his personal experiences as a Christian hermit in the Egyptian desert and he is one of the more important sources for the his-tory of early Christian monasticism in Egypt. Necessity and practicality would have compelled the residents of these humble settlements to recycle the jars in which wine may have originally been shipped and stored. Once empty of their original contents, however, these jars would have served ideally as water containers. Palladius, in fact, mentions that Cilician pots and water jars were used at a number of Christian desert communities and it is likely no coincidence that we have found fragments of shipment and storage jars of this type, the Late Roman Amphora 1 amphoras noted above, in great numbers at all of the putative Christian sites we studied in the Eastern Desert.

The large Red Sea ports hauled potable water from varying distances in the desert because water deriving from wells dug by the sea would have been too brackish for human consumption. We know in the case of Berenike that at least three forts ranging from 7.2 to 8.5 kilometers west of the city, two in Wadi Kalalat and one at Siket, supplied drinking water to the port and we have more to say about Siket in Chapter 15. At Myos Hormos, too, it seems drinking water came from either Bir Nakheil immediately west of the port or from Bir Kareim about thirty-five kilometers to the southwest or perhaps from both places. Evidence suggests that water was laboriously hauled by pack animals from the wells to the ports; there is no evidence that aqueducts were used.

Given the high rates of evaporation in the desert and increased salinity of water remaining after evaporation it was essential to store and protect it carefully. As we have already mentioned, modern average evaporation statistics in the Red Sea Governorate of Egypt are 2,500 millimeters per annum versus annual precipitation of four to five millimeters. With similar rates in the Greco-Roman period it was critical that water be ingeniously retrieved, carefully stored, and sparingly distributed. The wells and cisterns visible throughout the desert are testaments to Ptolemaic-Roman care for the water supplies. Protective lining of wells with stones or bricks allowed them to be deeper; these linings also minimized collapse thereby keeping the water more pure. Thick coatings of lime-based waterproof plaster covering carefully crafted water cisterns made of cobbles or fired bricks, combined with shelves at the tops on which would be affixed wooden and leather or cloth covers, reduced evaporation and kept the water cleaner by reducing the amount of dirt that might otherwise blow or be accidentally dropped into them.

Reliable figures on amounts of water stored are sporadic and derive only from our own calculations and those of our European colleagues. No ancient written sources from the region record the amounts of water available at any of these wells or cisterns. At the Ptolemaic station at Abu Midrik on the Berenike–Apollonopolis Magna road we estimate that the two circular cisterns there could hold approximately 88,000 liters though there is no way to determine if they ever actually did so or how often. The early Roman *praesidium* at the quarry at Umm Wikala held 8,800 liters while that at the Ptolemaic-early Roman station at Rod Umm al-Farraj (Fig. 13.4) on the Marsa Nakari–Edfu road held approximately 39,000 liters. French archaeologists report that the tanks at al-Muweih (ancient Krokodilo) on the Myos Hormos–Nile road had a theoretical maximum capacity of over 200,000 liters. A small cistern inside the main fort at Mons Claudianus, on the other hand, held a mere ten thousand liters.

S.E. Sidebotham

Fig. 13.4: The cistern at the Ptolemaic-early Roman station at Rod Umm al-Farraj.

KARL RICHARD LEPSIUS

Karl Richard Lepsius was born in Saxony in 1810. He was the founder of modern scientific archaeology and is best known for his catalogue of Egyptian archaeological remains and for establishing a chronology for Egyptian history. He studied Greek and Roman archaeology at Leipzig, Gottingen, and Berlin, where he received his doctorate in 1833. Before his first visit to Egypt he expanded upon Champollion's work on hieroglyphs. Sponsored by King Wilhelm IV of Prussia, Lepsius led a famous expedition to Egypt and Nubia between 1842 and 1845 the purpose of which was to record monuments and collect antiquities. The expedition was a milestone as it contributed greatly to our knowledge of Egyptian monuments (many now lost or badly damaged), language, mythology, and geography. Upon his return to Prussia, Lepsius was appointed professor at Berlin University and he published his findings in the monumental multi-volume *Denkmaler aus Ägypten und Äthiopen* (1849–1858). These tomes are comparable to the Napoleonic magnum opus *Description de l'Égypte*. In 1865 Lepsius became keeper of the Egyptian Antiquities Department in the Berlin Museum. In the same year he led another expedition to the Delta region of Egypt. His last visit to Egypt was to witness ceremonies surrounding the opening of the Suez Canal in 1869. He continued writing until his death in Berlin in July 1884.

Pipelines and Aqueducts

Overall the larger sizes and greater numbers of the Roman-era forts compared to their Ptolemaic predecessors suggest that there were more people and animals residing in and passing by these installations in the early centuries of the Christian era than previously. Evidence of aqueducts or other devices to divert, control, or deliver water from one point in the desert to another do survive though we do not always understand precisely their functions. Conduits could have been used for both water acquisition and distribution though the bulk of the evidence suggests that most pipelines were for distribution. There must have been numerous examples of piping water from sources to points of storage and distribution in the Eastern Desert in antiquity, but few have been identified or studied. Many are no doubt hidden by sand or, in some cases, no longer survive.

Lengths of pipes or evidence for their existence indicate conveyance of water from *hydreumata* inside *praesidia* to adjacent or nearby *lakkoi* in several examples including the large fort in Wadi Kalalat, at Abu Greiya (possibly ancient Jovis) on the Berenike–Coptos road and likely that in Wadi Safaga on the Via Nova Hadriana. French archaeologists have also found them at al-Zarqa (ancient Maximianon) on the Myos Hormos road and at Khashm al-Menih/Zeydun (ancient Didymoi) on the Berenike–Coptos route.

There are only two examples of terra-cotta and stone pipes built over distances of several hundred meters or more that have been recognized and studied in the Eastern Desert. One is late Roman and the other can be no more precisely dated than to the Roman era. Both examples carried water to military installations. The one at the late Roman fort at Abu Sha'r on the Red Sea coast north of Hurghada (see Chapter 3) brought water from a well about one kilometer southwest of the fort under pressure through a closed system of terra-cotta pipes coated on the outside with plaster (Figs. 13.5–13.6). This pipeline entered the fort through the main western gate, but its terminus inside the fort remains uncertain, though it may have been the headquarters *(principia)*, which was later in the fourth or early fifth century converted into a church. There was probably also a branch of this water pipeline that bifurcated just before reaching the west gate and headed north supplying the fort's large extramural bath.

The second example of a pipeline brought water about 477 meters from the well at Bir Abu Sha'r al-Qibli to a small *praesidium* which we excavated in part in 1993. This small fort had been a station on both the second century AD Via Nova Hadriana (see Chapter 3) and had also served the late Roman fort at Abu Sha'r which lay 5.5 kilometers to the east. Thus, a precise date for this pipeline cannot be established. The internal diameter of this plaster and rock conduit was about ten centimeters and water flowing through it would have filled several water tanks the remains of which can still be seen located outside the southern wall of the small *praesidium*.

Our surveys have also found evidence for the conveyance of water from inside forts to small extramural water tanks, presumably to supply varying numbers of passing pack animals. Such external tanks can be seen at Deir al-Atrash ('Monastery of the Deaf One') on the Abu Sha'r/Mons Porphyrites–Nile road, at Abu Gariya on the Via Nova Hadriana, and at Abu

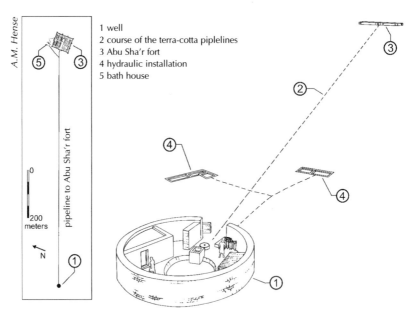

1 well
2 course of the terra-cotta piplelines
3 Abu Sha'r fort
4 hydraulic installation
5 bath house

A.M. Hense

pipeline to Abu Sha'r fort

0
200
meters

N

Fig. 13.5 Pipeline leading from a well to the late Roman fort at Abu Sha'r, about one kilometer away, on the Red Sea coast north of Hurghada.

S.E. Sidebotham

Fig. 13.6: Pipeline from a well one kilometer from the main fort at Abu Sha'r.

Greiya (ancient Jovis?) on the Berenike–Coptos road. There are also large, but extremely damaged, remains of hydraulic tanks both east and west of the main fort walls of the large *praesidium* in Wadi Kalalat near Berenike. Moreover, there is a large unfortified hydraulic installation in Wadi Abu Shuwehat on the southern route between Mons Claudianus and the Nile at Kainepolis (Figs. 13.7–13.8). Here there was at least one large well surrounded by a low stone wall, no doubt to keep animals from approaching too close to the source and also to prevent waterborne sediments from clogging the water source. One or more terra-cotta conduits, now in fragmentary states of preservation, fed water from this well to numerous troughs made of terra-cotta and plaster associated with a series of animal tethering lines that accommodated traffic hauling stone from Mons Claudianus to the Nile. A small hole part way up and through the eastern perimeter wall at the *praesidium* of Maximianon on the Myos Hormos–Nile road possibly conveyed water for extramural consumption by animals or liquefied waste from the fort interior to the exterior.

There has been some debate about the function of the so-called 'aqueduct' leading from the hydraulic complex in Wadi Umm Diqal toward the main settlement at Mons Claudianus. Earlier visitors believed that the long stone walls were the remains of an aqueduct, but recent investigations by a French-directed team that excavated and surveyed extensively in this region between 1987 and 1993 do not support this identification. More likely, the walls diverted wadi floods (*seyul/seyal* in Arabic) away from important architectural features or graves; possible parallels have been reported near Bir Nakheil west of Myos Hormos and in Wadi Qattar on the Abu Sha'r/Mons Porphyrites–Nile road; our survey has not seen these. Others of similar function survive in Libya and in the ancient Kingdom of Kush in what is today Sudan.

In 1826 J.G. Wilkinson, the same British traveler who drew the first plan of Berenike, noted a well and small length of possible aqueduct leading away from it toward lower ground in Wadi Abu Greiya (ancient Vetus Hydreuma) (Fig. 13.9), the first stop on the road leading from Berenike to the Nile. This well and putative aqueduct lay immediately south and at the base of the mountain atop which perches a facility our survey named 'Hill Top Fort Number 5.' Our survey work in the area has not revealed the conduit or wall that appears on Wilkinson's plan, but comparison of

S.E. Sidebotham

Fig 13.7: Water distribution system and animal tethering lines at the large unfortified hydraulic installation in Wadi Abu Shuwehat.

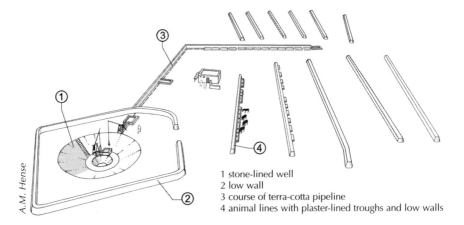

A.M. Hense

1 stone-lined well
2 low wall
3 course of terra-cotta pipeline
4 animal lines with plaster-lined troughs and low walls

Fig. 13.8: Water distribution system and animal tethering lines at the large unfortified hydraulic installation in Wadi Abu Shuwehat.

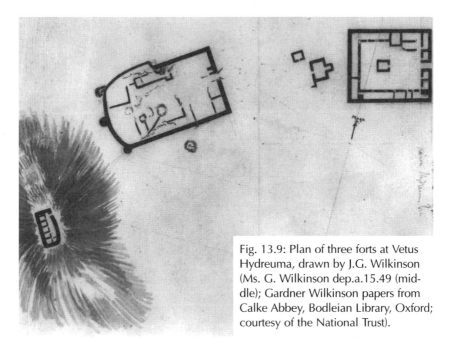

Fig. 13.9: Plan of three forts at Vetus Hydreuma, drawn by J.G. Wilkinson (Ms. G. Wilkinson dep.a.15.49 (middle); Gardner Wilkinson papers from Calke Abbey, Bodleian Library, Oxford; courtesy of the National Trust).

Wilkinson's numerous other plans and maps of antiquities that he drew in the Eastern Desert with actual remains have proven him to be generally accurate and reliable. Thus, we have no reason to doubt the existence of the wall or conduit he drew though we might argue with him about the function. Perhaps Wilkinson's now missing feature was a water diversion wall similar to that found in Wadi Umm Diqal in the Mons Claudianus area or some type of conduit designed to transport water from the well near the hilltop forts downhill and eastward toward the two large low-lying wadi forts in Wadi Abu Greiya about two or three kilometers away following the wadi floor. The nearest fort to the well and now missing wall is early Roman in date, precisely the period when travel along the road between Berenike and the Nile would have been at its peak and extra water would have been required for human and animal visitors.

Water Lifting Devices

Water lifting devices may also have been used at several Eastern Desert installations including Deir al-Atrash and the lower fort at al-Heita, both on the Abu Sha'r/Mons Porphyrites–Nile road, perhaps at Abu Zawal, noted above, at Gerf (likely the ancient Aristonis) on the Berenike–Coptos road and at Abu Sha'r al-Qibli on the Via Nova Hadriana also noted above. Called a *shaduf* in Arabic today (Fig. 13.10), a *kelon* in Greek and a *telo, tolleno,* or *ciconia* in Latin, this device can still be found along the Nile and was used to convey water from a lower elevation to a higher. A *shaduf* is basically a long pole with a bucket-like device at one end and a counterweight, often made of mud or clay, on the other, resting on a vertical beam that allows the long pole to dip down into the water source.

Waterwheels, *saqyas* in Arabic, *mechane* in Greek, were also used in the Eastern Desert in Roman times (Fig. 13.11). These devices were animal-powered waterwheels that had pots attached to lift water to higher ground. British excavators believe that such a device was probably used at Mons Porphyrites to draw water from a well just below the main fort. There are

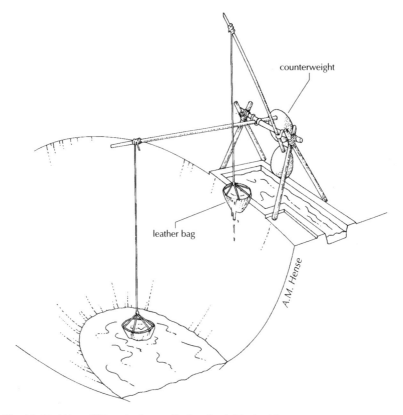

counterweight

leather bag

A.M. Hense

Fig. 13.10: Water lifting device, called a *shaduf* in Arabic

remains of *saqya* pots and references to women operating a waterwheel in some ostraca from the quarries at Mons Claudianus, from the station at Didymoi on the Berenike–Coptos route and from Maximianon on the Myos Hormos–Coptos road. *Saqya* pots and fragments have been found especially at late Roman/Byzantine sites in Egypt and papyri and other texts record their use throughout the land at that time. A large Roman-era station on the Mons Porphyrites/Mons Claudianus/Abu Sha'r–Nile road with extensive hydraulic facilities and animal tethering lines is today called al-Saqqia (Pl. 13.5) which may suggest the use of waterwheels here in Roman times.

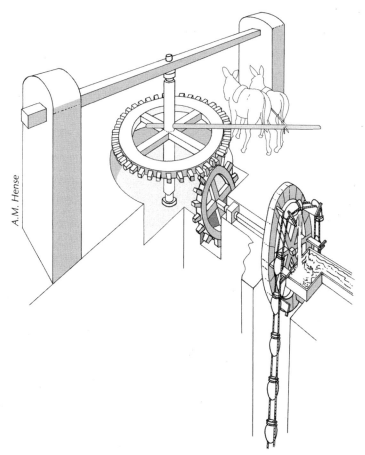

Fig. 13.11: Drawing of a waterwheel, called a *saqya* in Arabic.

Water Uses

Water would have been used to irrigate desert gardens, which are known to have existed from archaeological remains and from references in ostraca especially along the Myos Hormos–Nile road. There is also evidence for such desert cultivation at and near Berenike and near the *praesidium* at Abu Sha'r al-Qibli. As we noted earlier, courtyards of houses at the Roman emerald mining settlement of Sikait preserve small stone boxes that may have contained trellises used to support growing crops or to protect young saplings (see Chapters 10 and 12).

There are also references in various Christian literary sources to desert cultivation. In the fourth and fifth centuries, the *Historia Monachorum in Aegypto*, Athanasius' *The Life of St. Antony*, and Palladius' *Historia Lausiaca* all report that monks residing in the desert had their own gardens that produced fruits, vegetables, and some grains to make bread. The practice was probably more widespread in antiquity than we realize as analysis of mud bricks used in structures in the Eastern Desert shows pollen from locally cultivated plants mixed with the bricks.

Small-scale industrial activities in the desert also required water. Christian desert hermits wove baskets, ropes, and mats, and fibers used in their manufacture would have been soaked in water to make them more pliable. Brick making, metal working, gold refining, and glass working, all of which are activities known either in the Eastern Desert or at the Red Sea ports, would also have required water.

Possible pollution of water supplies as a result of their use in mining, quarrying, and industrial activities raises interesting and still to be studied questions about the impact on the health of those residing in the region. Ostraca indicate constant health problems of the eyes and gastrointestinal systems of many living in the Eastern Desert. Could some of these problems be caused by pollution of the water sources?

Few formal bathing facilities have been excavated in the Eastern Desert and most if not all have been found in Roman military contexts. More will probably be discovered as additional sites come under excavation. Thus far archaeologists have identified five baths in the region. Our excavations partially uncovered a relatively large one just outside the north gate of the late Roman fort at Abu Sha'r (Fig. 13.12). Another smaller one can be seen at the quarry settlement at Mons Claudianus (Fig. 13.13). The *praesidia* at

Fig. 13.12: Bathing facilities just outside the north gate of the late Roman fort at Abu Sha'r. Scale = one meter.

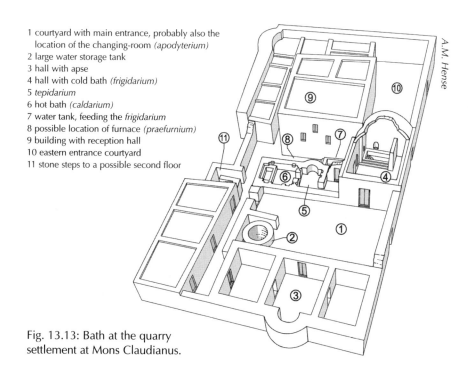

1 courtyard with main entrance, probably also the
  location of the changing-room *(apodyterium)*
2 large water storage tank
3 hall with apse
4 hall with cold bath *(frigidarium)*
5 *tepidarium*
6 hot bath *(caldarium)*
7 water tank, feeding the *frigidarium*
8 possible location of furnace *(praefurnium)*
9 building with reception hall
10 eastern entrance courtyard
11 stone steps to a possible second floor

Fig. 13.13: Bath at the quarry
settlement at Mons Claudianus.

Maximianon (Fig. 13.14) on the Myos Hormos–Nile road and at Didymoi on the Berenike–Coptos road also each preserve small baths. A fifth has been found near the large fort at Mons Porphyrites. Interestingly, excavations of two large civilian settlements in the region, the Red Sea ports of Berenike and Myos Hormos, have revealed no baths, but surely such communities must have possessed them. At Berenike our excavations immediately north of the Serapis temple recovered glass items used specifically for bathing and recycled kiln-fired bricks preserving remains of mortar, which must have had an original hydraulic function. These artifacts point to the possible presence nearby of a bathing facility.

Accommodations for animals hauling stone especially between quarries and mines in the desert on the one hand and the Nile on the other also provided water for their consumption. Such facilities are especially evident on roads between Mons Porphyrites and Mons Claudianus and the Nile, but also between Marsa Nakari and the Nile and the emerald mines at Sikait and the Nile. Good examples of these include Badia', Bab al-Mukhenig (Pl. 13.6), and Deir al-Atrash on the Mons Porphyrites–Nile road and Abu

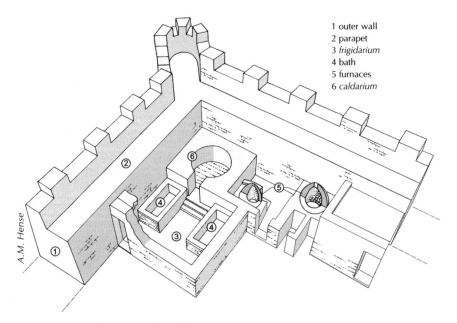

1 outer wall
2 parapet
3 *frigidarium*
4 bath
5 furnaces
6 *caldarium*

A.M. Hense

Fig. 13.14: Bath at Maximianon fort.

Greiya on the Mons Claudianus–Nile road. Farther south in the Eastern Desert the station at Rod Umm al-Farraj on the Marsa Nakari–Nile road and the one at Wadi Gemal East on the Sikait–Nile road are excellent examples. In addition to the watering facilities, tethering lines, as we have seen in Chapter 4, were also key features of these stations catering to traffic passing between quarries and mines on the one hand and the Nile on the other.

The methods used for water acquisition, storage, protection, and distribution in the Ptolemaic and Roman era in the Eastern Desert were undoubtedly similar to those used in earlier pharaonic times in the region. The most noteworthy differences would have been the generally larger scales and greater frequency with which these activities in the later period would have been conducted.

In Ptolemaic and Roman times it seems that mainly the military was responsible for all aspects of water procurement and distribution in the Eastern Desert. This is evident from the fact that most if not all of the important water sources known to the Ptolemaic and Roman officials were undoubtedly guarded or otherwise fortified. No surviving manuscripts of ancient authors discuss this and few of the thousands of ostraca and papyri found in the region are helpful in shedding light on this issue either. Inscriptions found at some of the *praesidia* and stops along the desert highways indicate that the periods of Ptolemy II Philadelphus (285–246 BC) and the Flavian emperors (AD 69–96) were ones of concern for water procurement and protection. There must have been additional eras of repair and refurbishment at the ports, mines, and quarries and at other peak periods of activity in the Eastern Desert. These would likely have been especially in the early Roman epoch from the emperors Augustus and Tiberius (30 BC–AD 37), the reigns of Trajan and Hadrian (AD 98–138), the rule of the Severan emperors (AD 193–217) and again in late Roman times beginning in the middle of the fourth century when there was an evident renaissance in the Red Sea trade and in gold mining activities in the region.

Clearly more survey and excavation must take place in the future in the Eastern Desert and along the Red Sea coast in order to have a better idea of how this important issue of water supply was handled.

The Roads from Berenike
to the Nile

The ancient Red Sea emporium of Berenike was the preeminent entrepôt at the northern end of the Red Sea for about eight centuries from
early Ptolemaic times until the late Roman period, that is, from early
in the third century BC until the sixth century AD. It was a local, regional, and
international hub for commerce in that period and, consequently, a number
of roads radiated from the city to various desert settlements and to several
points in the Nile Valley. Clearly, no overview of Egypt's Eastern Desert
would be complete without an examination of the road network emanating
from this pivotal port. Here we will concentrate on the main roads linking
Berenike to major emporia on the Nile at Apollonopolis Magna (Edfu) and
Coptos (Quft).

Ptolemaic Period

During the reign of Ptolemy II Philadelphus (285–246 BC), and later in the
third and second centuries BC, the central government made a sustained
effort to monitor and facilitate traffic penetrating from the Nile Valley into
the Eastern Desert and onward to the Red Sea coast. Part of this overarch-
ing Ptolemaic construction project included the foundation of Berenike and
other ports on the Red Sea shores of Egypt. Berenike's importance as a hub
for commerce flowing between the Mediterranean world on the one hand
and the Red Sea–Indian Ocean basins on the other allows us to appreciate
better the purpose and importance of the roads linking the city to the Nile.

In addition to founding various Red Sea ports, Philadelphus and his successors also ordered the construction of roads, wells, stations, fortified water points, and other facilities to assist travelers in the region and to support the military and police guarding it. In one instance Ptolemy II refurbished and completed a canal linking the Nile to the Red Sea in the region of Suez (Fig. 14.1); this canal, revitalized in Roman times, seems to have continued to operate in the Islamic period. Many of these structures, and part of the canal near its Nile terminus at Bablyon south of Cairo, survive in the archaeological record. It is from this Ptolemaic era and later that we have our first relatively focused picture of the appearance and location of the desert roads and the infrastructure that supported traffic along them.

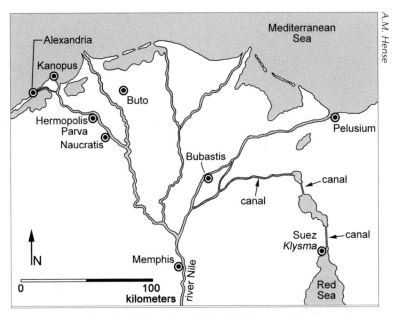

Fig. 14.1: Map showing the location of the Red Sea canal in the region of Suez.

Roads Leading to and from Berenike

There were several thoroughfares joining the Red Sea port of Berenike with her riverine counterparts and we examine one of these lesser-known and more southerly ones in Chapter 15. Undoubtedly, the most important and widely used roads linked Berenike to the Nile at Apollonopolis Magna and Contra Apollonopolis Magna in Ptolemaic times and then to Coptos in the Roman era. Actually, the latter route was merely an extension of the former and both roads intersected and, in one instance, coincided with the western end of yet another highway that linked Apollonopolis Magna with the Red Sea port at Marsa Nakari. Marsa Nakari, perhaps to be identified with the ancient emporium of Nechesia, lies about 150 kilometers north of Berenike. In addition, our surveys have shown that the roads from the Nile intersected and coincided with the Via Nova Hadriana near the stations in Wadi Abu Greiya (Vetus Hydreuma) and from there formed a single route leading to Berenike itself (Fig.14.2). Thus, it was important that this especially heavily used twenty-five kilometer stretch between Berenike and the forts in Wadi Abu Greiya be well maintained.

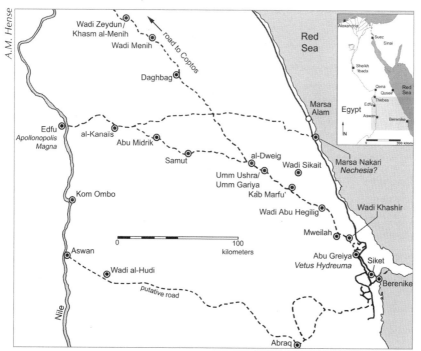

Fig. 14.2: Roads leading to and from Berenike.

All the extant archaeological and ancient written evidence indicates that the routes linking Berenike to the Nile were the earliest Greco-Roman thoroughfares in the Eastern Desert. The quotidian reasons for the roads and forts along them were to ensure safe passage of people, pack animals, and commodities between the Nile, the Red Sea, and the desert settlements in between and to facilitate monitoring of activities, and conveyance of official communications. Banditry was a problem that became serious especially, it seems, beginning in the late first to early second centuries AD. Ostraca found in excavations by the French along the Myos Hormos–Coptos road make this quite clear. An interesting novel written by Xenophon of Ephesus at about this time also refers to a large band of thieves who preyed on merchants involved in the commerce with India and Ethiopia. While such highway robbery could not be prevented, it could be contained and that was one of the purposes of these *praesidia*.

Berenike–Apollonopolis Magna (Edfu) Road

It is clear from our extensive archaeological surveys of the Berenike–Nile roads since 1990 that segments of them had been used as early as prehistoric times. In the Ptolemaic and Roman periods the road from Berenike comprised some cleared stretches similar in appearance to those surviving along the Via Nova Hadriana (see Chapter 3). A few segments were built up to pass over troublesome low spots in the desert floor. The 340 kilometer-long Ptolemaic highway between Berenike and Apollonopolis Magna was marked in some places with square-shaped cairns, wells *(hydreumata)*, and fortifications. The latter accommodated soldiers who monitored traffic along its course; the military also acted as a deterrent to those who would disrupt that traffic. In addition to watching over those traveling between the Nile and the Red Sea, these desert garrisons also provided protection to gold mining operations on or near the route including two our surveys discovered: a small one at Mweilah off the road northwest of the station in Wadi Khashir (likely the ancient Novum Hydreuma), and a second larger one called Samut near the large fort of the same name (Pl. 14.1 and Fig. 14.3). Our survey work suggests that the Samut mines operated during the second Achaemenid Persian occupation of Egypt (343–332 BC) and continued in use in Ptolemaic times.

The forts along the Berenike–Apollonopolis Magna road are, in general, square, rectangular or parallelogram in plan, though some appear rather rounded, with walls preserved least several meters high in a few cases. Some forts have external towers while others seem to lack them. Entrances are usually confined to a single portal. The forts are built of locally available cobbles and small boulders that are either stacked without any binding material or have a modicum of mud or clay that acts as an adhesive. The interiors of these forts have buildings and rooms constructed up against the inner faces of the main outer walls of the installation or have freestanding structures. The centers of the forts sometimes have the remains of wells; water cisterns may be found elsewhere in the fort interiors.

Some of the more outstanding examples of fortifications of Ptolemaic date, along the Berenike–Apollonopolis Magna route include the large one at Samut, not far from the gold mines of the same name mentioned above, and one at Abu Midrik (Fig. 14.4). The latter is a relatively small, very remote, and seldom-visited site today that preserves two deep, circular water

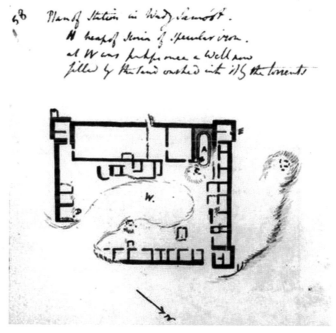

Fig. 14.3: Plan of the station at Samut on the Berenike–Apollonopolis Magna road, drawn by J.G. Wilkinson (Ms. G. Wilkinson sect. XXXVIII.39 page 58; Gardner Wilkinson papers from Calke Abbey, Bodleian Library, Oxford; courtesy of the National Trust).

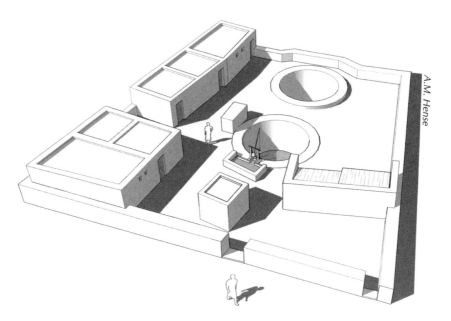

A.M. Hense

Fig. 14.4: Artist's reconstruction of the Ptolemaic protected water stop at Abu Midrik.

cisterns capable of holding about 88,000 liters of water. In neither case do we know the ancient names of these stations. Another noteworthy site, refurbished in Roman times, is the rather easily accessible fort at al-Kanaïs, a modern Arabic name meaning 'the Churches,' whose Greek epithet has been preserved to us as Hydreuma to epi tou Paneiou. We have discussed this site in several previous chapters.

Berenike–Coptos (Quft) Road

Judging by the large number of stops, the road between Berenike and Coptos was very likely considered by Roman authorities and civilians alike to be the most important in the entire Eastern Desert and one requiring more protection than any other road east of the Nile. In fact, of all the ancient desert highways in the area it was this one leading to Berenike that several ancient sources discuss at some length. Pliny the Elder was the first to describe it in detail and provided names of stops and stations and distances between them, though it is doubtful that he personally ever traveled along it. Pliny was followed by later documents such as the *Antonine Itinerary*, compiled in the third century AD, and the *Peutinger Table*, somewhat later than the *Itinerary*, and which have somewhat different lists of stops. The discrepancies between Pliny and these later sources regarding the names and locations of stops and stations undoubtedly indicate that some of Pliny's stations had fallen out of use, perhaps because water sources had dried up, and had been replaced by others by the time the *Antonine Itinerary* and *Peutinger Table* were compiled. It is also possible that the increased banditry and barbarian raids noted on the Myos Hormos–Nile road in the late first and early second centuries AD also affected the Berenike–Nile road at that time; these stations would not have been recorded by Pliny as they had not yet been constructed. These stations would have appeared in the *Antonine Itinerary* and the *Peutinger Table* as these documents were compiled after the second century AD. An even later document called the *Ravenna Cosmography* also lists stations on the Berenike–Coptos road, but it seems to be nothing more than a copy of one or more of the earlier documents we have already noted. The maps, itineraries, the appearance and marking of the roads, and the presence of *praesidia* themselves would not, however, have provided sufficient information for an independent traveler to attempt a desert crossing on his own; guides would have been essential.

The Romans, being very practical, also tended to overlap various roads with one another whenever possible. In the case of the highways radiating out from Berenike into the desert and toward the Nile, there was a great deal of this. The very southern end of the Via Nova Hadriana overlapped with the Apollonopolis Magna/Coptos route leading to Berenike, and the western end of the Myos Hormos–Nile road coincided with the main Berenike–Nile road terminating at Coptos. In addition, the first 170 kilometers of highway leaving Berenike in the Ptolemaic period toward the northwest also served the Romans at least to the area near the *praesidium* of al-Dweig (perhaps the ancient Falacro). The Beau Geste type structure at al-Dweig, near the bifurcation point of the Apollonopolis Magna–Coptos route, with its fine walls, catwalks, and towers as well as two entrances, is in an excellent state of preservation (Pls. 14.2–14.3 and Fig. 14.5) and, from the pottery our surveys recovered here, seems to be Roman in date.

Farther along the road toward Coptos is the rather large, but badly damaged early Roman fort at Daghbag, which also guarded the adjacent gold mines with their industrial sized grinding facilities (noted in Chapter 9).

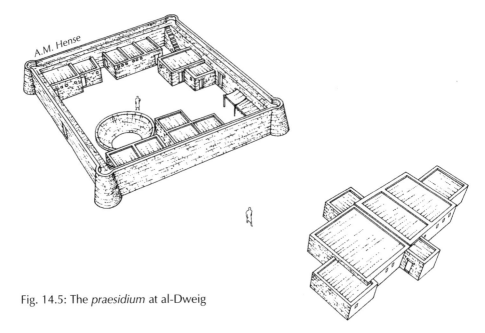

Fig. 14.5: The *praesidium* at al-Dweig

This may be the site of Compasi mentioned by Pliny. Although poorly preserved, the fort in Wadi Menih/Khawr al-Jer, perhaps to be associated with
the ancient Aphrodito (Figs. 14.6–14.7), has a spectacular setting and is,
without doubt, today the most inaccessible of all forts along the
Berenike–Coptos route due to the presence of sizeable sand dunes on its
northern approaches. Portions of a first century AD inscription in Latin
carved onto a rectangular-shaped block can still be seen swept into the fort's
interior from the gate by floods over the centuries (Fig. 14.8). According to
the Latin text, now almost totally effaced, but recorded by J.G. Wilkinson in
the 1820s, Aphrodito fort was dedicated at the same time that the *praesidia*
at Siket, near Berenike, and in Wadi Zeydun/Khashm al-Menih (ancient
Didymoi) were erected, that is, during the period of the Flavian emperors
(AD 69–96).

    The old Ptolemaic thoroughfare from near the fort at al-Dweig to Apol-
lonopolis Magna continued to be used in early Roman times, but fell out of
use soon thereafter. We do not understand why this happened, but it was
replaced by a longer road—about a twelve- to thirteen-day trip of approximately 380 kilometers—from Berenike to Coptos.

Fig. 14.6: The fort in Wadi Menih/Khawr al-Jer, perhaps to be associated with the ancient Aphrodito.

Fig. 14.7: Detail of Fig. 14.6 above.

S.E. Sidebotham

Fig. 14.8: Bedouin sitting next to the inscription that has washed into the fort from the front gate (Wadi Menih al-Heir/Khawr al-Jer).

GEORG AUGUST SCHWEINFURTH

Georg August Schweinfurth was born in December 1836 in Riga, Latvia (then part of the Russian Empire). Best known as a German botanist, ethnologist, and traveler in East Africa, he was educated at universities in Heidelberg, Munich, and Berlin (1856–1862). His major interests were botany and paleontology. In 1863 Schweinfurth traveled to the Red Sea, the region between there and the Nile, and then onward to Khartoum. He returned to Europe in 1868. Greatly impressed with his accomplishments, Humboldt Stiftung sponsored him to lead an expedition, beginning in January 1869 up the White Nile. He discovered the Uele River and made important contributions to our knowledge of the flora and fauna of Central Africa. Schweinfurth settled in Cairo in 1875 where he lived off and on until 1879. There he founded the Société Khediviale de Géographie. He spent much of the period 1876 to 1888 in the Eastern Desert. His importance for us was the resulting publication many years later of *Auf unbetretenen Wegen in Aegypten*. He returned to Berlin in 1889 and visited Eritrea in 1891, 1892, and 1894. Schweinfurth died in Berlin in September 1925.

The Berenike–Apollonopolis Magna and Berenike–Coptos roads preserve some cairns and graves along their courses, but our extensive surveys
of these thoroughfares over the years have noted surprisingly few signal or
watch towers. Some route sections preserve cleared tracks flanked by
windrows similar to those we described along the Via Nova Hadriana in
Chapter 3. This is especially true of the section between Berenike and the
first major stop along the road toward the Nile at Vetus Hydreuma (in Wadi
Abu Greiya) where some of the best-preserved segments survive. These
portions vary substantially from about 5.1 to 32.3 meters wide (Fig. 14.9)
and pass just north of the small *hydreuma* at Siket, 7.2 kilometers west
northwest of Berenike, which we will discuss in Chapter 15. Most of the
Berenike–Nile roads when viewed today, however, lack these cleared tracks.

In the Roman era, the Ptolemaic route and stations between Berenike and
al-Dweig were repaired, old forts were renovated, new forts were constructed, and wells were refurbished or new ones excavated. The erection of
cairns of piled stones marking the courses of the routes as well as some
watch and signal towers complemented the heightened security precautions

S.E. Sidebotham

Fig. 14.9: Berenike-Vetus Hydreuma road.

especially in the period between the Flavian emperors (Vespasian, Titus, Domitian) who reigned from AD 69–96 and the rules of Trajan and Hadrian (AD 98–138), but later as well. The best preserved of such watch and signal towers survive on the trans-desert road joining Myos Hormos and Coptos and we discussed these in Chapter 4, though additional examples can be found on some of the other routes in the Eastern Desert including a few on the Berenike–Nile and Abu Sha'r/Mons Porphyrites–Nile roads.

The distances between stations varied greatly and they do not seem to have been placed, in some cases, at ranges that the average traveler or caravan would necessarily find convenient; in some instances they were much closer and rarely in others much father than an average day's journey. Stations lay on low ground in areas where water supplies were readily available and where they were most needed to monitor activities. Few stations were erected on high terrain as Roman strategy did not to attempt to control the entire region, but, rather, to manage water points and communication arteries, both of which lay on low ground.

Numerous and well-preserved *praesidia* punctuated the course of the Roman thoroughfare between al-Dweig and Coptos. These *praesidia* contained cisterns fed from wells either inside or somewhere outside their walls. Cisterns were carefully constructed of local stones or fired brick and coated with a waterproof lime mortar several centimeters thick.

Some of the more impressive Roman installations between Berenike and Coptos include five forts at Vetus Hydreuma (Pl. 14.4), which was the first major stop on the road from Berenike laying about twenty-five kilometers northwest of the port. One of those in the low-lying wadi seems to have been Ptolemaic and was dramatically enlarged in early Roman times. Others of note along the road include the small early Roman (at least) era stations in Wadi Abu Hegilig South with two well-preserved oval shaped cisterns and another at Umm Ushra/Umm Gariya. Both these small *praesidia* seem to have had water piped into their internal cisterns from nearby mountain runoff.

Between the forts in Wadi Abu Hegilig South and Umm Ushra/Umm Gariya are the impressive remains of the huge fort in Wadi Gemal (Figs. 14.10–14.11). This installation, probably to be associated with Apollonos in Pliny the Elder's list of stops that appears in his *Natural History*, was one of the largest in the Eastern Desert and judging by the pottery we collected

Fig. 14.10: The impressive remains of the huge fort in Wadi Gemal (ancient Apollonos).

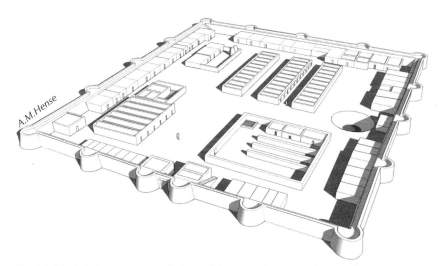

Fig. 14.11: Artist's reconstructed view of the huge fort in Wadi Gemal.

here during several surveys, was active from at least the first to sixth centuries AD. Although most of two outer walls have been washed away by floods over the centuries, the two remaining enceintes, whose original lengths have also suffered water damage, indicate a fort of impressive dimensions by Eastern Desert standards: at least 0.92 hectares (almost 2.5 acres) in area. In addition to providing protection to and monitoring of travelers between the Nile and the Red Sea, the fort in Wadi Gemal also offered security to a number of nearby desert communities including Ka'b Marfu' (see Chapters 6 and 10) and several large and lucrative emerald mining centers. The important emerald mining settlements in Wadi Sikait and Wadi Nugrus, for example (see Chapter 12), would have relied on the garrison in Wadi Gemal in case there was need of military help.

One other site worthy of mention, though not a fort or other officially sanctioned stop on the road, is a small but fascinating rock shelter in Wadi Menih located between the stations of Aphrodito (in Wadi Menih al-Heir) and Didymoi. Here the visitor finds a small natural cave where Pan, known as Min to the Egyptians, the patron deity of desert voyagers, was venerated. Numerous travelers in antiquity rested here to escape the enervating sun and heat. Many of these transients left doodlings and graffiti in many different languages attesting their passing and we discussed a few of these in some detail in Chapter 7.

There is ample evidence from examination of pottery found at some of the *praesidia*, from along the road itself and from some of the graves flanking it that the Berenike–Coptos route continued in use until at least the sixth century AD at which time Berenike itself ceased to function. After the Muslim Arab conquest of Egypt in AD 641 there is little evidence that this route was still used though portions of some of the other trans-desert routes continued to carry traffic. At that time the faithful making the *hajj* traveled to ports on the Red Sea for conveyance to Jeddah for the short onward overland journey to Mecca.

Estimating the number of soldiers, police, and civilian laborers that lived and worked at the numerous road stations, forts, mines, and quarries can never be known precisely. Nevertheless, the sheer numbers and dimensions of such facilities suggest that the size of the population of the Eastern Desert in early and late Roman times was large and seems not to have been equaled either before or since. We have examined this issue and some of these roads in previous chapters including the Via Nova Hadriana (Chapter 3), the Abu Sha'r/Mons Porphyrites–Nile road (Chapter 4), and the route linking Quseir al-Qadim/Myos Hormos on the Red Sea with Coptos on the Nile (Chapter 4).

The Last Frontier
The Southernmost Sites in the Eastern Desert

The extreme south is the least known and, therefore to us, the most intriguing part of the Eastern Desert (Fig. 15.1). Compared to the northern regions, this area is even more inhospitable, the water sources scarcer, the terrain more unforgiving, and the heat more intense. Due to these impediments, and the need for special and difficult-to-obtain military permits, this part of the desert has been little explored. Some hardy Westerners ventured into this arid landscape in the nineteenth and early twentieth centuries and recorded their encounters with the Bedouin. To their surprise, they saw many traces of ancient human activity, ranging on the one hand from drawings and doodlings on rock faces, and broken pottery to settlements, fortifications, and temples on the other. Certainly, of all the vast stretches of the Eastern Desert, this hauntingly beautiful region offers the greatest future potential to reveal new archaeological remains, sites that until now are known only to the local 'Ababda and Bisharin Bedouin.

Prehistory

European explorers during the past 170 years or so have discovered that people lived in the southernmost areas of the Eastern Desert beginning from at least six thousand years ago. Finds of pottery indicate that groups of nomads and hunters in the late Paleolithic period left the Nile Valley, at least temporarily, and traveled to Abraq if not farther afield. Petroglyphs

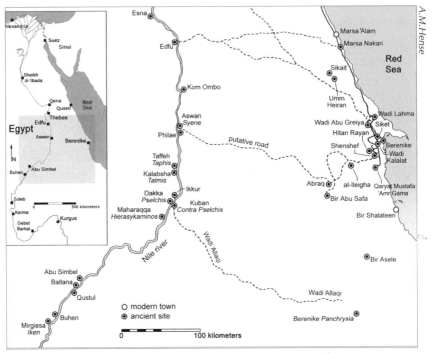

Fig. 15.1: Map showing the location of the southernmost sites in the Eastern Desert mentioned in this chapter.

depict cattle and boats the Nile Valley inhabitants used to navigate the river.

Around 3500 BC in Lower Nubia, the area south of Aswan up to the Second Cataract, people of the so-called A-Group emerged. Possessing a culture distinct from contemporary Egypt, from about 3200 BC onward they were middlemen in the exchange of exotic goods between Egypt and the far south. Along the trade route through Lower Nubia gold, ivory, incense, ebony, and panther skins streamed into Egypt. Nubia itself produced large quantities of cattle, something that remained an export from the region for thousands of years to come.

Activity during this time increased substantially in the Eastern Desert, as remains of hundreds of tumuli found in the region south of Abraq and many rock drawings in the same area indicate. The cemetery of Bir Asele shows more organized types of burials. As we pointed out in Chapter 8, parallels for this Predynastic (before about 3000 BC) cemetery are known from the Sinai, which makes it less likely that a local group constructed it. On the other hand, all pottery finds from the Bir Asele cemetery are of Nubian style. Pharaonic Egyptians greatly preferred burial in the Nile Valley. Perhaps these graves in the Bir Asele necropolis belonged to some group of individuals, cooperating in extensive mining or commercial operations in the region.

Pharaonic Period

Over four centuries following the unification of Upper and Lower Egypt in about 3000 BC, the early pharaohs undertook a series of military campaigns against the population in Lower Nubia. A victory inscription of King Sneferu (2575–2551 BC) of the Fourth Dynasty, father of Khufu (2551–2528 BC) the builder of the largest pyramid at Giza, describes an Egyptian military campaign, which resulted in the capture of thousands of prisoners and the removal of one hundred thousand head of cattle. The kings of the early Egyptian dynasties took full control of the resources and trade of this southern region, which probably caused a drastic decline in the economy of the A-Group people. Combined with climatic changes, this economic collapse resulted in a sudden depopulation of the area, which allowed the Egyptians to move in. Settlements and trade posts, like the fortified town of Buhen, were built to control direct commerce with the far south. As happened many times in the coming millennia, Egypt lost control of the area in the second half of the Fifth Dynasty (2465–2323 BC) and retreated north of the First Cataract. The decimated population quickly recovered, probably assisted by an influx of settlers from the south. This new cultural phase, called the C-Group, established small kingdoms and chiefdoms along the Nile. The C-Group people built mud-brick huts and placed their dead in low, round burial mounds. In addition to the fine red pottery comparable to that made by their predecessors, they also produced polished black and gray dishes and bowls, decorated with colored geometric patterns. Most of the wealth of these C-Group peoples was based on cattle breeding, as reflected in the many clay figurines of bulls and cows, and the burial of sheep, goats, and oxen with the deceased.

Around 2200 BC the names of the small kingdoms and chiefdoms emerged in autobiographical texts recorded in the tombs of Egyptian high officials. Directly south of Aswan, the small states called Wawat, Irtjet, and

Setju had somewhat uncomfortable relations with their huge northern neighbor (Fig. 15.2). These chiefdoms are clearly described as "foreign lands" in inscriptions in the tomb of Harkhuf, the governor of Upper Egypt. These texts contain an account of the travels of Harkhuf, who led several expeditions to the south. The goal of his journeys, each of which took over seven months, was to explore the road to the land of Yam. This relatively large and prosperous kingdom south of the three aforementioned ones had a much friendlier relationship with Egypt. Praised by the pharaoh, Harkhuf brought back from Yam large quantities of exotic goods. His autobiography sums up an impressive list, containing hundreds of donkeys laden with ebony, panther skins, and elephant tusks among many other exotic items. On his last voyage, Harkhuf succeeded in bringing a 'dancing pygmy' at the personal request of the boy-king Pepy II (2246–2152 BC).

As we know from the autobiography of Weni, Harkhuf's predecessor, these chiefdoms provided troops to support the Egyptian army during military campaigns in the far south and north. Because of the fame of its

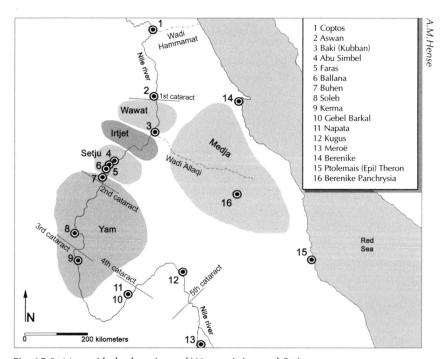

Fig. 15.2: Map with the locations of Wawat, Irtjet, and Setju.

archers, one of the names the Egyptians gave to Nubia was *Ta-Seti* (Land of the Bow). Another group, the Medjay, inhabitants of the Eastern Desert south of Aswan, also supplied Egypt with soldiers. Medjay, the people of the land of Medja, in about 2200 BC began a long relationship with Egypt, and their soldiers played an important role in crucial events in the next thousand years of Egyptian history.

Egyptian expeditions late in the Old Kingdom (2649–2152 BC), searching for mineral resources, trade opportunities, or loot, also entered Nubia uninvited on a regular basis. A rock inscription of governor Weni in the middle of the Eastern Desert, halfway along Wadi 'Allaqi, some 250 kilometers southeast of Aswan, shows that these expeditions sometimes reached into the heart of the desert.

During a century of chaos, following the end of the reign of king Pepy II, a new state emerged on Egypt's southern border. The Kingdom of Kerma, called Kush by the Egyptians, had devoured most former chiefdoms, thereby creating a mighty political power that had a less submissive attitude toward Egypt. Moreover, inhabitants of the Eastern Desert occasionally raided settlements in Upper Egypt and robbed travelers. The Egyptian pharaohs of the Middle Kingdom (2040–1640 BC) reacted by pushing the border southward during several military campaigns. In earlier times Egypt obtained most of its gold from Wadi Hammamat (see Chapter 4), but as early as the reign of Senwosret I (1971–1926 BC), Egypt began to open gold mines in numerous places in Wadi 'Allaqi. To intimidate the Kushite rulers, to secure the trade with the far south, and to protect the gold mines in Wadi 'Allaqi, the Egyptians built eleven massive fortresses at strategic points along the Nile in Lower Nubia. The imposing mud-brick fort that dominated the plain near Buhen clearly had a propagandistic function, with its double walls and enormous towers punctuated with myriads of loopholes for archers. A little south of this fort, the Egyptians built the giant commercial center of Iken. Protected by a stone wall, Iken handled virtually all trade between Egypt and the south. In contrast to Buhen, other fortresses were built specifically for defensive purposes.

For the first time, there also emerged fortifications in the southern part of the Eastern Desert. Wadi al-Hudi, about twenty-five kilometers southeast of Aswan, became an extensively exploited mining area (see Chapter 12). A fort and a fortified settlement were built here to protect the important amethyst mines. There are indications that Wadi al-Hudi was part of the territory of the Medjay. Relations between Egypt and the Medjay were good, as they now served in large numbers in the Egyptian army. A delegation likely of Medjay is reported to have visited the Egyptian royal court, shortly thereafter followed by a Medja prince and his entourage.

Around 1640 BC the Egyptian central government collapsed with the invasion of the Hyksos in the north thereby initiating the so-called Second Intermediate Period. At that time Egypt abandoned its forts in Lower Nubia and withdrew from the region. Egypt was then divided into two parts. As the Hyksos ruled the north and controlled vassal kings in Middle Egypt, only the south remained under independent Egyptian kings based in Thebes.

In about 1560 BC the Hyksos tried to invoke the help of the Kingdom of Kush to destroy what remained of independent Egyptian territory. A letter in which this cooperation was proposed was, however, intercepted and brought to the Theban king. After the defeat and expulsion of the Hyksos, this epistle probably served as a *casus belli* to deal with the Kushites. Systematically, Egypt conquered the territory of Kush culminating in about 1502 BC in the complete destruction of the capital at Kerma. The conquest of Nubia was completed during the reign of Thutmose II, around 1480 BC. Some old forts were restored and new ones were built in the vicinity of the Fifth Cataract. Egyptian settlers, soldiers, officials, and merchants resided in small settlements spaced along the Nile. The gold mines in the interior delivered the main wealth to New Kingdom Egypt. Those in Wadi 'Allaqi were then in their heyday, which lasted until the end of the reign of Ramesses II (1290–1224 BC). Estimates suggest that these mines produced over eighty-five percent of all of the gold used in New Kingdom Egypt. Many rock inscriptions left by scribes, soldiers, and officials are evidence of the extensive traffic through this long wadi leading deep into the Eastern Desert. To make those travels far into the arid region possible, deep wells had to be dug. We discussed some of these in Chapter 13.

The Viceroy of Kush, usually a close confidant of the pharaoh, was administrative head of the huge Nubian region. The territory seems to have been divided into districts. On the walls of his Theban tomb, Viceroy Huy, a contemporary of Tutankhamun (1333–1323 BC), receives three 'Chiefs of Wawat' and six 'Chiefs of Kush.' During the rule of the Viceroys, temples were built at Abu Simbel, Soleb, and Gebel Barkal, and many other places. Egyptian control over Nubia rapidly ceased after the reign of Ramesses II, although the Egyptians managed to retain the strategic town of Baki until the reign of Ramesses X (1112–1100 BC). With the collapse of Egyptian power, the mines in Wadi 'Allaqi were abandoned, and a considerable number of the inhabitants, both Egyptian and native, gradually drifted back to Egypt.

Again, there emerged an unknown number of independent kingdoms, which slowly resumed their intermediary role in the trade between Egypt and the south. As excavations have demonstrated, there was a drastic change in burial customs of the local chiefs. Even during Egyptian occupation in the New Kingdom, most of the local elite retained the traditional practice of placing the dead in burial mounds. But in the ninth century BC, the elite started to build small pyramids with offering chapels. The deceased were mummified and placed in stone sarcophagi in large burial chambers underneath the chapel. The cause of this sudden change is unknown, but it may be that missionary activities of Egyptian priests of Amun, who fled the civil war in Egypt, had something to do with it.

In approximately 780 BC, all of Nubia was united in the Kingdom of Napata, with Meroë as capital. King Piye of this powerful new state succeeded in 730 BC in adding to his territories most of the weakened and divided Egyptian provinces, up to the Nile Delta. Piye and his successors of the Twenty-fifth Dynasty presented themselves as Kings of Upper and Lower Egypt. They also restored and expanded numerous dilapidated Egyptian temples, both in Egypt and in Napata. But some fifty years later the Assyrians, who had invaded Egypt in 671 BC, drove king Taharqa back to Napata. After several military campaigns the end came with the destruction of the town of Napata in 593 BC by pharaoh Psamtek II (595–589 BC) of the revived Egyptian state.

Thereafter, Napata began to orientate itself increasingly toward the south and gradually lost its Egyptian influences. This new direction can be seen most dramatically in the written language; a Meroitic script, which has still not been deciphered, replaced the Egyptian hieroglyphs. Eventually the Kingdom of Meroë emerged with its capital at Meroë city. This metropolis served both as a religious and administrative center. In the fifth century BC the Greek historian Herodotus records an espionage mission of so-called

Fish-Eaters sent by the Persian King Cambyses to the Kingdom of Meroë. In his account of the 'Fish-Eaters,' who were inhabitants of the Nile banks near Elephantine, Meroë is described as a fairy tale-like city, inhabited by the most pious and longest-living people in the world. A well in the city produced flower-scented water that extended the life of anyone who drank it. Prisoners were put in irons of gold, and the dead were buried in transparent coffins of crystal.

Ptolemaic Era

After the New Kingdom (ended 1070 BC), mining and commercial activities in the southern portion of the Eastern Desert rapidly declined. It was not until the third century BC, in the Ptolemaic period, that some mines and trade routes were re-opened. In 275 BC, King Ptolemy II sent a large army into Nubia to recapture the long-lost gold mines of Wadi 'Allaqi. In this region the settlement of Berenike Panchrysia was built, creating the southernmost town of Ptolemaic Egypt now known. More hostile actions followed back and forth, until a peace treaty at the end of the century improved relations. Egypt maintained control of the gold mines in Wadi 'Allaqi, and trade between Meroë and Egypt rapidly increased.

Meroë exported ivory, spices, hides, and wild animals to Egypt. Major discoveries of iron deposits around the capital led to a substantial iron industry; the Kingdom of Meroë had yet another highly prized export article. In return for these products the Meroites received Hellenistic manufactured goods as well as wine, grain, and olive oil. Hellenistic designs were adopted and modified according to local taste in architecture, pottery, and stone carvings.

Abraq

The fort of Abraq sits on a flat plateau, overlooking a large wadi along what seems to be the southernmost Ptolemaic trade route to the Red Sea coast north of Meroë (Pls. 15.1–15.2). This massive fortress, over 160 meters wide, may have been built to protect a trade route; the nearby well was probably the main reason for the location of the stronghold. Pictographs and graffiti, which include gazelles, elephants, cows, camels, warriors on horseback, and Christian crosses cover large boulders and the wadi walls near the well.

The fortress was built on a bluff that rises over fifty meters above the wadi floor. Where the bluff has a gentler slope, and is easier to climb, the outer defensive wall is over two meters thick and four meters high. In the center of the fortress, a natural rise of the rock facilitated construction of a citadel, some six meters above the level of the outer wall on the wadi side. This central building has twenty-eight rooms surrounding a large courtyard. Smaller buildings were constructed inside the outer southern wall, and at the southwestern corner a large tower once overlooked the entrance path to the fort. This path zigzags on the steep western side of the rock from the wadi floor to the entrance gate, close to the central building.

Early travelers like the Frenchman Linant de Bellefonds, who visited the fort at Abraq in 1832, and the American Colston who saw it about twenty years later, considered the stronghold an elephant hunting station. It is, however, unlikely that elephants were hunted here in the Ptolemaic period, when environmental circumstances in this area closely resembled those of the present day. It is plausible that the elephants depicted near the well are memorials of travelers coming from the south, or even records of animals imported from the south and passing Abraq en route to the Nile Valley.

Al-Ileigha

An ancient trade route from the Red Sea port of Berenike, probably leading to Aswan via Abraq, once passed by the gold mines at al-Ileigha. Gold was extracted from large open pits here for the first time in the Ptolemaic period. On the hills surrounding the mines are stone foundations of simple huts, which are still visible. A large housing complex was probably the core of the fairly large settlement. The date of the buildings is still unclear; in addition to pottery of the Ptolemaic period, survey work has recovered quantities of Islamic shards dating ninth to the eleventh centuries AD.

Roman Period

During the Roman period, military units from various parts of that Mediterranean-wide empire were stationed in Egypt. There was a good reason for bringing foreign units, some of which had to travel thousands of kilometers. To avoid loyalty problems during revolts of the local population, non-Italian auxiliary troops were often sent to regions far from their homeland (Pl. 15.3).

The total Roman force in Egypt varied over time, but at its peak in the first century AD it comprised three legions plus auxiliaries totaling about twenty thousand troops, a number that was probably somewhat larger in the fourth century AD. Mounted soldiers with horses, and later camels, became more important as the numbers of raids and attacks by desert tribes increased and Roman forces had to react quickly over great distances. The large-scale breeding of camels in the second century AD gave the Romans a mount more adapted to the desert. The effect of this new 'vehicle' was a somewhat mitigated by the fact that within fifty years the marauding desert Blemmyes started to use the camel as well.

The bow was an important weapon for desert troops and excavations at Berenike and Sikait produced many types of bronze and iron arrowheads. Palmyrene troops, as we have seen in Chapters 6 and 7, had garrisons in both Berenike and Coptos in the early third century AD and inscriptions indicate that some of these were archers. This comes as no surprise as Palmyra, a desert caravan city in Syria, was famous for its mounted archers. These specialized troops would have been ideally suited to protect the important trade routes in Egypt's Eastern Desert. What better locations to station them than at the terminal points of one of the most important desert roads: that linking Berenike to Coptos?

So far, a *cohors Ituaeorum* is the only unit whose presence near Berenike during the first century AD can be archaeologically proven. A fragmentary papyrus dated to the reign of Nero (AD 54–68), and found in our excavations at Berenike, records an official contract or dispute in which one of the parties served in this cohort. The Ituraeans, originating from northeast Palestine, are known to have served in various military units in Egypt and elsewhere in the Roman East. Another text found in Berenike shows the presence of two officers of the *ala Thracum Herculiana* in late second or early third century AD Berenike. The nominal size of an *ala quingenaria* was five hundred horsemen, while that of an *ala milliaria* was upward of one thousand in the first century AD. In Egypt, however, cavalry were dispersed over the area in smaller units, sometimes as small as thirty to sixty horsemen or camel riders.

As we noted in Chapter 7, some personal names of military men are known through documents recording their transactions, again at Berenike. The commander, Tiberius Claudius Dorion, for instance, was a successful businessman in addition to being a soldier. Notes of a Roman customs

office written on ostraca during the first three quarters of the first century
AD and found in a Roman trash dump in Berenike indicate that he ordered
shipments of trade goods at least sixteen times.

With the enormous upsurge of activity in the southern area of the Eastern Desert in the Roman period came the need to protect the re-opened
mines, trade routes, and Red Sea ports like Berenike. Several measures were
taken. Garrisons were stationed in posts from Aswan to Berenike. The
Romans constructed forts near the towns in the Dodekaschoinos. These
included auxiliary forts on the east bank of the Nile opposite Taphis, Talmis,
and especially at Pselchis, where the western entrance to the Wadi 'Allaqi
had to be protected. Near the Red Sea port of Berenike fortifications were
built on the plain west of the city.

The approaches to Berenike were very heavily guarded. Thus far, ten forts
have been documented within a thirty-five-kilometer radius of this large Red
Sea emporium. In addition to the two nearby forts in Wadi Kalalat there was
also, only about 7.2 kilometers to the west–northwest, another small *praesidium* at Siket, and some twenty-five kilometers to the northwest, five more forts
in Wadi Abu Greiya (ancient Vetus Hydreuma). These plus a hill top fort at
Shenshef and another fort in Wadi Lahma, which may have fallen out of use
before early Roman times, guarded the northern road leading to the port.
Berenike probably had its own garrison as well. This substantial military presence may appear to be 'overkill' to the modern visitor. Besides the sporadic
encounters with snakes and scorpions any major danger seems unthinkable
here in antiquity, without vehicles, paved roads, or sufficient water resources.
The dangers in Roman times were real, however, and sometimes army-sized.
In addition to pirates roaming the Red Sea, and small bands looking for caravans to loot, now and then large armies entered Roman territory. The Roman
authorities did not soon forget the devastating attack of a large Meroitic army
less than a decade after Egypt became part of the Roman Empire in 30 BC.

Wadi Kalalat and Siket

The Roman garrisons in the southern part of the Eastern Desert were
housed, as was the case throughout the region east of the Nile as a whole,
in fortifications. The dimensions and plans of the structures varied
greatly, and depended on the functions and sizes of the garrisons. The
large *praesidium* in Wadi Kalalat, with its giant *hydreuma*, measures about

WEAPONS AND ARMOR

Our excavations and those of others have produced much evidence of military presence in the southern parts of the Eastern Desert. Egyptians, Greek mercenaries, Romans and their many auxiliary troops, Blemmyes and other desert tribes all had specific weaponry. This is the reason so many different types of arrowheads, the most common type of military equipment, are found in excavations. Besides the bronze flat arrowhead with two barbs, more complex ones of iron have been unearthed at Berenike, at the emerald mining site of Sikait, and at forts in their environs. This type of arrowhead was already used in pharaonic times. The more complicated arrowheads, with three or four blades, were fairly common in the Roman arsenal and are ubiquitous on military sites all over the Roman Empire. Similar arrowheads have been excavated, for example, in the *limes* areas of Scotland, Syria, and Palestine.

Scale armor is another indication of the presence of soldiers. Excavations have recovered parts of iron and bronze scale armor at both Sikait and Berenike. These scales were linked together with small bronze rings, and attached with threads to a thick linen shirt. Scale armor was relatively simple to produce, but required a great deal of maintenance. Especially in the east, soldiers wore scale armor throughout the early and late Roman periods (Figs. 15.3–15.4), alongside the more flexible chain mail.

Even some units of Roman cavalry became heavily armored. From the later second century AD on, Rome increasingly put into action more and more heavily mailed cavalry, the *cataphractarii* and *clibanarii*. Both the men and their mounts were covered in a complex combination of chain mail, plate armor, and scale armor. It is unlikely that cavalry like this was ever used in the Eastern Desert, in view of the rough terrain, the heat, and the enormous weight of this type of armor. It is more probable that the scale armor belonged to the equipment of the lighter armored horse- or camel-archers. These mounted archers formed the bulk of the late Roman armies, especially in remote border territories like the Eastern Desert.

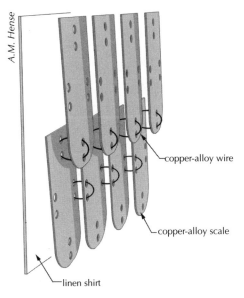

copper-alloy wire

copper-alloy scale

linen shirt

A.M. Hense

Fig. 15.3: Construction of scale armor.

S.E. Sidebotham

Fig. 15.4: Bronze scale armor found in Sikait (fourth–fifth century AD). Scale = five centimeters.

80 by 90 meters. The small *praesidium* at Siket, about 7.2 kilometers west northwest of Berenike, with a *hydreuma* in its center, on the other hand, measures only approximately 24 by 32 meters. The fort at Siket provided Berenike with some water and also protected the considerably less dangerous northern approaches to the city. The strength of the contingent at Siket was probably not more than ten men who were undoubtedly sent out in rotation from nearby Berenike, whereas we estimate that the garrison size in the large *praesidium* in Wadi Kalalat may have been several score soldiers.

The installations in Wadi Kalalat indicate that both dangers and available numbers of soldiers dictated the size of the forts. In the late second century AD the larger fort (see Chapter 13) was abandoned and a new smaller one was built less than a kilometer to the northeast (Fig. 15.4). This latter structure measured only about 30 by 40 meters. Although the dangers had grown, the number of soldiers was reduced below a level that made the defense of the large fort either unnecessary or impossible. On the other hand, this might also indicate that the emphasis in garrison composition had shifted to mounted troops and that the main body of the horse- and camel-soldiers was now stationed closer to or in Berenike itself. That the small fort in Wadi Kalalat was more focused on defense is shown by the remnants of a low rampart, which once surrounded it. Roman forts in northern areas of the empire where the ground was more solid were surrounded by one or more ditches, which made attackers more vulnerable to the missiles of the defenders. In the loose and dry soil of the Eastern Desert, digging a trench around the fort would have undermined the walls. A low rampart five to ten meters distant from the outer perimeter enceinte of this smaller fort, with a steep angled inside and a gentle slope on the outside, created the same effect.

The typical Roman fort in the Eastern Desert usually, but not invariably, had a rectilinear ground plan. Larger ones had a tower attached at each corner and sometimes along the walls between the corner towers themselves. Towers of similar size flanked the main gate of the larger installations. Large forts that had intermediate towers along the walls did so at intervals usually not greater than forty meters. This was necessary to provide archers and javelin throwers with good fields of fire up to the foot of the wall, and to protect it against undermining, or more likely scaling, by enemy troops. Staircases at the inside corners of the perimeter walls provided access to the walls and towers.

Larger forts like the one in Wadi Kalalat also had staircases or ramps leading up to catwalks and parapets. Walls and towers were of the same height, usually about four to five meters, and were built of locally gathered, unworked cobblestones and small boulders. Only crucial parts, like the lintel, doorposts, and threshold of the main gate, were made of large hewn stone, in the case of those near Berenike usually gypsum or anhydrite, brought from nearby quarries. In addition to this, at least some forts near Berenike had monumental inscriptions above their main gates. The inscription over the entrance of the fort at Siket was found almost intact (Figs. 15.5–15.6 and Pls. 15.5–15.6). It was inscribed in a massive carefully crafted triangular shaped stone, almost 2.5 meters wide and 1.07 meters high, and according to the Latin text, the construction took place in year nine of the reign of the Roman emperor Vespasian (AD 76/77). The inscription fragments found at the main gate of the large *praesidium* in Wadi Kalalat, carved in Greek rather than Latin, identified the builder as Servius Sulpicius Similis, Roman prefect (governor) of Egypt in the early second

Fig. 15.5: Fallen columns that once supported the inscription over the gate of the *praesidium* at Siket.

Fig. 15.6: The inscription block from the *praesidium* at Siket, just after excavation.

century AD during the reign of the emperor Trajan (AD 98–117). Similis was also actively involved in other building projects in the Eastern Desert.

Although the *praesidium* at Siket is small, much attention was, of course, given to the strength of the gate (Pl. 15.7). Massive stone doorposts protected the edges of the double doors. A large stone with two holes, placed behind the threshold, facilitated locking the gate at floor level. The almost three-meter-high wooden doors probably had handles on the inside for heavy bolts. The doors of the forts in the environs of Berenike were over fifteen centimeters thick, as proven by finds in the gates of the Wadi Kalalat strongholds. Excavations recovered many fragments of iron nails in the gate areas of Siket and Wadi Kalalat. Some of these nails may have served as fastenings for armor plating on the outside of the doors. During abandonment of the forts, the wooden gates were dismantled and undoubtedly stripped of their armor; the timber was, likely, recycled, probably at Berenike.

Wadi Shenshef

The largest, southernmost settlement built in the Eastern Desert during the Roman period that we know of was in Wadi Shenshef (Pls. 15.8–15.9). This is a late Roman site whose floruit was the fifth to sixth centuries AD. The ruins nestle along the lower and middle slopes of both sides of a wadi of the same name about twenty-one to twenty-two kilometers south–southwest of Berenike and approximately twelve kilometers in a straight line due west of the Red Sea. Several ancient mountain tracks marked by stone cairns, and comprising portions that were artificially built-up and hacked away from the edges of precipices, lead north from the heart of Shenshef to Wadi Kansisrub. From there one ancient desert track heads to Berenike via the two Roman forts in Wadi Kalalat while another leads to the contemporary site at Hitan Rayan, about ten kilometers in a straight line to the northwest. Due to its remote and mountainous location, the last six kilometers leading into Shenshef from the north must be traversed on foot or using camels, horses, or donkeys as it is completely inaccessible to vehicular traffic. Comprising approximately three hundred structures of various sizes and functions, and at least five hundred doughnut-shaped tombs, the bulk of the settlement stretches for about eight hundred meters east–west by 275 meters north–south; in addition there are numerous outbuildings including guard posts, signal and guard towers *(skopeloi)*, and tombs scattered beyond these

VLADIMIR SEMIONOVITCH GOLÉNISCHEFF

Vladimir Semionovitch Golénischeff was born in St. Petersburg in 1856. At an early age Golénischeff showed a great interest in oriental culture and ancient languages. When he was only fourteen years old, Golénischeff purchased his first Egyptian object, which was the start of a large collection of antiquities. From 1875–1879 he studied at St. Petersburg University, at the department of oriental languages. Publication of a paper on the subject of a papyrus, which the young scholar had found in the Hermitage Museum, was regarded as a great success.

In 1881 Golénischeff discovered a well-preserved papyrus of the Middle Kingdom (2040–1640) containing the famous "Tale of the Shipwrecked Sailor," a masterpiece of ancient Egyptian literature.

In 1886 he became a curator of the Egyptian department of the Hermitage, where he arranged a catalogue of the museum's Egyptian collection.

Golénischeff embarked for Egypt for the first time in 1879; during his sixty visits to Egypt he examined the most important archaeological complexes and assembled many antiquities, which were finally sold to the Russian government and transferred to the Pushkin Museum of Fine Arts in Moscow in 1911. Golénischeff's travels also brought him to the Eastern Desert. In the winter of 1884–1885 the Russian Egyptologist carried out an epigraphic inspection of the Wadi Hammamat. He never returned to Russia after the revolution of 1917 and settled in Nice, France. In Cairo where he was cataloguing the papyri in the Egyptian Museum for some time, he became Professor of Egyptology at the University in 1924. He died in Nice in 1947.

limits. The better-preserved structures in this wadi settlement survive to heights of two to three meters and include doors with lintels, windows, and interior shelving (Figs. 15.7–15.8). They are built of locally obtained metadiorite/metagabbro and aplite, the latter quarried nearby.

Shenshef is the largest, best-built, and best-preserved ancient settlement within a fifty kilometer radius of Berenike. Yet, despite detailed surveying and limited excavations, its raison d'être remains uncertain. Some of the earlier travelers to Berenike were also aware of Shenshef and provided brief

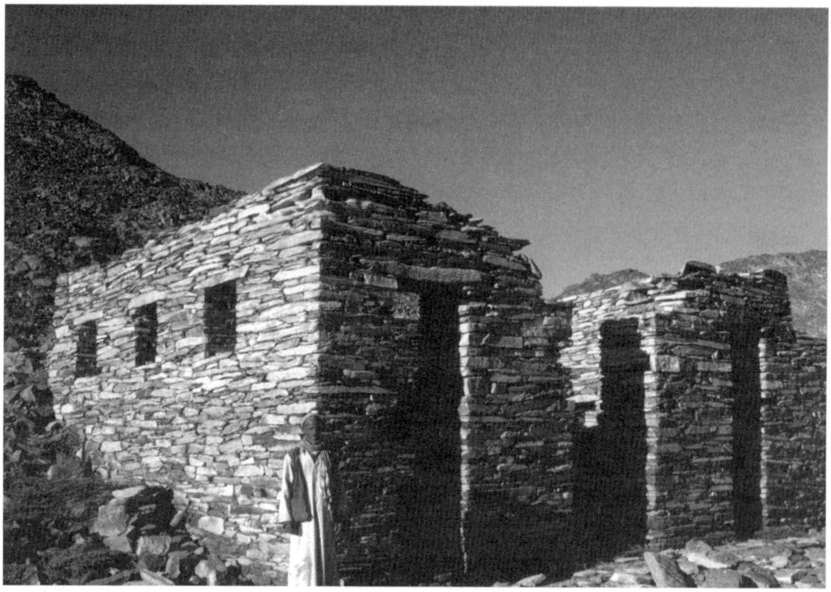

S.E. Sidebotham

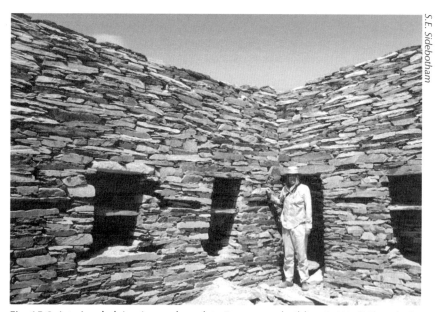

Fig. 15.7: Well-preserved structure in the late Roman-era community in Wadi Shenshef with doors, lintels, and windows.

S.E. Sidebotham

Fig. 15.8: Interior shelving in one large late Roman-era building in Wadi Shenshef.

descriptions of the remains; they were also puzzled by what function the site may have had. R.E. Colston in 1887 and G. Daressy in 1922 thought Shenshef was an Arab village and J. Ball in 1912 wrote that Shenshef was "a slave dealer's stronghold where slaves were herded till they could be shipped to Berenice." These interpretations are highly unlikely. The best overall description until the 1990s was that of G.W. Murray who published a brief account in 1926. Murray was also intrigued by the purpose of this large settlement in the desert. He speculated that inhabitants from Berenike resided here in the autumn, presumably because adverse winds curtailed sailing at that time of year from the port, but this cannot be substantiated. Murray also believed that Shenshef acted as a warehouse for precious commodities eventually destined for trade through Berenike.

The presence of water on or near the surface of Wadi Shenshef in proximity to the settlement for much of the year would have allowed the cultivation of a great deal of food, a fact borne out by the botanical finds and numerous grain grinding stones recovered during our surveys and excavations there. Whether this permitted a high degree of self-sufficiency let alone export of food to Berenike remains to be determined.

Excavations have indicated close contacts between Shenshef and many distant lands by way of Berenike. Imported items such as amphoras from the Eastern Mediterranean, mainly Cyprus and Cilicia in southern Turkey, black pepper from south India, and a sapphire from Sri Lanka arrived at Shenshef via Berenike. Finds of these and other high status artifacts suggest that an element of Shenshef's population was fairly well-to-do. Our excavations have also recovered quantities of the so-called Eastern Desert Ware, associated with a population from the Eastern Desert of Upper Egypt and Lower Nubia. Perhaps these people were some of the city's residents.

Hilltop Fort at Shenshef

Overlooking the late Roman settlement of Shenshef, to the east and crowning a high hill about ninety meters above, are the remains of a late first century BC-early first century AD fort that extends—oddly and uniquely for forts in the Eastern Desert—from a hilltop down into a saddle and up to another hilltop (Fig. 15.9 and Pls. 15.10–15.11). Virtually all of the late Roman Shenshef settlement as well as the Red Sea are visible from this mountain redoubt. The presence of a fifth–sixth century AD civilian settlement beneath a fort several hundred years older, and which appears not to have been in operation when the civilian settlement functioned, is an enigma that we cannot explain.

The superbly situated, but oddly shaped fort at Shenshef, with an overall length of nearly 120 meters, appears architecturally to have undergone two distinct building phases. Though it remains unexcavated, certain facts about its use can be understood from examination of surviving surface features. The northwestern-most portion of the fort sits atop a summit that immediately overlooks the later civilian settlement and from which there is also an excellent view of the Red Sea. This seems to be the older and is certainly the smaller of the two sections—measuring 56.1 meters north–south by about 39 meters east–west. This northwestern section has a massive four-meter-wide gate on the west that leads down a steep path to the wadi floor. This northwestern portion also contains virtually all the internal buildings now visible in either fort section; most surface pottery (late first century BC–early first century AD) was also found here.

The later addition to the fort, which extended toward the south–southeast down into a saddle and up to another hilltop to the south, contained virtually no pottery or interior structures; it cannot, therefore, be dated. A portal about 1.7 meters wide, torn through the southeastern portion of the

Fig. 15.9: Profile of the hilltop fort at Shenshef.

S.E. Sidebotham

original curtain wall of the northern/earlier fort, joined it to the later addition. Strangely, the walls of the later addition do not actually join those of the earlier. Where they should exist there are, instead, gaps, 1.8 meters wide on the east and 2.32 meters wide on the west, which may have been entrances into the later addition. In both fort sections, walls tended to be thicker than they were high.

The great differences in dates of apparent occupation of this fort with those of the civilian settlement below and to the west indicate that this hilltop installation was originally positioned to oversee a broad area and was not intended to guard a specific location. There is no indication at this time that the fort, originally occupied at the turn of the Christian era, remained in use when the civilian settlement below functioned four hundred to six hundred years later. Hilltop forts in the Eastern Desert are unusual. Our surveys over the years have identified only about eight of approximately eighty forts in the region that are situated on high ground.

Indigenous Peoples and 'Immigrants' in the Eastern Desert in Ptolemaic and Roman Times

From Ptolemaic times on, the Egyptian territory of Lower Nubia regained prosperity as a result of good administration and improved agricultural techniques. The Nile town of Hierasykaminos (Maharraqa) marked the border with Meroitic Nubia. The 120-kilometer stretch of land between Hierasykaminos and Aswan was called the Dodekaschoinos ('Land of the Twelve Miles' in Greek). The main goal of Ptolemaic recolonization of Lower Nubia was to facilitate access to the re-activated gold mines of Wadi 'Allaqi.

Shortly after Rome took control of Egypt in 30 BC, the long period of peace came to an end. The overly ambitious Roman governor Cornelius Gallus forced Meroitic envoys in 29 BC to sign a treaty that made the Meroitic part of Lower Nubia a Roman protectorate. The premature end of the governor, and the military debacle of his successor Aelius Gallus in Arabia, gave the Meroitic king an opportunity to turn the tables. A Meroitic army of thirty thousand men led by Queen Amanirenas defeated the Roman garrison in the Dodekaschoinos, occupied Philae, and looted Aswan. Only six years later a Roman army defeated the Meroitic troops and destroyed their capital, Napata. After renewed hostilities, the Roman emperor Augustus called a peace conference on the Aegean island of Samos. As a consequence, the Romans left that part of the Meroitic kingdom that they had occupied and the border was once again fixed at the town of Hierasykaminos. The following period of peace with Rome brought Meroë a short span of renewed international contacts and trade with Roman provinces, but the kingdom slowly lost its grip on Meroitic Nubia. This area became more or less independent, while the Nobadae and Blemmyes emerged and took control. Farther south the ancient empire of Meroë faded away during the following centuries.

We do not know much about the inhabitants of the southern Eastern Desert in this era of Ptolemaic and Roman history. Those living on the coast were called, understandably, *Ichthyophagoi* (Fish-Eaters). These people dwelt in scattered caves, according to Agatharchides, who lived in the second century BC, but whose information dates from the preceding century. He further described the Fish-Eaters, who buried their dead under heaps of stones, as not very warlike. The *Periplus of the Erythraean Sea* also lists the Fish-Eaters. Farther inland, according to the *Periplus,* lived the tribes of the 'Wild-Flesh-Eaters' and 'Calf-Eaters.'

In the third century AD the Blemmyes and Nobadae started to loom large in the texts of ancient classical authors as menacing threats to Roman order, though they were certainly in the region earlier. In this period, the introduction of the camel had transformed their society drastically; previously pastoralists restricted to certain areas, they then became long-range raiders. In the 50s–70s AD Pliny the Elder described the Blemmyes in his *Natural History* as mythological beings. According to him, a typical Blemmye was headless with eyes and a mouth on his chest (Fig. 15.10). Members of these same desert tribes were characterized in about AD 200 by Julius Solinus, who borrowed much of his information unashamedly from Pliny and Pomponius Mela, as extremely mean, and able to capture wild animals just by leaping on them. The sixth century writer Procopius also recorded the devastation wrought by these tribes in the region.

In AD 250 the inhabitants of the Dodekaschoinos saw that Pliny's account of the grotesque features of these desert peoples was fanciful. The Blemmyes attacked in this year for the first time the towns of the Dodekaschoinos. Roman troops were able to repel their assaults, but subsequent attacks had

ARCHAEOLOGICAL TRACES OF THE BLEMMYES AND NOBADAE

"Then there is another island, south of the Brixontes, on which there are born men without heads who have their eyes and mouth in their chests. They are eight feet tall and eight feet wide." (Fig. 15.10). A catalogue entitled *Mirabilia Descripta (The Wonders of the East)* provides this account of grotesque, deformed people. When this collection of descriptions of people and beasts living in Africa and Asia was compiled in the early Middle Ages, Europe had basically lost all contact with, and with it most of its knowledge of, Africa and Asia. Writers of compilations like *The Wonders of the East* had to fall back on ancient books. The above-mentioned text was clearly based on the description of the Blemmyes by Pliny, who wrote his *Natural History*, an attempt to collect all knowledge of his time, in the first century AD. At the time Pliny wrote his encyclopedia, not much was known of the desert people east of the Dodekaschoinos.

Fig. 15.10: Blemmyes. Drawing by A.M. Hense (based on illustrations in *Cosmographia* [Basel 1544] by Sebastian, and the *Nuremberg Chronicle* [1493] by Hartmann Schedel).

more serious consequences. Eleven years after they launched their initial attack, the Blemmyes entered the Dodekaschoinos again, this time overrunning the weakened garrisons completely. Before the Roman general Julius Aemilianus succeeded in driving the Blemmyes back to the First Cataract, they had plundered many Egyptian cities. During the attack of Queen Zenobia of Palmyra in the north of Egypt in AD 270, the Blemmyes conquered the whole of Upper Egypt. Many Blemmyes stayed in the Egyptian towns of Ptolemais and Coptos in peaceful cohabitation with the Egyptians, even after the Romans regained most of their territory. The Dodekaschoinos had to be given up, however, and the Romans permanently abandoned the area in AD 289.

This changed only in the third century AD, when an army of Blemmyes attacked Roman territory for the first time. Roman accounts explicitly refer to the Blemmyes in their border conflicts in southern Egypt. Some early Coptic Christian stories also mention local Egyptian fear of the Blemmyes. Such an account we find in the story of the Coptic saint Apa Shenoute freeing prisoners from the raiding Bedouin. It is a wonder story in which Apa Shenoute made the arms of the Blemmyes, who intended to kill him, stiff and inflexible "like dry wood." Shenoute made his way to the king of the Blemmyes, who, confronted with the fate of his people, begged Apa Shenoute to restore his men's arms. The king gladly responded to Shenoute's demand to release all prisoners immediately.

Sources, both Roman and local, stress the ruthless savageness of these people and contrast them with those living in the civilized Egyptian territories. Relations with the Blemmyes were, however, much more complicated than these accounts suggest. During periods of peace, the Blemmyes lived in the towns of the Dodekaschoinos, and when those belonged to Blemmye territory, governed them well, adopting Roman administrative techniques. During these periods, trade must have flourished with Roman Egypt. And just like their forerunners the Medjay had done more than a thousand years earlier, the Blemmyes served in the army of the (Roman) rulers of Egypt.

Although mentioned frequently by their Roman contemporaries, identifiable archaeological traces of the Blemmyes and Nobadae are scarce. We know almost nothing of the Blemmyes in the first and second centuries AD. The Nobadae emerged during the first century AD in the Nile Valley south of the Dodekaschoinos. Until that time, the area was barely inhabited, but by about AD 200 the whole region was covered with settlements. The peoples responsible for the rapid development of the area were first dubbed the X-Group, later identified as the Nobadae; the Blemmyes and other local groups probably supplemented them. The X-Group, and the archaeological remains of settlements and burials, was more recently renamed the Ballana culture, which is the material culture shared by all the inhabitants of Nubia in this period. The Nobadae were organized in a village culture, without monumental buildings such as temples and palaces. The small villages were more or less independent, and governed by local monarchs and officials. The settlements produced agricultural products and cattle, which were bartered among the villages. There was also an important weaving industry in the villages. In trade with Roman Egypt, food was exchanged for luxury goods such as incense burners and glass vessels. The pottery of the Nobadae consisted of characteristic thin-walled and painted beakers and bowls. These delicate vessels are also described as 'eggshell ware.' The Ballana culture did not, as far as we can determine, have any written literature or history, but adopted the Meroitic script for administrative purposes. The houses had thick, red-painted mud-brick walls and vaulted ceilings. Windows were placed high in the walls, and stone staircases gave access to the roofs.

The only known monumental structures built by the Ballana culture were the royal tombs near Qustul and Ballana in the third and fourth centuries AD. Mounds, varying in diameter from three to twelve meters and up to 4.5 meters high, crowned many common tombs. The final resting places of the kings and the nobles were far larger, and each had an adjoining offering chamber. The dead were wrapped in a shroud, as was the practice in Meroitic times, and placed on a canopied wooden bier. Most grave goods consisted of locally made pottery, but iron weapons and beads were also common. Moreover, the royal tombs contained bronze lamps, glass vessels, and wooden boxes inlaid with ivory. In one tomb a Ballana king and queen were found wearing large silver crowns. Like the Blemmyes, the Nobadae worshiped the old Meroitic and pharaonic Egyptian gods. Isis, also very popular throughout many parts of the Roman Empire, was one of their most important deities, and her temple at Philae was the main sanctuary for both people until very late in antiquity.

The origin of the Blemmyes is uncertain. They may have entered the Eastern Desert during the early Roman period, but it seems more likely that they largely descended from earlier Eastern Desert tribes. Recognizable archaeological traces of the Blemmyes are still extremely scarce, although finds from our excavations at Berenike and Sikait may be evidence of their presence in the area. In the late Roman period, Berenike and Sikait counted many inhabitants of local origin, as shown by the large numbers of pottery shards of so-called Eastern Desert Ware, a handmade and burnished pottery, found in excavations there. It is still unclear if this pottery belonged to the Blemmyes, or to another, still unknown, desert people.

To keep the Blemmyes at bay, the Romans invited the Nobadae in AD 289 to colonize the Dodekaschoinos. In addition, they gave both Blemmyes and Nobadae permission to visit the Isis sanctuary at Philae. The Nobadae never really succeeded in taking over the whole of Lower Nubia from the Blemmyes. They also never controlled the Eastern Desert and were unable to obtain revenues from the gold and emerald mines there, which were completely in the hands of the Blemmyes. As a consequence, the royal jewelry of the Ballana culture was made of imported silver, rather than Blemmye gold. In AD 392 an edict of the Roman emperor Theodosius I (AD 379–395) proclaimed the closure of all pagan temples, including those of Philae. Confronted with this, the united armies of the Nobadae and Blemmyes attacked and conquered Upper Egypt, which they ruled until AD 452, at which time the Roman general Maximinus defeated them. The peace treaty stipulated that the Blemmyes and Nobadae could visit the temple of Philae again, and resume their worship of Isis. Until the sixth century the Blemmyes ruled over the Dodekaschoinos, and managed to keep this 'pagan' enclave, as the Nobadae were Christianized by then, relatively prosperous. The Blemmyes defended their last strongholds south of Aswan until their final defeat in AD 540 by king Silko of the Nobadae. Silko and his successors expanded their kingdom to the First Cataract. By AD 600 the conversion of Upper Egypt and Nubia was complete, and most Nubian temples were transformed into churches.

Even after their defeat along the Nile, the Blemmyes retained control over a large part of the Eastern Desert. The Arab historian al-Taghribirdi (AD 1411–1470) recounts how in AD 854 the natives "of the remotest part of Upper Egypt" refused to pay their yearly tribute of five hundred slaves, dromedaries, and several giraffes and elephants to the Muslim ruler of Egypt. The desert tribes then plundered towns as far as Esna and Edfu. As in Roman days, a large punitive expedition was sent to the south. Although the account of al-Taghribirdi on the battle that followed was probably tendentious, it suggests that the Blemmyes still had a considerable camel corps. The creation of three small Nubian Christian kingdoms followed the downfall of the Blemmyes. The Arab conquest of Egypt in AD 641 brought new conflicts between these southern kingdoms and Egypt, but they succeeded for centuries in warding off occupation. The Kingdom of Makouria achieved friendly relations with the Fatimids in Egypt, and the intense trade with Upper Egypt promoted the prosperity of the land. Faras became the cultural and religious center, while in many places churches and monasteries were built. In the tenth century the Kingdom of Makouria had even gained enough power to occupy Upper Egypt. The heyday of this Christian kingdom came to an end, however, shortly thereafter, and around AD 1300 it was completely overrun by Egyptian Muslims. The southernmost kingdom, Alodia, retained its independence until the fifteenth century.

Enigmatic Settlements in the Eastern Desert

As we noted in Chapter 10, in the course of the fourth and fifth centuries AD communities whose functions have yet to be determined emerged in the Eastern Desert. Although the most spectacular, Shenshef is only one of over a dozen settlements found thus far which cannot be connected to any mine, quarry or road. Some ten kilometers northwest of Shenshef the contemporary settlement of Hitan Rayan was built in a long narrow wadi. The buildings here are much simpler, and are probably the stone foundations for tents or huts of wood, hides, and matting. The structures recall those found at Eastern Desert mining sites. Our archaeological surveys in the area, however, have not detected any mines or quarries. Both Shenshef and Hitan Rayan were built during the latest period of habitation at Berenike in the later fourth, fifth and sixth centuries AD.

Our archaeological survey discovered a settlement in Wadi Umm Atlee (Figs. 15.11–15.12) in winter 1998. This site lies approximately thirty-five kilometers southwest of Berenike and about thirteen kilometers in a straight line west of the Red Sea. We named the remains Qaryat (Village of) Mustafa

'Amr Gama in honor of the 'Ababda Bedouin who revealed the site's location to the survey. The village comprises 109 structures or parts of buildings
that extend up two branches of the wadi; it covers a total area of about 240
meters north–south by 390 meters east–west. There are a few doughnut-
shaped tombs of ancient date on the surrounding ridges above the wadi.
Evidence of water damage sustained over the years suggests that the settlement was originally somewhat larger. Buildings were probably mainly used
for human habitation, food storage, and animal pens. The community had
an estimated population of 122.

The structures comprising this site include mainly unpretentious small
one and two room buildings and a smattering of three and four room edifices that are mainly rectilinear, a few round or oval, in plan. Surviving walls
are made of locally available and unworked cobbles and small boulders and
average 0.7–1.2 meters high, and only about 0.5 meters thick. In some
places natural rock faces form building walls. The low walls and little surviving tumble beside them suggest that they were not originally much
higher. Thus, most of the superstructures were probably made of less per-

S.E. Sidebotham

Fig. 15.11: Some of the buildings in the enigmatic late Roman period settlement of
Qaryat Mustafa 'Amr Gama in Wadi Umm Atlee.

S.E. Sidebotham

Fig. 15.12: Some of the buildings in the enigmatic late Roman period settlement of Qaryat Mustafa 'Amr Gama in Wadi Umm Atlee.

manent materials that have long since disappeared, perhaps wooden frames covered by hides, cloth, or mats as is the current practice of the 'Ababda Bedouin in the area today. Analysis of the site and the surface finds collected there, including pottery and some dipinti painted in red on the shoulders and necks of amphora fragments, indicates occupation in the fifth to mid sixth centuries AD. No definitive identification of the purpose of the site is possible though it might have been one of the many Christian *laura* communities known from literary sources to have been active in the Eastern Desert at that time. *Laura* settlements comprised numbers of cells (small rooms) loosely grouped together sometimes, but not always, in combination with a church. Monks and Christian recluses would reside in these communities for varying lengths of time. The recovery of numerous amphora fragments styled Late Roman Amphora 1, made in Cyprus and Cilicia (the southern and southeastern coast of modern Turkey) in southern Asia Minor, suggests frequent contacts with Berenike, the nearest port through which such jars could have been trans-shipped.

The site of Qaryat 'Ali Muhammad Husayn, which we also named after one of our 'Ababda guides, counts at least eight rather large buildings in four different areas. There is no evidence of what its purpose might have been. It may have served as a stop on the route between Hitan Rayan and Vetus Hydreuma (Wadi Abu Greiya) as the buildings are dispersed over the wadi and not clustered in a group.

It seems from the late fourth century AD on that several groups sought refuge and relative safety in the Eastern Desert. One of these hiding places may have been the settlement of Umm Heiran not far from the large Roman emerald mining town of Sikait (see Chapter 12). Tucked away in a narrow wadi dissecting Wadi Gemal, this settlement numbered over 190 small buildings, and one larger structure, which may have been a church or administrative building. A small cemetery lay northeast of the settlement.

Survey work has discovered about ten other sites in the Eastern Desert whose similarity in locations, plans, appearances and construction techniques of buildings, and dates of activity parallel those of Qaryat Mustafa 'Amr Gama, Hitan Rayan, and Umm Heiran. Their functions also remain enigmatic, but identification as Christian hermit *(laura)* communities is possible. In late Roman Egypt, the desert was a refuge for those who sought to avoid taxes, public service, or religious persecution. Large numbers of Christian monks, recluses, and hermits resided in the deserts especially in the early fifth century and these enigmatic settlements may be evidence of their activities.

All graves found near these putative 'Christian' settlements were late Roman 'ring-cairn' (doughnut) tombs. The number of graves seems rather small compared to the sizes of most settlements, which suggests that these sites were only used for short periods of time. Alternatively, as mentioned in Chapter 8, it is also possible that many of the dead were returned to the Nile Valley, which is only logical if the inhabitants were not local desert people. Most of the pottery found in these settlements is of Nile Valley or foreign, non-Egyptian, origin. The number of local hand-made pottery shards, the so-called Eastern Desert Ware, is remarkably small, which makes it likely that the population of these settlements consisted largely of Egyptians from the Nile Valley or Red Sea coastal towns.

It is possible that some, if not all, of these enigmatic desert settlements were communities where groups of prospectors would gather and start their expeditions, looking for gold or other valuable deposits. As most auriferous deposits had already been discovered during the New Kingdom, this is unlikely and no gold mines have been found associated with any of these settlements. It is also unlikely that these sites were military marching camps. The army built few of these in the late Roman period. The settlements we have found are not fortified and are not situated in any tactically or strategically important locations.

Suggestions for Further Reading

Chapter 1

Prehistoric

M.A. Hoffman, *Egypt Before the Pharaohs: The Prehistoric Foundations of Egyptian Civilization* (Austin: University of Texas Press, 1991).

B. Midant-Reynes, *The Prehistory of Egypt* (Oxford: Blackwell Publishing, 2000).

Pharaonic Period

J. Baines and J. Málek, *Cultural Atlas of Ancient Egypt* (New York: Checkmark Books, 2000).

J.H. Breasted, *A History of Egypt from the Earliest Times to the Persian Conquest* (London: Hodder & Stoughton, 1937).

P.A. Clayton, *Chronicle of the Pharaohs: The Reign-by-Reign Record of the Rulers and Dynasties of Ancient Egypt* (London: Thames and Hudson Ltd, 1994).

I. Dodson and D. Hilton, *The Complete Royal Families of Ancient Egypt* (London: Thames and Hudson Ltd, 2004).

T.G.H. James, *An Introduction to Ancient Egypt* (London: British Museum Publications Ltd, 1979).

I. Shaw, ed., *The Oxford History of Ancient Egypt* (New York: Oxford University Press, 2000).

I. Shaw and P. Nicholson, *The British Museum Dictionary of Ancient Egypt* (London: British Museum Press, 1995).

T.A.H. Wilkinson, *Dictionary of Ancient Egypt* (London: Thames and Hudson Ltd, 2005).

T.A.H. Wilkinson, *Early Dynastic Egypt* (New York-London: Routledge, 2006).

C. Ziegler, ed., *The Pharaohs* (London: Thames and Hudson Ltd, 2002).

Ptolemaic Era

A. Bouché-Leclercq, *Histoire des Lagides,* reprint ed. (Aalen: Scientia Verlag, 1978).

A.K. Bowman, *Egypt After the Pharaohs 332 BC–AD 642: From Alexander to the Arab Conquest* (Berkeley: University of California Press, 1986).

M. Chauveau (trans. D. Lorton), *Egypt in the Age of Cleopatra. History and Society under the Ptolemies* (Ithaca-London: Cornell University Press, 2000).

P.M. Fraser, *Ptolemaic Alexandria* (Oxford: Clarendon Press, 1972).

G. Hölbl, *A History of the Ptolemaic Empire* (London-New York: Routledge, 2001).

A.E. Samuel, *The Shifting Sands of History: Interpretations of Ptolemaic Egypt* (Publications of the Association of Ancient Historians 2) (Lanham-New York-London: University Press of America, 1989).

Roman Period

R. Alston, *Soldier and Society in Roman Egypt: A Social History* (London-New York: Routledge, 1995).

R.S. Bagnall, *Egypt in Late Antiquity* (Princeton: Princeton University Press, 1993).

A.K. Bowman, *Egypt After the Pharaohs 332 BC–AD 642: From Alexander to the Arab Conquest* (Berkeley: University of California Press, 1986).

R.B. Jackson, *At Empire's Edge: Exploring Rome's Egyptian Frontier* (New Haven-London: Yale University Press, 2002).

A.C. Johnson, *Roman Egypt.* Volume 2 of T. Frank, ed., *An Economic Survey of Ancient Rome* (Baltimore: The Johns Hopkins Press, 1936).

J. Lesquier, *L'Armée romaine d'Égypte d'Auguste à Dioclétien (MIFAO 41)* (Cairo: IFAO, 1918).

N. Lewis, *Life in Egypt Under Roman Rule* (Oxford: Clarendon Press, 1983).

Chapter 2

Topography and Geology of the Red Sea and Eastern Desert

A.J. Edwards and S.M. Head, eds., *Key Environments-Red Sea* (Oxford: Pergamon Press, 1987).

K.A. Kitchen, "Red Sea Harbours, Hinterlands and Relationships in Pre-classical Antiquity," in J. Starkey, P. Starkey and T. Wilkinson, eds., *Natural Resources and Cultural Connections of the Red Sea (Society for Arabian Studies Monographs* No. 5)(BARis 1661)(Oxford: Archeopress, 2007): 131–141.

B.M. Sampsell, *A Traveler's Guide to the Geology of Egypt* (Cairo: American University in Cairo Press, 2004).

R. Said, *The Geology of Egypt* (Amsterdam-New York: Elsevier, 1962).

Prehistoric and Early Dynastic Rock Graffiti

P. Červíček, *Felsbilder der Nord-Ethbai, Oberägyptens und Unternubiens* (Wiesbaden: Steiner Verlag, 1974).

S. Redford and D.B. Redford, "Graffiti and Petroglyphs Old and New from the Eastern Desert," *Journal of the American Research Center in Egypt* 26 (1989): 3–49.

D. Rohl, ed., *The Followers of Horus Eastern Desert Survey Report.* Volume I (Thames View, Abingdon, Oxon: ISIS, 2000).

H.A. Winkler, *Rock Drawings of Southern Upper Egypt I* (London: Egypt Exploration Society, 1939).

Ptolemaic History (General)

A. Bouché-Leclercq, *Histoire des Lagides,* reprint edition (Aalen: Scientia Verlag, 1978).

P.M. Fraser, *Ptolemaic Alexandria* (Oxford: Clarendon Press, 1972)

G. Hölbl, *A History of the Ptolemaic Empire* (London-New York: Routledge, 2001).

Bedouin of the Eastern Desert

J.J. Hobbs, *Bedouin Life in the Egyptian Wilderness* (Austin, TX: University of Texas Press, 1989).

G.W. Murray, *Sons of Ishmael. A Study of the Egyptian Bedouin* (London: George Routledge & Sons, Ltd., 1935).

L.A. Tregenza, *The Red Sea Mountains of Egypt* (London-New York-Toronto: Oxford University Press, 1955).

Ancient Maps, Geographers, and Itineraries

O.A.W. Dilke, *Greek and Roman Maps* (Ithaca, NY: Cornell University Press, 1985).

B. Salway, "Travel, *Itineraria* and *Tabellaria*," in C. Adams and R. Laurence, eds., *Travel and Geography in the Roman Empire* (London-New York: Routledge, 2001): 22–66.

R.K. Sherk, "Roman Geographical Exploration and Military Maps," *Aufstieg und Niedergang der römischen Welt 2.1* (1974): 534–562.

J.N. Wilford, *The Mapmakers. The Story of the Great Pioneers in Cartography from Antiquity to the Space Age* (London: Pimlico, 2002).

Early European Explorers

J. Starkey and O. El Daly, eds., *Desert Travellers from Herodotus to T.E. Lawrence* (Durham: Astene Publications, 2000).

Chapter 3

The Via Nova Hadriana, Antinoopolis, Hadrian, and Antinoos

A.R. Birley, *Hadrian: The Restless Emperor* (London-New York: Routledge, 1997).

M.T. Boatwright, *Hadrian and the Cities of the Roman Empire* (Princeton: Princeton University Press, 2000).

R. Chevallier, *Les voies romaines* (Paris: Picard, 1997)

L. Del Francia Barocas, *Antinoe Cent'Anni Dopo. Catologo della mostra Firenze Palazzo Medici Riccardi 10 luglio – 1° novembre 1998. Istituto Papirologico "G. Vitelli" Firenze* (Florence: Istituto Papirologico "G. Vitelli", 1998).

R. Lambert, *Beloved and God: The Story of Hadrian and Antinous* (New York: Carol Publishing Group, 1992).

S.E. Sidebotham and R.E. Zitterkopf, "Survey of the Via Hadriana by the University of Delaware: The 1996 Season," *Bulletin de l'Institut français de Archéologie Orientale* 97 (1997): 221–237.

S.E. Sidebotham and R.E. Zitterkopf, "Survey of the Via Hadriana: The 1997 Season," *Bulletin de l'Institut français de Archéologie Orientale* 98 (1998): 353–365.

S.E. Sidebotham, R.E. Zitterkopf and C.C. Helms, "Survey of the Via Hadriana: The 1998 Season," *Journal of the American Research Center in Egypt* 37 (2000): 115–126.

S.E. Sidebotham and R.E. Zitterkopf, "Surveying the Via Nova Hadriana: The Emperor Hadrian's Desert Highway in Egypt," *Minerva* 17, no. 3 (May/June 2006): 34–35.

E. Speller, *Following Hadrian: A Second-century Journey through the Roman Empire* (London: Review, 2002).

M. Yourcener, *Memoirs of Hadrian* (New York: Farrar, Straus and Young, 1954).

The Fort at Abu Sha'r and Nearby Installations

R.S. Bagnall and J.A. Sheridan, "Greek and Latin Documents from 'Abu Sha'ar, 1990–1991," *Journal of the American Research Center in Egypt* 31 (1994): 159–168.

R.S. Bagnall and J.A. Sheridan, "Greek and Latin Documents from 'Abu Sha'ar, 1992–1993," *Bulletin of the American Society of Papyrologists* 31 (1994): 109–120.

L. Bender Jørgensen, "The Late Roman Fort at Abū Sha'ār, Egypt: Textiles in Their Archaeological Context," *Textiles In Situ Their Find Spots in Egypt and Neighbouring Countries in the First Millennium CE (Riggisberger Berichte* 13) (2006): 161–174.

L. Mulvin and S.E. Sidebotham, "Roman Game Boards from Abu Sha'ar (Red Sea Coast, Egypt)," *Antiquity* 78, no. 301 (September 2004): 602–617.

S.E. Sidebotham, "Preliminary Report on the 1990–1991 Seasons of Fieldwork at 'Abu Sha'ar (Red Sea Coast)," *Journal of the American Research Center in Egypt* 31 (1994): 133–158.

S.E. Sidebotham, "University of Delaware Archaeological Project at 'Abu Sha'ar: The 1992 Season," *Newsletter of the American Research Center in Egypt* 161/162 (Spring/Summer 1993): 1–9.

S.E. Sidebotham, "University of Delaware Fieldwork in the Eastern Desert of Egypt, 1993" *Dumbarton Oaks Papers* 48 (1994): 263–275.

S.E. Sidebotham, J.A. Riley, H.A. Hamroush, and H. Barakat, "Fieldwork on the Red Sea Coast: The 1987 Season," *Journal of the American Research Center in Egypt* 26 (1989): 127–166.

W. Van Neer and S.E. Sidebotham, "Animal Remains from the Fourth–sixth Century AD Military Installations near Abu Sha'ar at the Red Sea Coast (Egypt)," Jennerstrasse 8, ed., *Tides of the Desert – Gezeiten der Wüste – Contributions to the Archaeology and Environmental History of Africa in Honor of Rudolph Kuper* (14 *Africa Praehistorica*. Monographs on African Archaeology and Environment)(Bonn: Heinrich-Barth-Institut, 2002): 171–195.

The Cities and Inscriptions of Tentyris, Coptos, Apollonopolis Magna, and Syene on the Nile

A. Bernand, *Les Ports du désert. Recueil des inscriptions grecques d'Antinooupolis, Tentyris, Koptos, Apollonopolis Parva et Apollonopolis Magna* (Paris: Centre national de la Recherche scientifique, 1984).

Coptos L'Egypte antique aux portes du désert. Lyon, museé des Beaux-Arts 3 février–mai 2000 (Lyon: Museé des Beaux Arts/Paris: Réunion des museés nationaux, 2000).

S.C. Herbert and A. Berlin, eds., *Kelsey Museum of the University of Michigan, University of Assiut Excavations at Coptos (Qift) in Upper Egypt, 1987–1992* (Journal of Roman Archaeology Supplementary Series number 53)(Portsmouth, RI: Journal of Roman Archaeology, 2003).

The Coptos Tariff

F. Burkhalter, "Le 'Tarif de Coptos' La douane de Coptos, les fermiers de l'*apostolion* et le préfet du désert de Bérénice," *Topoi* Supplement 3 (2002): 199–233.

The Red Sea–Indian Ocean Trade

D. Peacock and D. Williams, eds., *Food for the Gods. New Light on the Ancient Incense Trade* (Oxford: Oxbow Books, 2007).

M.G. Raschke, "New Studies in Roman Commerce with the East," *Aufstieg und Niedergang der römischen Welt* 2.9.2 (1978): 604–1378.

S.E. Sidebotham, *Roman Economic Policy in the Erythra Thalassa 30 BC–AD 217 (Mnemosyne* supplement no. 91)(Leiden: E.J. Brill, 1986).

J. Starkey, P. Starkey and T. Wilkinson, eds., *Natural Resources and Cultural Connections of the Red Sea (Society for Arabian Studies Monographs* No. 5)(BARis 1661)(Oxford: Archeopress, 2007).

G.K. Young, *Rome's Eastern Trade International Commerce and Imperial Policy, 31 BC–AD 305* (London-New York: Routledge, 2001).

Sir John Gardner Wilkinson

J. Thompson, *Sir Gardner Wilkinson and His Circle* (Austin, TX: University of Texas Press, 1992).

Chapter 4

Predynastic, Pharaonic, Ptolemaic, and Roman Quarries, Wadi Hammamat

V.M. Brown and J.A. Harrell, "Topographical and Petrological Survey of Ancient Roman Quarries in the Eastern Desert of Egypt," in Y. Maniatis, N. Herz, and Y. Basiakos, eds., *The Study of Marble and Other Stones Used in Antiquity – ASMOSIA III Athens: Transactions of the 3rd International Symposium of the Association for the Study of Marble and Other Stones used in Antiquity* (London: Archetype Publications, 1995): 221–234.

J. Couyat and P. Montet, *Les inscriptions hiéroglyphiques et hiératiques du Ouâdi Hammâmât* (Cairo: IFAO, 1912).

G. Goyon, *Nouvelles inscriptions rupestres du Wadi Hammamat* (Paris: Librairie d'Amérique et d'Orient Adrien-Maisonneuve, 1957).

D. Farout, "La carrière du wHmw Ameny et l'organisation des expéditions au ouadi Hammamat au Moyen Empire," *Bulletin de l'Institut français de Archéologie Orientale* 94 (1994): 143–172.

J.A. Harrell, "A Stone Vessel Quarry at Gebel Umm Naqqat," *Egyptian Archaeology* 24 (2004): 34–36.

J.A. Harrell, "Pharaonic Stone Quarries in the Egyptian Deserts," in R. Friedman, ed., *Egypt and Nubia Gifts of the Desert* (London: The British Museum Press, 2002): 232–243.

J.A. Harrell and V.M. Brown, "A Late-period Quarry for Naoi in the Eastern Desert," *Egyptian Archaeology* 14 (1999): 18–20.

J.A. Harrell and V.M. Brown, "Rock Sawing at a Roman Diorite Quarry in Wadi Umm Shegilat, Egypt," in J.J. Herrmann, Jr., N. Herz, and R. Newman, eds., *Asmosia 5: Interdisciplinary Studies on Ancient Stone* (London: Archetype Publications, 2002): 52–57.

J.A. Harrell and L. Lazzarini, "A New Variety of *Granite Bianco e Nero* from Wadi Barud, Egypt," in J.J. Herrmann, Jr., N. Herz, and R. Newman, eds., *Asmosia 5: Interdisciplinary Studies on Ancient Stone* (London: Archetype Publications, 2002): 47–51.

J.A. Harrell, V.M. Brown, and L. Lazzarini, "Breccia Verde Antica: Sources, Petrology, and Ancient Uses," in L. Lazzarini, ed., *ASMOSIA VI Proceedings of the Sixth International Conference Venice, June 15–18, 2000. Interdisciplinary Studies on Ancient Stone* (Padova: Bottega d'Erasmo, 2000): 207–218.

T. Hikade, "Expeditions to the Wadi Hammamat During the New Kingdom," *Journal of Egyptian Archaeology* 92 (2006): 153-168.

Mons Porphyrites and Its Environs

V. Maxfield, D. Peacock, eds., *The Roman Imperial Quarries Survey and Excavation at Mons Porphyrites 1994–98.* Volume 1: *Topography and Quarries* (London: Egypt Exploration Society , 2001).

G.W. Murray, "An Archaic Hut in Wadi Umm Sidrah," *Journal of Egyptian Archaeology* 25 (1939): 38–39.

D. Peacock and V. Maxfield, eds., *The Roman Imperial Quarries Survey and Excavation at Mons Porphyrites 1994–1998*. Volume 2: *The Excavations* (London: Egypt Exploration Society, 2007).

Mons Claudianus and Its Environs

H. Cuvigny, "The Amount of Wages Paid to the Quarry-Workers at Mons Claudianus," *Journal of Roman Studies* 86 (1996): 139–145.

V.A. Maxfield and D.P.S. Peacock, eds., *Survey and Excavation Mons Claudianus 1987–1993*. Volume 2 *Excavations:* Part I (*FIFAO* 43)(Cairo: IFAO, 2001).

V.A. Maxfield and D.P.S. Peacock, eds., *Survey and Excavations. Mons Claudianus 1987–1993*. Vol. 3: *Ceramic Vessels and Related Objects from Mons Claudianus* (*FIFAO* 54) (Cairo: IFAO, 2006).

D.P.S. Peacock, V.A. Maxfield, eds., *Mons Claudianus. Survey and Excavation* I. *Topography and Quarries (FIFAO* 37)(Cairo: IFAO, 1997).

S.E. Sidebotham, "Newly Discovered Sites in the Eastern Desert," *Journal of Egyptian Archaeology* 82 (1996): 181–192.

Wadi Umm Wikala (Mons Ophiates)

S.E. Sidebotham, H. Barnard, J.A. Harrell and R.S. Tomber, "The Roman Quarry and Installations in Wadi Umm Wikala and Wadi Semna," *Journal of Egyptian Archaeology* 87 (2001): 135–170.

Roman Roads and Stations between the Quarries and the Nile

H. Cuvigny, ed., *La route de Myos Hormos. L'armée romaine dans le désert Oriental d'Égypte (FIFAO* 48/1 and 48/2)(Cairo: IFAO, 2003).

S.E. Sidebotham, "Caravans Across the Eastern Desert of Egypt: Recent Discoveries on the Berenike–Apollonopolis Magna–Coptos Roads," in A. Avanzini, ed., *Profumi d'Arabia. Atti del Convegno (Saggi di Storia antica* 11)(Rome: "L'Erma" di Bretschneider, 1997): 385–394.

S.E. Sidebotham, "Newly Discovered Sites in the Eastern Desert," *Journal of Egyptian Archaeology* 82 (1996): 181–192.

S.E. Sidebotham, "From Berenike to Koptos: Recent Results of the Desert Route Survey," *Topoi* 10 (2002): 415–438.

S.E. Sidebotham, R.E. Zitterkopf and J.A. Riley, "Survey of the 'Abu Sha'ar-Nile Road," *American Journal of Archaeology* 95, no. 4 (1991): 571–622.

R.E. Zitterkopf and S.E. Sidebotham, "Stations and Towers on the Quseir–Nile Road," *Journal of Egyptian Archaeology* 75 (1989): 155–189.

Arthur E.P. Weigall

J. Hankey, *A Passion for Egypt A Biography of Arthur Weigall* (London-New York: I.B. Tauris Publishers, 2001).

A.E.P. Weigall, *Travels in the Upper Egyptian Deserts* (Edinburgh-London: William Blackwood and Sons, 1913).

George William Murray

G.W. Murray, *Dare Me to the Desert* (New York-South Brunswick: A.S. Barnes and Co., Inc., 1968).

G.W. Murray, *Sons of Ishmael A Study of the Egyptian Bedouin* (London: George Routledge & Sons, Ltd., 1935).

Chapter 5

T.M. Herbich, "Magnetic Survey," in S.E. Sidebotham and W.Z. Wendrich, eds., *Berenike 1999/2000. Report on the Excavations at Berenike, Including Excavations in Wadi Kalalat and Siket, and the Survey of the Mons Smaragdus Region* (Los Angeles: Cotsen Institute of Archaeology, 2007): 22–29.

Leo A. Tregenza

L.A. Tregenza, *Egyptian Years* (London-New York-Toronto: Oxford University Press, 1958).

L. Tregenza, *Harbour Village Yesterday in Cornwall* (London: William Kimber, 1977).

L.A. Tregenza, *The Red Sea Mountains of Egypt* (London-New York-Toronto: Oxford University Press, 1955).

Chapter 6

Amethyst Mines in Wadi Abu Diyeiba

J.A. Harrell and S.E. Sidebotham, "Wadi Abu Diyeiba: An Amethyst Quarry in Egypt's Eastern Desert," *Minerva* 15, no. 6 (November–December 2004): 12–14.

J.A. Harrell, S.E. Sidebotham, S. Marchand, R.S. Bagnall, J.E. Gates, and J. L. Rivard, "The Ptolemaic to Early Roman Amethyst Quarry at Abu Diyeiba in Egypt's Eastern Desert," *Bulletin de l'Institut français de Archéologie Orientale* 106 (2006): 127–162.

Mons Porphyrites

V.A. Maxfield, "Stone Quarrying in the Eastern Desert with Particular Reference to Mons Claudianus and Mons Porphyrites," in D.J. Mattingly and J. Salmon, eds., *Economies Beyond Agriculture in the Classical World* (London-New York: Routledge, 2001): 143–170.

V. Maxfield and D. Peacock, eds., *The Roman Imperial Quarries Survey and Excavation at Mons Porphyrites 1994–1998.* Volume 1: *Topography and Quarries* (London: Egypt Exploration Society, 2001).

D.P.S. Peacock and V.A. Maxfield, *The Imperial Quarries. Survey and Excavation at Mons Porphyrites, 1994–1998.* Volume 2: *The Excavations.* 82nd Excavation Memoir of the Egypt Exploration Society (London: Egypt Exploration Society, 2007).

Mons Claudianus

V.A. Maxfield and D.P.S. Peacock, eds., *Survey and Excavation Mons Claudianus 1987–1993.* Volume 2: *Excavations:* Part I (*FIFAO* 43)(Cairo: IFAO, 2001).

V.A. Maxfield and D.P.S. Peacock, eds., *Survey and Excavations. Mons Claudianus 1987–1993.* Vol. 3: *Ceramic Vessels and Related Objects from Mons Claudianus* (*FIFAO* 54) (Cairo: IFAO, 2006).

D.P.S. Peacock and V.A. Maxfield, eds., *Survey and Excavations Mons Claudianus 1987–1993.* Volume 1: *Topography and Quarries* (*FIFAO* 37)(Cairo: IFAO, 1997).

Mons Ophiates

S.E. Sidebotham, H. Barnard, J.A. Harrell and R.S. Tomber, "The Roman Quarry and Installations in Wadi Umm Wikala and Wadi Semna," *Journal of Egyptian Archaeology* 87 (2001): 135–170.

Sikait and Nugrus

B.C. Foster, J.-L.G. Rivard, S.E. Sidebotham, and H. Cuvigny, "Survey of the Emerald Mines at Wadi Sikait 2000/2001 Seasons," in S.E. Sidebotham and W.Z. Wendrich, eds., *Berenike 1999/2000. Report on the Excavations at Berenike, Including Excavations in Wadi Kalalat and Siket, and the Survey of the Mons Smaragdus Region* (Los Angeles: Cotsen Institute of Archaeology, 2007): 304–343.

J.-L. Rivard, B.C. Foster, and S.E. Sidebotham, "Emerald City," *Archaeology* 55, no. 3 (May–June 2002): 36–41.

S.E. Sidebotham, H.M. Nouwens, A.M. Hense, and J.A. Harrell, "Preliminary Report on Archaeological Fieldwork at Sikait (Eastern Desert of Egypt), and Environs: 2002–2003," *Sahara* 15 (2004): 7–30.

Ka'b Marfu'

S.E. Sidebotham, H. Barnard, L.A. Pintozzi, and R.S. Tomber, "The Enigma of Ka'b Marfu': Precious Gems in Egypt's Eastern Desert," *Minerva* 16, no. 1 (January/February 2005): 24–26.

Bir Kareim

D. Whitcomb, "Bir Kareim," in D.S. Whitcomb and J.H. Johnson, eds., *Quseir al-Qadim 1980 Preliminary Report (American Research Center in Egypt Reports,* Volume 7)(Malibu, California: Undena Publications, 1982): 391–396.

Myos Hormos–Nile Road

H. Cuvigny, *Ostraca de Krokodilô. La correspondence militaire et sa circulation (O. Krok. 1–151). Praesidia du désert de Bérénice* II (*FIFAO* 51)(Cairo: IFAO, 2005).

H. Cuvigny, ed., *La route de Myos Hormos. L'armée romaine dans le désert Oriental d'Égypte* (*FIFAO* 48/1 and 48/2)(Cairo: IFAO, 2003).

R.E. Zitterkopf and S.E. Sidebotham, "Stations and Towers on the Quseir–Nile Road," *Journal of Egyptian Archaeology* 75 (1989): 155–189.

Berenike

S.E. Sidebotham and W.Z. Wendrich, eds., *Berenike 1994. Preliminary Report of the 1994 Excavations at Berenike (Egyptian Red Sea Coast) and the Survey of the Eastern Desert* (Leiden: CNWS, 1995).

S.E. Sidebotham and W.Z. Wendrich, eds., *Berenike 1995. Preliminary Report of the 1995 Excavations at Berenike (Egyptian Red Sea Coast) and the Survey of the Eastern Desert* (Leiden: CNWS, 1996).

S.E. Sidebotham and W.Z. Wendrich, eds., *Berenike 1996. Report of the 1996 Excavations at Berenike (Egyptian Red Sea Coast) and the Survey of the Eastern Desert* (Leiden: CNWS, 1998).

S.E. Sidebotham and W.Z. Wendrich, eds., *Berenike 1997. Report of the 1997 Excavations at Berenike and the Survey of the Egyptian Eastern Desert, including Excavations at Shenshef* (Leiden: CNWS, 1999).

S.E. Sidebotham and W.Z. Wendrich, eds., *Berenike 1998. Report of the 1998 Excavations at Berenike and the Survey of the Egyptian Eastern Desert, including Excavations in Wadi Kalalat* (Leiden: CNWS, 2000).

S.E. Sidebotham and W.Z. Wendrich, eds., *Berenike 1999/2000. Report on the Excavations at Berenike, Including Excavations in Wadi Kalalat and Siket, and the Survey of the Mons Smaragdus Region* (Los Angeles: Cotsen Institute of Archaeology, 2007).

S.E. Sidebotham and W.Z. Wendrich, "Berenike: Archaeological fieldwork at a Ptolemaic-Roman port on the Red Sea coast of Egypt: 1994–1998," *Sahara* 10 (1998): 85–96.

S.E. Sidebotham and W.Z. Wendrich, "Berenike: Archaeological fieldwork at a Ptolemaic-Roman port on the Red Sea coast of Egypt: 1999–2001," *Sahara* 13 (2001–2002): 23–50.

Myos Hormos

D. Peacock, L. Blue, eds., *Myos Hormos – Quseir al-Qadim Roman and Islamic Ports on the Red Sea.* Volume 1 *Survey and Excavations 1999–2003* (Oxford: Oxbow Books, 2006).

D.S. Whitcomb and J.H. Johnson, eds., *Quseir al-Qadim 1978 Preliminary Report* (Cairo-Princeton: American Research Center in Egypt, 1979).

D.S. Whitcomb and J.H. Johnson, eds., *Quseir al-Qadim 1980 Preliminary Report (American Research Center in Egypt Reports* vol. 7)(Malibu, CA: Undena Publications, 1982).

Christian Remains

R.S. Bagnall and J.A. Sheridan, "Greek and Latin Documents from 'Abu Sha'ar, 1990–1991," *Journal of the American Research Center in Egypt* 31 (1994): 159–168.

R.S. Bagnall and J.A. Sheridan, "Greek and Latin Documents from 'Abu Sha'ar, 1992–1993," *Bulletin of the American Society of Papyrologists* 31 (1994): 109–120.

D.J. Chitty, *The Desert a City* (Crestwood, NY: St. Vladimir's Seminary Press, 1966).

M. Dunn, *The Emergence of Monasticism. From the Desert Fathers to the Middle Ages* (Oxford: Blackwell Publishers, Ltd., 2000).

W. Harmless, *Desert Christians. An Introduction to the Literature of Early Monasticism* (Oxford: Oxford University Press, 2004).

J. Kamil, *Coptic Egypt History and Guide*, revised ed. (Cairo: American University in Cairo Press, 1990).

O.F.A. Meinardus, *Monks and Monasteries of the Egyptian Deserts*, revised ed. (Cairo: American University in Cairo Press, 1989).

D. Peacock, L. Blue, eds., *Myos Hormos – Quseir al-Qadim Roman and Islamic Ports on the Red Sea*. Volume 1: *Survey and Excavations 1999–2003* (Oxford: Oxbow Books, 2006).

T. Power, "The 'Arabians' of pre-Islamic Egypt," in J. Starkey, P. Starkey, and T. Wilkinson, eds., *Natural Resources and Cultural Connections of the Red Sea (Society for Arabian Studies Monographs* No. 5)(British Archaeological Reports International Series 1661)(Oxford: British Archaeological Reports, 2007): 195–210.

S.E. Sidebotham, "Late Roman Berenike," *Journal of the American Research Center in Egypt*, 39 (2002): 217–240.

S.E. Sidebotham, "Preliminary Report on the 1990–1991 Seasons of Fieldwork at 'Abu Sha'ar (Red Sea Coast)," *Journal of the American Research Center in Egypt* 31 (1994): 133–158.

S.E. Sidebotham, "University of Delaware Archaeological Project at Abu Sha'ar: The 1992 Season," *Newsletter of the American Research Center in Egypt* 161/162 (Spring/Summer 1993): 1–9.

S.E. Sidebotham and W.Z. Wendrich, "Berenike: Archaeological Fieldwork at a Ptolemaic-Roman port on the Red Sea Coast of Egypt: 1999–2001," *Sahara* 13 (2001–2002): 23–50.

S.E. Sidebotham, H. Barnard, and G. Pyke, "Five Enigmatic Late Roman Settlements in the Eastern Desert," *Journal of Egyptian Archaeology* 88 (2002): 187–225.

S.E. Sidebotham, R.E. Zitterkopf, and J.A. Riley, "Survey of the 'Abu Sha'ar-Nile Road," *American Journal of Archaeology* 95, no. 4 (1991): 571–622.

General on Religion in the Eastern Desert

S.H. Aufrère, "Religious Prospects of the Mine in the Eastern Desert in Ptolemaic and Roman Times (= Autour de l'univers mineral VIII)," in O.E. Kaper, ed., *Life on the Fringe. Living in the Southern Egyptian Deserts during the Roman and Early Byzantine Periods. Proceedings of a Colloquium Held on the Occasion of the 25th Anniversary of the Netherlands Institute for Archaeology and Arabic Studies in Cairo 9–12 December 1996* (Leiden: CNWS, 1998): 5–19

G. Hölbl, *Altägypten im römischen Reich. Der römische Pharao und seine Tempel III. Heiligtümer und religiöses Leben in den ägyptischen Wüsten und Oasen* (Mainz: Philipp von Zabern, 2005): 4–34.

C. Traunecker, "Le Panthéon du Ouadi Hammâmât (Inscription n° 58)," *Topoi Supplement* 3 (2003): 355–383.

Bir Abu Safa

S.E. Sidebotham, G.T. Mikhail, J.A. Harrell, and R.S. Bagnall, "A Water Temple at Bir Abu Safa (Eastern Desert)," *Journal of the American Research Center in Egypt* 41 (2004): 149–159.

Louis Maurice Linant de Bellefonds

L. de Bellefonds, *L'Etbaye pays habité par les Arabes Bicharieh, géographie, ethnologie, mines d'or* (Paris: A. Bertrand, 1868).

Chapter 7

Pharaonic Egypt

K.A. Bard, R. Fattovich, and C. Ward, "Sea Port to Punt: New Evidence from Marsa Gawasis, Red Sea (Egypt)," in J. Starkey, P. Starkey, and T. Wilkinson, eds., *Natural Resources and Cultural Connections of the Red Sea* (*Society for Arabian Studies Monographs* No. 5)(BARis 1661) (Oxford: Archeopress, 2007): 143–148.

H. Frost, "'Ports' Cairns and Anchors. A Pharaonic Outlet on the Red Sea," *Topoi* 6, no. 2 (1996): 869–902.

A. Lucas and J.R. Harris, *Ancient Egyptian Materials and Industries*, 4th ed. (London: Histories & Mysteries of Man Ltd, 1989).

P.T. Nicholson and I. Shaw, eds., *Ancient Egyptian Materials and Technology* (Cambridge: Cambridge University Press, 2000).

A.M.A.H. Sayed, *The Red Sea and its Hinterland in Antiquity. A Collection of Papers Published in the Arabic and European Periodicals* (Alexandria: Dar al-Ma'rifa al-Gam'iya, 1993).

Ptolemaic Egypt

S.M. Burstein, "Ivory and Ptolemaic Exploration of the Red Sea: The Missing Factor," *Topoi* 6, no. 2 (1996): 799–807.

P.M. Fraser, *Ptolemaic Alexandria* (Oxford: Clarendon Press, 1972).

J. Hatzfeld, *Les trafiquants italiens dans l'orient hellénique* (Paris: E. de Boccard, 1919).

G. Hölbl, *A History of the Ptolemaic Empire* (London: Routledge, 2001).

H.H. Scullard, *The Elephant in the Greek and Roman World* (Ithaca, NY: Cornell University Press, 1974).

Red Sea–Indian Ocean Trade

V. Begley, ed., *The Ancient Port of Arikamedu: New Excavations and Researches 1989–1992* Vol. I (*Mémoires Archéologiques* 22) (Pondicherry, India: École française d'Extrême-Orient, 1996).

V. Begley, ed., *The Ancient Port of Arikamedu: New Excavations and Researches 1989–1992*, Volume II (*Mémoires Archéologiques* 22.2) (Paris: École française d'Extrême-Orient, 2004).

A. Dalby, *Food in the Ancient World from A to Z* (London-New York: Routledge, 2003).

D. Peacock and D. Williams, eds., *Food for the Gods. New Light on the Ancient Incense Trade* (Oxford: Oxbow Books, 2007).

M.G. Raschke, "New Studies in Roman Commerce with the East," *Aufstieg und Niedergang der römischen Welt* 2.9.2 (1978): 604–1378.

J.-F. Salles and A.V. Sedov, *Qani': Le port antique du Hadramawt entre la Mediterrannée, l'Afrique et l'Inde. Fouilles russes 1972, 1985–1989, 1991, 1993-1994 (Indicopleustoi)* (Turnhout: Brepols, 2008).

S.E. Sidebotham, *Roman Economic Policy in the Erythra Thalassa 30 BC–AD 217* (*Mnemosyne* supplement no. 91) (Leiden: Brill, 1986).

G.K. Young, *Rome's Eastern Trade. International Commerce and Imperial Policy, 31 BC-AD 305* (London-New York: Routledge, 2001).

Coptos

S.C. Herbert and A. Berlin, eds., *Kelsey Museum of the University of Michigan, University of Assiut Excavations at Coptos (Qift) in Upper Egypt 1987-1992*, (Portsmouth, RI: Journal of Roman Archaeology, 2003).

Roman Banking

J. Andreau, *Banking and Business in the Roman World* (Cambridge: Cambridge University Press, 1999).

The Periplus of the Erythraean Sea

S. Belfiore, *Il Periplo del Mare Eritreo di anonimo del I sec. d.C. e altri testi sul commercio fra Roma e l'Oriente attraverso l'Oceano Indiano e la Via della Seta* (Rome: Società Geografica italiana, 2004).

L. Casson, *The Periplus Maris Erythraei. Text with Introduction, Translation, and Commentary* (Princeton: Princeton University Press, 1989).

Nabataeans

G. Markoe, ed., *Petra Rediscovered. Lost City of the Nabataeans* (New York: Harry N. Abrams, 2003).

J. Taylor, *Petra and the Lost Kingdom of the Nabataeans* (Cambridge, MA: Harvard University Press, 2002).

Yavanas

H.P. Ray, "The Yavana Presence in Ancient India," *Journal of the Economic and Social History of the Orient* 31 (1988): 311–325.

K. Zvelebil, *The Smile of Murugan. On Tamil Literature of South India* (Leiden: E.J. Brill, 1973).

Ships and Harbor Facilities

S.E. Sidebotham, "Archaeological Evidence for Ships and Harbor Facilities at Berenike (Red Sea Coast), Egypt," in R.L. Hohlfelder, ed., *The Maritime World of Ancient Rome. Proceedings of "The Maritime World of Ancient Rome" Conference held at the American Academy in Rome 27–29 March 2003 (Memoirs of the American Academy in Rome Supplementary Volume VI)* (Ann Arbor: The University of Michigan Press, 2008): 305–324.

Personal Names from Berenike

R.S. Bagnall, C. Helms and A.M.F.W. Verhoogt, *Documents from Berenike*. Volume I. *Greek Ostraka from the 1996–1998 Seasons (Papyrologica Bruxellensia* 31)(Brussels: Fondation Égyptologique Reine Élisabeth, 2000).

R.S. Bagnall, C. Helms, A.M.F.W. Verhoogt, A. Bülow-Jacobsen, A. Cuvigny, and U. Kaplony-Heckl, *Documents from Berenike*. Volume II. *Texts from the 1999–2001 Seasons (Papyrologica Bruxellensia* 33)(Brussels: Fondation Égyptologique Reine Élisabeth, 2005).

Graffiti in the Eastern Desert

A. Bernand, *Pan du désert* (Leiden: E.J. Brill, 1977).

F. De Romanis, "Graffiti greci da Wādi Menīh al-Hēr. Vestorius tra Coptos e Berenice," *Topoi* 6, no. 2 (1996): 731–745.

F. de Romanis, *Cassia, Cinnamomo, Ossidiana. Uomini e merci tra Oceano Indiano e Mediterraneo* (*Saggi de Storia antica* 11) (Rome: "L'Erma" di Bretschneider, 1996).

Locations of Ancient Red Sea Ports

G.M. Cohen, *The Hellenistic Settlements in Syria, the Red Sea Basin, and North Africa* (Berkeley, Los Angeles, London: University of California Press, 2006): 305–343.

Arabian Caravan Routes

P. Crone, *Meccan Trade and the Rise of Islam* (Princeton: Princeton University Press, 1987).

K. Kitchen, "Economics in Ancient Arabia from Alexander to the Augustans," in Z.A. Archibald, J. Davies, V. Gabrielsen, and G.J. Oliver, eds., *Hellenistic Economies* (London-New York: Routledge, 2001): 157–173.

M. Maraqten, "Dangerous Trade Routes: On the Plundering of Caravans in the Pre-Islamic Near East," *Aram* 8 (1996): 213–236.

F. Millar, "Caravan Cities: The Roman Near East and Long-Distance Trade by Land," in M. Austin, J. Harries, and C. Smith, eds., *Modus Operandi. Essays in Honour of Geoffrey Rickman* (London: Institute of Classical Studies, School of Advanced Study, 1998): 119–137.

D. Potts, "Trans-Arabian Routes of the Pre-Islamic Period," in J.-F. Salles, ed., *L'Arabie et ses Mers bordières. I. Itinéraires et Voisinages* (*Travaux de la Maison de l'Orient* No. 16)(Lyon: Maison de l'Orient Méditerranéen, 1988): 127–162.

Transport in Roman Egypt

C. Adams, *Land Transport in Roman Egypt. A Study of Economics and Administration in a Roman Province* (Oxford: Oxford University Press, 2007).

Myos Hormos/Quseir al-Qadim

D. Peacock and L. Blue, eds., *Myos Hormos–Quseir al-Qadim. Roman and Islamic Ports on the Red Sea.* Volume 1: *Survey and Excavations 1999–2003* (Oxford: Oxbow Books, 2006).

D. Whitcomb, "Quseir al-Qadim and the Location of Myos Hormos" *Topoi* 6, no. 2 (1996): 747–772.

D.S. Whitcomb and J.H. Johnson, eds., *Quseir al-Qadim 1978 Preliminary Report* (Cairo-Princeton, 1979).

D.S. Whitcomb and J.H. Johnson, eds., *Quseir al-Qadim 1980 Preliminary Report* (*American Research Center in Egypt Reports* volume 7) (Malibu, CA: Undena Publications, 1982).

Berenike

R.T.J. Cappers, *Roman Foodprints at Berenike Archaeological Evidence of Subsistence and Trade in the Eastern Desert of Egypt* (Monograph 55) (Los Angeles: Cotsen Institute of Archaeology, 2006).

S.E. Sidebotham, "Late Roman Berenike," *Journal of the American Research Center in Egypt* 39 (2002): 217–240.

S.E. Sidebotham and W.Z. Wendrich, "Berenike: Archaeological Fieldwork at a Ptolemaic-Roman Port on the Red Sea Coast of Egypt: 1994–1998," *Sahara* 10 (1998): 85–86.

S.E. Sidebotham and W.Z. Wendrich, "Berenike Archaeological Fieldwork at a Ptolemaic-Roman Port on the Red Sea Coast of Egypt 1999–2001," *Sahara* 13 (2001–2002): 23–50.

S.E. Sidebotham and W.Z. Wendrich, eds., *Berenike 1994. Preliminary Report of the 1994 Excavations at Berenike (Egyptian Red Sea Coast) and the Survey of the Eastern Desert* (Leiden: CNWS, 1995).

S.E. Sidebotham and W.Z. Wendrich, eds., *Berenike 1995. Preliminary Report of the 1995 Excavations at Berenike (Egyptian Red Sea Coast) and the Survey of the Eastern Desert* (Leiden: CNWS, 1996).

S.E. Sidebotham and W.Z. Wendrich, eds., *Berenike 1996. Report of the 1996 Excavations at Berenike (Egyptian Red Sea Coast) and the Survey of the Eastern Desert* (Leiden: CNWS, 1998).

S.E. Sidebotham and W.Z. Wendrich, eds., *Berenike 1997. Report of the 1997 Excavations at Berenike and the Survey of the Egyptian Eastern Desert, including Excavations at Shenshef* (Leiden: CNWS, 1999).

S.E. Sidebotham and W.Z. Wendrich, eds., *Berenike 1998. Report of the 1998 Excavations at Berenike (Egyptian Red Sea Coast) and the Survey of the Eastern Desert, including Excavations in Wadi Kalalat* (Leiden: CNWS, 2000).

S.E. Sidebotham and W.Z. Wendrich, eds., *Berenike 1999–2000. Report on the Excavations at Berenike, including Excavations in Wadi Kalalat and Siket, and the Survey of the Mons Smaragdus Region* (Los Angeles: Cotsen Institute of Archaeology, 2007).

W.Z. Wendrich, R.S. Tomber, S.E. Sidebotham, J.A. Harrell, R.T.J. Cappers, and R.S. Bagnall, "Berenike Crossroads: The Integration of Information," *Journal of the Social and Economic History of the Orient* 46, no. 1 (2003): 46–87.

Giovanni Battista Belzoni

G.B. Belzoni, *Narrative of the Operations and Recent Discoveries within the Pyramids, Temples, Tombs, and Excavations in Egypt and Nubia* (London: John Murray, 1820).

D. Manley and P. Rée, *Henry Salt Artist, Traveler, Diplomat, Egyptologist* (London: Libri Publications Limited, 2001).

S. Mayes, *The Great Belzoni. The Circus Strongman who Discovered Egypt's Ancient Treasures* (London: Taurisparke Paperbacks, 2003).

A. Siliotti, ed., *Belzoni's Travels, Narrative of the Operations and Recent Discoveries in Egypt and Nubia* (London: The British Museum Press, 2001).

Vienna Papyrus

S. Belfiore, *Il Periplo del Mare Eritreo di anonimo del I sec. d.C. e altri testi sul commercio fra Roma e l'Oriente attraverso l'Oceano Indiano e la Via della Seta* (Rome: Società Geografica Italiana, 2004): 235–244.

L. Casson, "P. Vindob. 40822 and the Shipping of Goods from India," *Bulletin of the American Society of Papyrologists* 23 (1986): 73–79.

H. Harrauer and P.J. Sijpesteijn, "Ein neues Dokument zu Roms Indienhandel, P. Vindob. G 40822," *Anzeiger der Österreichischen Akademie der Wissenschafter*, phil.–hist. Kl. 122 (1985): 124–155.

D. Rathbone, "The 'Muziris' Papyrus (SB XVIII. 13167): Financing Roman Trade with India," *Bulletin de la Société Archéologique d'Alexandrie* 46 (2000): 39–50.

Chapter 8

Demography in the Roman Period
W. Scheidel, *Death on the Nile. Disease and the Demography of Roman Egypt*
(Leiden-Boston-Köln: Brill, 2001).

Graves and Burials
F.G. Aldsworth, "The Buildings at Shenshef," in S.E. Sidebotham and W.Z.
Wendrich, eds., *Berenike 1997. Report of the 1997 Excavations at Berenike
and the Survey of the Egyptian Eastern Desert, including Excavations at
Shenshef* (Leiden: CNWS, 1999): 385–418.
F.G. Aldsworth and H. Barnard, "Survey of Hitan Rayan," in S.E. Side-
botham and W.Z. Wendrich, eds., *Berenike 1995. Preliminary Report of the
Excavations at Berenike (Egyptian Red Sea Coast) and the Survey of the East-
ern Desert* (Leiden: CNWS, 1996): 411–440.
F.G. Aldsworth and H. Barnard, "Survey of Shenshef," in S.E. Sidebotham
and W.Z. Wendrich, eds., *Berenike 1996. Report of the 1996 Excavations at
Berenike (Egyptian Red Sea Coast) and the Survey of the Eastern Desert* (Lei-
den: CNWS, 1998): 427–443.
H. Barnard, "Human Bones and Burials," in S.E. Sidebotham and W.Z.
Wendrich, eds., *Berenike 1996. Report of the 1996 Excavations at Berenike
(Egyptian Red Sea Coast) and the Survey of the Eastern Desert* (Leiden:
CNWS, 1998): 389–401.
V.A. Maxfield, "The cemetery and adjacent structure," in D.P.S. Peacock
and V.A. Maxfield, eds., *Survey and Excavation Mons Claudianus
1987–1993*. Volume 1: *Topography and Quarries (FIFAO 37)* (Cairo:
IFAO, 1997): 137–138.
D. Peacock and A. Macklin, "The Necropolis and Burials," in V. Maxfield
and D. Peacock, eds., *The Roman Imperial Quarries Survey and Excavation
at Mons Porphyrites 1994–1998*. Volume 1: *Topography and Quarries* (Lon-
don: Egypt Exploration Society, 2001): 26–36.
S.E. Sidebotham, "Survey of the Hinterland," in S.E. Sidebotham and W.Z.
Wendrich, eds., *Berenike 1997. Report of the 1997 Excavations at Berenike
and the Survey of the Egyptian Eastern Desert, including Excavations at
Shenshef* (Leiden: CNWS, 1999): 349–369.

S.E. Sidebotham, "Survey of the Hinterland," in S.E. Sidebotham and W.Z. Wendrich, eds., *Berenike 1998. Report of the 1998 Excavations at Berenike and the Survey of the Egyptian Eastern Desert, including Excavations in Wadi Kalalat* (Leiden: CNWS, 2000): 355–377.

S.E. Sidebotham, H. Barnard, and G. Pyke, "Five Enigmatic Late Roman Settlements in the Eastern Desert," *Journal of Egyptian Archaeology* 88 (2002): 187–225.

S.E. Sidebotham, R.E. Zitterkopf and C.C. Helms, "Survey of the Via Hadriana: The 1998 Season," *Journal of the American Research Center in Egypt* 37 (2000): 115–126.

Pollution in Antiquity

J.D. Hughes, *Pan's Travail: Environmental Problems of the Ancient Greeks and Romans* (Baltimore: The Johns Hopkins University Press, 1994).

James Burton

W.R. Dawson and E.P. Uphill, *Who was who in Egyptology* (London: Egypt Exploration Society, 1995).

J. Thompson, *Sir Gardner Wilkinson and His Circle* (Austin, TX: University of Texas Press, 1992).

Chapter 9

Gold Mining

J.H. Breasted, *Ancient Records of Egypt*. Volumes 1–5 (Urbana-Chicago: University of Illinois Press, 2001).

A. and A. Castiglioni, and J. Vercoutter, *Das Goldland der Pharaonen. Die Entdeckung von Berenike Pancrisia* (Mainz: Philipp von Zabern, 1998).

H. Cuvigny, "The Amount of Wages Paid to the Quarry-Workers at Mons Claudianus," *Journal of Roman Studies* 86 (1996): 139–145.

J.A. Harrell and V.M. Brown, "The Oldest Surviving Topographical Map from Ancient Egypt: (Turin Papyri 1879, 1899, and 1969)," *Journal of the American Research Center in Egypt* 29 (1992): 81–105.

J.A. Harrell and V.M. Brown, "The World's Oldest Surviving Geological Map: The 1150 BC Turin Papyrus from Egypt," *Journal of Geology* 100 (1992): 3–18.

R. Klemm and D.D. Klemm, "Chronologischer Abriß der antiken Goldgewinnung in der Ostwüste Ägyptens," *Mitteilungen des deutschen Archäologischen Instituts Abteilung Kairo* 50 (1994): 189–222.

D.D. Klemm, R. Klemm, and A. Murr, "Ancient Gold Mining in the Eastern Desert of Egypt and the Nubian Desert of Sudan," in R. Friedman, ed., *Egypt and Nubia. Gifts of the Desert* (London: The British Museum Press, 2002): 215–231.

D. Klemm, R. Klemm, and A. Murr, "Gold of the Pharaohs–6000 years of gold mining in Egypt and Nubia," *Journal of African Earth Sciences* 33 (2001): 643–659.

C. Meyer and L. Heidorn, "Three Seasons at Bîr Umm Fawâkhîr in the Central Eastern Desert," in O.E. Kaper, ed., *Life on the Fringe. Living in the Southern Egyptian Deserts during the Roman and early-Byzantine Periods. Proceedings of a Colloquium Held on the Occasion of the 25th Anniversary of the Netherlands Institute for Archaeology and Arabic Studies in Cairo 9–12 December 1996* (Leiden: CNWS, 1998): 197–212.

C. Meyer, L.A. Heidorn, W.E. Kaegi, and T. Wilfong, *Bir Umm Fawakhir Survey Project 1993. A Byzantine Gold-Mining Town in Egypt (Oriental Institute Communications* no. 28) (Chicago: The Oriental Institute of the University of Chicago, 2001).

F. Millar, "Condemnation to Hard Labour in the Roman Empire, from the Julio-Claudians to Constantine," *Papers of the British School at Rome* 52 (1984): 124–147.

R. Shepherd, *Ancient Mining* (London-New York: Institution of Mining and Metallurgy by Elsevier Applied Science, 1993).

F.H. Thompson, *The Archaeology of Greek and Roman Slavery* (London: Duckworth/The Society of Antiquaries of London, 2003).

J. Vercoutter, "The Gold of Kush," *Kush* 7 (1959): 120–153.

Giovanni Battista Brocchi

G.B. Brocchi, *Giornale delle osservazioni fatte ne'viaggi in Egitto, nella Siria e nella Nubia* 2 volumes (Bassano: Presso A. Roberti Tip. Ed Editore, 1841).

Chapter 10

J-P. Adam, *Roman Building Materials and Techniques* (London: B.T. Batsford, 1994).

B. Adams, *Predynastic Egypt*, (Aylesbury: Shire Publications Ltd., 1988).

C.E.P. Adams, "Supplying the Roman Army: *O. Petr.* 245," *Zeitschrift für Papyrologie und Epigraphik* 109 (1995): 119–124.

H. Cuvigny, ed., *La route de Myos Hormos L'armée romaine dans le désert Oriental d'Égypte* (FIFAO 48/1 & 48/2) (Cairo: FIFAO, 2003).

J.A. Harrell, V. M. Brown and M. S. Masoud, "An Early Dynastic Quarry for Stone Vessels at Gebel Manzal al-Seyl, Eastern Desert," *Journal of Egyptian Archaeology* 86 (2000): 33–42.

M.A. Hoffman, *Egypt Before the Pharaohs* (London: Routledge & Kegan Paul, 1980).

V. Maxfield and D. Peacock, eds., *The Roman Imperial Quarries Survey and Excavation at Mons Porphyrites 1994–1998.* Volume 1: *Topography and Quarries* (London: EES, 2001).

V.A. Maxfield and D.P.S. Peacock, eds., *Survey and Excavations. Mons Claudianus 1987–1993.* Vol. 3: *Ceramic Vessels and Related Objects from Mons Claudianus* (*FIFAO* 54) (Cairo: IFAO, 2006).

D. Meredith, "Berenice Troglodytica, *Journal of Egyptian Archaeology* 43 (1957): 56–70.

C. Meyer, L.A. Heidorn, W. Kaegi and T. Wilfong, *Bir Umm Fawakhir Survey Project 1993: A Byzantine Gold Mining Town in Egypt (Oriental Institute Communication* 28) (Chicago: Oriental Institute of Chicago, 2000).

D.P.S. Peacock, V.A. Maxfield, eds., *Survey and Excavations Mons Claudianus 1987–1993.* Volume 1: *Topography & Quarries* (*FIFAO* 37) (Cairo: IFAO, 1997).

D. Peacock, L. Blue, eds., *Myos Hormos – Quseir al-Qadim. Roman and Islamic Ports on the Red Sea.* Volume 1: *Survey and Excavations 1999–2003* (Oxford: Oxbow Books, 2006).

S.E. Sidebotham, "Late Roman Berenike," *Journal of the American Research Center in Egypt* 39 (2002): 217–240.

S.E. Sidebotham, "Newly Discovered Sites in the Eastern Desert," *Journal of Egyptian Archaeology* 82 (1996): 181–192.

S.E. Sidebotham, H. Barnard and G. Pyke, "Five Enigmatic Late Roman Settlements in the Eastern Desert," *Journal of the American Research Center in Egypt* 88 (2002): 187–225.

S.E. Sidebotham, H. Barnard, J.A. Harrell, and R.S. Tomber, "The Roman Quarry and Installations in Wadi Umm Wikala and Wadi Semna," *Journal of Egyptian Archaeology* 87 (2001): 135–170.

S.E. Sidebotham, H.M. Nouwens, A.M. Hense, and J.A. Harrell, "Preliminary Report on Archaeological Fieldwork at Sikait (Eastern Desert of Egypt), and environs: 2002–2003," *Sahara* 15 (2004): 7–30.

S.E. Sidebotham, J.A. Riley, H.A. Hamroush, and H. Barakat, "Fieldwork on the Red Sea Coast: The 1987 Season," *Journal of the American Research Center in Egypt* 26 (1989): 127–166.

S.E. Sidebotham and W.Z. Wendrich, "Berenike: Archaeological Fieldwork at a Ptolemaic-Roman Port on the Red Sea Coast of Egypt: 1994–1998," *Sahara* 10 (1998): 85–96.

S.E. Sidebotham and W.Z. Wendrich, "Berenike Archaeological Fieldwork at a Ptolemaic-Roman Port on the Red Sea Coast of Egypt 1999–2001," *Sahara* 13 (2001–2002): 23–50.

G. Webster, "Roman Windows and Grilles," *Antiquity* 33 (1959): 10–14.

W.Z. Wendrich, "Fringes are Anchored in Warp and Weft: The Relations between Berenike, Shenshef and the Nile Valley," in O.E. Kaper, ed., *Life on the Fringe Living in the Southern Egyptian Deserts during the Roman and early-Byzantine Periods. Proceedings of a Colloquium Held on the Occasion of the 25th Anniversary of the Netherlands Institute for Archaeology and Arabic Studies in Cairo 9–12 December 1996* (Leiden: CNWS, 1998): 243–251.

D.S. Whitcomb and J.H. Johnson, eds., *Quseir al-Qadim 1980 Preliminary Report (American Research Center in Egypt Reports* Vol. 7) (Malibu, CA: Undena Publications, 1982).

Chapter 11

L. de Bellefonds, *L'Etbaye pays habité par les arabes Bicharieh. Géographie, ethnologie, mines d'or* (Paris : A Bertrand, 1868).

R.T.J. Cappers, *Roman Foodprints at Berenike Archaeological Evidence of Subsistence and Trade in the Eastern Desert of Egypt* (Monograph 55) (Los Angeles: Cotsen Institute of Archaeology, 2006).

J.J. Hobbs, *Bedouin Life in the Egyptian Wilderness* (Austin, TX: University of Texas Press, 1989).

L. Keimer, "Notes prises chez les Bišarīn et les Nubiens d'Assouan," *Bulletin de l'Institut d'Égypte,* tomes 33–35 (1950–1953) (Cairo: Le Caire Imprimerie de L'Institut d'Égypte, 1952–1954).

C.B. Klunzinger, *Upper Egypt: Its People and Products* (London-Glasgow-Edinburgh: Blackie & Son, 1878).

K. Krzywinski and R.H. Pierce, eds., *Deserting the Desert a Threatened Cultural Landscape between the Nile and the Sea* (Bergen: Department of Botany, Department of Greek, Latin and Egyptology, 2001).

G.W. Murray, *Sons of Ishmael. A Study of the Egyptian Bedouin* (London: George Routledge & Sons, Ltd, 1935).

A. Paul, *A History of the Beja Tribes of the Sudan* (Cambridge: Cambridge University Press, 1954).

T.C. Skeat, "A Letter from the King of the Blemmyes to the King of the Noubades," in *Journal of Egyptian Archaeology* 63 (1977): 159–170.

L.A. Tregenza, *Egyptian Years* (London-New York-Toronto: Oxford University Press, 1958).

L.A. Tregenza, *The Red Sea Mountains of Egypt* (London-New York-Toronto: Oxford University Press, 1955).

Chapter 12

Amethysts

J.A. Harrell and S.E. Sidebotham, "Wadi Abu Diyeiba: An Amethyst Quarry in Egypt's Eastern Desert," *Minerva* 15, no. 6 (November/December 2004): 12–14.

J.A. Harrell, S.E. Sidebotham, S. Marchand, R.S. Bagnall, J.E. Gates and J.-L. Rivard, "The Ptolemaic to Early Roman Amethyst Quarry at Abu Diyeiba in Egypt's Eastern Desert," *Bulletin de l'Institut français de Archéologie Orientale* 106 (2006): 127–162.

A. Lucas and J.R. Harris, *Ancient Egyptian Materials and Industries,* 4th revised ed. (London: Histories and Mysteries of Man Ltd, 1989).

I. Shaw, "Pharaonic Quarrying and Mining: Settlement and Procurement in Egypt's Marginal Regions," *Antiquity* 68, no. 258 (1994): 108–119.

I. Shaw, "Wadi el-Hudi," in K.A. Bard and S.B. Shubert, eds., *Encyclopedia of the Archaeology of Ancient Egypt* (London-New York: Routledge, 1999): 871–872.

I. Shaw and R. Jameson, "Amethyst Mining in the Eastern Desert: A Preliminary Survey at Wadi el-Hudi," *Journal of Egyptian Archaeology* 79 (1993): 81–97.

Beryls/Emeralds

B.C. Foster, J.-L. G. Rivard, S.E. Sidebotham and H. Cuvigny, "Survey of the Emerald Mines at Wadi Sikait 2000/2001 Seasons," in S.E. Sidebotham and W.Z. Wendrich, eds., *Berenike 1999/2000. Report on the Excavations at Berenike, Including Excavations in Wadi Kalalat and Siket, and the Survey of the Mons Smaragdus Region* (Los Angeles: Cotsen Institute of Archaeology, 2007): 304–343.

J.A. Harrell, "Archaeological Geology of the World's First Emerald Mine," *Geoscience Canada* 31, no. 2 (June 2004): 69–76.

W.F. Hume, *Geology of Egypt*. Volume 2: *The Fundamental Pre-Cambrian Rocks of Egypt and the Sudan; their Distribution, Age and Character*. Part I. *The Metamorphic Rocks* (Cairo: Government Press, 1934): 109–125.

S.E. Sidebotham, H.M. Nouwens, A.M. Hense and J.A. Harrell, "Preliminary Report on Archaeological Fieldwork at Sikait (Eastern Desert of Egypt), and Environs: 2002–2003," *Sahara* 15 (2004): 7–30.

J. Sinkankas, *Emerald and Other Beryls* (Prescott, Arizona: Geoscience Press, 1989).

Jewelry and Mummy Portraits

E. Doxiadis, *The Mysterious Fayum Portraits. Faces from Ancient Egypt* (Cairo: American University in Cairo Press, 1995).

C. Riggs, *The Beautiful Burial in Roman Egypt. Art, Identity, and Funerary Religion* (Oxford: Oxford University Press, 2005).

S. Walker, ed., *Ancient Faces. Mummy Portraits from Roman Egypt* (New York: Metropolitan Museum of Art and Routledge, 1997).

S. Walker and M. Bierbrier, *Ancient Faces. Mummy Portraits from Roman Egypt* (London: British Museum Press, 1997).

Frédéric Cailliaud
F. Cailliaud, *Voyage à l'oasis de Thèbes et dans les déserts situées à l'orient et à l'occident de la Thébaïde fait pendant les années 1815, 1816, 1817 et 1818* (Paris: Imprimerie royale, 1821).

Chapter 13

K. Krzywinski and R.H. Pierce, eds., *Deserting the Desert a Threatened Cultural Landscape between the Nile and the Sea* (Bergen: Department of Botany, Department of Greek, Latin, and Egyptology, 2001).

S.E. Sidebotham, "Ptolemaic and Roman Water Resources and their Management in the Eastern Desert of Egypt," in M. Liverani, ed., *Arid Lands in Roman Times. Papers from the International Conference (Rome, July, 9th–10th 2001)* (Rome: Edizioni all'Insegna del Giglio, 2003): 87–116.

S.E. Sidebotham, H. Barnard and G. Pyke, "Five Enigmatic Late Roman Settlements in the Eastern Desert," *Journal of Egyptian Archaeology* 88 (2002): 187–225.

Richard Pococke
R. Pococke, *A Description of the East and Some Other Countries* (London: Printed for the author, 1743–1745).

Karl Richard Lepsius
W.R. Dawson and E.P. Uphill, *Who Was Who in Egyptology* (London: Egypt Exploration Society, 1995).

R. Lepsius, *Letters from Egypt, Ethiopia, and the Peninsula of Sinai* (London: Henry G. Bohn, 1853).

Chapter 14

Berenike
R.S. Bagnall, C. Helms and A.M.F.W. Verhoogt, *Documents from Berenike. Volume 1: Greek Ostraka from the 1996–1998 Seasons (Papyrologica Bruxellensia* 31) (Brussels: Fondation Égyptologique Reine Égyptologique, 2000).

R.S. Bagnall, C. Helms and A.M.F.W. Verhoogt, *Documents from Berenike. Volume 2: Texts from the 1999–2001 Seasons (Papyrologica Bruxellensia* 33)(Brussels: Fondation Égyptologique Reine Élisabeth, 2005).

R.T.J. Cappers, *Roman Foodprints at Berenike. Archaeobotanical Evidence of Subsistence and Trade in the Eastern Desert of Egypt* (Los Angeles: Cotsen Institute of Archaeology, 2006).

S.E. Sidebotham, "Late Roman Berenike," *Journal of the American Research Center in Egypt* 39 (2002): 217–240.

S.E. Sidebotham, "Reflections of Ethnicity in the Red Sea Commerce in Antiquity: Evidence of Trade Goods, Languages and Religions from the Excavations at Berenike," in P. Lunde and A. Porter, eds., *Trade and Travel in the Red Sea Region. Proceedings of Red Sea Project I Held in the British Museum October 2002 (Society for Arabian Studies Monographs* no. 2) (British Archaeological Reports International Series 1269) (Oxford: British Archaeological Reports International Series, 2004): 105–115.

S.E. Sidebotham and W.Z. Wendrich, eds., contributors, *Berenike 1994. Preliminary Report of the 1994 Excavations at Berenike (Egyptian Red Sea Coast) and the Survey of the Eastern Desert* (Leiden: CNWS, 1995).

S.E. Sidebotham and W.Z. Wendrich, eds., contributors, *Berenike 1995. Preliminary Report of the 1995 Excavations at Berenike (Egyptian Red Sea Coast) and the Survey of the Eastern Desert* (Leiden: CNWS, 1996).

S.E. Sidebotham and W.Z. Wendrich, eds., contributors, *Berenike 1996. Report of the 1996 Excavations at Berenike (Egyptian Red Sea Coast) and the Survey of the Eastern Desert* (Leiden: CNWS, 1998).

S.E. Sidebotham and W.Z. Wendrich, eds., contributors, *Berenike 1997. Report of the 1997 Excavations at Berenike and the Survey of the Egyptian Eastern Desert, including Excavations at Shenshef* (Leiden: CNWS, 1999).

S.E. Sidebotham and W.Z. Wendrich, eds., contributors, *Berenike 1998. Report of the 1998 Excavations at Berenike and the Survey of the Egyptian Eastern Desert, including Excavations in Wadi Kalalat* (Leiden: CNWS, 2000).

S.E. Sidebotham and W.Z. Wendrich, eds., contributors, *Berenike 1999–2000. Report on the Excavations at Berenike, Including Excavations in Wadi Kalalat and Siket and the Survey of the Mons Smaragdus Region* (Los Angeles: Cotsen Institute of Archaeology, 2007).

S.E. Sidebotham and W.Z. Wendrich, "Berenike: Archaeological Fieldwork at a Ptolemaic-Roman Port on the Red Sea Coast of Egypt: 1994–1998," *Sahara* 10 (1998): 85–96.

S.E. Sidebotham and W.Z. Wendrich, "Berenike Archaeological Fieldwork at a Ptolemaic-Roman Port on the Red Sea Coast of Egypt 1999–2001," *Sahara* 13 (2001–2002): 23–50.

S.E. Sidebotham and W.Z. Wendrich, "Berenike: Roman Egypt's Maritime Gateway to Arabia and India," *Egyptian Archaeology* 8 (1996): 15–18.

S.E. Sidebotham and W.Z. Wendrich, "Berenike, Roms Tor am Roten Meer nach Arabien und Indien," *Antike Welt* 32, no. 3 (2001): 251–263.

S.E. Sidebotham and W.Z. Wendrich, "Berenike: A Ptolemaic-Roman Port on the Ancient Maritime Spice and Incense Route," *Minerva* 13, no. 3 (May/June 2002): 28–31.

W.Z. Wendrich, R.S. Tomber, S.E. Sidebotham, J.A. Harrell, R.T.J. Cappers and R.S. Bagnall, "Berenike Crossroads: The Integration of Information," *Journal of Economic and Social History of the Orient* 46, no. 1 (2003): 46–87.

Berenike–Nile and Marsa Nakari–Nile Roads

A. Bernand, *Pan du désert* (Leiden: E.J. Brill, 1977).

R.S. Bagnall, J.G. Manning, S.E. Sidebotham and R.E. Zitterkopf, "A Ptolemaic Inscription from Bir 'Iayyan," *Chronique d'Égypte* 71, no. 142 (1996): 317–330.

F. de Romanis, *Cassia, Cinnamomo, Ossidiana Uomini e merci tra Oceano Indiano e Mediterraneo* (*Saggi di Storia antica* vol. 9) (Rome: "L'Erma" di Bretschneider, 1996).

S.E. Sidebotham, "Caravans Across the Eastern Desert of Egypt: Recent Discoveries on the Berenike–Apollonopolis Magna–Coptos Roads," in A. Avanzini, ed., *Profumi d'Arabia. Atti del Convegno* (*Saggi di Storia antica* 11) (Rome: "L'Erma" di Bretschneider, 1997): 385–393.

S.E. Sidebotham, "From Berenike to Koptos: Recent Results of the Desert Route Survey," *Topoi* supplement 3 (2002): 415–438

S.E. Sidebotham, "Survey of the Hinterland, in S.E. Sidebotham and W.Z. Wendrich, eds., *Berenike 1997. Report of the 1997 Excavations at Berenike and the Survey of the Egyptian Eastern Desert, including Excavations at Shenshef* (Leiden: CNWS, 1999): 349–369.

S.E. Sidebotham and R.E. Zitterkopf, "Routes Through the Eastern Desert of Egypt," *Expedition* 37, no. 2 (1995): 39–52.

Ancient Maps

C. Adams and R. Laurence, eds., *Travel and Geography in the Roman Empire* (London-New York: Routledge, 2001).

O.A.W. Dilke, *Greek and Roman Maps* (Ithaca, NY: Cornell University Press, 1985).

R.K. Sherk, "Roman Geographical Exploration and Military Maps," *Aufstieg und Niedergang der römischen Welt* 2.1 (1974): 534–562.

J.N. Wilford, *The Mapmakers. The Story of the Great Pioneers in Cartography From Antiquity to the Space Age* (London: Pimlico, 2002).

Georg August Schweinfurth

G.A. Schweinfurth, *Auf unbetretenen Wegen in Aegypten* (Hamburg-Berlin: Hoffmann und Campe Verlag, 1922)

Chapter 15

Kush and Nubia

D.A. Welsby, *The Kingdom of Kush. The Napatan and Meroitic Empires* (London: The British Museum Press, 1996).

D.A. Welsby, *The Medieval Kingdoms of Nubia. Pagans, Christians and Muslims along the Nile* (London: The British Museum Press, 2002).

Blemmyes

R.T. Updegraff, "The Blemmyes I, the Rise of the Blemmyes and the Roman Withdrawal from Nubia Under Diocletian (with Additional Remarks by L. Török)," *Aufstieg und Niedergang der römischen Welt* 2.10.1 (1988): 44–106.

Abraq

S.E. Sidebotham, "Survey of the Hinterland," in S.E. Sidebotham and W.Z. Wendrich, eds., *Berenike 1994. Preliminary Report of the 1994 Excavations at Berenike (Egyptian Red Sea Coast) and the Survey of the Eastern Desert* (Leiden: CNWS, 1995): 85–101.

S.E. Sidebotham and R.E. Zitterkopf, "Survey of the Hinterland," in S.E. Sidebotham and W.Z. Wendrich, eds., *Berenike 1995. Preliminary Report of the 1995 Excavations at Berenike (Egyptian Red Sea Coast) and the Survey of the Eastern Desert* (Leiden: CNWS, 1996): 357–409.

Hitan Rayan

F.G. Aldsworth and H. Barnard, "Survey of Hitan Rayan," in S.E. Sidebotham and W.Z. Wendrich, eds., *Berenike 1995. Preliminary Report of the
1995 Excavations at Berenike (Egyptian Red Sea Coast) and the Survey of the
Eastern Desert* (Leiden: CNWS, 1996): 411–440.

S.E. Sidebotham. H. Barnard and G. Pyke, "Five Enigmatic Late Roman
Settlements in the Eastern Desert," *Journal of Egyptian Archaeology* 88
(2002): 187–225.

Siket

R.S. Bagnall, A. Bülow-Jacobsen and H. Cuvigny, "Security and Water on the
Eastern Desert Roads: the Prefect Iulius Ursus and the Construction of
Praesidia under Vespasian," *Journal of Roman Archaeology* 14 (2001):
325–333.

L.A. Pintozzi, "Excavations at the *Praesidium et Hydreuma* at Siket," in S.E.
Sidebotham and W.Z. Wendrich, eds., *Berenike 1999/2000. Report on the
Excavations at Berenike, Including Excavations in Wadi Kalalat and Siket,
and the Survey of the Mons Smaragdus Region* (Los Angeles: Cotsen Institute of Archaeology, 2007): 358–367.

S.E. Sidebotham, "Survey of the Hinterland," in S.E. Sidebotham and
W.Z. Wendrich, eds., *Berenike 1998. Report of the 1998 Excavations at
Berenike and the Survey of the Egyptian Eastern Desert, including Excava-
tions in Wadi Kalalat* (Leiden: CNWS, 2000): 355–377.

Small Praesidium in Wadi Kalalat

A.E. Haeckl, "Excavations at the Smaller *Praesidium* in Wadi Kalalat," in
S.E. Sidebotham and W.Z. Wendrich, eds., *Berenike 1999/2000. Report on
the Excavations at Berenike, Including Excavations in Wadi Kalalat and
Siket, and the Survey of the Mons Smaragdus Region* (Los Angeles: Cotsen
Institute of Archaeology, 2007): 344–357.

S.E. Sidebotham, "Survey of the Hinterland," in S.E. Sidebotham and
W.Z. Wendrich, eds., *Berenike 1994. Preliminary Report of the 1994 Exca-
vations at Berenike (Egyptian Red Sea Coast) and the Survey of the Eastern
Desert* (Leiden: CNWS, 1995): 85–101.

Large Praesidium in Wadi Kalalat

R.S. Bagnall, "Inscriptions from Wadi Kalalat," in S.E. Sidebotham and W.Z. Wendrich, eds., *Berenike 1998. Report of the 1998 Excavations at Berenike and the Survey of the Egyptian Eastern Desert, including Excavations in Wadi Kalalat* (Leiden: CNWS, 2000): 403–412.

S.E. Sidebotham, "Survey of the Hinterland," in S.E. Sidebotham and W.Z. Wendrich, eds., *Berenike 1994. Preliminary Report of the 1994 Excavations at Berenike (Egyptian Red Sea Coast) and the Survey of the Eastern Desert* (Leiden: CNWS, 1995): 85–101.

S.E. Sidebotham and R.E. Zitterkopf, "Survey of the Hinterland," in S.E. Sidebotham and W.Z. Wendrich, eds., *Berenike 1995. Preliminary Report of the 1995 Excavations at Berenike (Egyptian Red Sea Coast) and the Survey of the Eastern Desert* (Leiden: CNWS, 1996): 357–409.

S.E. Sidebotham, H. Barnard, D.K. Pearce and A.J. Price, "Excavations in Wadi Kalalat," in S.E. Sidebotham and W.Z. Wendrich, eds., *Berenike 1998. Report of the 1998 Excavations at Berenike and the Survey of the Egyptian Eastern Desert, including Excavations in Wadi Kalalat* (Leiden: CNWS, 2000): 379–402.

Shenshef

F.G. Aldsworth, "The Buildings at Shenshef," in S.E. Sidebotham and W.Z. Wendrich, eds., *Berenike 1997. Report of the 1997 Excavations at Berenike and the Survey of the Egyptian Eastern Desert, including Excavations at Shenshef* (Leiden: CNWS, 1999): 385–418.

F.G. Aldsworth and H. Barnard, "Survey of Shenshef," in S.E. Sidebotham and W.Z. Wendrich, eds., *Berenike 1996. Report of the 1996 Excavations at Berenike (Egyptian Red Sea Coast) and the Survey of the Eastern Desert* (Leiden: CNWS, 1998): 427–443.

R.T.J. Cappers, "The Archaeobotanical Remains from Shenshef," in S.E. Sidebotham and W.Z. Wendrich, eds., *Berenike 1997. Report of the 1997 Excavations at Berenike and the Survey of the Egyptian Eastern Desert, including Excavations at Shenshef* (Leiden: CNWS; 1999): 419–426.

D.A. Gould, "Excavations at Shenshef," in S.E. Sidebotham and W.Z. Wendrich, eds., *Berenike 1997. Report of the 1997 Excavations at Berenike and the Survey of the Egyptian Eastern Desert, including Excavations at Shenshef* (Leiden: CNWS, 1999): 371–383.

G.W. Murray, "Note on the Ruins of Hitân Shenshef, Near Berenice," *Journal of Egyptian Archaeology* 12 (1926): 166–167.

W.J. Van Neer and A.M.H. Ervynck, "The Faunal Remains from Shenshef and Kalalat," in S.E. Sidebotham and W.Z. Wendrich, eds., *Berenike 1997. Report of the 1997 Excavations at Berenike and the Survey of the Egyptian Eastern Desert, including Excavations at Shenshef* (Leiden: CNWS, 1999): 431–444.

S.E. Sidebotham, "Survey of the Hinterland," in S.E. Sidebotham and W.Z. Wendrich, eds., *Berenike 1994. Preliminary Report of the 1994 Excavations at Berenike (Egyptian Red Sea Coast) and the Survey of the Eastern Desert* (Leiden: CNWS, 1995): 85–101.

C.E. Vermeeren, "Wood and Charcoal from Shenshef," in S.E. Sidebotham and W.Z. Wendrich, eds., *Berenike 1997. Report of the 1997 Excavations at Berenike and the Survey of the Egyptian Eastern Desert, including Excavations at Shenshef* (Leiden: CNWS, 1999): 427–429.

Enigmatic/Christian Desert Settlements

O.F.A. Meinardus, *Coptic Saints and Pilgrimages* (Cairo-New York: American University in Cairo Press, 2002).

O.F.A. Meinardus, *Two Thousand Years of Coptic Christianity* (Cairo: American University in Cairo Press, 1999).

S.E. Sidebotham, H. Barnard and G. Pyke, "Five Enigmatic Late Roman Settlements in the Eastern Desert," *Journal of Egyptian Archaeology* 88 (2002): 187–225.

T. Power, "The 'Arabians' of Pre-Islamic Egypt," in J. Starkey, P. Starkey, and T. Wilkinson, eds., *Natural Resources and Cultural Connections of the Red Sea (Society for Arabian Studies Monographs* No. 5)(British Archaeological Reports International Series 1661)(Oxford: British Archaeological Reports, 2007): 195–210.

Al-Ileigha

S.E. Sidebotham, "Survey of the Hinterland," in S.E. Sidebotham and W.Z. Wendrich, eds., *Berenike 1994. Preliminary Report of the 1994 Excavations at Berenike (Egyptian Red Sea Coast) and the Survey of the Eastern Desert* (Leiden: CNWS, 1995): 85–101.

Roman Military Equipment

M.C. Bishop and J.C.N. Coulston, *Roman Military Equipment from the Punic Wars to the fall of Rome* (London: B.T. Batsford, 1993).

Prehistoric Period

M.A. Hoffman, *Egypt Before the Pharaohs. The Prehistoric Foundations of Egyptian Civilization* (Austin, TX: University of Texas Press, 1991).

Vladimir Semionovitch Golénischeff

V. Golénischeff, "Une excursion à Bérénice," *Recueil de Travaux relatifs à la philologie et à l'archéologie égyptiennes et assyriennes* 13 (1890): 75–96.

Index